Feng Shui FOR DUMMIES®

2ND EDITION

by David Daniel Kennedy

Foreword by His Holiness Grandmaster Professor Lin Yun

WILEY

Wiley Publishing, Inc.

Feng Shui For Dummies®, 2nd Edition

Published by
Wiley Publishing, Inc.
111 River St.
Hoboken, NJ 07030-5774
www.wiley.com

For general information on our other products and services, please contact our Customer Care Department within the U.S. at 877-762-2974, outside the U.S. at 317-572-3993, or fax 317-572-4002.

For technical support, please visit www.wiley.com/techsupport.

Wiley also publishes its books in a variety of electronic formats. Some content that appears in print may not be available in electronic books.

Library of Congress Control Number: 2010939969

ISBN: 978-0-470-76932-4

Manufactured in the United States of America

10 9 8 7 6 5 4 3

WILEY

About the Author

David Daniel Kennedy is a professional Feng Shui consultant, teacher, author, and speaker whose client list ranges from individuals and small businesses to Fortune 500 companies. He specializes in helping people make simple, highly effective life changes that dramatically improve their wealth, relationships, and happiness.

Mr. Kennedy's unique, engaging, and entertaining approach and his ability to make Eastern concepts easily accessible have helped establish him as one of the best-known experts on Feng Shui. He has authored several highly regarded books on the subject; in partic- ular, *Feng Shui For Dummies* has become a standard in the field and is used as teaching material at numerous Feng Shui schools. Mr. Kennedy is also the author of *Feng Shui Tips for a Better Life* (Storey Publishing), *Feng Shui for Abundance* (Sounds True), and the *Feng Shui Home Study Course,* a self-study audio program (Sounds True). In addition, he has appeared on dozens of televi- sion and radio programs and traveled around the world for speaking engage- ments and creative workshops.

Mr. Kennedy has brought transformation to thousands of students around the world and has been the personal mentor of numerous successful Feng Shui consultants. He has dedicated his life to the study of personal growth and, under the tutelage of Grandmaster Lin Yun Rinpoche, experienced the transformational art of Feng Shui.

About the Author's Mentor

His Holiness Grandmaster Professor Lin Yun Rinpoche was highly regarded as the leading authority on Feng Shui. His school — the Black Sect Tantric Buddhist Feng Shui school — is the most widely practiced Feng Shui school in the United States. For the past 40 years, Grandmaster Lin Yun lectured extensively on the subject of Feng Shui at many distinguished universities, businesses, and professional organizations throughout the world. Because of his introduction, transmission, and continuous promotion, Feng Shui has drawn tremendous interest, and its popularity continues to grow worldwide. Numerous Feng Shui authors, teachers, and consultants were disciples and/ or students of Grandmaster Lin Yun, a man whose pioneering contribution to spreading the knowledge of Feng Shui earned him the reputation as the father of Feng Shui in the West. In 1997, Grandmaster Lin Yun received an honorary PhD in Human Psychology from Northern California Graduate University. In 1998, he was enthroned as His Holiness of Black Sect Tantric Buddhism in its fourth stage of development by the spiritual head of the Tibetan Bon religion, H.H. 33rd Menri Trizin Lungtok Tenpai Nyima.

Dedication

The author dedicates this book to his teacher and mentor, H.H. Grandmaster Professor Lin Yun Rinpoche, without whom this book would not be possible. Professor Lin devoted his life to helping others and is the individual most responsible for making Feng Shui known publicly in the West. He improved the lives of countless people, including the author's.

Through his teaching and personal guidance, he gave people around the world the opportunity to enjoy a happier, more prosperous life by sharing his profound knowledge of human nature, karma, and transcendental solutions to life's many difficulties.

In loving memory,

Grandmaster Professor Thomas Lin Yun, 1932–2010

Author's Acknowledgments

The author gratefully acknowledges these individuals for their assistance and guidance:

His Holiness Grandmaster Professor Lin Yun Rinpoche, Feng Shui and spiritual teacher, for writing the foreword to this book, bringing Feng Shui to the West, changing his life in virtually every way, and tirelessly helping others have better, happier lives through Feng Shui. He is the source of the life-changing knowledge in this book. Errors and omissions, however, are solely the responsibility of the author.

Khadro Crystal Chu Rinpoche, leader of Black Sect Tantric Buddhism in its fifth stage and CEO of the Yun Lin Temple, for her abundant support; Sarah Rossbach, whose books introduced Feng Shui to an English-speaking audience; Frances Li, the staff and volunteers at the Yun Lin Temple and the Lin Yun Monastery; Teacher Ho Lynn Tu; colleagues Seann Xenja, technical editor Eileen Conti Weklar (for her input, support, and wisdom), Shena Huang, Chris Wen-Chiao Li, the other translators of Professor's workshops, Ileen Weiss Nelson for her love and support, Robert Chui, Shelley Sparks, Nancy SantoPietro, the late James Moser; his Feng Shui students and clients.

Editorial wizard Doug Childers, whose input, wisdom, and support have resulted in a far better text.

The very talented and organized Wiley staff: Acquisitions Editor Tracy Boggier for believing in this project and shepherding it to conclusion, Senior Project Editor Georgette Beatty for her support and input, Senior Copy Editor Jen Tebbe for her excellent work and unflagging contribution, and the many others at Wiley who contributed to this project. Thanks to all.

Professional artist Chi Chung, for creating illustrations for both editions that are fitting, clear, and wonderfully matching the spirit of the book.

As Grandmaster Lin Yun taught, "Even a sage has many teachers." In addition to Grandmaster Lin Yun Rinpoche, the author wishes to thank Lama Ole Nydahl, Haidakhan Baba, Sadhguru, chi kung Grandmaster Zhang Yuanming, chi kung Grandmaster Tu Jin-Sheng, and teacher Hart DeFouw.

His beautiful partner.

Publisher's Acknowledgments

We're proud of this book; please send us your comments at `http://dummies.custhelp.com`. For other comments, please contact our Customer Care Department within the U.S. at 877-762-2974, outside the U.S. at 317-572-3993, or fax 317-572-4002.

Some of the people who helped bring this book to market include the following:

Acquisitions, Editorial, and Media Development

Senior Project Editor: Georgette Beatty
    (Previous Edition: Alissa Schwipps)

Acquisitions Editor: Tracy Boggier

Senior Copy Editor: Jennifer Tebbe
    (Previous Edition: Mary Fales)

Assistant Editor: David Lutton

Technical Editor: Eileen Conti Weklar

Editorial Manager: Michelle Hacker

Editorial Assistant: Jennette ElNaggar

Art Coordinator: Alicia B. South

Cover Photo: ©iStockphoto.com/pixhook

Cartoons: Rich Tennant
    (`www.the5thwave.com`)

Composition Services

Project Coordinator: Katherine Crocker

Layout and Graphics: Joyce Haughey, SDJumper, Christin Swinford

Proofreaders: Jessica Kramer, Evelyn Wellborn

Indexer: Estalita Slivoskey

Illustrator: Chi Chung

Special Help
    Todd Lothery

Publishing and Editorial for Consumer Dummies

> **Diane Graves Steele,** Vice President and Publisher, Consumer Dummies

> **Kristin Ferguson-Wagstaffe,** Product Development Director, Consumer Dummies

> **Ensley Eikenburg,** Associate Publisher, Travel

> **Kelly Regan,** Editorial Director, Travel

Publishing for Technology Dummies

> **Andy Cummings,** Vice President and Publisher, Dummies Technology/General User

Composition Services

> **Debbie Stailey,** Director of Composition Services

Contents at a Glance

Table of Contents

Foreword

*F*rom the time I was about 15 or 16 years old, I began studying with Black Sect Tantric Buddhist masters Hui Chieh-fu and Cheng Kuei-ying. In addition to spiritual studies, meditation, calligraphy, poetry, painting, secret cures, holistic healing, and divination, I was most captivated by the study of Feng Shui. In later years, I spread the teaching of Feng Shui to Taiwan, Hong Kong, Europe, the United States, and other parts of the world. In the last 40 years, I have combined the knowledge of modern architecture, space design, psychology, medicine, spirituality, healing, folkloric cultures of China and Taiwan, Chinese philosophies, Buddhism, and the knowledge of traditional and modern Feng Shui schools and theories to establish a new school in the study of Feng Shui, which is the Black Sect Tantric Buddhist Feng Shui school*. From 1973 to the present, I have been lecturing, teaching, and providing Feng Shui consultations and spiritual guidance in Asia, Europe, the United States, Australia, and Africa.

Many books are now available on the study of Feng Shui, and each one has its own specialty and value. Now that I have read David Daniel Kennedy's second edition of *Feng Shui For Dummies,* I feel that this guide is like an instamatic camera, readily usable and easily understood by anyone and everyone without the need for a teacher.

I am truly happy to see that the second edition of *Feng Shui For Dummies* is coming out. That proves the wide circulation and popularity of this book. From reading this book, the reader can completely understand the true meaning, explanation, techniques, and applications of Feng Shui through the Octagon, Five Elements, Methods of Minor Additions for Adjustments, and the power of the Three Secrets Reinforcement. This book also places special emphasis on the visible elements of Feng Shui, namely the chi (or energy) of the land, the shape of the land and/or lot, the shape of the house, the floor plan, the interior factors, and the exterior factors. Furthermore, the reader can understand the Five Elements and how to apply them to the Feng Shui adjustments, how to use the Methods of Exterior and Interior Chi Adjustments to bless a house, and the Method of Minor Additions to make modifications and improvements to his or her living and working environments. There are more features adding to the second edition of the book, which makes the book even more instrumental, such as Feng Shui for multifamily living; Feng Shui adjustments and transcendental cures for wealth, health, and relationship issues in our daily lives; an action plan for Feng Shui in your house; information on selecting a new home by using Feng Shui principles; and tips for finding a qualified Feng Shui consultant.

The publication of the second edition of *Feng Shui For Dummies* is much anticipated. The author, Mr. Kennedy, has a smooth penmanship and clear, precise ideas. His writing style and concepts are concise, refreshing, and easy for the reader to understand and accept. This book contains the theories from the Black Sect Tantric Buddhist Feng Shui perspective as well as meditation methods to improve one's spiritual powers, practical applications, and both mundane and transcendental solutions. Through this book, the author has made great contributions to society. These contributions can help many people who feel at a loss, and they can strengthen the stability of society, increase the well-being of the nation, and create happiness in mankind. Therefore, the publication of Mr. Kennedy's new book is indeed a great and joyous event for the Black Sect Tantric Buddhist Feng Shui school.

By His Holiness Grandmaster Professor Lin Yun
Translated by Crystal Chu and Mary Hsu

Referred to as Grandmaster Lin Yun's Feng Shui school in this book.

Introduction

●●●

*T*ake a look around you. What do you see? Whether or not you're aware of it, your environment is profoundly affecting your health, wealth, family life, relationships, and even your destiny.

Feng Shui (pronounced fung shway) is the ancient Chinese art of improving every part of your life by enhancing your environment according to principles of harmony and energy flow. Since the mid-1990s, Feng Shui has rapidly gained popularity in the West. Today, more and more people from all walks of life are practicing Feng Shui and experiencing the positive benefits of auspicious placement. Many successful individuals now create harmony and happiness in their relationships; increase their prosperity; and dissolve chronic patterns of failure, difficulty, and stress by rearranging their living and working environments according to Feng Shui principles.

Implementing the practical and effective Feng Shui methods in this book allows you to see your surroundings in a new light and notice how your home influences your job, your relationships, your personal health, and every other aspect of your daily experience. You're able to make new connections between obstacles in your physical space and recurring difficulties in your financial, professional, emotional, or creative life. By following Feng Shui principles, you can have a home environment that helps you achieve success, happiness, and prosperity. In short, through Feng Shui, you can experience how a harmonious environment allows more positive energy to flow through your whole life. And most important, you can understand why Feng Shui has been practiced for thousands of years — because it works!

Feng Shui is neither superstitious magic nor a passing fad. The Chinese have known for millennia that your physical surroundings affect both your inner and your outer life. They recognize the relationship between good Feng Shui and success, prosperity, and happiness. For example, the location of your bed affects your marriage, and the position of your desk affects your attention and work performance — which can mean the difference between a job promotion or demotion. Used by emperors and sages of the East for thousands of years, the Feng Shui principles I present in this book are as effective today as ever. And now you can find out how to make them work for you, too!

About This Book

Although many Feng Shui books crowd the bookstore shelves, finding the right one for you can be a real challenge. Some of the books are more suitable for advanced practitioners and scholars; others contain valuable yet highly complex details of historical, cultural, and theoretical significance. Trying to determine which ones actually work for you can sidetrack you from the pressing goal at hand — changing your home and life for the better.

Enter *Feng Shui For Dummies,* 2nd Edition, your do-it-yourself guide to no-kidding, cut-to-the-chase, hit-the-ground-running Feng Shui. I wrote this book with you, the on-the-go reader, in mind. In it, I guide you through the fascinating, mysterious art of Feng Shui and give you the practical information you need to improve your environment and life — starting now. I've shoe-horned and packed every page with the most effective tips and techniques available — methods that address the issues and concerns you encounter in your daily life (don't worry; I explain them clearly throughout this book). I've used these methods in my own life and have seen them work for many. So roll up your sleeves and prepare for action!

The easy, practical steps to effective Feng Shui involve

- ✔ Feeling and assessing the energy of your home. (It's easier than you may think!)
- ✔ Recognizing specifically how your environment is affecting your life right now — and is it ever. Your jaw will drop in amazement as you recognize amazing correlations between home features described in this book and the reality of your daily life.
- ✔ Properly implementing specific solutions to change your environment so you can feel the before-and-after differences as soon as possible.

For each feature of your home environment that I address, I describe the ideal state and function of that feature. (When I use the word *environment* in this book, I mean your personal environment, not the rain forest or the ozone layer.) I then show you how your situation may vary from these ideal principles and explain the potential negative consequences. But I don't leave you high and dry. Instead, I provide you with practical solutions for each problem and tell you which parts of your life benefit when you perform these solutions.

Conventions Used in This Book

I use the following conventions throughout the text to make things consistent and easy to understand:

- ✔ Key words and phrases in bulleted lists and the action parts of numbered steps appear in **boldface.**

- ✔ New terms appear in *italic* and are followed closely by an easy-to-understand definition; I also use italics for emphasis.

- ✔ All Web addresses appear in `monofont`.

Some additional important conventions are as follows:

- ✔ The Feng Shui method I present — called Grandmaster Lin Yun's Feng Shui school — is unique in several respects. First, it combines ancient Eastern concepts and modern Western approaches. Second, it's very practical and emphasizes easy-to-implement solutions that require as little time and effort as possible. For more on this type of Feng Shui and how it differs from traditional Feng Shui (which is also effective and valid), see Chapter 1.

- ✔ When I use the term *Life Area* throughout the book, I'm referring to specific areas of your physical space (such as the Wealth Area), not areas of your life (such as your financial situation). Life Areas are sections of the Feng Shui Octagon that you place on the plan of your home or lot; see Chapter 3 for more information.

- ✔ The Three Secrets Reinforcement I present in Chapter 6 is an important part of all cures. It should always be performed in conjunction with the physical part of a cure, even when a particular cure doesn't explicitly say to do so.

- ✔ All hanging cures (such as faceted crystal spheres and wind chimes) should be hung from a red ribbon or string cut to a multiple of 9 inches in length, even if this step isn't specifically noted within the description of such a cure.

What You're Not to Read

I like to think that you're going to read every single word I've written in this book, but I also know that you're busy and eager to start applying Feng Shui's secrets right away. If you're short on time, feel free to skip the sidebars (those gray-shaded boxes sprinkled throughout the chapters); they're full of interesting information but aren't essential to your understanding and application of Feng Shui.

Foolish Assumptions

In this book, I make several assumptions about you, the reader.

- ✔ You're interested in finding out how your surroundings affect you and how you can affect them — and improve your life by doing so.
- ✔ You want to make your home more harmonious and beautiful, improve your luck, nurture your relationships, and increase your prosperity.
- ✔ You don't want to be overwhelmed by overly mysterious or complex theories and methods that require years of study.
- ✔ You have an open mind and are ready to discover new and interesting ways to understand the world and improve your situation.
- ✔ You're eager to act, get moving, and make things happen.

Feng Shui is action-oriented; you get as much out of it as you put into it. When you prime a pump, it takes a bit of initial effort before the water starts to flow. In the same way, after you prime your Feng Shui pump by arranging your spaces according to Feng Shui principles, the energy of harmony, creativity, and abundance starts to flow into every part of your life.

How This Book Is Organized

Like all *For Dummies* books, *Feng Shui For Dummies,* 2nd Edition, is organized to make tons of useful information easily accessible. This book includes five main parts. Here's how I divvy it up.

Part 1: Getting Started: Feng Shui Made Clear

Part I explains the basic Feng Shui principles you need in order to apply the practical methods found throughout this book. I explain what Feng Shui is — and what it isn't. I also explain how the main schools of Feng Shui differ from each other and where Grandmaster Lin Yun's Feng Shui school — the one this book uses — fits into the general scheme of Feng Shui. In addition, I define core concepts of Feng Shui, show you how to map the energy of your personal space by using the Feng Shui Octagon, and help you harness the energies of the Five Elements.

Part II: Energizing Your Home's Exterior

Part II deals with the great outdoors — the outside of your home, that is. Just as you live in your home, your home lives in the land or property it sits on. From your neighborhood to your street and right up to your front door, I show you how to align the energies of nature to assist your personal progress. In addition, this part explains how to recognize positive and negative home positions on lot and landscape, counteract nearby negative features, and use the beneficial effects of vegetation and flowing water.

In this part, I also delve into the vital matter of shapes. The shapes of your lot, your home, and even the rooms within your home powerfully influence your life path in that residence. Additionally, I show you how to make the most of your approach — the path by which energy (and money) either flows in to nourish your dwelling or is blocked, creating a lack of vitality.

Part III: Feathering the Nest: Nurturing and Nourishing Indoor Spaces

Part III takes you indoors to consider your home's interior. I show you how to read your home's floor plan to see how the layout is benefiting or harming your life. I walk you through each room and give you practical tips for improving its energy. In addition, I explain the importance of features such as doors, stairs, windows, and beams. I also explain how to improve your home's energy with lighting, color, and everyday maintenance. If you live in an apartment, condominium, or other multiunit structure, I provide special guidance for you in this part, too.

The last chapter in this part includes suggestions for creating the unfair advantage just about everyone can use at work. Whether you work at home or in a cubical on your office building's 23rd floor, I show you how to apply easy Feng Shui cures to make the most of your work environment.

Part IV: Going to the Next Level: Using Feng Shui for Life Change

In Part IV, I start with a quick and effective action plan for using Feng Shui; then I provide tips for getting what you want with Feng Shui in the areas of wealth, relationships, and health. I also give you tips for selecting your next home with the help of Feng Shui.

Also in this part, I present ceremonies that help you clear unwelcome energies from your home and increase your good fortune. (And no, this isn't a recipe for getting rid of your significant other!) In addition, Part IV deals with a unique and effective branch of Feng Shui: performing special cures directly on yourself, instead of on your home, to enhance your personal energy.

Part V: The Part of Tens

The Part of Tens provides ten key principles for getting the most out of your Feng Shui cures. I also include ten hints for choosing a qualified Feng Shui consultant and ten pointers for selling a home with the help of Feng Shui. Closing out Part V is a special treat: ten calligraphy blessings for your home created by my mentor, Grandmaster Lin Yun.

Icons Used in This Book

In the margins of this book are several helpful icons that can make your Feng Shui journey easier:

If you want to tackle more-involved Feng Shui tips, follow the special cures given next to this icon. These remedies are some of the most potent solutions around.

This icon indicates a real-life Feng Shui story that illustrates some aspect or result of using Feng Shui. I share such stories because you can discover a lot from the experiences of others.

This icon sits next to key details you need to keep in mind in order to have success with your Feng Shui cures.

Text marked with this bull's-eye icon gives helpful Feng Shui pointers and information.

This icon tells you when to sit up and take notice. Something in your environment may be harming you, and changing it can save you a heap of trouble down the road.

Where to Go from Here

You may not choose to read this book from cover to cover, although you can read it this way if you want. For first-time Feng Shui-ers, Chapter 1 answers the question: "What is Feng Shui?" Its overview gives you the understanding you need to implement the practical suggestions found throughout the book. If you're familiar with the basic concepts of Feng Shui, you can use the table of contents or the index to jump directly to the chapter that provides the information you're looking for. Also, be sure to follow the references I provide within the book; they lead you to related material located in other chapters.

The helpful illustrations throughout the text clarify key points and demonstrate how you should perform specific cures. If an illustration differs from your particular situation, simply adapt the suggested remedy to fit your circumstances. On the other hand, in many cases, specific details can mean the difference between an effective solution and one that produces less-than-adequate results. For instance, if I recommend using a bamboo flute, don't use a chopstick and expect to get the same result! When I emphasize particular details as being critically important, I recommend sticking with them to the best of your ability.

Part I
Getting Started: Feng Shui Made Clear

The 5th Wave   By Rich Tennant

"Honey! The puppy just placed a new water element on the floor. Do you want me to clean it up or just balance the Feng Shui with a fire element?"

In this part . . .

Feng Shui is the study of the interaction between you and your environment. Feng Shui in action is jumping out of your current mold and applying tips, tricks, and techniques to reform your living environment, forge a new relationship with your space, and become happier in the process. Intriguing, no?

To get started practicing Feng Shui, you need some of the basics. Then you can move on to the really heavy Feng Shui firepower. In this part, I give you the lowdown on Feng Shui and the key principles that make it work. You're then fortified to move on and discover how to map the energy of your home (trust me, it's easier than it sounds). You can also grab an armful of effective Feng Shui changes (also known as cures) that you can apply anywhere you want. Last but not least, I let you in on one of the biggest Feng Shui secrets around: how to use the inner power of intention and motivation to make your Feng Shui solutions zing!

Chapter 1

Discovering the World of Feng Shui

*E*veryone appreciates the benefits of beautiful, comfortable living environments. America's flourishing landscaping and decorating industries attest to this fact. But Feng Shui says your interior and exterior surroundings affect not only your material comfort but also your physical and mental health, relationships, and worldly success. Feng Shui (pronounced fung shway) examines how the energy of your environment (including your neighborhood, property, and home) intimately interacts with and influences your personal energy. Your personal energy flow determines how you think and act, which in turn affects how well you perform and succeed in your personal and professional life. Feng Shui affects you every moment of the day — whether you're aware of it or not.

The purpose of this book is to help you perform effective Feng Shui corrections. In this chapter, I present a brief overview of Feng Shui methods and show you how Feng Shui can bring increased abundance, improved relationships, and better health to your life.

If you're new to Feng Shui, try to keep an open mind as you read. (A closed mind is bad Feng Shui!) When you're ready, select the methods and techniques that are most appropriate for your particular circumstances.

Demystifying Feng Shui

If you've read other Feng Shui books, you may find seemingly contradictory advice a bit confusing. Before I delve into the essence of Feng Shui, I want to help clear up some common Feng Shui misconceptions. Feng Shui isn't

- A method of Oriental design that guarantees get-rich-quick results from mystically rearranging your furniture.
- A superstitious, New Age belief system that's disconnected from the reality of your daily life.
- A simple home and garden makeover.
- A magical quick fix to be tackled in one afternoon.
- A luxury only the rich and famous can afford.
- A method chiefly concerned with the interior of your home. (In Feng Shui, your interior and exterior environments are equally important.)

Now on to the million-dollar question: What is Feng Shui?

- On the surface, Feng Shui is simply the interaction of humans and their environments. Taken a step further, Feng Shui allows you to strategically influence these interactions to achieve specific life improvements by positioning or designing your surroundings in harmony with principles of natural energy flow. As a result, you can achieve harmony with your surroundings. Feng Shui helps you right where you live and work.

- Feng Shui is the study of the relationships between the environment and human life. Feng Shui principles were discovered by the Chinese, and Feng Shui has been practiced for centuries to design environments that enhance conditions for harmony, well-being, and success in life.

- Feng Shui is often referred to as the art of placement. How you position yourself on the globe and in your particular region, and how you orient yourself to your surroundings, help determine your life experience at every level. Feng Shui offers a unique way of looking at yourself and your environment. It also provides ways to bring balance, comfort, and harmony into your environment in a manner that's difficult to achieve by other means.

Interesting bits of historical Feng Shui confirmation are starting to emerge. For example, recent scientific research indicates that more than 28,000 years ago, Neanderthal cavemen (located in present-day Croatia) chose which caves to live in based on three criteria: The caves held the high ground in the area, the surrounding area was easily seen from the entrance of the cave, and the water source was easily accessible. Interestingly, all three criteria are in harmony with the basic principles of Feng Shui, which has evolved and become more sophisticated along with humankind. The survival of these early humans significantly depended on how well they adapted to their surroundings — a fact that shows that even our primitive ancestors were aware of the effects of placement in their environment. Well, trust me when I say that Feng Shui is as relevant and beneficial to humankind today as it was more than 28,000 years ago.

The Meaning of the Term Feng Shui

Feng Shui is a term composed of two Chinese words: *feng* (wind) and *shui* (water). Wind and water are natural elements that flow, move, and circulate everywhere on Earth. They're also basic necessities for human survival. Wind — or air — is the breath of life; without it, you die in moments. Water is the liquid of life; without it, you die in days. The combined qualities of wind and water determine the climate, which historically has determined mankind's food supply and in turn affects people's lifestyle, health, energy, and mood. These two fundamental flowing elements have always profoundly yet subtly influenced human individuals and societies.

The essence of these life-giving elements is *chi,* or life force. Wind and water are important carriers of chi, and their flowing quality reflects their essential nature. Feng Shui is the art of designing environments that attract and harness the beneficial flow of chi, and this flow supports and enhances one's personal chi or life force. (Find out more about the energy called chi in Chapter 2.)

The environment rules! Feng Shui factors have determined the path of human culture

Many respectable, successful, and highly intelligent Western individuals are recognizing and applying in their own lives the basic premise behind Feng Shui — that your immediate environment affects you on a daily basis and can influence your long-term destiny. One individual who's deeply aware of these ideas has written a great book on the topic. Jared Diamond, biologist and author, won the Pulitzer Prize for Nonfiction for his book *Guns, Germs, and Steel: The Fates of Human Societies* (W.W. Norton & Company). Written after years of research, Diamond's book explains why some societies and peoples developed farming, then writing, then steel, and finally higher technologies, while other societies remained in hunter-gatherer mode.

Previous theories that attempted to explain this difference of cultures included racial factors, intelligence differences among peoples, and an evolutionary head start (or the lack of one). After examining all of these factors, Diamond decided that none of them satisfactorily explained the puzzling differences in human cultural and technological progression. Though his book doesn't discuss Feng Shui, he finally comes to this conclusion: Throughout human history, the dominant factor that has determined the evolutionary destiny and rate of progress among human societies has been the quality and types of environments in which they've lived. Feng Shui strikes again!

Ancient Chinese Secrets: The Big-Picture View of Feng Shui

Feng Shui is rooted in a holistic worldview. It sees all things and creatures as part of a natural order, a vast environment that's, alive and in flux, ever moving and changing. All things in this natural order are equally alive and possess an energetic value or component. Everything — plants, animals, people, and things — exists in a vast landscape that swirls with vital energy.

The same energy that flows through the world flows through you as well. In fact, according to this view, your essence — the part of you that makes you alive, unique, and vital — is this energy. And your body is the vehicle or environment through which this energy flows.

Feng Shui divides the vast environment or landscape that is the universe into more manageable units — like human beings and their homes, property, living rooms, and bedrooms. You can't control the Feng Shui of the world at large, but you can design your personal environment according to the same universal principles of energy flow by which planets spin in their orbits and galaxies wheel through space. I delve deeper into this energy, which is the basis for Feng Shui, in Chapter 2.

The historical origins of Feng Shui

Feng Shui has been practiced in one form or another for several thousand years. Its origins reach back to China's ancient shamanic practices and nature-based religions. The earliest Feng Shui comprised a mixture of divination, ritual, magic, and ancestor worship. It was practiced as a means of integrating one's earthly life, embedded in nature, with the world of chi or energy. In ancient times, gravesites were carefully selected according to energetic (or Feng Shui) principles with the thought that happy ancestors were more likely to promote favorable fortunes for their descendents. Eventually these principles were brought into common use and applied for the benefit of the living to improve the quality of their daily lives.

Feng Shui energy principles were also used to predict the weather; to determine the best

times to plant crops; and to fix dates, times, locations, and positions for building sites. These principles were even applied to decide when to wage war and where battles should be fought.

Systems similar to Feng Shui have evolved in other cultures throughout the world. In India, practices used to create harmony with the environment are called *Vastu Shastra* and *Sthapatya Veda* (both methods of aligning human spaces with the natural forces of the universe). The Japanese use a related method. Going back in time, Celtic and medieval European cultures used magical methods such as *geomancy* (literally "earth magic") to influence their relationship with their environment, align themselves with the power of the land, and improve their earthly lives.

Unearthing Basic Feng Shui Principles

Examining a few basic Feng Shui concepts, such as yin and yang and the Three Realms of Influence, can help get you started thinking in Feng Shui terms and help you better understand your environment and its effects on you. (***Note:*** If you're already aware of the basics of Feng Shui, you can skim the rest of this chapter and go straight to Chapter 3.)

The ancient Chinese not only determined that the universe was composed of two complementary energy principles — yin and yang — but also assigned three categories into which these two essences flowed — Heaven, Earth, and Human. The ancient philosophers made an intensive study over many generations to discover how these interconnected categories could be manipulated or influenced in order to improve one's personal life, fortune, and destiny. Feng Shui was developed out of this prolonged and profound consideration. Read on to further examine these primary elements.

Yin and yang

Everything in the universe is made up of two opposite yet complementary principles or qualities: yin and yang. *Yin* symbolizes the passive side of nature, and *yang* represents the active side. But yin and yang don't exist independently; they simply describe the two primary qualities in which all existing things partake. Therefore, nothing is 100 percent yin or 100 percent yang; all things contain relative amounts of both yin and yang energy.

Figure 1-1 shows the symbolism of yin and yang interacting. The white fish symbolizes yang, and the black fish shows yin. Note how each quality carries the color of its opposite within itself, showing that within all things is the seed for potential change.

Figure 1-1:
The interaction and harmony between yin and yang.

Things with characteristics such as passivity, receptiveness, silence, darkness, and inwardness represent yin. In contrast, things with active, hard, projecting, loud, and bright characteristics represent yang. Neither is better than the other, and both are necessary for life and the universe to exist. As philosophical concepts, yin and yang poetically describe the dualistic world. Nothing is completely good or pure, just as no one is totally evil or without redeeming qualities. Everything that exists is in some way a mixture of yin and yang. This is an important basis of Feng Shui thinking.

In Feng Shui terms, a too-yang environment is disturbing and leads to the loss of peace and harmony. For example, a bedroom facing a noisy street can rob you of the quality rest you need because there's too much disturbance or yang energy present for restful sleep. On the other hand, an overly yin area — like an office looking out onto a dark narrow alley — can cause you to become overly subdued and lethargic and can limit your energy and efficiency. Similarly, an overly yin entrance to a residence — one that's hidden and dark — may not attract enough money or energy. Note that the yin and yang levels are relevant to the specific environments; each environment has an appropriate balance of yin and yang energies.

Yin and yang can also describe activities, events, and even emotions. For instance, a funeral is usually yin in nature (think quiet, sober, and subdued). On the other hand, the Super Bowl is the epitome of yang energy (think active, colorful, noisy, and intense). If you're overly yang, your emotional state is angry or explosive. But if you're overly yin, you can become withdrawn or depressed. To help you counteract or enhance certain qualities and tendencies, you can design your environment according to Feng Shui. At their essence, all the Feng Shui cures you discover are ways of balancing the yin and yang within you and your environment.

The Three Realms of Influence

Another important Chinese model for looking at life is called the *Three Realms of Influence.* This concept relates to Feng Shui because Feng Shui excels as a way of influencing the destiny with which a person starts. Three realms of the universe influence you — Heaven, Earth, and Human. These areas are both literal (they actually exist) and figurative (they symbolically influence you). To get the most out of your life circumstances, you want positive conditions in each of these Realms. On the other hand, a powerful way of improving your circumstances is to pay close attention to these Realms and begin to move into alignment with the best that they can offer.

Through the centuries, the Three Realms of Influence have become associated with three types of luck, one for each realm. According to Chinese belief, aligning your life — your activities and thoughts — with the natural order of all three Realms brings you improved luck and success. Feng Shui is a fundamental method that follows this principle. The following sections help you better understand each of the Three Realms of Influence.

How the East came West

During the latter half of the 20th century, the Oriental mindset infiltrated the West in several different waves. In the 1950s and early 1960s, the Beat Generation discovered Zen Buddhism, meditation, and haiku poetry, and in the 1970s, Oriental martial arts (including karate and kung fu) started to gain popularity. In the 1970s and 1980s, acupuncture, acupressure, macrobiotics, yoga, and tai chi also became very popular; their use and influence continue to grow by leaps and bounds. In the 1990s, Feng Shui burst onto the scene, and its popularity has grown enormously. More than just a passing fad, the main reason for this surge in Feng Shui awareness is that people in the West started to experience amazing and exciting results from the applications of Feng Shui in their lives. Many Westerners have experienced the positive life benefits that come from arranging their homes and offices according to the timeless principles of Feng Shui. And all the Oriental systems I mention (martial arts, acupuncture, tai chi, and so on) are based on the same fundamental insights into the energy (chi) that flows everywhere, in the environment, in your body, and throughout the universe.

Analyzing the Western approach to life in light of the Three Realms of Influence shows that most people rely first on themselves and their associates or family (Human luck), then on providence (Heaven luck), and very little (if at all) on environmental circumstances (Earth luck) — that's Feng Shui to you and me — mainly because they don't know it exists. In reality, all three Realms are equally important. By waking up to the power and influence of Feng Shui, you can increase your luck and grow into your fullest potential.

The Heaven Realm

Heavenly energy physically influences you daily through the climate, atmosphere, and air quality. Miracles and other unexpected interventions from above are considered to be the workings of heaven. (Perhaps you've heard someone exclaim, "The heavens opened!" when describing an inspiration or a narrow escape from danger.) The Heaven Realm is also connected to you through the place and time of your birth.

Positive timing, which is somewhat easier to control than heavenly help, also falls under the category of the Heaven Realm. To have Heaven luck is to have proper or auspicious timing for your endeavors. To realize your greatest chances for prosperity and good fortune, plans should be started at the best possible times (the times with the most favorable chances for success).

The Earth Realm

The Earth Realm provides humans with all the materials needed to sustain life: food, shelter, clothing, and so on. According to Feng Shui, the way humans position and orient themselves relative to their surroundings affects their welfare and destiny enormously. Applying Feng Shui to your environment maximizes the positive influences and minimizes the negative influences of the environment on your life. Early Chinese thinkers described the good fortune achieved by powerful and positive positioning as Earth luck. (Of course, humans affect the Earth as well. The best practice of Feng Shui helps humans live in harmony with the environment.)

The Human Realm

The third Realm that affects your life is the Human Realm. In addition to auspicious timing (Heaven luck) and proper positioning (Earth luck), *you* need to have the best possible energies, thoughts, and actions. By the same token, associations with the right people help create success in your endeavors. The actions you and your associates undertake — and the harmony between all parties — is the factor that completes the picture. To be blessed with Human luck, you need to have the best energies in yourself and surround yourself with the right people who support you in your efforts.

Five top factors affecting your fortune

Another way to look at life's equation for success is to consider a historical concept from Chinese culture called the Five Factors That Contribute to Life Fortune. This information has been distilled over several centuries of empirical observations by Chinese sages with a burning question on their minds: What are the key factors for human success? The Five Factors concept is the abridged version of their answer.

I explain these factors, in order of importance, in this list:

- ✔ **Fate (or destiny):** The time in history, the country you're born into, your family type, and the socioeconomic status of your family are all elements that combine to set you on a particular life path from the start. Feng Shui scholars believe that this factor includes the date, time, and location of your birth. In theory, fate exerts about 70 percent influence over one's life destiny. Three types of fate generally affect humans: good, fair, and poor. Traditionally, you're stuck with the type of fate you're handed at birth. The best you can do is work to improve your basic situation by using the four other factors (so read on).

- ✔ **Luck:** According to the Five Factors concept, luck is neither chance nor random coincidence striking like a bolt out of the blue. Luck is a discernible, if mysterious, pattern of influences on your life path. Some people seem to have a luckier path through life than others do. If destiny is the time, place, direction, and speed with which you hit the road at birth, your luck is the pattern of events that affects you as you head down your path.

- ✔ **Feng Shui:** The third key factor affecting the quality of your life is your placement (positioning) on the Earth. How you situate yourself in life affects you so strongly that the ancient seers rated it as number three on life's hit parade. Here's the payoff: If your fate and luck are poor (or even if they're wonderful), you can improve things by properly applying Feng Shui in your life and environment. In fact, practicing good Feng Shui is one of the best ways (besides winning the lottery) to maximize one's fate and luck, whether positive or negative.

✔ **Charitable actions and good deeds:** The positive actions you undertake — especially to help others — are the fourth important factor that influences the quality of your life. Performing good deeds, without hope of reward or recognition, makes your actions more beneficial to you and others. To employ this factor, perform one good deed per day.

✔ **Education and self-improvement:** This factor refers to improving one's knowledge, character, and moral fiber. To improve yourself in this way invites good people, events, and well-being into your life.

As you can see from the preceding list, when determining causes of success in life, the influence of Feng Shui ranks as the third most important factor. If the ancient Chinese were correct (and why shouldn't one take the longest continuously existing civilization on the planet seriously), your environmental surroundings can affect your success more than the good deeds you do or even the attempts you make to improve yourself. Can the environments in which you spend your time have massive and pervasive effects on your thoughts, feelings, actions, and life results? My answer is an emphatic yes!

Of the Five Factors, the first one on the list you can do something about is your Feng Shui. Think about this for a second: You can't choose which family you're born into, and you can't change your luck pattern on a whim. But you can plant some beautiful flowers in your garden or start changing the colors in your home. Both are Feng Shui methods you can implement today and see the positive results tomorrow, or not long after. The truth is that all Five Factors affect you all the time. The point to grasp is that Feng Shui (the interaction between you and your environment) affects you powerfully. Arranging your environment to your advantage is one of the most powerful methods of life improvement the human species has yet discovered.

Understanding the Schools of Feng Shui

Though many schools of Feng Shui exist, all of them maintain the same basic purpose: Gaining life improvement by improving the energy of the environment. Most traditional schools of Feng Shui use a combination of two basic methods: the Landform Method and the Compass Method.

A lesser-known school of Feng Shui is called *BTB* or *Black Sect Feng Shui,* which is the type of Feng Shui used in this book. My teacher, Grandmaster Lin Yun, further developed this style and brought it to the West. (***Note:*** When I refer to BTB in this book, I'm referring to Grandmaster Lin Yun's Feng Shui school.) I fill you in on the basics of the different schools of Feng Shui and help you distinguish between the two in the next sections.

Landform and Compass Method Feng Shui

Landform Feng Shui reads the lay of the land and notes the contour, climate, shape, and other factors to determine the best locations for living and working. For example, in China, living with a mountain at your back and with your house facing south was recognized over the centuries as a safer living position. Why? This positioning helped the residents on at least three levels:

- ✔ It gave protection from warring bands of infidels pillaging the countryside.

- ✔ It provided a strong psychological feeling of support and stability, a continuous influence that helped the family's fortune grow over time.

- ✔ It was a protective barrier against the storms and cold that could sweep down from the north in the winter. (This barrier helped preserve the croplands and the personal health of the occupants.)

The Landform Method was easier to apply in the countryside, but even today, many of its observations are still highly useful for city living.

Compass Method Feng Shui studies the directions (east, west, north, and south) that your front door and other key parts of your home face and compares these directions with your personal life directions, which are calculated from the time and date of your birth. Simple and complex formulas exist to determine your positive and negative directions. Other areas of the house that are aligned to positive directions include the bed, the stove, the desk, and the back door. The Compass Method says that these directions (as well as timing) are some of the most critical factors affecting your Feng Shui.

Note: I don't use the Compass Method in this book, so you can set aside any concerns you may have about cardinal or personal directions and how they affect your home and life. I respect this method, but I use a different approach.

Grandmaster Lin Yun's Feng Shui school

One of the chief characteristics of Grandmaster Lin Yun's Feng Shui school is its eclectic nature. With roots in the teachings of India, China, and Tibet, it pulls from multiple sources, weaving together a combination of traditional Feng Shui, Grandmaster Lin Yun's energy theories, and Chinese folklore. This school also benefits from the addition of Western concepts and explanations from various fields, including physiology, psychology, ecology, and sociology. Its working philosophy is that the best result comes from a marriage of Eastern and Western viewpoints and knowledge.

Grandmaster Lin Yun's Feng Shui school is

- ✔ An easy-to-grasp and easy-to-apply form of Feng Shui

- ✔ Highly practical and effective
- ✔ Focused on creating beneficial results quickly with the least expenditure of time and money

I follow the teachings of Grandmaster Lin Yun's Feng Shui school. In addition, I focus intently on solutions that produce noticeable effects but are relatively easy to perform. Feng Shui is one of the most effective methods available to change your circumstances and achieve more of what you really want out of life. You can put it into practice immediately, generate great results, and create a brand-new flow of life and energy. Also, with Feng Shui, no life scenario is hopeless or unworkable; you can always do something to improve your situation — if you so choose.

Distinguishing the schools from each other

A key tenet of Grandmaster Lin Yun's Feng Shui teachings is to honor and respect all other Feng Shui schools and practitioners and to refrain from criticizing other methods. Those who follow Grandmaster Lin Yun's teachings don't proclaim the method as superior to others; rather, they respect the differences and seek to learn from them. By the same token, Grandmaster Lin Yun's approach to Feng Shui does have its own special characteristics that distinguish it from other schools. Grandmaster Lin Yun's Feng Shui school differs from traditional Feng Shui methods in that

- ✔ **There's an "internal" rather than "external" compass.** Traditional Feng Shui employs a physical compass to diagnose key directions of the home and relate them to the residents through astrological calculations. Grandmaster Lin Yun's school doesn't use a physical compass to read the Feng Shui of a site. Instead, the practitioner uses an internalized or memorized compass traditionally called the *compass of the heart*. This *Feng Shui Octagon* (also known as the *Ba-Gua*) is one of several methods for mapping the energies of homes and properties. (Chapter 3 has details on how to apply the Feng Shui Octagon to your environment.)

When you apply the Feng Shui method in this book, you don't need to know which earthly direction your door or any other part of your home faces.

- ✔ **It employs a spiritual approach rather than a traditional one.** Traditional Feng Shui schools employ a traditional approach to the art and use traditionally styled solutions, such as employing positive and negative cardinal directions. Grandmaster Lin Yun's approach draws from traditional sources and adds spiritual methods such as the Three Secrets Reinforcement, which are a key part of the cures you perform. (Chapter 6 has more details about the Three Secrets Reinforcement.)

- ✔ **It places a unique emphasis on Relative Positioning.** Traditional Feng Shui uses the birth date and time of the residents or the completion date of the home to determine Feng Shui factors. Grandmaster Lin Yun's Feng Shui school instead emphasizes the *Theory of Relative Positioning,* which states that the areas of the environment that are physically closest to you affect your energy the most (Chapter 2 has more on this theory). The *Mouth of Chi* focuses on the energy of the main entrance as a primary influencing factor (see Chapter 9 for details).

✔ **It uses the power of intention and visualization.** Grandmaster Lin Yun's school differs from traditional Feng Shui schools in that it emphasizes using the power of intention to dramatically enhance the effects of the Feng Shui cures you apply. It also considers mind as a sixth sense, employing visualization in addition to the traditional five (sight, hearing, touch, smell, and taste). In Chapter 6, I detail how to use intention and visualization to make your cures highly effective.

✔ **It offers personal cures.** Unlike traditional Feng Shui schools, which focus on environmental changes and astrological timing, Grandmaster Lin Yun's Feng Shui school not only employs these factors but also adds a remarkable variety of cures you can apply directly to your own body and mind. I share these amazingly effective personal cures in Chapter 22.

✔ **It considers self-development to be key.** Self-development, or bettering yourself as a human being, is paramount in Grandmaster Lin Yun's approach, in contrast with many traditional Feng Shui schools. According to Grandmaster Lin Yun's Feng Shui school, to derive the fullest benefits of Feng Shui, you must cultivate harmonious, balanced energy not only within your environment but also within yourself. Meditation and energy practices are some of the best ways to do this inner cultivation. I recommend starting a meditative practice; use a technique from your own tradition or one found in this book (see Chapter 22 for step-by-step meditation instruction).

Note: If you read other Feng Shui books, keep in mind that other schools of Feng Shui may use different principles and methods. This difference is okay; no one Feng Shui approach has a monopoly on value and effectiveness.

Looking at Feng Shui Factors That You Can Use to Your Advantage

By correctly applying the easy and sensible Feng Shui principles I present in this book, you can reverse negative patterns and strengthen positive ones to maximize your chances of success. When you improve your environment, you can also improve essential areas of your life such as relationships, career, wealth, and family connections. You may be amazed at how life obstacles can be cleared away with simple energy shifts that you can perform in your home.

The following list describes some important ways that Feng Shui is influencing you right now. By reading this book, you can discover how to use all of these factors — and more — to your advantage:

- ✔ **Your front door:** This area receives most of the subtle energy in your home. It influences your opportunities and the amount of income you command. (See Chapter 9 for more information.)

- ✔ **The ability to see your front door from the street:** You may have to struggle hard for the opportunities you receive if your front door is hidden from plain view. (Head to Chapter 9 for more information.)

- ✔ **Your bed position:** This condition influences your love life and health to an amazing (and unseen) degree. (Flip to Chapter 11 for details.)

- ✔ **The placement of your stove:** This location can influence your cash flow and physical health. A chronically dirty stove can significantly affect your financial status. (Flip to Chapter 12 for the scoop.)

- ✔ **The locations of bathrooms:** This situation can result in a loss of money or significant health issues. (See Chapter 13 for more info.)

- ✔ **The air quality and lighting levels:** These circumstances directly affect your thinking patterns and endorphin levels, which in turn influence your performance, attitude, and results. (Chapter 15 has more information.)

- ✔ **The colors you see:** The colors around you powerfully influence your moods, energy level, and effectiveness. (See Chapter 15 for the scoop.)

- ✔ **Your desk position:** This situation can make or break your career. The desk is a top Feng Shui factor for success on the job. (Chapter 17 has details.)

- ✔ **The people who previously lived in your home:** They probably left behind some invisible vibes when they moved. The subtle traces of their feelings and experiences — if negative — may hinder you for the first several years you live in the home. (Chapter 20 has more details.)

 A Midwestern dentist located in a small town was frustrated due to his difficulties in hiring additional staff to expand his practice. After performing Feng Shui in his office, he was pleasantly surprised to find that quality hygienists came out of the woodwork to apply for positions. Ultimately, changing the Feng Shui of your environment creates new options and choices. Feng Shui can open up a whole new realm of possibilities for you if you let it.

Finding Life Solutions with Feng Shui

When you have a problem, you can seek solutions through multiple avenues. For example, if you have a problem with your car, you can buy a new car, repair it yourself, have someone else repair it, hope the problem goes away, or live with the issue. Each option holds advantages and disadvantages. The option you choose depends on your level of cash on hand, your expertise with cars, and your current life status. In almost any situation, you can choose from a range of solutions. You almost never have only one road to follow.

For general life problems, your solutions can include

- Working harder and/or smarter (or acquiring new information)
- Calling in an expert
- Calling on a higher power and praying
- Trying to learn from the situation, becoming a better person and building character
- Improving the environment to create change (in other words, performing Feng Shui adjustments)

You may be surprised to find out that the best choice on the list is often the last one: Adjust the Feng Shui of your home to change your situation and resolve your problem. In the following sections, I outline the types of Feng Shui approaches you can use and the range of cures available to you.

Selecting a Feng Shui approach

Grandmaster Lin Yun's school of Feng Shui involves identifying energetic problems (or opportunities for improvement) in your environment and coming up with a solution that's viable for your needs, including your taste, budget, aesthetic values, and temperament.

You can apply Feng Shui to your life in two basic ways: generally and specifically. Though both approaches are effective, the general approach can sometimes lead to frustration and confusion. I recommend the specific approach because of its clarity, power, and straightforward progress toward tangible results. However, as usual in Feng Shui, the best method is the one that feels right for you and creates the results you need.

The general approach: Improving the environment at random

With the general approach to Feng Shui, you start by looking at your house in Feng Shui terms, without first taking your current life needs into account. Then you apply solutions to improve the overall energy of the environment with the general intention of making things better for you and your home.

I consider this method a general approach because you're not analyzing your life to determine the results you want to create. Yes, this approach produces results, but because you don't set specific intentions first, those results may not be as powerful or as targeted as you desire. Using a general approach to Feng Shui can therefore make it more difficult to know how well your cures are working or what additional improvements you need to make.

The specific approach: Setting your goals and achieving them

If you're looking for powerful results, I recommend you take the specific approach to Feng Shui. This approach requires you to perform two steps:

1. **Examine your life and pinpoint the parts of your life (relationship, work, money, and so on) that aren't working as desired and are crying out for improvement.**

   Now's the time to decide specifically how you want these areas to improve. (See the following section for help getting started.)

2. **Adjust your environment to achieve specific changes in different parts of your life.**

   Use the information packed into this book to determine how you can adjust your environment, pick the cures that work for you and your lifestyle, and implement them.

Overall, the specific approach is effective and is focused on getting you the results you want. You know your goals and targets, and you can hone in on and achieve them. Instead of just making general improvements to the environment and hoping they can help, you know the specific, practical purpose of each cure, which enhances the power of the cure. The specific approach puts you in the driver's seat. You get to decide which areas of your life to improve and which areas are fine for now. Because you set goals and implement changes to reach them, you can easily track your results to see how well your Feng Shui is working. Finally, you can adjust your cures over time to fine-tune the energy for even better results.

Choosing the Life Areas to improve

When you're ready to begin using Feng Shui to improve your life, you can start by deciding exactly what you want to change or improve. Don't worry about addressing every possible Feng Shui issue in your home (after all, no home is perfect). Instead, focus on how your environment is currently helping or halting your progress.

More significantly, focus on what you can do now. By taking proper action, sooner or later you'll create new results. Start by filling out Table 1-1 to find out what parts of your life you want to improve first through Feng Shui (see Chapter 3 for more about the Life Areas listed in the table). This life-assessment exercise gives you a clear look at the status of several parts of your life and helps you decide which ones you want to improve. For each Life Area listed in the first column, write one or two words describing the general situation for that part of your life in the middle column. Use the third column to prioritize the urgency of improvement by assigning 1 (high priority), 2 (medium priority), or 3 (low priority) to each Life Area. (***Tip:*** Photocopy the worksheet before using it so you can use it again later.)

Table 1-1	Life-Assessment Exercise	
Life Area	*Description*	*Priority (1, 2, 3)*
Wealth/Money		
Marriage/Partnership		
Health		
Career		
Fame/Reputation		
Family		
Children		
Helpful People		
Knowledge		

After you complete the life-assessment exercise, select (from the ones you've rated as high priorities) the one Life Area you want to focus on immediately. Keep this Life Area firmly in mind. As you read this book, notice the cures you can perform to improve this part of your life. This awareness keeps you focused on finding practical techniques you can implement right away.

Taking steps to Feng Shui success with a range of available cures

You can perform a wide range of possible cures to transform a Feng Shui malady. For any situation, cures may range anywhere from simple, quick, and easy (like rearranging your existing furniture) to complex, difficult, and expensive (like buying a new house). In this book, I keep things as easy and inexpensive as possible.

Feng Shui isn't inherently cheap, but you can find creative ways to implement low-cost Feng Shui cures in many situations. Most importantly, choose practical solutions for your situation.

Be sure to get a scale drawing of your home and lot (or at least one that's close to scale) to use with this book. (Hey, if you're going to practice Feng Shui, do it right.) Find the architectural drawings you stashed in the garage or make a drawing of your home including the internal walls and the doors. This tool is your guide when using Feng Shui to actually make something happen (instead of just thinking about making a change).

In the following list, I present nine steps you can use to implement powerful Feng Shui changes. I use the life example of improving one's marriage in each step to help you understand how to apply the steps.

1. **Choose which Life Area you want to work on first.**

   Refer to Table 1-1 to see what I'm talking about. In this example, say you want more harmony and closeness with your partner.

2. **Make a commitment to see new results (changes!) in your life in the chosen area.**

   You need to make changes in your home or on your property to get the new results you desire, so commit yourself to finding and correcting the imbalances. Or, following the example, add positive energy to Marriage Areas if no problems are obvious. At this point, you may want to recruit your spouse to help make the Feng Shui changes; this is a beneficial approach for all of your Feng Shui endeavors (not just the marriage cures!).

3. **Scan your environment to see where you need to implement Feng Shui adjustments.**

   So to improve your marriage, for example, you may note the placement of your bed and the colors in your bedroom.

4. **Select the best cure options for each environmental problem you notice.**

   You may choose to cure the situation by moving your bed to the best possible position in the room and improving the colors as needed.

5. **Implement the chosen cures.**

   In this example, you physically move the bed and install the new colors.

6. **Perform the Three Secrets Reinforcement for each cure you do.**

   This one's self-explanatory provided you know all about the Three Secrets Reinforcement. I explain this important internal step, which empowers the cures you perform, in Chapter 6.

7. **Pay attention to changes that occur in your life after you implement your cures.**

   Keep on the lookout for the new effects you desire. Ideally, you and your spouse will experience greater harmony and increased communication after you put your cures in place.

   Keep a written record of the cures you do and the results you get (see Chapter 18.)

8. **Based on the feedback you get from your life, perform additional cures for the same area of your life as needed.**

   If things have improved somewhat but you want further benefits, apply some more marriage cures.

9. **Start the whole process again, focusing on another area of your life.**

   Now that you have a success under your belt, you can target another aspect of your life — such as career or income — that you want to improve.

Intention: The real power behind Feng Shui

Feng Shui can be divided into two parts — the visible and the invisible — both of which are important for success in life and in Feng Shui.

✔ Visible factors include the chi (life force energy) of the land, as well as the walls, doors, streets, and other tangible elements that we analyze and alter using Feng Shui.

✔ The invisible factors include *predecessor influences* (the energies of the people who previously lived in your home), ghosts and spirits, and other intangible qualities of the environment.

✔ The most important invisible factor is *intention,* or the simultaneous strong desire and visualization of what you want a cure to produce. Everything you do in life involves an intention and an action.

✔ The action is the physical side of the process. In Feng Shui, this means some tangible activity, like moving your bed to a better location, changing a wall color, or decorating with healthy potted plants.

✔ Intention is the invisible, or spiritual, side of Feng Shui. It's the reason why you move the bed. Specifically, it's the life change you hope to accomplish when you make this adjustment. Intention includes two parts: what you want and how clearly you want it. If you move the bed to improve your marriage and you visualize the improvement while changing the bed position, your cure will be much more effective. (See Chapter 6 for powerful methods of empowering your intention.)

How and when results come isn't something you can control directly (refer to Chapter 18 for info on results). However, keep in mind that even if you see quick or immediate benefits from your cures, they continue to work indefinitely and provide you with ongoing energy and results for years to come — unless of course you move, in which case there's even more important Feng Shui work to do (particularly before you move). Chapter 20 has the skinny on this vital Feng Shui topic.

Getting Additional Help

Occasionally, a situation is so burdened with Feng Shui problems that you can't decide where to begin. Or you may perform some good cures and see incremental improvement but feel that you still have a long way to go. If you need help to tackle your issues fully, you can take a Feng Shui course or you can call in a professional consultant for assistance (see Chapter 24 and the appendix for details). Meanwhile, make any improvements that you can right now and better your odds of creating positive effects — inevitably, things will begin to shift in the right direction.

Chapter 2

Mastering the Principles of Feng Shui

· ·

In This Chapter

▶ Exploring chi (energy) and its variations

▶ Flowing with and nurturing your life energy

▶ Positioning yourself auspiciously

▶ Getting to know the Three Life Pillars

▶ Providing a little Feng Shui 101

· ·

Feng Shui teaches you to become aware of your environment and to apply energetic principles to your surroundings. Whether you know it or not, you're affected by the Feng Shui of your environment at all times. The energies of your residence and workplace constantly contribute to your successes and/or failures in life. When you practice Feng Shui, you intentionally interact with your environment instead of being passively influenced by it. The information in this book opens your Feng Shui perception. With it, you start to see how to make practical changes in your living and working environments to improve your life situation, and you make these changes according to principles and techniques discovered in China and refined over centuries.

An underlying premise of Feng Shui is that energy flows smoothly in a harmonious environment and is obstructed in a disharmonious environment. Whether this premise seems mystical or academic to you, this Feng Shui concept is a reality that continuously affects your life in direct, tangible ways. So prepare to explore some unusual ways of thinking about life, energy, and feeling, and get ready to perceive living environments in a way that gives you new levels of understanding and control over your life.

In this chapter, I introduce the essential principles of Feng Shui that explain how and why *cures* (alterations to your environment that result in desired life changes; see Chapter 4) work. You can certainly get results without mastering all of these principles, but this crash course in Feng Shui concepts helps you make sense of all the advice that follows in this book. Start reading, and you'll soon find yourself growing and changing with your environment. Feng Shui can be fun! So strap yourself in for an adventure in the realms of space (your space, that is), energy, and improved living circumstances. Houston, we have liftoff!

Chi: The Energy of Feng Shui

Chi (pronounced chee) is the fundamental principle without which Feng Shui (or you and me for that matter) can't exist. This Chinese word has no direct English translation; instead, it refers to several meanings at once: cosmic energy, life force, breath, and vapor. (In this book, when I say energy, I'm referring to chi.) Chi is the invisible energy that animates all living things. It flows continuously through pathways (or *meridians*) in your body (the practices of acupuncture and Oriental medicine are based on these flows; see Figure 2-1 for a stylized view of human energy circulation); if chi were to stop flowing through you for even one second, you'd cease to exist (at least in human form). Chi also flows through your home and through the Earth, the heavens, the atmosphere, and the cosmos. (Based on Chinese folklore, energy channels that run inside the Earth are called dragon veins. These veins are similar to the body's energy meridians, and the chi that flows through them is metaphorically called the breath, or energy, of the dragon.)

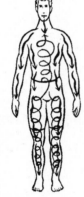

Figure 2-1:
Energy
flowing
within the
body.

The flow of chi in your environment affects every aspect of your life: your health, your outlook, your decision making, and even your sex life. The flow of chi in turn is influenced by the interior and exterior elements of your physical environment. Colors, shapes, orientation, lighting, objects and their positions and arrangements, the use of space, the degree of cleanliness, and many other factors all affect and collectively determine your home's energy flow. And this flow (or lack thereof) affects you continually, conditions your experience in your home and workplace, and significantly influences your future for good or for ill.

Millions of people worldwide and thousands of people with whom I've worked over the years are applying the principles and practices of Feng Shui in their daily lives and are experiencing positive results. Whether you prefer the philosophical approach to understanding chi ("This whole chi metaphor really gives me a useful new way to look at and reorganize my life") or you take the tangible route ("Whoa, I'm really feelin' something here"), you can receive profound and practical benefits by arranging your living and working environments according to Feng Shui principles. Start by examining the ways that your body absorbs chi on a daily basis. Chi comes to you from multiple environmental sources that include

- The food you eat
- The air you breathe
- The water you drink
- The land and its vegetation
- The Sun, Moon, and other celestial bodies
- Your living environment
- Your working environment
- Your relationships

These multiple sources in the environment supply your body with energy (chi) to sustain itself. Your body then transforms that energy and directs it into multiple activities: digestion, breathing, moving, thinking, working, sensing, worrying, complaining, watching TV, and a myriad of other human activities. But all of these activities are powered by the same basic energy that flows through your system, your environment, and the universe itself.

A new, yet old, way of seeing the world

Perhaps you're wondering, "How real is this mysterious, all-important force called chi?" Many Westerners don't understand chi because modern science doesn't acknowledge that it exists. The rationalist worldview denies the reality of whatever can't be weighed on a scale or measured by an instrument. By this logic, a life force that animates all living things doesn't exist because no meter exists to measure it. By further extension, happiness, sadness, joy, love, and pain aren't real for the same reason. Yet the most sophisticated instrument in the universe already exists that possesses functions for registering the flow of chi. This instrument is the human being, and the functions are feeling and intuitive sensing.

An interesting fact about chi is that it works for you whether or not you believe it's real (kind of like gravity and oxygen). For example, how exactly are you able to move your arm? Modern science says that the food you digest releases energy (calories of heat) that powers your cells and enables your nerves to fire and your muscles to contract. Voilà! You can grab your morning cup of coffee. But how exactly does this process occur? And why, when the body dies, can't you simply shove a hamburger into it — or zap it with electricity — and make it rise and walk again? These mysteries drive both science and religion.

(continued)

(continued)

Chinese theory explains the phenomenon of movement from a different perspective. Your life force — your personal chi — originally came from your parents. (Before your parents, it came from the universe, but that's a longer story.) Chinese theory says that the chi activates your brain to perceive and think and then flows through the body, allowing the body to move and function. "Gimme a cup of coffee!" Mr. Brain says. And the chi stimulates the muscles of your arm to grasp the cup, lift it to your lips, and swallow the sips. But even when you're buzzing on coffee, you're still running on chi, like everything else in the universe.

Or look at it this way: Modern electricity is essentially electrons flowing through wires. Electricity leaves a power plant at very high voltages. When it reaches your home, the energy has stepped down enough to power your home's wiring without blowing it out. This basic energy is then adapted to run a wide variety of appliances (furnace, air conditioner, refrigerator, computer, stereo, TV, and so on) that perform a diverse range of functions. By now you're used to it, dependent on it, and probably even take its numerous benefits for granted — until the power goes out or the monthly bill arrives — and yet you don't really understand exactly what it is. In fact, no one really does! The most interesting thing about electricity is that you know how to harness it, but you ultimately don't know what it is. (So you call it electricity.) The same can be said for chi: You ultimately don't know what chi is, but you know it's the energy that runs your body; courses through your emotions; and dances mysteriously in your thoughts, inspirations, and dreams.

And remember, even the greatest masters of the East haven't completely conquered the subtlest mysteries of the life force. Nor have the greatest Western scientists. They simply find workable theories that allow them to effectively manipulate forces they ultimately don't understand or need to understand. (Scientists are still searching for about 95 percent of the mass of the universe, which they've termed *dark matter* and *dark energy,* so if you happen to find it under your bed, please let them know.)

For the purposes of this book, visualize chi as a river of energy that runs through your home and your body. Where the river flows smoothly and powerfully, you're able to navigate the path of life with confidence and power, and you tend to be fortunate, happy, and successful. But where the river is blocked or stagnant, you can get bogged down and overwhelmed by obstacles, problems, and frustrations.

The Types of Chi

According to Feng Shui theory, several varieties of chi exist, all of which affect you on one level or another. The following sections cover some of the more important varieties.

The chi of the heavens

Heavenly chi includes the chi of the weather, the sky, the stars, and other heavenly bodies. Chi of the sky and atmosphere includes climatic influences that affect humans and other life-forms. Cosmic chi is the energy of outer space and its celestial bodies: the Sun, the Moon, and the stars.

The chi of the Earth

The chi of the Earth is the realm of Feng Shui. The most important factor in Feng Shui is whether the chi of a parcel of land is healthy and supportive of the humans who live in the area. The chi of the Earth can either be lively, vibrant, and nourishing (such as in Hawaii and old-growth redwood forests), or it can be arid, barren, and hostile (such as in Antarctica and the Dead Sea). The chi in a hostile area is unsupportive of human life and can actually drain life from the people who stay in the area for long periods of time.

The chi of homes and living environments

The interaction between the chi of a living environment and the chi of the humans within that environment is Feng Shui. The way your home is situated can mean the difference between experiencing long-term happiness and good fortune versus missed opportunities and a more difficult life path.

The chi of humans

The chi states of people are measured against an ideal chi state and have many variations. Human chi states are classified according to their demeanor or dominant behavior patterns. For example, someone who's prickly, pushy, and displays sharp edges around others has porcupine chi; a person who's physically present but mentally absent has daydreamer's chi. (The lights are on, the dog is barking, but no one's home.)

The Flows of Chi

An important thing to remember about chi is that it flows like wind and water. Think of the flow of chi in your body and in your home as a river of energy. The main intake of this energy river for your body is your mouth; the main source of it in your home is the front door. To manipulate the flow of chi in your environment is to practice Feng Shui. Ideally, your flows of chi should meet the characteristics described in the next sections.

The ideal chi state for the physical body

For the human body, the ideal state of chi is strong, smooth, and positive energy that's uplifted and evenly distributed through the body — it flows from the ground (feet) up to the head. You receive chi from many sources, including through your mouth. Food, air, light, and chi all enter the body through the mouth to provide nourishment, sustenance, and energy. (The fact that your mouth plays a key role in your ideal chi state reveals why breathing exercises and changing what you eat for the better are so important.) Figure 2-1 shows chi entering through the mouth and flowing within the body. The best chi condition occurs when chi flows strongly through the whole body without any blocks, distortions, or flow problems.

The ideal chi state for the home

Ideally, the chi in a home circulates smoothly and freely through every part of the home, filling it with positive energy. This energy — which comes mainly through the front door — is the energetic income of the home. The front door is the main energy source because this point is where people enter. (See Chapter 9 for details on creating a welcoming entry into your home.) When your home chi is ideal and flowing (as in Figure 2-2), it conducts sufficient energy to provide you with beneficial life circumstances. In other words, you prosper and flourish, and life is good. But if the home contains obstructions (for example, if the front door is blocked), the flow of chi is disrupted, and areas of the home can become energetically depleted, which in turn affects the people who live in the home. Generally, a home that has depleted or distorted energy patterns results in disharmony and various life problems.

Figure 2-2:
Energy
circulating
in the home
and land.

The positive and negative traits of chi flow

The beneficial characteristics of ideal chi flow for your body or your environment are as follows:

- ✔ Powerful (it's appropriately strong enough to nourish the situation)
- ✔ Positive (the quality of the energy is beneficial for humans)

- ✔ Uplifting (it promotes growth and causes life to flourish)
- ✔ Flowing (it's moving and circulating, not stuck or stagnant)
- ✔ Smooth (the flow is even and balanced, not buffeting or abrupt)

The negative characteristics of either human or home chi flow include the following:

- ✔ Rushing (it comes too fast, is unbalancing, and can lead to injuries)
- ✔ Stagnant (it prevents your goals from happening)
- ✔ Blocked (it can stop you in life)
- ✔ Leaking (it leads to loss of energy)
- ✔ Piercing (it can threaten your health and welfare)

Cultivating Chi

You know that everything affects your energy, so what can you do about it? According to ancient Chinese philosophy, one of the most important things in life is cultivating one's chi. So consider chi cultivation your personal Feng Shui mission.

You cultivate chi in the same way you cultivate anything else — with time, attention, and patience. For example, to cultivate a vegetable garden, you do the following: Pay close attention to how the garden is doing; feed, water, and care for it; protect it from pests and intruders; continuously create the conditions where the things you want (plants, wildlife, and so on) can flourish. You may also want to increase your knowledge of gardening techniques and principles and maybe plant a few vegetable seeds while you're at it.) Read on to find out how to apply the cultivation principle to your own personal chi.

Benefits and rewards of chi cultivation

Chi is life, so cultivating your chi enhances and improves your life in all areas and expands your sphere of influence in life, at home, in relationships, and at work. The many desirable results of chi cultivation include

- ✔ Improved physical health
- ✔ Enhanced mental health
- ✔ Increased intellectual ability and wisdom
- ✔ Increased spiritual and psychic power

✔ Better luck

✔ Improved family and personal relationships

✔ Character benefits, such as becoming calmer, more tolerant, more patient, more honest, and so on

Eight factors that affect your personal chi

You can cultivate your personal chi by proactively addressing or manipulating the eight main factors that affect it:

✔ Your inner self

✔ The people around you

✔ Your environment

✔ Events

✔ Your conduct

✔ Your spiritual demeanor

✔ The political climate

✔ Other factors (including those that are unknown)

These factors influence everyone to one degree or another. However, your personal Feng Shui is one of the easiest of the eight factors to change. So forget about trying to change other people (it doesn't work anyway) and focus on improving yourself and your personal environment. Cultivate your own chi, take responsibility for your personal Feng Shui, and then watch the positive changes stream into your life.

Positioning: Your Place in the Scheme of Things

Positioning is how you relate personally to any environment in which you find yourself. A Feng Shui principle is that the importance of a position is determined by the amount of time you spend in the positioned area. On average, humans spend one-third of their time working (usually at a desk), one-third sleeping (in bed), and one-third saving the planet, I mean, taking care of everything else in their lives. You may not have thought about it before reading this, but the positions of your bed and desk determine your physical orientation during two-thirds of your life. Needless to say, these positions have a strong effect on your health, happiness, success, and financial fortune.

Two positioning principles — the Theory of Relative Positioning and the Commanding Position method — help you understand the concept. (In Chapters 11, 12, and 17, you can find cures to help you gain powerful positioning.)

Understanding the Theory of Relative Positioning

The type of Feng Shui I practice is from Grandmaster Lin Yun's Feng Shui school, which teaches the Theory of Relative Positioning for orienting and analyzing your environment. This method is easier for many people to pick up quickly (compared to some traditional Feng Shui approaches that rely on the physical compass to determine directions for positioning) because you don't need to perform complex directional calculations.

Two principles guide the Theory of Relative Positioning:

✔ **Local interrelations are more important than global positioning.** The first principle of the Theory of Relative Positioning says that the interaction between the parts of your environment (meaning their orientation relative to each other) is more important than their orientation to any absolute direction (east, west, north, or south). In practical usage, this school emphasizes the interrelationships between your home and your neighbors, your driveway and the street, your home and your lot, and numerous other parts of your environment over the importance of compass directions. (*Note:* Grandmaster Lin Yun's school does consider the compass method to be a valid and effective Feng Shui system but prefers its own unique method for analyzing and diagnosing the environment.) This method has the added benefit of getting you to examine more closely and understand more deeply the energetic connections that exist between the various parts of the environment in which you live and how interrelated they really are. This system also helps you see the interactions of all the parts of your personal life and understand more clearly the ways in which they affect you.

✔ **What's closer to you is more important than what's farther away.** The second principle of the Theory of Relative Positioning is that the closer an area of the environment is to the human beings in it (that's you!), the more that area affects that person and his or her life experience. Keep in mind that the closer an area of your environment is, the more it affects you.

Using the Commanding Position method

The main idea of the Commanding Position is to sit, stand, or otherwise situate yourself in the best and most powerful position available in any situation. For example, the Commanding Position in a car is the driver's seat because you have complete control of the vehicle (unless of course the person riding shotgun is packing a real shotgun).

The Commanding Position helps keep you safe, strong, and in charge. Many modern Westerners have forgotten the need for protection or for taking extra precautions in life, but the truth is that, on a basic level, you're still the same being who fought to survive in the jungles, forests, and savannas a hundred thousand years ago (albeit slightly less hairy and maybe a tad more evolved). The evolutionary advantage still goes to the person in the more protected and empowered position.

An example of classic positive Feng Shui home positioning

One powerful way to apply the Commanding Position to your home is with the classic armchair position. Say a hill or mountain sits behind your home, providing a solid backing in life. Imagine that another, slightly lower hill sits to the left of the home and that a third hill (one that's even lower yet still substantial) sits to the right of the home. In front of the home is an open place with a pleasant view, including a view of water in the middle distance (see the following figure). This position protects the home on three sides, keeping out intruders and protecting the residents, and the home's inspiring front view bodes well for good fortune.

The Commanding Position provides fundamental assistance to these parts of your life:

- ✔ Overall fortunes (home position on lot and landscape)
- ✔ General success (bed position)
- ✔ Career and projects (desk position)
- ✔ Health and money (stove position)
- ✔ Social life (living room couch position)

In the interior of the home, the Commanding Position has applications in several key areas. In order of importance, these areas are the bed, the stove, the desk, the dining table, and the couch. The following guidelines give you the interior Commanding Position principles in a nutshell:

- ✔ Situate yourself as far as practical from the main entrance to the space.
- ✔ See the entrance from wherever you're situated (command the room visually).
- ✔ See the widest possible part of the room.
- ✔ Avoid situating yourself in the direct onward path of the door into the space.

I show you how to put the Commanding Position principle into action with your bed in Chapter 11, your stove in Chapter 12, your living room in Chapter 13, and your desk in Chapter 17. For more on the Commanding Position for the home, see Chapter 7.

Presenting the Three Life Pillars

I created the term *Three Life Pillars* based on Grandmaster Lin Yun's teachings to embrace the fundamental Feng Shui concept that the three most vital parts of any residence are the front door, the master bed, and the stove. By focusing on the Three Life Pillars of your home, you can ensure that the basic energy of your home and life stays strong and solid. If you have Feng Shui issues in just one of these three areas, multiple life problems can result; if you have issues in two or three of the Life Pillars — who ya gonna call? Shui Busters! See Chapter 19 for an in-depth exploration of the Three Life Pillars for improving your life.

Recognizing the importance of the entry

The front door — the *Mouth of Chi* — is the first and greatest of the Three Life Pillars. The front door is the chief entry point for your home's energy;

it affects money, relationships, health, people, and so on. The condition of the front door tells a good deal about your life and sets the tone for the Feng Shui of the entire home. If the conditions of your front door prevent sufficient energy from entering the home, all parts of your life can suffer. In Chapter 9, I cover the front door and entryway in great detail.

Improving the place of rest and rejuvenation

The second Life Pillar is the master bed, which relates directly to rest, relationships, and health. It also relates to your financial success because your sleeping position and the quality of your rest affect your ability to acquire money. You can find out more information about the master bed and bedroom in Chapter 11.

Activating your home's energy generator

The Third Life Pillar and chief energy generator of the home is the stove, which creates health and prosperity. In the kitchen, the position of the stove and the cook are vitally important to your health and finances. I cover the stove, the kitchen, and the position of the cook in Chapter 12.

The Psychology of Feng Shui

Attitude determines the potential for success in any endeavor, including performing Feng Shui in your home. How you approach your Feng Shui practice helps determine how much it contributes to increased energy and success. Use the following attitudes and modes of thinking to attain success and fulfillment through your Feng Shui efforts.

Know that improvement is possible in any situation (especially yours)

Like gravity, Feng Shui works equally for all things. The same energy is available, and the same principles apply, whether you're rich or poor; happy or sad; atheist, Buddhist or Christian. No situation is hopeless, and something can be done to remedy any environment and life circumstance. At the most, you may need to move. Moving is a Feng Shui remedy, as long as you choose the right place — the right change of environment can change your life. (See Chapter 20 for the lowdown on how to avoid key Feng Shui pitfalls when choosing a home.) No matter who you are, whether you're Donald Trump or Donald Duck, you can benefit from arranging your living and working environments according to Feng Shui principles. The results may be subtle; they may be dramatic. But you can see positive results either way.

Maximize your current situation

The idea of maximizing your current situation follows on the heels of improving any situation. A special magic derives from pulling out all the stops and tweaking everything available. When you know you've done all (not almost all) that you can, a burden lifts, your psyche shifts, and the situation definitely changes. Something new and unexpected comes into the picture. And you — sitting in the catbird seat (the best possible Feng Shui position) — are able to grab opportunity by the collar and slide gracefully into a realm of greater harmony, prosperity, and happiness.

The saying "pray as if everything depends on God and work as if everything depends on you" echoes this Feng Shui principle: Take action as if the Feng Shui of your home determines your life course. Apply every reasonable option and then stretch it a bit further. Then enjoy fabulous results.

Action without knowledge is never a recipe for success. Feng Shui is not merely furniture juggling or aesthetic interior decorating. Feng Shui combines aesthetics with time-tested energy principles. So take the reins. Apply the principles in this book with wisdom. Choose the appropriate cure(s) after observing your environment and considering your needs. And above all, listen to your intuition.

Recognize that you're the center of the equation

Whether you believe in science or in a higher power, life is still a mystery. No one controls all the events in his or her life. However, you have free will, so you can take positive action to influence the areas you want to affect. In Feng Shui, you're the central factor in your environment. And your actions can make the differences that lead to substantial and beneficial life changes.

Choose to take action

After you realize that you can act to improve your situation, the next step is to decide to get moving. The decision to act is made by anyone who ever accomplishes anything worthwhile in life. Now it's your turn. Look closely at your present situation; you're reading a book that gives you easy, practical methods for creating changes that can lead to a better life. All you need to do is put these methods to use.

Be open to change and receiving the new

When you put Feng Shui into action, prepare for changes! Some life shifts may be dramatic and sudden; others may be subtle and gradual. The key is to be open to new things and ideas, to be willing to act, and to be receptive to change. Remember that the mind is like a parachute — it works best when open. The people who get the best results from Feng Shui proceed with an open mind, a positive outlook, and a clear intention (qualities that are also Feng Shui principles).

Basic Pointers for Feng Shui Success

If you do nothing else, at least apply the following Feng Shui principles (consider them Feng Shui 101):

- ✔ **Enliven the door and entrance.** The door is the key point of the entire home. Appoint it well — there's a lot of leverage at this spot. Find out more in Chapter 9.

- ✔ **Energy must flow.** If your situation is blocked or stagnant, you may find it hard to get and keep moving. Keep your pathways (hallways, driveways, and so on) open and clear for free-flowing energy.

- ✔ **Improve your master bed position and quality.** The bed is the most important place in the home after the door; it affects all parts of life, including the key areas of health and marriage. You can improve your life by improving the Feng Shui of your bed. (See Chapter 11 for details.)

- ✔ **Protect your back.** Take the Commanding Position for strength and safety. See Chapters 7, 10, 11, 13, and 17 for more information on this concept.

- ✔ **Cleanliness is next to godliness.** A clean home provides you with fresh, clean energy — the kind you need to stay truly happy, healthy, and vigorous.

- ✔ **Improve balance and harmony at every opportunity.** Whenever and wherever you detect a lack of balance in your space, make an effort to correct it with Feng Shui cures. You may be surprised by the benefits.

Chapter 3

Unveiling the Secrets of the Octagon

In This Chapter

▶ Getting to know the Nine Life Areas of the Octagon

▶ Applying the Octagon map to your space

▶ Troubleshooting your floor plan

▶ Using the Octagon to make positive life changes

*I*n Feng Shui, a fundamental part of the ballgame is to discover *where* in your environment you should make necessary changes to get the results you want (followed closely by *which* changes to actually make; for more on this, see Parts II and III). An important way you find out where to make your changes is by energetically mapping your space to see which parts of your environment correspond to which parts of your life so you can get busy making changes.

Feng Shui lore contains many different mapping methods. I focus on two of the more prominent mapping systems, both of which you use to improve your space. These two systems can be used independently of each other, but they're also related:

✔ **The Feng Shui Octagon** (traditionally called the *Ba-Gua*) gives you a visual mapping method you can apply to any space. It helps you divide your home into nine areas, which I refer to as *Life Areas*.

✔ **The Five Elements** is an energy system with many different applications, including how it relates to your space. See Chapter 5 for more on the Five Elements.

In this chapter, I show you how to overlay the Octagon on your home floor plan. (Refer to Chapter 17 for pointers on using the Octagon in your office.) By applying the Octagon to your home, you acquire a strong tool for identifying where to take action to create your desired life changes. (After you have a grasp on this chapter's basic methods of analyzing the energy characteristics of your space, go to Chapter 4 for the Mr. Fix-It toolbox of cures to make the appropriate life and energy changes.)

Discovering the Magic of the Octagon

Using the Feng Shui Octagon, or Octagon for short, is an instrumental element of Feng Shui analysis. It enables you to discern how the parts of your space (home, property, and so on) are affecting the corresponding parts of your life. All spaces affect you; the important question is this: Which spaces affect what? The Octagon provides a vital key to answering this question.

The Octagon is an *energetic map* (a tool used to diagnose energy qualities in your space) that applies the wisdom of the I-Ching (an ancient book of Chinese knowledge) to human spaces. Using the Octagon, you divide any definable space, such as your home or lot, into nine sections — eight sides plus the center — each with its own corresponding set of influences and energies. ***Note:*** A definable space must have specific boundaries and a discernible main entrance.

I recommend you commit the Octagon to memory so you can apply it mentally to your rooms and home. Doing so helps you more easily discern their Feng Shui qualities.

The Octagon divides the floor plan into nine parts: the eight parts around the sides (traditionally called *guas* in Chinese), and the center. Each of the parts (or Life Areas) hosts a different energy corresponding to a specific aspect of your life. If your home is square, the sizes of these parts are equal, like a tic-tac-toe grid. In irregularly shaped homes, the sizes of the parts may vary a little. (Although the actual size of each of the nine parts is less important than what's happening energetically in them.) The Octagon enables you to first locate the parts of your life you need to (or just want to) work on and then proceed with knowledge and awareness.

For example, suppose you need more money (hard to believe, I know). First, use the Octagon to locate the part of your home that affects wealth; then assess the energy conditions of this area and make changes or adjustments (*cures*) to improve its energy. (This process is Feng Shui in action; you use it throughout the book to make simple and effective changes.)

The nine Life Areas of the Octagon and their corresponding locations in your environment are as follows (orient yourself from the main entrance of the space):

- ✔ **Helpful People:** Located in the right-front area of the space
- ✔ **Career:** Located in the center front
- ✔ **Knowledge (Self-Development):** Located in the left front
- ✔ **Family:** Located in the center-left side
- ✔ **Wealth (Money):** Located in the back left

✔ **Fame (Reputation):** Located in the back center

✔ **Marriage (Partnership):** Located in the back right

✔ **Children:** Located in the center-right side

✔ **Health:** Located in the center of the Octagon

Look at Figure 3-1 to see the nine Life Areas of the Octagon — eight sides and the center. In the following sections, I go through each of the Areas along with their life associations and other important correlations. (For actually placing the Octagon on your floor plan, see the "Placing the Octagon on your home's main floor plan" section later in this chapter.) I also include correlations for the business world in case you want to place the Octagon on your floor plan at work or in your home office.

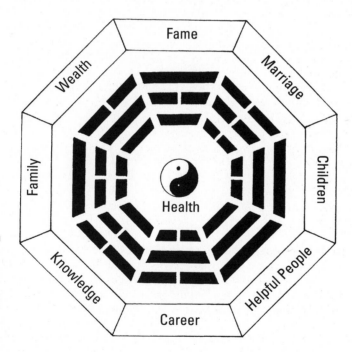

Figure 3-1:
Feng Shui Octagon showing the nine Life Areas.

Locations of the Octagon Areas in Figure 3-1 are in relation to the front door and the front of the home. So when I say "back left of the home," the position is figured as if you're standing in the front door of the home and looking inside.

You can also use the Octagon for physical healing and good health, so in the following sections, I also list the body parts that correspond to each Area of the Octagon. For example, the Marriage Area is connected with the internal organs, so the proper cure placed in the Marriage Area can help heal an organ that's out of balance.

Time for a personal disclaimer. I'm not a qualified healthcare practitioner! (I'm not even a witch doctor.) So don't use Feng Shui cures as substitutes for professional medical care. If you have a medical problem, consult a qualified health professional. Meanwhile, you can also use Feng Shui cures in both a proactive and a supplementary fashion.

In Feng Shui, everything is energetic and interrelated with everything else. Color is another form of energy and has profound effects on your life. Feng Shui associates certain colors with each area of the Octagon. I include the associated colors for each Life Area in the following sections, and in Chapter 15, I give you specific tips for how to use color to create changes in your environment.

In Feng Shui, no one Life Area is more important than any other. The Areas all interact and, when aligned to Feng Shui principles, contribute to a balanced, full, and prosperous life. Deciding which Life Area to focus on at any given time is up to you and ultimately depends on which corresponding part of your life you want to remedy or enhance. Also, the correlations given for each issue are by no means the only ones. For example, family issues are affected not only by the Family Area of the Octagon but also by rooms where the family spends time together, such as the living and dining rooms. In other words, natural energetic overlaps exist.

The Helpful People Area of the Octagon

Location: Right front

Chinese name: Ch'ien (pronounced chyen)

Colors: Gray, white, and black

Body part association: Head

Because anyone and everyone can be a helpful person, adjusting the *Helpful People Area* of a space can benefit all of your life relationships. Enhancing this Area can improve your networking, relationships with business associates (colleagues, employees, clients, customers, suppliers, and so on), and even your friendships. This Area is also associated with the fortunes of male members of the family, such as a husband, father, son, or brother.

The Helpful People Area also relates to any travel you do. If you travel a lot or plan to travel more and want to be safe on your trips, I suggest you enhance this Life Area with the Feng Shui cures detailed throughout this book.

The Career Area of the Octagon

Location: Front center

Chinese name: Kan (pronounced kahn)

Colors: Black and midnight blue

Body part association: Ears and kidneys

The *Career Area* of the Octagon concerns your work, career success, and how you make a living. Performing cures in this Life Area is a great idea if you want to find a better job, get a promotion, have better relationships with your co-workers, or receive increased recognition at work.

The Career Area of the home can affect your career as much as your business office does. Because it's in the front of your home, this Area is also connected to your relationship with the world outside of your home. (And what is a career if not a relationship to the outer world?) Obviously, this Area is a key Feng Shui location for any workplace.

The Knowledge Area of the Octagon

Location: Front left

Chinese name: Gen (pronounced guhn)

Colors: Blue, green, and black

Body part association: Hand

Also called the *Self-Development Area,* the *Knowledge Area* affects the mental/inner/spiritual areas of your life. If you desire to become smarter, wiser, or quicker-witted, look here. Because this Life Area is associated with knowledge, information, and insight, it's also linked with your spiritual/religious life, personal growth, and self-development, so adjusting the Knowledge Area can be very helpful for these parts of your life.

In a business context, the Knowledge Area is concerned with business data, competitive intelligence, good decision making, and computer networks. If you deal with the Internet and its deluge of data, curing this Life Area can help you keep up with the continuous change and flow of information.

The Family Area of the Octagon

Location: Center left

Chinese name: Jen (pronounced jen)

Colors: Green and blue

Body part association: Foot

The *Family Area* concerns your nuclear family as well as all of your relatives. Family is the Feng Shui area to work on if you seek to resolve interpersonal family conflicts or promote family harmony.

In business, the Family Area affects both employees and management. It also relates to customers, vendors, and others who regularly interact with the business (think of them as the extended family of the business).

The Wealth Area of the Octagon

Location: Back left

Chinese name: Sun (pronounced shuhn)

Colors: Purple, green, red, and blue

Body part association: Hips

The *Wealth Area,* also referred to as the *Money Area,* correlates directly to the prosperity and abundance in your life; it concerns your cash flow and financial status. For financial improvement, focus your attention here. (Because most people approach Feng Shui for this issue, I call the Wealth Area the Feng Shui end zone.) Keep in mind that in addition to the Wealth Area, your front entrance and your kitchen stove also strongly affect your money chi (see Chapters 9 and 12). And of course, in a business site, the Wealth Area is of primary concern.

The Fame Area of the Octagon

Location: Back center

Chinese name: Li (pronounced lee)

Color: Red

Body part association: Eyes

The *Fame Area* affects fame, acclaim, and public attention. I'm talking about the Hollywood type of fame, complete with paparazzi, talk show appearances, and magazine articles (although harmonizing this Feng Shui space can't guarantee these results). Yet this Life Area also has a more practical, mundane side. Fame also means your personal reputation. Your personal reputation is determined by how your peers, neighbors, and community see you. Not everyone can be famous, after all. (You didn't really want to deal with the paparazzi anyway, did you?) Everyone, including you, has a reputation of some kind. Having a good reputation brings many benefits in life; a poor reputation is an obvious stumbling block.

The Fame Area also influences how you envision your life, so it's good to enhance this Area if you're setting goals or planning your future.

In the business world, the Fame Area relates to marketing, public relations, market position, and word of mouth about your company. To improve your business or corporate reputation, be sure to pay some Feng Shui attention to this Life Area.

The Marriage Area of the Octagon

Location: Back upper-right

Chinese name: Kun (pronounced kuhn)

Colors: Pink, red, and white

Body part association: Internal organs

The *Marriage Area* is related to the status of your marriage or relationship with a significant other. If you're with someone, it affects the quality of your existing relationship; if you're single, it affects your ability to find a new partner. According to Feng Shui energetics, this Area is associated with the nurturing energy of the Earth and is also connected to the females in the household — the wife, mother, daughters, sisters, and so on.

In business, the Marriage Area is called the *Partnership Area,* and it affects your primary business partnerships, whether internal business partnerships (such as two partners who own a business together) or the key external partnerships with which the business engages.

The Children Area of the Octagon

Location: Center right

Chinese name: Dui (pronounced dway)

Color: White

Body part association: Mouth

The *Children Area* is connected to the health, well-being, and progress of your children. If you're having trouble conceiving a child, apply Feng Shui cures to this area. The Children Area also affects your creative offspring, whether artistic or otherwise.

In a business, the Children Area connects to the employees, specifically their welfare, success, and contribution to the enterprise.

The Health Area of the Octagon

Location: Center

Chinese name: Tai Chi (pronounced ty chee)

Colors: Yellow and earth tones

Body part association: Any body part not associated with the other eight areas

The *Health Area* of the Octagon is primarily concerned with physical health. Enhance this area with Feng Shui cures if you want to boost your physical vitality and stamina. Because this Life Area's position is in the center of the Octagon, the Health Area also relates to the self (that's you!) and affects all parts of your life at once. The Health Area is the hub of the wheel connecting all the different parts of your life; the energies of the other eight Life Areas all pass through and connect to the center.

In a business, the Health Area relates to the physical health of the people in the business and to the financial health of the business itself.

Orienting the Octagon

You always want to set up the Octagon in relation to the main front door of the home, never to a side, back, or garage door. Each home has only one front door, which in Feng Shui terms is called the *Mouth of Chi;* it's where the main flow of energy enters the home. (For more on the Mouth of Chi, see Chapter 9.) For individual rooms, orient the Octagon according to the main door to the room.

In the sections that follow, I describe the various places where you can position the Octagon, including your home's floor plan, your home's upper and lower floors, your lot, and the individual rooms of your home.

Placing the Octagon on your home's main floor plan

The following steps help you place the Octagon on the main floor plan of your home. *Note:* If your home has a complicated shape, you may want to practice the following exercise on a simple, square-shaped home drawing before applying it to your floor plan. Also check out the later "Missing areas and projections" section to understand how irregularities in your floor plan affect the Octagon and, therefore, you.

1. **Determine which wall is the front wall of the home.**

   The front wall is the one that contains your front door.

2. **Draw a line that runs from left to right directly through the plane of the front door on your floor plan.**

   This *line of the front door* is important for two reasons: It helps you orient and place the Octagon, and it tells you which parts of the structure are energetically in front of the front door.

3. **Determine whether your door is in the right (Helpful People Area), middle (Career Area), or left (Knowledge Area) part of the front wall of the home.**

   A door on the right-hand side of the front wall of the home (viewed from outside the home looking in) is in the Helpful People Area of the Octagon. A door in the middle of the front wall is in the Career Area. Finally, a door on the left-hand side is in the Knowledge Area. In this Feng Shui system, these three Octagon Areas are the only ones that can contain the front door (meaning the front door can never be in the Wealth Area or Children Area, for example). Take a look at Figure 3-2 to see the possibilities.

4. **Mark the front three Areas of the Octagon across the line of the front door.**

   The line of the front door is a left-to-right line drawn on your floor plan that contains the front door. The Helpful People Area is always in the front right, the Career Area is always in the front center, and the Knowledge Area is always at the front left.

5. **Mark the rest of the Octagon on the floor plan accordingly.**

   See Figure 3-3 for an example. If you prefer, you can simply write in the Life Areas in their respective positions; drawing an actual octagon shape on the floor plan is optional.

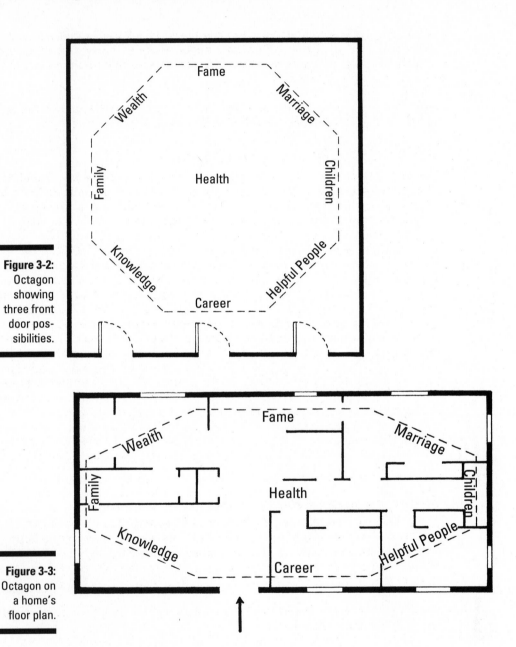

Figure 3-2: Octagon showing three front door possibilities.

Figure 3-3: Octagon on a home's floor plan.

Placing the Octagon upstairs and down

The main floor of your home is generally the most important in terms of Octagon assessment. But suppose you want to put the Octagon on other floors, such as a second or third floor or basement? *Note:* There's no need to place the Octagon on nonliving areas such as crawl spaces and attics, but you should regard an attached garage as part of your home's floor plan and include it in your Octagon analysis.

You have two methods to choose from when placing the Octagon on floors other than main floors, and I outline them for you in the next sections.

Method 1: Corresponding to the main floor

The main method in Grandmaster Lin Yun's Feng Shui school is to orient the Octagon on the floor in question exactly as it's oriented on the main floor. In other words, this method says that the Octagon on all other floors stays consistent with the Octagon position on the main floor.

Assume the new floor you're working with is the same size and shape as the main floor. As in the method given earlier in this chapter for placing the Octagon on the main floor of your home, use your front door as the beginning point to orient the Octagon properly. After correctly placing the Octagon on the main floor, you can easily determine each of the Life Areas for the other floor. In the case of a second floor space, each Life Area should be directly above its corresponding position on the main floor. So the Wealth Area on the second floor should be right above the Wealth Area of the main floor, the Fame Area should be directly over the Fame Area on the main floor, and so on for all nine Life Areas. Correspondingly, when using this method to place the Octagon on a basement or lower floor, the Life Areas should be directly below the same Life Areas as on the main floor.

When the Octagon is placed on a floor other than the main one, the Helpful People, Career, and Knowledge Areas all go along the same front line of the home as on the main floor.

Method 2: Corresponding to the floor's main entrance

An alternate method for placing the Octagon on other floors is to orient it from the internal entrance to the floor. This technique is handy if the floor is oddly shaped or markedly different in size or shape from the main floor. It's also helpful to use when the floor's entrance is offset so that its front line doesn't correspond to the front line of the main floor.

Keep the following points in mind when orienting the Octagon to correspond to the floor's main entrance:

✔ The entrance (or main door) of any floor other than the ground floor (any floor accessed by stairs) is its landing (see Figure 3-4).

✔ Internal stairways constitute missing areas of the Feng Shui Octagon of both floors connected by the stairway. (I tell you all about missing areas in the later related section.)

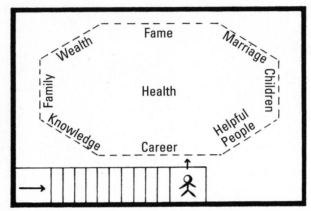

Figure 3-4:
Octagon
on a floor
entered by a
staircase.

Placing the Octagon on other spaces

The Feng Shui Octagon is applicable to any space that you can define (or determine the perimeter of) and that has a clear front (or main) entrance. An Octagon reading can be centered on your home itself, but you can also place the Octagon on other key spaces in your life, such as your bedroom, kitchen, or garden, giving you an increasingly detailed understanding of Feng Shui causes and effects.

Two additional ways you can use the Octagon to analyze your environment and change its influences include placing the Octagon

> ✔ **On your lot:** You can place the Feng Shui Octagon on your property plan to determine which parts of the lot to adjust to improve the corresponding parts of your life (see Figure 3-5). I give cures for your lot in Chapter 7.

> ✔ **On the individual rooms of your home:** Figure 3-6 illustrates how the Octagon can be used for any and all rooms of the home. Note that the most important room is the master bedroom (see Chapter 11 for more on the master bedroom.) Feng Shui lore says that the Octagon of your bedroom affects your life even more so than the Octagon of your home and property.

A powerful Feng Shui technique is to use the Octagon to perform cures for the same issue in every room of the home at once. For example, if you want to increase your wealth, you can perform cures in the Wealth Area of each room of your home. This method has the potential to improve your home and your life dramatically.

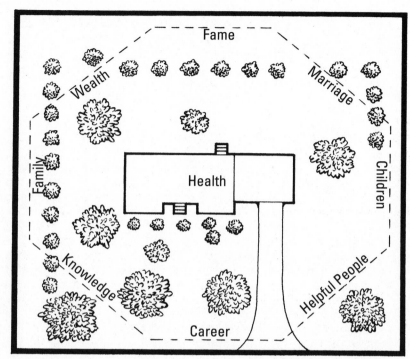

Figure 3-5:
Octagon on
a lot plan.

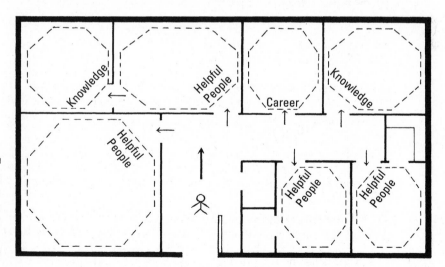

Figure 3-6:
Octagon
placed on
each room
of a home.

Troubleshooting Octagon Placement

For many homes, placing the Octagon on the floor plan is easy and straightforward. However, questions arise in several common situations. I cover a few of these situations in the following sections.

Missing areas and projections

The ideal home shape is a regular one — square or rectangle. A regular shape supports a natural, positive balance. An irregular home shape isn't necessarily negative, but it can bode either good or ill for the home's occupants depending upon the shape and the Feng Shui cures you use (or fail to use).

Missing areas of your floor plan are negative features that block chi flow in the corresponding Life Area. *Projections,* on the other hand, represent extra areas where energy circulates, providing additional chi, and thereby improving one's fortune in that Life Area. You can have both at once in the same floor plan. To illustrate, if you have a missing area in the Children Area of the Octagon and a projection in the Fame Area, you're likely to have a good reputation but may have problems with your children (or with conceiving children). These principles hold true for the shape of your lot as well. For clarity on whether your home or lot shape has either missing areas or projections, refer to Chapter 8.

Entrances with turns

If you enter the home in one direction yet turn to continue into the body of the home in another direction, the situation can be a little tricky. In such cases, I suggest you orient the Octagon to accommodate the main layout of the home (as shown in Figure 3-7).

Angled entrances

A front door at a 45-degree angle presents two possible ways to place the Octagon on the floor plan. Which is correct? The solution comes in two steps:

1. **Determine which of the two sides of the home experiences greater traffic flow (either by foot or by vehicle).**

2. **Place the Octagon at a 90-degree angle to this direction.**

   See Figure 3-8 for two examples and turn to Chapter 14 for more information about the Feng Shui challenges caused by angled doors.

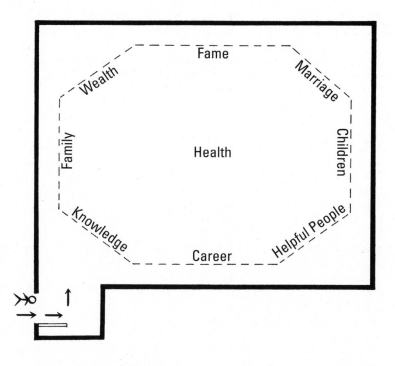

Figure 3-7:
Octagon on
a home with
an unusual
entrance.

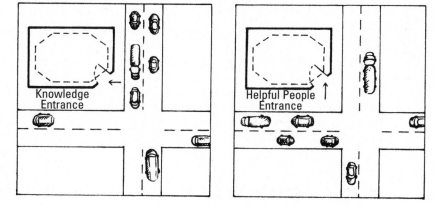

Figure 3-8:
Octagon on
a home with
an angled
entrance.

Complex or oddly shaped floor plans

If your floor plan is complex or has an unusual shape, correctly placing the
Octagon may be difficult. A potential solution for such cases is to place the
Octagon on each room in the home. This way, if your home consists of, say,
ten rooms, you now have ten Marriage Life Areas in which to put cures to
enhance your relationship rather than just one.

What if you're still stuck with placing the Feng Shui Octagon? The first thing to realize is that the Octagon method, although important, isn't the be-all, end-all of Feng Shui analysis. Many solutions in this book don't require using the Octagon; you can still perform powerful Feng Shui cures without it. (As an example, the Three Life Pillars that I describe in Chapters 2 and 19 don't rely on the Octagon.) So free yourself from the idea that there's no way to make Feng Shui progress without correctly placing the Octagon onto your floor plan. Nothing could be further from the truth. If you're really unable to place the Octagon in a way that makes sense to you, use the Octagon troubleshooting methods I mention in the previous sections. In the meantime, also consider calling in a professional to help you. After all, if your home is that confusing, it may have a number of other issues that could use resolution. Flip to Chapter 24 and the appendix for tips on finding and working with a Feng Shui consultant.

Changing Your Life with the Octagon

After you're able to place the Octagon correctly, the next step is to put it to use. A good way to use the Octagon is to select the Life Areas that correspond to the most important life changes you want to make. If you want to increase family harmony, the Family Area is a good place to begin. After discovering what affects family energy in this book, go to the Family Area(s) of your home, quiet down, and take a look around. Things may jump out at you and clamor for changes and cures.

Another good way to use the Octagon is to look for correlations between each Octagon Area of the home and the corresponding life patterns you're experiencing. For example, if the Wealth Area contains a toilet and your money is draining away, the correlation may be easy to make. Curing the toilet in this Life Area can bring about noticeable improvement in your financial circumstances. Feng Shui is nothing if not practical.

Chapter 4

Picking Up Your Feng Shui Tools

. . . .

In This Chapter

▶ Defining Feng Shui cures

▶ Examining cures in three phases

▶ Surveying the different types of cures

▶ Performing the Method of Minor Additions to create major results

. . . .

Changing the way *chi* (energy) circulates in your home and life is where the rubber meets the road in Feng Shui. You change chi by performing *cures,* which are simple Feng Shui adjustments to your environment that positively shift the energy of your home or lot. Feng Shui cures support positive changes in any part of your life that you want to improve (flip to Chapter 1 for help selecting the parts of your life you want to focus on).

The enormous array of solutions in Feng Shui can seem a little bewildering at first, so I focus on the ones I've found to be the simplest, easiest, and most effective. This chapter presents an overview designed to familiarize you with the basic cures, how they work, and how you can improve on them. These are simple, effective Feng Shui methods that you can apply without arduous training or the need to learn Chinese. Well, what are you waiting for? It's time to put Feng Shui into action!

So What Is a Feng Shui Cure?

At the simplest level, Feng Shui cures are ways of changing your life by altering your space. You can also say that cures are solutions to Feng Shui problems that may be causing real-life problems (or they can be enhancements for parts of your life that are already in good shape). Performing cures changes the flow of energy in your space, shifting the chi in your environment — and in you — to a more beneficial and balanced energy state. The following sections outline the motivations behind Feng Shui cures as well as five different types of cures you can perform.

Motivations for performing Feng Shui cures

You can use Feng Shui cures to fix an environmental problem, improve a part of your life that needs it, or further improve a part of your life that's already in good shape. If you're looking for motivation or inspiration, check out these three reasons for performing cures:

- ✔ **To remedy an energetically weak or problematic aspect of your surroundings:** Say you assess your bedroom using Feng Shui principles and discover that your bed sits in a position that's bad for your health. You connect this situation to health problems you've been having. If you were an ostrich, you'd simply stick your head in the sand and hope the problem goes away. (Unfortunately, Ostrich Feng Shui works only until you feel the need to breathe; when you pull your head out, the problem is still there.) But because you're a person and not an ostrich, you want your environment to support your health, so you decide to perform a cure.

- ✔ **To remedy a life problem or improve a part of your life that's challenging or troubling you:** In keeping with the bedroom example, say you've been arguing a lot with your spouse or significant other lately, and you therefore decide you want to perform a cure to improve your relationship. The next step is to consult the Marriage Life Area of your home, lot, bedroom, and so on and perform specific cures to improve this Life Area by fixing an existing Feng Shui defect (perhaps an exit door in the Marriage Area is allowing chi to leak away from the relationship).

    If you can't detect any relevant Feng Shui problems, you can perform a cure that energetically enhances or activates the Life Area you're targeting (in this case, the Marriage Area). For example, place fresh flowers or something with the color pink in the Marriage Area of the bedroom or other parts of the home. (Refer to Chapter 3 for the scoop on all nine Life Areas of the Feng Shui Octagon.)

- ✔ **To further empower or strengthen an aspect of your life that's already strong:** These are proactive cures, and I'm a firm believer in them. Say your career is going gangbusters. Your latest movie hits number one at the box office, your latest song tops the charts, your music video has made you an icon, and your new fashion line is all the rage in Paris. What, you want a Pulitzer Prize, too? Well, go for it! To assist your career, you can perform cures in the Career Areas of your home, lot, bedroom, and other applicable spaces.

Five types of Feng Shui cures

To remedy or enhance any life situation, you have a range of options from which to choose. The Feng Shui cure you select depends on the nature of the problem, your particular goals, and your financial circumstances. Each level of cure has advantages and disadvantages and requires varying expenditures of time, energy, and (yes, sometimes) cash. As with many decisions, budget is often the bottom line. ("These solid-gold, diamond-encrusted bathroom fixtures would make marvelous Feng Shui accouterments. But I think I'll go with the brass ones instead.")

The following list gives you five levels of solutions, arranged from most to least expensive, that you can use to bring your home into tiptop Feng Shui shape.

- ✔ **Move to a different home or build a new one.** This cure is one of the most radical ones you can perform. It also can be expensive, so if you choose this option, make sure you do it right (meaning make sure your new home has better Feng Shui than your old one; see Chapter 20 for help in this very important process).

- ✔ **Perform major remodeling or landscaping to fix the problem.** This cure can be an excellent option, provided you perform it according to valid Feng Shui principles. Failing that, it may be quite problematic. This solution, like moving to a different home, has obvious drawbacks: expense, time investment, and inconvenience. Plus, sometimes remodeling or landscaping is trickier than just starting over with a new place. Consider calling in a professional Feng Shui consultant for assistance with your renovations (see Chapter 24 and the appendix for help finding one). After all, nothing's worse than financing a noncure worth tens of thousands of dollars.

- ✔ **Devise an energetic placement or adjustment that changes the chi flow.** Such placements and adjustments are cost-effective ways of solving Feng Shui problems that don't require you to make structural changes to your home. Most cures in this book fit into this category. I focus on practical methods you can use now to create noticeable, desired effects later so you can perform cures with minimal expense.

- ✔ **Conduct a blessing ceremony to change, clear, or shift the energy.** Feng Shui ceremonies work on the overall energy state of your home and/or property at once, giving them great power. Ceremonies work purely on an energetic level, affecting the invisible elements of the site, including spiritual and emotional energies as well as energetic residue left by previous occupants (or spillover from surrounding occupants). Blessing ceremonies help remove negative energies, calm chaotic chi, and instill prosperity and well-being. They're one of the most effective and least expensive Feng Shui methods. Although blessing ceremonies typically involve no physical changes to the site, they can profoundly and positively affect your physical and mental health, well-being, and safety. I present solutions of this type in Chapter 21.

✔ **Adjust your personal chi directly.** This method involves special personal-energy-adjustment practices that you can use to change your life experience directly without necessarily having to alter your home or environment. Personal chi cures work on your inner environment (your body, mind, and spirit) much like blessing ceremonies do for your external environment (your home and lot). These potent cures are also highly effective and usually quite inexpensive. I include several of these solutions in Chapter 22.

Using the Three Phases of Your Cures

All Feng Shui cures work in two realms at the same time: the *visible* (or material) realm and the *invisible* (or intangible) realm. They do this work through three phases. Phases I and III relate to the invisible realm, whereas Phase II has to do with the visible realm. By paying equal attention to all three parts of a cure, you'll get maximum benefits and results from your cures. The sections that follow outline the three phases.

Phase 1: Setting the intention for the cure

The first phase of a cure involves deciding what you want to change in your life and why. You can decide what to change either by looking at your home or by looking at your life.

✔ In the first approach, you look at your home to discover what Feng Shui challenges or problems currently exist in your environment. Then you apply the appropriate remedies.

✔ In the second approach, you examine different aspects of your life — finances, career, relationships, health, and so on — and decide which part you most want to improve and transform. After zeroing in on a specific part of your life, you then perform specific cures to improve the part of your home that supports that part of your life. As I detail in Chapter 1, I generally recommend starting with this approach.

Whichever approach you use, you must have a clear, strong intention behind each Feng Shui cure you perform. You must know exactly what you want to change or improve in your life and why. Doing a cure because you read about it in a Feng Shui book and it seemed like a good idea isn't as powerful a reason for the cure as having a compelling desire to make a specific change in your life. Vague, ambiguous, or wishy-washy cure intentions tend to produce less dramatic results. (I cover intention in more detail later in this chapter and in Chapter 6.)

Phase II: Performing the physical activity of the cure

The second phase of a cure relates to the visible realm. It involves making the physical change in your environment that the cure calls for (for example, painting a room a new color or rearranging your furniture). This visible part of the cure typically accounts for around 20 to 30 percent of the cure's power. The invisible portions of the cure (Phase I: Intention and Phase III: Reinforcement) together supply an additional 70 to 80 percent of the cure's effectiveness.

Phase III: Reinforcing your intention and activity with spiritual energy

The third phase of a cure deals with your thoughts and emotions as you perform the cure. In this phase, you use special methods to reinforce both the intention you set in the first phase of the cure and the physical change you made in the second phase.

The secret of effective Feng Shui is your intention. The intention and reinforcement of a cure generates 70 to 80 percent of the cure's effectiveness. So take a closer look at this thing called intention.

- ✔ On one level, intention is your awareness of your personal reasons for performing a cure and your desire to accomplish it. What do you want the cure to create, and how strongly do you want it to happen? These questions are a matter of intention.

- ✔ On a second level, intention encompasses a combination of sincerity, will, visualization, and faith. These factors work synergistically to activate or reinforce the physical portion of a cure, taking its power to new heights.

Note: The combination of intention, action, and reinforcement can create cures with more than 100 percent effectiveness, meaning a cure can not only fix a particular life problem but also make things better than they were before the problem started.

Cures aren't mere mechanical adjustments that you make in an environment. Feng Shui changes involve your heart and mind as well as your home and lot. If you feel that you don't fully understand just yet, that's okay. As you perform your cures and practice the Three Secrets Reinforcement (a special method of activating your intentions for cures; see Chapter 6), you start to understand how this process creates new energy states and life paths.

Opening the Feng Shui Toolbox: Creating Your Cures

You have six key methods at your disposal for performing cures. The method you implement depends on your particular needs and wishes, budget, and sense of aesthetics. The next sections outline these methods.

Creating positive placement

Creating positive placement means putting things in their right places or most favorable locations. Good or bad placement affects you in important ways. The arrangement of things in your environment determines how chi circulates through your environment, and this chi flow directly affects your body and mind.

Items that require positive placement for best life results include not only your home itself but also your bed, desk, and stove.

- Your bed location (see Chapter 11) affects many areas of life, including your marriage, your level of pep and vitality, and your income.

- The placement of your office desk (see Chapter 17) is important because it dictates where and how you sit and appear, as well as how you interact with the people and energy entering your office.

- The stove (see Chapter 12) is vital for both your health and your finances.

Adding what's needed, minor and otherwise

Another category of cures involves adding objects to your environment. These cures range from planting a new tree or constructing a flower bed to adding furniture or a mobile or installing a mirror. See the later "Making Minor Additions to Bring about Major Changes" section for detailed explanations of many different additional cure tools you can apply for fun and profit.

Think of the cures in this category as the acupuncture needles of Feng Shui. The proper addition at the right point in your space can create dramatic changes in the energy of that space and its corresponding part of your life.

Adjusting by repairing, cleaning, and changing

This category involves altering and adjusting existing items in your home to improve their energy value. Examples of this type of cure include repairing broken objects; replacing burned-out light bulbs; and, of course, cleaning. What's important about these changes? Simply this: Whatever's out of order in your environment subtly or profoundly influences disorder in a corresponding part of your life. Broken, dirty, or unmaintained features of your home provide a continuous subconscious influence of malfunction and decay. So be sure to dig into Chapter 15, where you can find many types of adjusting cures.

Using ceremony to create new energy states

Ceremony was the first, and most powerful, human art form, and it's still an essential part of human experience. A woman putting on her makeup and a dash of perfume before a date; a man putting on his power suit for an important meeting; a pitcher tugging his baseball cap with every new batter; even fans and players singing the national anthem before each game. What are these habits if not ceremonies — ritual actions performed to trigger specific effects? But awareness of the power of ceremony has been pushed out of modern society due to the current fixation on technology and science. Feng Shui, however, hasn't forgotten the effectiveness of ceremonies. It still makes good use of their ability to unite the material world in which we live with the unseen realms of energy to which we're also connected.

Feng Shui ceremonies are energy procedures that change the spirit and feeling of your home's chi. They purify unseen (but definitely felt!) negativity, remove bad luck, provide protection, create new beginnings, and add cheerful energy to your environment. I detail some vital ceremony procedures in Chapter 21.

Making personal Feng Shui adjustments

Believe it or not, you can use Feng Shui to adjust not only your living space but also yourself. These personal cures are some of the most powerful and direct ways to create transformation in your life. They're traditionally shared only with those who are sincere of heart and mind, and are transmitted by word of mouth from teacher to student. I share some of these "secret solutions" in Chapter 22.

Employing meditative methods

Cultivating your inner energies and peace of mind through internal meditative methods may be just as important for your long-term progress as performing environmental Feng Shui cures. After all, no matter how much you change your exterior environment, the fact is that your life is what you make of it. In the end, that's always an inside job. Meditation sharpens the mind and helps you develop wisdom and perspective that make you more effective in life. Turn to Chapter 22 for a meditative method that calms and balances your mind and improves your body's energy flow.

Making Minor Additions to Bring about Major Changes

For cures that call for you to add something to your environment, the Method of Minor Additions is one of the easiest approaches you can take. It operates on the principle of *xie di* (shyeh dee), which means "a little bit." This principle is akin to using a few ounces of positive energy to deflect a thousand pounds of negative force. For example, say you're walking across the street and look up to see a speeding car coming right at you. Do you go into your immovable martial arts stance, lean forward with your hands outstretched, and prepare to stop the car in its tracks? Or do you step lightly out of the way? If you chose the second option, by golly, I think you're starting to get it.

Minor Additions cures involve adding one of several kinds of *natural chi* (such as light, sound, or water) to adjust the energy of a location. These cures allow you to create tangible, desired changes without the need for remodeling or turning your current home around on its foundation to face a different direction. Minor Additions cures are simple, practical, and effective. They work immediately, and you can feel their energetic effects on the environment and on you.

Minor Addition cures use the energies of the following (see the appendix for cure sources):

- Light
- Sound
- Living energy (or spirit)
- Water
- Color
- Movement
- Weight

- ✔ Bamboo
- ✔ Power
- ✔ Fragrance
- ✔ Touch

Note: The Method of Minor Additions isn't the only important Feng Shui method; all methods have their uses at the proper place and time. However, it is a method that's easy to comprehend and put into action, so I cover it in detail in the sections that follow.

Light cures

Light cures come in three main types: lights, faceted crystal spheres, and mirrors. These cures add beneficial energy qualities to spaces in need, including additional light, brilliance, expansion, and cheer. Lighting levels and lighting quality naturally affect humans in many ways, a fact that makes light cures a powerful tool in your Feng Shui toolbox.

Lights

Lights, such as overhead lights, lamps, and incandescent lights, can easily add brightness and cheer to an area. With light, the general rule is this: The brighter the light, the better. Lights used in Feng Shui cures don't have to be on at all times, but they should remain in good working condition. If the bulb in your Feng Shui cure burns out, the cure is nullified, so replace a burned-out bulb at once to maintain the cure.

Faceted crystal spheres

Faceted, leaded-glass crystal spheres have many useful Feng Shui applications. They shift the energy of a space by

- ✔ Adding light, expansion, and new energy.
- ✔ Redirecting energies toward a more beneficial direction.
- ✔ Harmonizing confusing or chaotic flows of energy.
- ✔ Protecting you from poison arrows of energy by refracting and diffusing energy flows. (I fill you in on poison arrows in Chapter 7.)
- ✔ Empowering and aiding in visualizations.
- ✔ Attracting and drawing energy to a location.
- ✔ Looking so darned beautiful. (Beauty is an important Feng Shui element.)

When sunlight hits a faceted crystal sphere that's made from leaded glass, prismatic rainbows scatter beautifully throughout the space (see Figure 4-1) —

an effect you can't get from a natural quartz crystal. (Smooth, nonfaceted crystal spheres don't have the same energy qualities as faceted, leaded-glass crystals either, which is why I don't recommend using them.)

Figure 4-1:
Various
cure tools.

 For the purposes of this book, when I refer to *crystals,* I'm referring to faceted, leaded-glass crystal spheres (rather than crystal crocks or geodes, which are mined from the Earth). I recommend using spheres that are 40 or 50 millimeters in diameter (1.5 to 2 inches). Generally, larger is better, but purchase what you can afford. Turn to the appendix for help obtaining good-quality crystals.

 Crystals aren't the place to skimp on quality. I recommend buying the best faceted, leaded-glass crystal you can afford. The best quality I've found is in the crystal made by the world-famous Swarovski brand. Swarovski crystal is made in Austria and tends to cost a bit, but it's worth it. However, if you're strapped for cash, you can find high-quality crystal from South America and the Middle East that's nearly as good as Swarovski and somewhat cheaper.

Mirrors

Mirrors are like the Swiss Army Knife of Feng Shui — an extremely useful tool. They're best used in one of four shapes: square, rectangular, octagonal, or circular. Square and rectangular mirrors (refer to Figure 4-1) symbolize balance, whereas circular mirrors represent wholeness, oneness, and unity.

Octagonal mirrors denote power and have the positive symbology of representing the Feng Shui Octagon (which I cover in Chapter 3).

When it comes to shape, rectangular or square mirrors are best for mirrors that hang on doors or get used for regular viewing (and not just for décor). As for size, large mirrors generally create stronger cures than smaller mirrors.

Depending on the need, you can use mirror cures to

- ✔ Add light and brightness
- ✔ Attract new energy to a space
- ✔ Repel negative or harmful chi
- ✔ Redirect an energy flow
- ✔ Expand an area by energetically creating more space
- ✔ Magnify or strengthen one's image
- ✔ Empower a Life Area of the Octagon for a particular life need
- ✔ Restore a missing area of a room or home (see Chapter 8 for details about missing areas)

Always check a mirror out before purchasing one. You want to avoid buying mirrors with visible ripples or flaws in the glass. Mirrors symbolize your self-image and clarity of mind, so distorted mirrors can have subtle and unpleasant effects on your psyche. To check a mirror for visible distortions, stand to one side, look into the mirror, and then pick out a specific reflected object. Holding your eye steady on the object, sway your body back and forth evenly from left to right. If the object seems to move in a wavelike manner or appears deformed in any way, the mirror is distorted. Such a mirror is better replaced or not bought in the first place.

The ideal mirror comes with or without a frame and is a plain, flawless surface (although a small bevel around the edges is fine). Avoid using mirrors that are smoked, darkened, or oddly shaped. Also steer clear of mirror tiles and mirrors that have etchings or any other embellishments on them.

Note: Feng Shui recommends replacing antique mirrors that are scratched, pitted, or marred. If you're attached to the beauty of an antique mirror frame whose glass is flawed or visibly aged, keep the frame and replace the mirror portion.

Sound cures

Sound cures are very effective for clearing old, negative energy and bringing new, positive energy into a space. You can choose from two types of sound cures: ones with a ringing quality and ones with an alerting type of sound.

Ringing cures are more powerful, but you can use almost any sound-emitting tool to create a cure. Tools for ringing cures include wind chimes, bells, and gongs. Modern ringing devices include telephones, alarm clocks, and classroom bells, which never fail to grab your attention.

Sound cures create beneficial effects by

- ✔ Stimulating new energy.
- ✔ Awakening, arousing, and alerting.
- ✔ Calling forth a message.
- ✔ Sending a reply.
- ✔ Strengthening the energy of a location, person, or Life Area.
- ✔ Providing protection. (Burglar alarms are just glorified bells.)
- ✔ Creating harmony, peace, and balance.

Wind chimes

Wind chimes can be used for a multitude of curing purposes, both indoors and out. Chimes help attract new energy, stimulate opportunities, and blow away obstacles in your life. Be sure to hang your wind chimes from a red ribbon or cord for the greatest effect (see the nearby "The special powers of the red ribbon" sidebar for details).

Sound quality — the clarity and tone of the ring — is the most important chime factor, but the sound should also be something that's pleasant to you. If it's not, the cure won't be as effective in adjusting your energy. So listen to your chimes before purchasing them to ensure a high-quality, pleasant-sounding ring. Also, don't hang a chime that you don't love simply because someone gave it to you. (One home's chime is another's aggravation.)

The best wind chimes to use for your cures are made of metal and chime clear, resonating tones (refer to Figure 4-1). Metal chimes truly ring; those made of other materials don't and thus have less curing power. Brass is the favored metal for chimes.

If the chimes inside your home don't ring, don't worry! Interior wind chimes are still very effective. If you want, you can activate a wind chime by ringing it as you pass by, creating chi on demand.

Bells and gongs

A brass bell is a good cure for an area where a wind chime is inappropriate. You can place it on a desk or counter and activate it by ringing it when needed. Gongs are excellent solutions for entrances to homes, properties, or buildings.

The special powers of the red ribbon

When hanging Feng Shui cures such as faceted crystal spheres, wind chimes, or mobiles, always use a red string, ribbon, or cord for best results. The color red is the most potent, transformative color in Feng Shui. It symbolizes fire and the energy that makes changes happen. (See Chapter 9 for information on red front doors.)

In addition to the color red, another key factor is to cut your hanging ribbon or string to a multiple of 9 inches in length. This multiple could be 9 inches, 18 inches, 27 inches . . . you get the idea. Why multiples of nine? Nine is the most powerful number in Feng Shui theory; it symbolizes completion and peak accomplishment. Therefore, using a red cord cut to a multiple of 9 inches in length adds the two peak energies of color and number to your cures, providing additional oomph. This ribbon application is an important and integral part of your cures, so be sure to include it.

Living cures

Living cures utilize the vitality and energy of plants, vegetation, and even animals to boost the chi of a space. They provide nourishing, healthy chi for your home or office. Living cures are also easy to perform, highly effective, and aesthetically pleasing.

Plants and flowers

Plants add color to your space and symbolize new life and growth. The best plants to use for cures are full, lush, and vibrant. Rounded leaves are generally better than long, pointed ones. Avoid daggerlike plants, such as cacti, which create symbolic spears in your environment. If you have plants that are sparse, weak, sickly, or dying, heal them or replace them as soon as possible with fresh, healthy plants — preferably those with flowers and/or fruits because these plants create more effective cures than those without.

To get the best results, go out and buy a new, fresh, vibrant plant specifically for a Feng Shui cure instead of using a plant you already own. (However, if plants you already own are all you can afford, by all means use them.) Freshly cut flowers make another great living energy cure because they stimulate life, cheer, and positive chi. Just be sure not to let them wilt and die on the premises.

Generally, an odd number of plants creates a stronger, more active energy than an even number. However, an even number of plants is still effective.

Get rid of dead, dying, and dried plants

Dead or wilting plants, flowers, and decorative sticks (except for bamboo flutes) create negative Feng Shui because they're anti-life signs. Even dried wreaths and flower arrangements, however beautifully designed, symbolize death to the subconscious mind and can create a subtle drag on your energy. Dried flowers are dead, regardless of how nice they look or how much you paid for them, and according to Feng Shui principles, they can negatively influence your environment and you. A strong cure for this situation is to replace dead and dried flowers with living, colorful plants or flowers. Replacing death with life is a wonderfully symbolic act, and you can feel the positive, energizing effects of this cure immediately.

You can use artificial plants (preferably silk ones) for cures, but make sure they look real because if they don't, the cure they provide becomes nil. The best silk plants are indistinguishable from the real ones except to the touch, and they always seem fresh, thereby symbolizing continuing life. (*Note:* A nice touch is to put a convincing silk plant in a pot of real soil.)

Fish

Aquariums, which combine water and living energy, are powerful Feng Shui cures. They spruce up an area wonderfully, bringing in new vitality and stimulating energy flow. They're also natural mood-enhancers. Aquariums are renowned for bringing luck and good fortune to a residence and generating a stream of wealth for the occupants, which is why so many restaurants — one of the most difficult of all businesses to succeed in — use them.

Aquariums also contain fish that continuously circulate, are apparently peaceful, and never get stuck. They stimulate a similar flow in your life, flexibility and ease in your endeavors, and fewer blocks and obstacles. Also, bright, lively, multicolored fish represent you getting along with many different types of people.

To maintain the positive chi of your aquarium, make sure your fish remain healthy, the water stays clean rather than murky, and any fish that die are replaced as soon as possible with healthy new ones.

An even stronger aquarium cure given by Grandmaster Lin Yun is to fill your tank with nine goldfish, eight of them red and one black. If one of these fish dies, replace it with a new one of the same color at once. If the black fish dies, it means a misfortune headed your way has caught the fish instead of you.

Creating good luck with plant symbology

An exciting aspect of using plants as cures is discovering the specific symbolism of various plants. The following plants are renowned for their positive effects when placed in one's environment:

✔ **Bamboo** is the king of plants. When grown or displayed on the premises, bamboo denotes safety, harmony, and a strong future. The Chinese say that when one lives with bamboo, one's life will improve in stages over time.

✔ Because the green **jade plant** resembles the jade stone, this plant is considered one of good luck or good fortune and wealth.

✔ The **money plant** *(Lunaria annua)* is a Feng Shui favorite, symbolizing wealth and abundance coming to its owners.

For more on specific plant symbology, flip to Chapter 7.

Water cures

Water represents connection, sustenance, wealth, and the flow of life. Humans have always chosen to live near sources of water, but today, sealed inside homes and workplaces, most people are cut off from contact with naturally flowing water. As a result, they lose something psychologically and energetically profound.

The Feng Shui solution to this lost influence of water is to perform *water cures* that add water to your environment, either on the property or inside the home. Flowing water creates soothing sounds (the babbling brook), and the movement of water over stones and rocks (streams and waterfalls) instigates a healthy, refreshing release of negative ions, which provides a sense of well-being and makes breathing easier. Still-water features help create calm, tranquil environments and represent wisdom and clarity.

Fountains and waterfalls

Fountains and waterfalls create a new energy flow in any environment. Moving water is both surprising and pleasant to encounter indoors, and a well-placed fountain has a refreshing and beneficial effect in any home.

 Despite moving water's benefits, you should avoid placing a fountain in the Fame Area of the Feng Shui Octagon (see Chapter 3). The Fame Area is the natural location of the fire element, and because water puts out fire, a fountain in this Life Area can have a dampening effect on your reputation.

The best fountains are ones in which you can see the flow of water and in which the water pools visibly instead of disappearing immediately. A particularly potent fountain is one in which the water's flow performs work, such as turning a water wheel. Flowing water means flowing money, and this factor symbolizes that money not only comes to you but also that your funds are effective and create results. Another nice energetic touch is a fountain that incorporates a light in its design.

Ponds and pools

Still bodies of water represent stored wealth on the property as well as clarity and depth of knowledge. Ponds, lakes, and swimming pools generally enhance the chi of a property. However, the following key principles should be observed:

- ✔ The body of water shouldn't be too large compared to the home, or else it can energetically overwhelm the home and weaken the occupants' chi.

- ✔ A sharp angle of a swimming pool pointed toward the home resembles a cutting edge and can stimulate accidents in the residence.

- ✔ A crescent-shaped pond positioned with the tips of the crescent pointing away from the home symbolizes money leaving the site.

- ✔ Kidney shapes are positive because they're rounded, and the kidney relates directly to the water element in the body. Kidney-shaped ponds are best situated so they appear to hug the home, meaning wealth gathers and remains in the home.

- ✔ The clearer your still-water feature, the better your finances and clarity of mind. Murky water on the property can result in funky financial deals and confusion.

Color cures

Color cures are a powerful way to change a mood or activate the emotions and subconscious mind for success. Color affects every aspect of life, and opportunities for using it to improve your home's energy are innumerable. You can use color to adjust the energy of an entire room by painting the walls, adding it in various ways to a Life Area for energetic effects, or using it in your clothing to adjust your personal Feng Shui.

The Feng Shui color representations and attributes noted in Table 4-1 are listed in the order of the Life Areas of the Feng Shui Octagon (see Chapter 3), starting with the Family Area and moving clockwise. Naturally, many different color systems exist throughout the world (Western, Indian, and Native American, just to name a few). Add this color information to your existing knowledge and make choices about which color schemes are right for you. For more on color, see Chapters 5 and 15.

Table 4-1	Key Colors and Their Attributes
Color	*Symbolizes*
Green	New life, new beginnings, growth, energy, vitality, spring, hope.
Purple	Wealth, royalty, the extreme value of red. (A Chinese saying, "That's so red it's purple," denotes purple's great energy and power.)
Red	Power, protection, energy, activity. (Red is the most active of all colors and is used in many ways in Feng Shui.)
Pink	Love, the heart, marriage, motherhood.
White	Cleanliness, purity, righteousness, death. (The Chinese wear white mourning gowns when grieving departed loved ones.)
Gray	Neutrality, absence of color, hidden things, benefactors.
Black	Power, authority, absorbing energy, respect. (Too much black represents despair and gloom.)
Blue	Knowledge, the sky, royalty, life, hope.
Yellow, earth tones	Health, the Earth, ground, connection.

Mobile cures

Mobile cures create new flows of energy, harmonize and balance chaotic energy, stimulate action and new thinking, and clear stagnation. You perform them by placing mobile objects in key places for specific energetic reasons. Mobile objects swirl and move, stimulating and circulating energy while projecting a uniquely calming effect. They rely on air currents for their movements and take several forms.

Mobiles

Mobiles are an excellent addition to a space needing circulation, movement, or clearing. A mobile's gentle, swaying rotation soothes, settles, and diffuses sharp energies (like those caused by the protruding corner of a desk, counter, bookshelf, or wall). You can also use mobiles to fill an area that lacks definition or create balance by bringing down or filling in a ceiling that's too high.

Flags and banners

Flags add unique qualities of color and symbolism to your cures. A green flag (favored in Feng Shui) denotes health, vitality, life, and money. Other colors can be used according to your needs and the design of the space (see Chapter 15 for details). Designs or emblems on your flag or banner are fine as long as they appeal to you. Such emblems may include your family crest, a state or national flag, your alma mater or favorite football team, sunflowers, ladybugs, or any other image that pleases or energizes you. Use your gut feeling as a final arbiter when choosing your Feng Shui flags.

Windsocks

Because they combine motion with color, windsocks help stimulate, activate, and enliven dead energy areas such as alleys and dead-end roads.

 Road traffic moving too quickly past a home (excess chi) pulls away a home's chi, but placing a windsock (or three) in strategic locations, such as near the offending road, can calm the negative effects of this excess chi and stabilize the area.

Pinwheels and whirligigs

Pinwheels are a quick, inexpensive way to enliven a garden path or draw chi along a driveway or walkway. Whirligigs are small, yet effective, energy generators that are also useful for calming or counteracting excess traffic chi.

Weight cures

Weight cures provide needed weight or solidity to a space by literally adding substantial mass or presence to a site, generating feelings of stability and calm. Weight cures can also be used to emphasize or give form to a certain area or point. For example, a heavy rock or statue can be used to energetically strengthen a needy area of a property or complete a missing area of a home (check out Chapter 8 for details on missing areas). A weight cure can also be a heavy desk or other piece of furniture. It can even be an outbuilding that's added to the property, like a greenhouse, garage, or toolshed (refer to Chapter 7 for the best locations for outbuildings).

The significance of flagpoles and light poles

A commonly recommended cure in many Feng Shui situations is to place a flagpole or light pole in a key location. Besides adding color, motion, and light energy to the area, flagpoles and light poles play another very important role: They act as Earth needles, tapping into the chi of the Earth and bringing it to the surface to provide vital, nourishing energy. Tapping into the Earth's chi in this way is an important function in Feng Shui. Energy with an upward motion promotes life and growth, whereas downward energy promotes decay and decline. Flagpoles and light poles thus have dual effects of uplifting and enlivening.

Tip: A hollow flagpole is more powerful than a solid one because a hollow pole acts as an attractor for Earth energy, uplifting the chi of the Earth, which in turn blesses and uplifts the property.

A more mystical form of a weight cure is called a *yu bowl* (pronounced you). A yu is a small bowl with a shallow base, wide body, and shallow mouth (refer to Figure 4-1). If a yu bowl is properly prepared, it can cure many problems. I explain how to prepare a yu bowl in Chapter 22.

Bamboo flute cures

Bamboo flutes are sometimes passed over by those not aware of their benefits, but they're one of the most powerful, significant, and effective cure tools available. *Bamboo flute cures* are potent remedies for numerous life problems. My clients use them and report amazing life changes as a result. The proper type of bamboo flute cure

- **Delivers peace and safety:** Bamboo is renowned in Chinese culture for bringing luck and strength if grown or displayed on the premises.

- **Provides support:** Everyone can use more support in life, and bamboo, one of the strongest and hardiest of plants, is a potent energetic symbol of support for your ongoing endeavors.

- **Fights off evil spirits:** Whether you call them spirits, ghosts, heebie-jeebies or just plain-old bad vibes, humans can sense negative energies. When hung as shown in Figure 4-2, the bamboo flute, representing the symbolic angle of a sword, helps scare away negative energies and promote calmness and peace of mind.

- **Drives away evil, negative, and scandalous persons:** The flute cure is a powerful way to banish or nullify the negative energy of those who harm, harass, or harangue you.

Angling your flute

An important aspect of a flute's power is the angle at which it hangs (the hanging angle associates with the angles of the Feng Shui Octagon that I describe in Chapter 3). To understand this, visualize the Feng Shui Octagon not placed on a floor plan as usual but placed vertically on a wall. The actual angle at which you hang your flute depends upon the angle of the Octagon sector or Life Area you want to remedy or enhance.

For example, if you want to accentuate wealth, hang a flute in the Wealth Area. To make such a Wealth flute cure even more potent, you can also hang this flute at the Wealth Angle. This additional detail makes a real difference in the cure's effect. Table 4-2 explains how to hang a bamboo flute at the proper angle for any Life Area you want to empower. Refer to Figure 4-2 for the visuals.

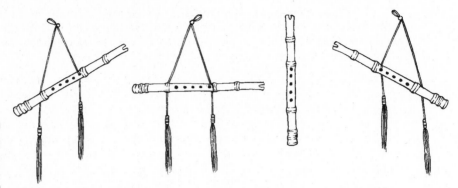

Figure 4-2:
Flute
positions.

Table 4-2	Beneficial Angles for Hanging Bamboo Flutes
Life Area to Empower	*Hanging Direction/Orientation*
Wealth or Helpful People	45-degree angle; left side lower, right side higher
Marriage or Knowledge	45-degree angle; right side lower, left side higher
Children or Family	Vertical; smaller sections of the flute pointing downward
Fame or Career	Horizontal
Health	Use any of the four preceding angles

Paying attention to important flute pointers

Here's a list of key things to consider when purchasing and hanging your flute:

✔ The bamboo flute I recommend for your cures is straight (rather than curved or bent) and made from a special kind of bamboo, where each section is longer than the previous one. This symbolizes life climbing upward step by step, things getting better for you tomorrow than they are today, and so on. The bamboo flute cure is more effective when you use a flute that's made from real bamboo as opposed to another type of wood (or plastic, yikes!).

✔ The sections of bamboo are segmented by the visible ridges in the bamboo stalk (refer to Figure 4-2 to see what I mean.) The ridges themselves are a key part of the flute's energy, symbolizing power and strength. For maximum effectiveness, use a bamboo flute that has its ridges still intact. If the ridges are sanded off (making the bamboo flute smooth and unsegmented), the result is a much weaker (and unrecommended) solution.

✔ Flute cures are most effective when the flute is hung by a red ribbon cut to a multiple of 9 inches in length with two red tassels, one on each end. When you hang the ribbon, you connect the two tassels to the two points where the ribbon attaches to the flute (again, refer to Figure 4-2). Leave the ribbon on the flute even if you hang it vertically. (See the earlier "The special powers of the red ribbon" sidebar for more information on using red ribbons.)

✔ Hang your flute with the shorter bamboo segments lower (closer to the floor), the longer bamboo segments higher (closer to the ceiling), and the mouthpiece on top. (Obviously this doesn't apply when you hang a flute horizontally.) This powerful hanging method symbolizes upward growth over time and increasing fortune in each successive stage of your life. (The correct and incorrect ways to hang flutes are shown in Figure 4-3.)

✔ The Yun Lin Temple supplies the highest quality and only type of bamboo flute that I recommend. To purchase one (which comes with a red ribbon attached) call 510-841-2347 and ask for the bamboo flute (the Temple carries only one kind).

✔ Treat any bamboo flute used for a cure with respect. A flute that's handled roughly, played with casually, or blown into is de-energized; it becomes an object of décor rather than a genuine Feng Shui artifact.

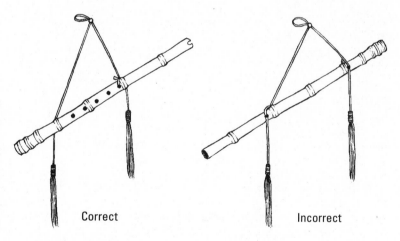

Figure 4-3:
Correct and
incorrect
ways to
hang
bamboo
flutes.

Correct   Incorrect

Powered cures

Powered cures often utilize electrical objects such as appliances featuring generators or motors. The energy generated by these appliances can be used to activate particular parts of your space. Powered cures are used mainly to generate energy or create activity in a specific Life Area of the Feng Shui Octagon (see Chapter 3).

Firecrackers can also be used as a powered cure. Symbolic firecrackers located over the front door (on the inside of the home), can help protect the home and its occupants. Depending on your intention when placing them, firecrackers can also activate new sources of revenue, enhance an occupation, and attract important business connections. (You can find a source for symbolic firecrackers in the appendix.)

Fragrance cures

Fragrance cures take advantage of your sense of smell. One of the most powerful and evocative senses, smell directly stimulates the limbic system and often triggers the instant recall of rich and long-forgotten memories. Pleasant odors are frequently related to good feelings, higher states of well-being, and increased awareness. In the East, it's commonly believed that good spirits prefer environments that have pleasant, uplifting odors. (And everyone associates bad smells with negative vibes!) Cures in the fragrance category include incense, essential oils, and flowers. (Flowers are also a living cure, as I explain earlier in this chapter.) Turn to Chapter 21 for some highly effective fragrance cure methods.

Incense

When using incense as an energy-adjustment tool, I strongly recommend high-quality incense rather than inexpensive brands that commonly incorporate synthetic oils and perfumes. Synthetic incense is not only less effective but also much less enjoyable. It can even be irritating to the senses.

Essential oils

With essential oils, quality is vital for effectiveness. When essential oils are processed, heat and exposure to light rapidly degrade their subtle molecular structure and destroy their vital qualities. With oils, you definitely get what you pay for, and quality essential oils are worth the extra price. Two excellent brands of oils are Young Living (www.youngliving.com) and Tisserand (www.tisserand.com).

Fragrant oils can improve your health and your mood as well as your environment. For more on the benefits and applications of fragrance, I recommend the excellent *Aromatherapy For Dummies* by Kathi Keville (published by Wiley).

Touch cures

Touch cures engage your kinesthetic sense to awaken or adjust your energy. For instance, place a green vine around the handrail of a stairway so each time you ascend or descend the stairs, your hand brushes the vine and tangibly connects to its symbolic life energy. Touch cures can give a boost to your recuperative powers and stimulate good health.

Chapter 5

Harnessing the Energies of the Five Elements

*I*n this chapter, I present a powerful method for understanding and shifting the energy of your environment — the *Five Elements*. According to Chinese energy theory, everything in the universe is made up of varying combinations of five *elements,* or forms of energy. The Five Elements are Wood, Fire, Earth, Metal, and Water. They're simply a further extension of the fundamental yin and yang principle I describe in Chapter 1. The Five Elements system offers a way of looking at the natural cycles of the world and bringing your life into greater balance with them. Energetically speaking, you contain a unique mixture of each of the Five Elements — and so does your environment.

In Grandmaster Lin Yun's Feng Shui school, each of the Five Elements has corresponding natural locations in a space, similar to the Feng Shui Octagon. If the Elements are situated in their natural positions in your home, the energy circulates and helps you achieve harmony and abundance. But each Element also has a location in the environment where it can conflict with another Element in the space. When Elements are situated in these negative locations, you may experience conflict, lowered income, and even psychological or physical health problems.

In this chapter, I explain the basic energies of each of the Elements, as well as their positive and negative placements. I also describe different cycles of the Five Elements and give you several ways to create powerful cures by using the energies of the Five Elements.

The Chinese Five Element system differs somewhat from the Western element system, which is typically composed of four elements (earth, wind, fire, and air), and from the Indian five element system (space, air, fire, water, and earth). The Chinese Five Element system is a profound system that isn't limited only to Feng Shui applications; you could study it for a lifetime and gain continuing benefits. Experts beneficially study and employ Five Element principles in cooking, traditional Chinese medicine, *chi kung* (energy exercises), meditative methods, martial arts, and more.

The Energies of the Five Elements

Each of the Five Elements — Wood, Fire, Earth, Metal, and Water — is a form of energy with unique characteristics, feelings, and various *correspondences* (meaningful and important connections) to the natural world. These correspondences include colors, organs, parts of nature, seasons of the year, and two-dimensional and three-dimensional shapes (see Table 5-1 for a quick summary). The Five Elements are also connected to the psychological and interpersonal aspects of human life.

Table 5-1	The Five Elements' Corresponding Physical Representations, Colors, & Shapes		
Element	*Physical Representations of the Element*	*Colors of the Element*	*Two- and Three-Dimensional Shapes of the Element*
Wood	Living tree, plant	Green, blue	Upright rectangle, column
Fire	Candle, fire-place, light	Red	Triangle, pyramid
Earth	Pottery	Yellow, earth tones	Square, cube
Metal	Metal sculpture or metal table	White	Circle, sphere, dome
Water	Fountain, stream, pond	Black, midnight blue	Undulating, wavy

In the following sections, I provide the correspondences of each of the Elements to help you understand how they function. I also explain their energetic qualities.

The energy of Wood: Growth

Wood chi is the energy of upward movement; it initiates new growth. Represented by the colors green and blue, the Wood Element is related to the liver, trees, and the season of spring. Its corresponding geometric shape is an upright rectangle or column; skyscrapers are common examples of Wood-shaped buildings. Wood is naturally located in the center of the left side of a space. It's good to apply when you want to add the energy of growth, expansion, and vitality to your life. Associated with new beginnings, Wood cures are like adding a touch of spring, the season in which you feel young, energetic, and motivated.

The energy of Fire: Expansion

Fire chi is upward-moving, burning, hot, bright, fiery energy. Of the five energies, Fire represents maximum expansiveness and activity — the peak of energetic intensity. Fire is related to the summer season, the color red, the heart, and actual fire. Its corresponding geometric shape is a triangle or pyramid. And Fire energy's natural position is in the back center of a space or location. Perform Fire cures when you want to create more expansion, heat, and power in your life and experience increased recognition.

The energy of Earth: Stability

Earth chi stabilizes, balances, and grounds you (pun intended). In times of intense life change, Earth helps you become centered. Earth is related to the harvest season, the color yellow (and other earth tones), the stomach, and actual earth. Its corresponding geometric shapes are the square, a horizontally positioned rectangle, and the cube. Earth's natural location is the center of a space. Perform Earth cures when you want to slow down in life, become more centered, and feel connected and stable.

The energy of Metal: Contraction

Metal chi is cold, contracting, dense energy associated with communication, creativity, detail, symbols, signals, and noise. Corresponding with the color white, metal is related to the lungs, the fall season, and metallic objects. Its geometric shapes are the circle, sphere, and dome. Metal is located in the center of the right-hand side of a space. Apply Metal cures when you want to improve communications, clarity, and precision, or when you want to stimulate your projects.

The energy of Water: Stillness

Water chi is the energy of maximum concentration and stillness. Water is the energy of things moving downward and coming to rest. It's related to the season of winter, to the colors black and midnight blue, and to the kidneys. The shapes of Water are elusive, imprecise, undulating forms that are flowing and difficult to describe. Water is naturally positioned in the center of the front side of a space. It embodies the energy of stillness (think lakes and ponds) and of movement (think rivers, streams, and oceans). In addition, in Feng Shui, Water traditionally relates in a big way to money ("cash flow"). Perform Water cures when you want more peace and clarity of mind or when you want to increase the flow of people, contacts, and money into your life.

Placing the Five Elements in Your Environment According to the Octagon

If you know the positions of the Feng Shui Octagon, finding the natural locations of the Five Elements is easy. (If you don't know these positions, take a look at Chapter 3.) The Five Elements are located on the Octagon as follows:

- ✔ **Wood:** The center-left part of the environment (Family Area)
- ✔ **Fire:** The center-back part (Fame Area)
- ✔ **Earth:** The center part (Health Area)
- ✔ **Metal:** The center-right part (Children Area)
- ✔ **Water:** The center-front part (Career Area)

The Cycles of the Five Elements

The Five Elements relate to and interact with each other according to two main cycles: the Creative (Generative) Cycle and the Destructive (Transformative) Cycle. (In advanced Feng Shui study, you find some additional cycles, but the Creative and Destructive Cycles contain all the transformational power you need.) You can use the Elements themselves as well as their Creative and Destructive Cycles for Feng Shui cures.

- ✔ In the Creative Cycle, the Elements create one another in a continual cyclical process.
- ✔ In the Destructive Cycle, the Elements cyclically consume each other in a similar process.

In the type of Feng Shui I present in this book, neither cycle is necessarily better than the other. The next sections describe in greater detail how the two Element Cycles work.

The Creative Cycle of the Five Elements

In the Creative Cycle, the Elements generate, create, or lead to one another in a continuous chain of creative energy (see Figure 5-1). The following ring-around-the-rosie example clearly illustrates the Creative Cycle:

- ✔ Wood, as it burns, is the fuel for Fire.
- ✔ Fire produces ashes, which return to and replenish the Earth.
- ✔ The Earth gives birth to Metal, which humans mine from the Earth.
- ✔ Metal, when heated sufficiently, becomes liquid like Water.
- ✔ Water nourishes Wood (the tree).

In the Creative Cycle, the Elemental energies change from one form into another.

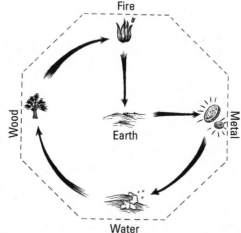

Figure 5-1:
The Creative
Cycle of
the Five
Elements.

The Destructive Cycle of the Five Elements

In the Destructive Cycle, the Elements energetically destroy or overcome each other in a continuous pattern (see Figure 5-2).

✔ Wood is cut by the Metal axe.

✔ Metal is burned by the blacksmith's Fire.

✔ Fire is extinguished by Water.

✔ Water is absorbed, subdued, and evaporated by the Earth.

✔ Earth is penetrated and consumed by growing trees (Wood).

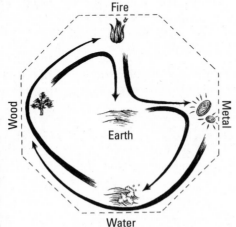

Figure 5-2:
The
Destructive
Cycle of
the Five
Elements.

Creator and Offspring Elements

The later "Using the Five Elements in Different Cure Methods" section shows you how to empower any Element simply by placing it in its natural location. However, you can also create cures by using the Element that creates the Element you want to empower; I call this Element the *Creator Element*. Another cure option is to use the Element created by the Element you want to help; I call this Element the *Offspring Element*. Table 5-2 gives you the Creator and Offspring Elements for each of the Five Elements.

Table 5-2   Creator & Offspring Elements of the Five Elements

Creator Element	Element Itself	Offspring Element
Water	Wood	Fire
Wood	Fire	Earth
Fire	Earth	Metal
Earth	Metal	Water
Metal	Water	Wood

Using the Five Elements in Different Cure Methods

The Five Elements theory explains how natural forces combine and interact to either help or hinder your life. When the Elements are located in their natural positions in your space and, more importantly, aren't located in positions of conflict with other Elements, balance is enhanced. When the Elements are in balance, your daily life reflects peace and harmony, but when your home has conflicts between Elements, you may experience disharmony and chaotic life patterns.

In the sections that follow, I go over four different cure methods you can apply to create powerful energetic shifts in your environment, with corresponding beneficial changes in your life.

When applying the Five Elements to create particular life results, you can use any of the following items (refer to Table 5-1 for a reminder of the Five Elements' correspondences):

- ✔ The physical representation of the Element
- ✔ The color of the Element
- ✔ The shape of the Element

Method 1: Placing Elements in their natural locations

With this cure method, you simply place a representation of a chosen Element in its natural location. You can use this method if you desire an increase in the Element's energy or if you want to stimulate the Life Area of the Octagon where the Element resides.

Suppose you want a boost in your reputation; simply add the Fire Element to the Fame Area of your home, yard, or a specific room. You can add a candle or the color red to the natural location of Fire, or you can place a triangular or pyramid-shaped object in the area.

Method 11: Removing or counteracting offending Elements

When any of the conflicts in the following list are present in your environment, watch out! An Element positioned in the natural location of a conflicting Element can create particular life problems. You may want to remedy these Element relationships, especially if they correspond to an aspect of your life you want to improve.

- ✔ Wood located in Earth's natural location can harm your health.
- ✔ Fire located in Metal's natural location can harm your communication.
- ✔ Earth located in Water's natural location can harm your career.
- ✔ Metal located in Wood's natural location can harm your family life.
- ✔ Water located in Fire's natural location can harm your reputation.

For best results, remove an Element from a position where it conflicts with another Element (one symbolically consumes and destroys the other), particularly if you're experiencing challenges in the corresponding Life Area. For example, Water destroys Fire, so a fountain (Water) located in the Fire location (Fame Area) of your home causes an Element conflict that can negatively affect your reputation. The cure? Simply remove the fountain. Who says Feng Shui needs to be complicated?

If a Destructive Element relationship can't be moved, you can still cure the problem in one of two ways:

- ✔ **Counteract the offending Element by adding a counter Element to the area in question to symbolically destroy the offending Element.** For instance, if a fireplace (Fire) is located in the Metal position of your home (the Children Area) and your child is experiencing problems in school, cure the fireplace by adding Water — which destroys Fire — to the Children Area. Try adding a fountain to the Metal position to dampen the effect of the fireplace and relieve the negative effects on your child. Instead of adding actual water, you can also use the color of Water by placing something black in the area, or you can use an object with Water's wavy, undulating shape. Better yet, use a black object with Water's shape. (But please, don't use black water. There is such a thing as going overboard!)

- ✔ **Add more of the attacked Element to its natural location to increase its strength and help it overcome the offender.** Continuing with the example of a fireplace in Metal's natural location, use this method by adding more Metal to its natural location to boost Metal's power. Accordingly, you can add an object made of metal, the color white, or something round or spherical to the Metal location. (You can combine these effects by adding a spherical white metal object, if you can find one.)

Method III: Utilizing Creator and Offspring Elements for added power

Another way to perform Five Elements cures is to add either the Creator or the Offspring Elements (or both) to an Element's natural position (see the earlier "Creator and Offspring Elements" section for the scoop on these Elements). For example, say you want to boost family expansion (with another kid!) and family unity. Wood is the Element you need to apply for these results. Water creates Wood, and Fire is the offspring of Wood. Therefore, to increase Wood, you can add either a fountain (Water) or the color red (Fire) to Wood's natural position.

Method IV: Combining all the Elements for power and creativity

To create balance, harmony, and power, you can add all Five Elements to any Element's natural position or to any room that needs its energy positively adjusted. This cure is good for a bedroom or living room, or even an office. With all Five Elements in place, you can create an atmosphere of wholeness, peace, and creativity. Place the Elements individually in the room or Life Area or install one item that contains all the Elements, such as a painting that presents each of the Element colors or an object that combines all the Elements in shape, color, and/or material.

Say you want to perform this cure using the three-dimensional Element shapes (refer to Table 5-1). In this case, you should add five objects to the space; one a column, another a pyramid, a third a cube, another a sphere, and the last one a wavy shape. This is just one of the many ways to carry out this cure; feel free to use your creativity and imagination along with the guidance in this chapter.

When combining all the Elements, no negative Destructive relationships ensue. When all the Elements are together, they work in harmony, so the situation is energetically complete and whole.

Applying Five Elements Cures for Life Change

So how do you use knowledge of the Five Elements to make things happen the way you want in your life? Just follow these steps:

1. **Map out the Five Element positions in your environment so you know the lay of the land.**

   You have to know the natural positions of each of the Elements before you can start making changes, but the environment you're working with can be any you want, be it your lot, your home's floor plan, or your bedroom. (Or how about all three? Now you're seeing the real power of Feng Shui!)

2. **Get rid of or counteract any significant Destructive Cycle situations that are occurring in the natural locations of any Elements.**

   This step can help you free yourself from natural forces that have unknowingly been holding you back for years. It's especially important to perform if the Destructive Cycle occurs in an Element area in which you're experiencing challenges (although taking care of as many Destructive Cycle situations as you can doesn't hurt either). Use the information in the earlier "Method II: Removing or counteracting offending Elements" section to help you perform this step.

3. **Decide what you want to positively change or improve in your life.**

   Here's a quick reference to help you decide which changes to make:

   - To improve growth and upward movement and to initiate new projects, cure the Wood position of your space.

   - To increase passion, heat, and power, cure the Fire position of your space.

   - To improve stability, balance, and harmony with the other Elements, cure the Earth position of your space.

   - To improve clarity, precision, and your communication abilities, cure the Metal position of your space.

   - To improve cash flow, increase connections with people, or boost wisdom, cure the Water position of your space.

   Apply the Three Secrets Reinforcement as part of each cure you do (see Chapter 6 for details).

The most powerful Five Elements cures involve using the Element shapes (three-dimensional shapes are even more powerful than two-dimensional ones). The next most powerful cure is to use an Element's color(s), and the third most powerful cure is to employ the Element itself. To see which shapes, colors, and physical representations correspond with each Element, refer to Table 5-1.

Chapter 6

Tapping the Inner Power of Feng Shui

In This Chapter

▶ Defining Feng Shui's outer and inner aspects

▶ Taking a look at intention's power and how to successfully apply it to cures

▶ Performing the Three Secrets Reinforcement

▶ Answering some common questions about Reinforcement

"What we are today comes from our thoughts of yesterday, and our present thoughts build our life of tomorrow: Our life is the creation of our mind."

—Guatama Buddha

You find out in Chapters 1 and 2 that Feng Shui and the Chinese energetic arts are all based on the concept of *chi* (the life force). Feng Shui is a system for harnessing this force to create a better life. As important and central as this energy is, there's another, deeper level to the process. All the energetic arts that make up the esoteric portion of China's cultural heritage — including kung fu, chi kung, tai chi, acupressure, alchemy, and Feng Shui — recognize the core principle of mind training as fundamental to realizing one's fullest potentials.

In the spiritual traditions of the East, mind training plays a preeminent role in self-development. The masters of the Far East realized that the inner world holds the key to one's happiness and success. Feng Shui masters also recognized that the external environment significantly affects one's inner world and outer life circumstances. This chapter introduces the application of Feng Shui principles directly to your inner life for the purpose of improving your fortune and destiny.

Introducing the Outer and Inner Aspects of Feng Shui

All the Chinese energetic arts have two parts:

- ✔ The outer part has to do with the physical and tangible concepts and performance (such as bed placement or land formation in Feng Shui).
- ✔ The inner part deals with the energetic nature of the art; at its peak, it involves the mind and spirit.

Grandmaster Lin Yun's Feng Shui school also refers to these parts as the *mundane* (outer) and the *transcendental* (inner) parts. Although studying both parts is the key to effective Feng Shui, the inner parts are the more hidden and potent aspects. They're typically taught to a teacher's family members and occasionally to the teacher's most sincere, highly cultivated, and long-standing students. Very few Feng Shui teachers today publicly teach the most inner parts of their art.

The Chinese masters called this inner, mind-cultivated power *yi*. There's no direct English translation for yi. Rather, it's a combination of intention, imagination, vision, belief, faith, positive expectation, and more. All of these elements are timeless spiritual principles, important for creating successful cures.

You use yi to effectively perform the Three Secrets Reinforcement (which I describe later in this chapter). To maximize your positive results, cultivating both the right intention for each cure and the most positive attitude and motivations surrounding each cure is essential. The rest of this chapter explores proper, powerful intentions and attitudes to supercharge your Feng Shui cures.

One effective way to build inner power is through regular meditation. Every cure directly benefits from the power you cultivate through meditation. Flip to Chapter 22 for some meditation methods you can apply immediately.

Discovering the Magic of Intention

Nearly everything you do in life requires *intention* — a combination of will, motivation, concentration, and desire. In Grandmaster Lin Yun's Feng Shui school, intention plays a key role: It's actually the starting point for your Feng Shui efforts. Intention not only sets the space and the "target" for the cure but it also contains the reason behind the cure and refers to the power of your intent.

To intend a result, you must first decide what you want. Then you need to focus your intention as you perform a cure in the part of your life you want to remedy or transform (see Chapter 3 for the scoop on the nine Life Areas of the Feng Shui Octagon).

If your intention is clear, your desired outcome is much more likely to occur. Why? Because intention magnifies the energy of cures, increasing their power and effectiveness in your life. Yes, Feng Shui cures work whether you perform them with focused intention or not because the external environment affects your inner and outer life. However, the most powerful Feng Shui results come from the combined application of the mundane and transcendental aspects that I describe in the preceding section. In other words, powerful results occur when physical changes are combined with strong intention and proper motivation.

Grandmaster Lin Yun's Feng Shui school has a special technique for empowering the intentions of your cures — thereby making them much more potent — called the *Three Secrets Reinforcement*. This is an easy-to-perform procedure that you apply with each and every Feng Shui cure you do. It takes just a couple minutes and uses the spiritual power of your body, speech, and mind to energetically strengthen your cures.

Applying the Power of Intention to Cures

Feng Shui works because its philosophy is based on the principles of energy flow, to which all environments are subject. However, you can add rocket fuel to your Feng Shui by connecting a particular intention to each cure that you perform. By applying specific intentions to cures, you infuse them with additional energy.

Here's the basic rundown of how to successfully apply the power of your mind to your cures:

1. **Know exactly what you want.**

2. **Have the proper positive attitude and motivation for yourself and others.**

3. **Visualize and feel the desired result before it happens.**

4. **Believe, without a doubt, that the results will happen.**

5. **Relax and allow the results to happen.**

To the degree that any of the preceding ingredients are missing, the effectiveness of your cure may be lessened. To the degree that these ingredients are present, the effectiveness of your cures is increased. In the next sections, I cover these ingredients in detail so you're absolutely clear about using this powerful aspect of Feng Shui practice.

For the best results, pay attention when you apply intention.

Know exactly what you want

Knowing what you want is a fundamental requirement in the realm of intention; the more clear you are about your goal, the better. If you're unclear about it, you can still get positive results, but they may be more general than particular. Clarity about your goals focuses your intention and empowers your cures to accomplish specific desired results. (You can still perform beneficial cures with general intentions, such as improving your health, increasing your wealth, bringing harmony into the home, and so on. The point is to have a strong, clear, and focused intention with each cure you perform.)

After knowing what you want, the next crucial factor is the strength of your desire. These two factors generate your intention. Weak, wishy-washy intentions (as in "it'd be nice for that to happen, but it's really okay if it doesn't") don't magnify your cures. Passion is what infuses your intentions with power and effectiveness. The greater your passion for achieving your goal, the more powerful your intention — and the more effective your cure.

When you practice Feng Shui, I recommend you write down your intentions. Be sure to write down not only what you want but also why you want it and how intently you want it. This simple step clarifies and focuses your intention, making your goal more real and the cure more meaningful, which produces better results. (See Chapter 1 for an exercise that has you write down the parts of your life that you want to improve.)

Have the right attitude and motivation

A second important component of your internal Feng Shui work is your attitude or motivation toward the cures you do. Attitude and motivation are a combination of awareness of the goal you want to accomplish and the feelings and desires that fuel your intention.

The nature of the motivation behind an action — whether it's positive or negative — determines whether the action creates positive or negative consequences for the doer. If your intention is negative, the cure may either backfire or do nothing.

Purity of motivation is key. Self-serving outcomes desired in opposition to and at the expense of others skew a Feng Shui cure. Desiring the best and most helpful results for yourself and everyone concerned, on the other hand, adds spiritual power to a cure. Seeing your own success benefiting others is therefore a recipe for a more successful Feng Shui cure. (The wider your blessing motivation, the more powerful and positive potential your cure contains. This insight is exemplified in the prayer, "May all beings be happy, may all beings be peaceful, may all beings be free.") Keep this principle in mind when doing your cures. Have a loving, caring heart and visualize something good happening with your cure that's beneficial to others and harmful to no one.

See and feel the result before it happens

Another important internal Feng Shui skill is *visualization,* which is simply internally seeing the results of your cures before they happen. Professionals of all types (including businesspeople, top athletes, and astronauts) use visualization to help them dissolve limitations, accomplish their goals, and excel in their chosen fields.

Visualizing an intention is almost a prerequisite for manifesting an intention in any field of endeavor, whether that field is art, science, business, or magic. In Feng Shui, visualization is a powerful way to exercise and build your intention.

The clarity with which you visualize an intention makes your goal more likely to happen as you foresee it. So visualizing the desired results of a cure — while you perform it — makes the cure substantially more effective. Visualize your internal pictures so vividly that it seems like you're actually emotionally and physically experiencing how wonderful and exciting your new life will be when the result is attained. (I share visualization tips in the next section.)

Believe completely that the result will happen

Grandmaster Lin Yun's Feng Shui school says that having a sincere heart is vital for effective cures. A sincere heart means you have full and complete belief that the cure you've implemented is working. When you know and feel what you want and you can visualize and feel it happening, the next step is to proceed in life with the confident assumption that your cures are effective as soon as you apply them. Seal the deal with certainty!

Belief is *not* a substitute for choosing your cures wisely and implementing them correctly. It's an added component on top of correct execution.

Don't make the mistake of waiting for your cures to start working. If you do, you're setting yourself up to fail. (Doubt is your enemy in the realm of Feng Shui cures, so you must realize that your cures are working from the moment you do them.) Your expectations create your future, and positive expectation opens the doors to success. Align your actions, thoughts, attitudes, and words to the new life situation or result that you desire; believe with complete faith and confidence; and then watch the results you desire come into being before your eyes.

Expecting a result isn't wishing upon a star and then sitting back and expecting a higher power to magically work everything out. Nor is it stubbornly folding your arms or dragging your heels with an "Oh yeah, prove it to me!" attitude, doubting the result until your Feng Shui cures cough up and give you what you want. Neither passive wishful thinking nor passive/aggressive skepticism is helpful.

A friend recently told me about the marvelous benefits she received after performing just two cures with a positive mindset. A year before our visit, she'd painted the door of her home red as well as the door of the rental home she owned. As she painted the doors, she visualized more prosperity and expected results. By the time she saw me, she'd just completed the purchase of a third home and a share in another home. Her personal transformation was obvious: Her energy was stronger and more vibrant, and she even looked younger than the last time I'd seen her. Did I mention she's happier? (And she hadn't yet had the opportunity to read this book!)

Relax and allow the results to happen

After you choose your intended result and perform the cures, it's time to relax and allow yourself to receive the results that you're seeking. You can never control the final outcome of anything in life, but you can set in motion a powerful process that possesses its own energy and unfolds in its own way. So just relax and let things happen. It's a matter of believing without pushing, of having faith that your intentions and actions, empowered by Feng Shui methods, are generating the desired results — even if you don't (and can't) know exactly how this process occurs. Final results may differ somewhat from your specific expectations, but they'll fulfill them in some tangible (and agreeable) form.

Of course, merely performing Feng Shui cures won't make you rich, successful, or famous. Feng Shui isn't a substitute for responsible and committed action toward your goals. Ultimately, you're still responsible for taking the proper actions in the world to make your dreams come true.

Revealing the Secrets of the Three Secrets Reinforcement

One of the most fundamental techniques taught by Grandmaster Lin Yun's Feng Shui school is the Three Secrets Reinforcement. It's not only the energizing and vitalizing portion of each cure you perform but it's also your key to creating successful cures. Feng Shui directs and optimizes the energy in your environment to improve your life, and the Three Secrets Reinforcement establishes the decisive energetic connection between your environment and yourself.

According to Grandmaster Lin Yun, "if you do your Feng Shui cures and forget to include the Three Secrets Reinforcement, your results will likely be weak; if you do your cures using the Three Secrets Reinforcement, your results will be very strong." Without the Three Secrets Reinforcement, a cure is like a flashlight operating on a weak battery. The beam of light can only be so bright and shine so far before it starts to fade. With the Three Secrets Reinforcement, that beam is like a laser cutting through any energetic obstacles in you and in your personal environment.

As I explain in the earlier "Introducing the Outer and Inner Aspects of Feng Shui" section, in Grandmaster Lin Yun's Feng Shui school, every cure involves two parts:

- ✔ **Visible (tangible) elements:** These are the changes you make in your physical environment, such as hanging a wind chime, moving your bed, and so on. The physical part of the cure provides only a fraction of the cure's effectiveness.

- ✔ **Invisible (spiritual) elements:** These are your goals, desires, energy, intention, motivation, visualization, and attitude. They provide the remaining portion of the cure's effectiveness.

The invisible part of a cure — strengthened by the Three Secrets Reinforcement — uses and focuses your intention and motivation to turbocharge the energy of the physical change. In fact, the invisible part of the cure contributes more to the cure's overall strength than the physical part does, so including the Three Secrets Reinforcement in each cure you perform is essential.

In the following sections, I describe the parts of the Three Secrets Reinforcement and what you need to perform cures with it.

Defining the Three Secrets Reinforcement

The Three Secrets Reinforcement adds the powers of body, mind, and speech to the physical Feng Shui adjustments of your environment. The three basic elements of it are the Body Secret, the Speech Secret, and the Mind Secret. Each element engages a different part of your body-mind system and channels its unique power into the Reinforcement. In the following sections, I detail each of the secrets individually; then in the later "Performing cures with the Reinforcement" section, I show you how to combine all three components into one simple-yet-potent package.

The Body Secret: The physical you

The Body Secret uses a *mudra,* a spiritual hand gesture, position, or action that aligns the energy of your body to help create the desired energetic effect. Hand gestures have a symbolic as well as an energetic value. To understand the power of hand gestures in daily life, consider how the infamous one-fingered salute can trigger anger and even violence in a total stranger; how both hands raised overhead can save your life in wartime; and even how clasping your hands in front of you can make you feel more relaxed, calm, and aware.

When applying the Body Secret in your Reinforcements, feel free to use a hand gesture from your personal spiritual tradition or any other gesture that feels comfortable and effective for you. I recommend any of the following mudras for your Reinforcements:

- **The Expelling or Ousting Mudra:** The Expelling or Ousting Mudra is often recommended for the Three Secrets Reinforcement because it creates wonderful blessings by removing obstacles from your life while simultaneously infusing positive energy into the situation. You perform this mudra by pointing your index and pinky fingers straight up and then holding your middle and ring fingers near your palm with your thumb. Then you repeatedly flick your middle and ring fingers out from your palm (see Figure 6-1a). Repeat this flicking motion for a total of nine times. (Note that women use their right hand for this mudra; men use their left.)

- **The Heart-Calming Mudra:** This mudra invokes peace, calm, and contentment. Perform it by placing your left hand on top of your right, with your palms facing up and the tips of your thumbs touching (see Figure 6-1b).

- **The Prayer Mudra (and other options):** Other sacred gestures that are effective in your Reinforcements include the Prayer Mudra (palms together, as shown in Figure 6-1c) or any other meditative or spiritual hand position that has personal meaning or simply feels good to you. If you don't practice a religion, you can create your own personal hand gesture or position, although I don't recommend starting a new religion based on your new hand gesture. Or you can simply stand or sit with your eyes closed in a comfortable, balanced position until you feel a sense of clarity and calm.

Don't worry about picking the right mudra. You simply need to choose a mudra you like for each Reinforcement that you perform. Any mudra that feels right to you can work (just remember that you only need to use one per Reinforcement).

To perform the Body Secret step of the Three Secrets Reinforcement, simply hold your hand gesture (if using the Expelling Mudra, flick nine times) as you perform the next two Secrets.

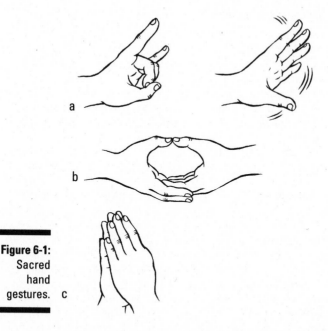

Figure 6-1:
Sacred
hand
gestures.

The Speech Secret: The power of the spoken word

The Speech Secret utilizes sacred words and sounds to enhance cures. All sounds and words have power, and sacred words have the most power of all. If you're wondering how spoken words can possibly affect your cures, think of how hearing a four-letter curse word can affect your mind and emotions and consider how other words can soothe, reassure, and calm turbulent emotions and distress. And yes, the clear intention with which you speak such words does affect their potency.

The sounds used in the Three Secrets Reinforcement are called *mantras* (sacred words of power). Mantras are ancient containers of spiritual vibrations, meanings, and intentions made potent through ceremonial use over time.

To perform the Speech Secret step of the Reinforcement, repeat your mantra or prayer aloud nine times.

Sacred speech isn't the same as affirmations or repeating sentences stating your desire. Affirmations are good to use, but mantras used in the method described in the later "Performing cures with the Reinforcement" section can be even more effective. Correctly used, a mantra uses sounds or words to take you beyond your conscious mind and connect you to your spirit, where the majority of your power resides.

I recommend that you use one of the following mantras when doing your Reinforcements:

✔ **The Six True Words:** The Six True Words are *Om Ma Ni Pad Me Hum* (pronounced ohm-mah-nee-pahd-mee-hum). This mantra, which also goes by the name *Mantra of Compassion,* has the power to improve luck, uplift your mind, correct negative thoughts, enhance wealth and prosperity, and help you perform better in your daily life.

✔ **The Heart-Calming Mantra:** The beneficial effects of this mantra include creating peace and calm, invoking feelings of ease and contentment, and releasing fears and anxieties. The Heart-Calming Mantra has four lines to recite (reciting the four equals one time through the mantra): Here's how to pronounce this mantra (the italics indicate stressed syllables):

- Gate gate (*gah*-tay *gah*-tay)

- Para gate (*pair*-uh *gah*-tay)

- Para sum gate (*pair*-uh *sum gah*-tay)

- Bodhi swaha (*boh*-dee *swa*-ha)

Feel free to substitute mantras, prayers, or chants from other spiritual traditions for your Three Secrets Reinforcements. Just be sure to repeat the one you select nine times when performing the Reinforcement.

The Mind Secret: The power of visualization

Whether you're consciously aware of it or not, you're continuously creating your future with mental visualization, so you may as well start using it to your advantage. Because many of your mental pictures are formed outside of your awareness, figuring out how to consciously direct them is highly beneficial in terms of creating positive results and life changes.

The Mind Secret is the most potent Secret of the Three Secrets Reinforcement (although all three parts are vital). It's also the part of the Reinforcement in which you mentally see your desire — your motivation for performing the cure — coming true. In other words, you must visualize in concrete and realistic detail the events, conditions, and scenes that you desire in your life.

The more clearly you see what you want, the more likely it is that you'll receive it. By visualizing what you want, you adjust your chi and powerfully propel yourself toward new actions, events, and outcomes. So see and feel the excitement and positive emotions you'll experience when you achieve your desire.

If you have difficulty visualizing clear mental images, don't worry. Instead, you can internally feel or mentally hear your desired results; the effect is the same as visualizing. The present imagining of your future desired results is what does the trick. The images you see, sounds you hear, and feelings you feel should be exciting, even thrilling. Actually see yourself in your mental pictures doing, achieving, and receiving the wonderful life benefits you deserve. If after visualizing, you feel "ho-hum" or indifferent about what you saw, do it again but with more gusto. To illustrate, if you want greater wealth, visualize or imagine your future wealth and the things you can enjoy with wealth flowing into your life. The pictures, feelings, or imaginings should be moving, involving, and exciting.

Grandmaster Lin Yun's Feng Shui school promotes two other important principles for increasing the power of your visualizations:

- ✔ **Detail is helpful for effective visualization.** See your desired goal occurring in as much detail as possible. Detailed visualization directs your body, mind, and energies to create the life scenarios you desire. Involve other senses internally for even more oomph. For instance, if your goal is a new car, you can visualize the model, the color, the year, the sleek design, and the details of the instrument panel. You can feel the leather grain of the seat, hear the purr of the engine as you see yourself driving to your office, and smell the new car scent (one of the greatest smells in the world).

- ✔ **See in your mind's eye that your desired life situation occurs in three stages of development.** New things in life don't often drop out of the sky the moment you ask for them. Most things in life have beginning, middle, and ending stages; your desired results will happen in the same manner. So I recommend this three-stage visualization method, which follows life's natural progression. It sets up energetic pathways that gracefully lead you into the new life situation you desire.

Say you want to buy a new car. The following steps demonstrate how you can put the three stages of development into effect to achieve your desire (see Figure 6-2):

- • **See the initial circumstances that lead to what you want.** You're at the dealership checking out and test-driving the car you really want, and you're saving money to get the car.

- • **Visualize the development phase of the process.** You pick out the exact car you want, acquire the down payment, and sign the loan papers. The whole process is smooth and enjoyable.

- • **See the wonderful completion of your goal.** You're roaring down the street in your new, fabulous ride with YO BABY on your license plate. Life is sweet!

Figure 6-2:
The three
steps of
visualization.

Performing cures with the Reinforcement

To perform an entire Feng Shui cure, you must do both of the following, gearing everything to the part of your life that you want to change:

- ✔ Include the physical aspect, which means physically altering the energy of your environment by choosing one of the many methods I describe in this book (such as hanging a crystal sphere, moving your bed, installing a mirror, and so on).

- ✔ Apply the Three Secrets Reinforcement immediately before or after you perform the physical part of your cure. (The next day works fine too if you forget.)

Here's how to do the Reinforcement in three easy steps:

1. **Perform the Body Secret.**

   Place your hands in the mudra of your choice.

2. **Perform the Speech Secret.**

   While holding the mudra, repeat the mantra of your choice nine times.

3. Perform the Mind Secret.

Visualize your intended desire transpiring in as much detail as possible.

Congratulations, you've just completed a cure! Now go perform another cure, take other productive and practical actions toward your goal, or simply relax.

 A watched pot never boils. Worrying about your cure after you've performed it is like planting a seed in the ground and standing around wondering whether it'll sprout. Go about your daily life and let the cure unfold in due course.

Frequently Asked Questions about the Three Secrets Reinforcement

In the sections that follow, I address some basic questions about the Three Secrets Reinforcement.

In what order should I perform the three steps of the Reinforcement?

The order of mudra, then mantra, then visualization (as explained in the earlier "Performing cures with the Reinforcement" section) is usually the easiest way for beginners to perform the Reinforcement. Alternatively, you can do all three steps at the same. As long as you involve all three parts, the effect will be the same.

 Belief and maximum inner involvement have more to do with the effectiveness of your Reinforcements than the order of the steps.

How long should my Reinforcements take?

You don't need to spend any particular period of time performing a Three Secrets Reinforcement. Internal intensity and realism are what creates results, not the length of time you perform your Reinforcements. A minute or two is certainly sufficient if you really feel the energy and emotion inside.

Is how I'm thinking and feeling during the Reinforcement important?

Absolutely! Be as focused and sincere as possible and trust the process. Perform each Reinforcement with sincerity, energy, intention, and powerful emotion. The element of sincerity is particularly fundamental for a high level of effectiveness with your cures. Involve your heart in what you're doing, and you'll do fine. Ideally, your visualizations are so exciting and powerful that your nervous system lights up like a Christmas tree. (Don't worry if you're not quite there yet. Sincerity effectively empowers a cure whether you're a master of visualization or a beginner acquiring a new skill.)

How do I know whether I'm doing the Reinforcement right?

Don't get caught up in performance anxiety over your Reinforcements. Every person has his or her own natural way that works. Perform a Reinforcement as well as you can. Release all concern and feel confident that your Reinforcement is effective, and it'll be effective. As with any skill, your ability will grow with practice.

How many times do I need to perform the Reinforcement?

Generally, you perform one Reinforcement per cure. (Several of my clients went around their homes reinforcing each of their cures every day! Not required, but not a bad ideal either. And though they received fabulous results with their Feng Shui, so did many of my other clients who performed a single Reinforcement for each cure following all the steps in this chapter.) The Reinforcement you perform with the cure empowers the cure energetically and is usually sufficient to hold the energy of the cure indefinitely.

If you want to apply the Three Secrets Reinforcement again for a cure (especially if a part of your life really needs a boost or you simply want the practice), feel free. An extra Reinforcement can't hurt. It may even improve your situation. (And if nothing else, it'll be good practice.) A general rule of thumb is to perform at least one supplemental Reinforcement for each cure you have in place every year or two.

The red envelope tradition

The red envelope tradition, which involves giving red envelopes containing money as gifts to friends and family on occasions such as weddings, birthdays, and the Chinese New Year, has long been practiced throughout Chinese history. It's a practice that stems from Chinese culture and folklore, and it symbolizes good luck, power, and protection from evil.

In Feng Shui, red envelopes that include a token or significant amount of money are respectfully offered to energetically protect the giver of Feng Shui cures. By giving a red envelope, you protect the consultant or teacher from harm for sharing his or her sacred (and traditionally exclusively oral) knowledge. You may use either Western stationary-style red envelopes or the Chinese version; both are equally effective. Just be sure that the envelopes are brand-new.

Note that the number of envelopes given is also important; a multiple of nine is traditional in Grandmaster Lin Yun's Feng Shui school because nine represents the highest and most powerful number of all. (Typically a minimum of one red envelope is given to the expert for each recommended cure.) If you're working with a Feng Shui consultant or teacher and aren't sure of the number of cures, or if you just want to show additional respect, you can give a multiple of nine envelopes (such as 18, 27, 36, and so on).

To perform the red envelope practice according to tradition, place money inside a new red envelope and then present the envelope to the person who provides you with Feng Shui analysis or cure information. (***Note:*** It's important that each envelope you're giving contain money. How you divide the money is less important than that each envelop contain some money.)

If you feel inclined to participate in the red envelope tradition in honor of what you pick up from this book — note that doing so is completely optional — you can send any sum of money in a new red envelope (again, a token amount or coin is fine) to your favorite charity.

Part II
Energizing Your Home's Exterior

The 5th Wave   By Rich Tennant

In this part . . .

Your outside environment (including your neighborhood, the property your home is on, and the environment your home is in) affects your life in a big way. That's why in Part II I show you secret ways to whip your lot into energetic shape without lifting a single shovel — unless you really dig diggin' in. I explain how to conduct beneficial new flows of natural energy into the front entry of your home. Meanwhile, you can paint your front door (and the neighbor's dog) Chinese red. (And you thought this was going to be all work and no play. Silly rabbit!)

Chapter 7

Harnessing Nature's Power to Enhance Your Outdoor Spaces

*W*hy focus on the outside of your home? Because with Feng Shui you can determine the quality of the energy (or *chi*) that affects you by observing the external environment. What you see as you come and go from one place to another affects you energetically and emotionally.

Imagine this: On your way to work, you experience the usual bump over the pothole in front of your driveway. You pass by the eyesore that is your neighbor's home, with its peeling paint and untended yard. Then, with a grumble, you pass the vacant lot at the end of the street that now serves as a local dumping ground for irresponsible citizens. Next, you're delayed in a traffic jam and late for an important meeting at work. By the end of the day, you only want to relax at home, but first you must face the rush hour traffic snarl again, pass the same neighborhood eyesores, and hit the same irritating pothole to get into your driveway. Sounds like a tough day, right? Experienced repeatedly over time, these conditions can provoke increasing irritability and energetic discomfort.

The same experience — specifically, continuous environmental influences on your psyche and life — happens on a more subtle level with smaller obstacles that you encounter daily as you move in and out of your personal environment (also known as your home). What's the point? Everything you see in your external environment, whether you notice it or not, affects you energetically. In this chapter, I show you how to read the energies of your surroundings and perform cures for the problem features found in the exterior of your home and property. Performing the cures in this chapter can increase the energy quotient of your property and smooth your path to increased success and happiness.

Note: A similar process occurs when you travel to and from your apartment or condominium. The exterior energy sets the tone for the building's chi, so pay close attention to it. Virtually all the information in this chapter applies to single-family residences as well as apartment and condominium living.

Looking around the Neighborhood

Your neighborhood is the context or local container of your personal environment — the space in which your home is contained. It plays a large role in determining the overall feel, mood, and energy of your home, as well as your personal energy when you're inside your home. The following sections help you get a sense of how the energy moves (or doesn't move) in your neighborhood and on your street.

Reading the chi of a neighborhood or place

Everyone (including you) can read energy. Sensing energy is a basic human ability; it doesn't require mystical training (although training and practice will improve your skill). You sense energy through your feelings, which tell you basic information about the energy of a place and whether that energy is positive or negative. Observing the following also helps you determine the nature of the energy surrounding you:

- ✔ **The local animals and wildlife:** Do you see healthy, bright animals and pets? For example, seeing a deer as you enter an area is a positive sign. A negative animal sign is a mangy, unleashed, roaming dog. As for a black cat crossing the road while smoking a cigarette and panhandling? That's definitely a bad Feng Shui sign.

- ✔ **The plants and vegetation:** Are they lush, vibrant, and healthy? Or are they sickly, brown, and dried up? Healthy plants are a sign of living, flourishing energy — the kind you want to surround yourself with. Dying plants symbolize a lack of abundant chi in the environment, which can make you wonder whether enough energy is present to support your life and success.

- ✔ **The people:** Seeing the inhabitants of a location can tell you a lot about the energy of a place. Are the people friendly, cheerful, and happy, or do they appear suspicious, dour, and unhappy? Generally, friendly people demonstrate a much higher quality of energy in the environment than unhappy and angry people.

✔ **The life patterns of the neighborhood:** Find out the general levels of harmony and happiness in your area. Notice how wealth is distributed and whether personal lawsuits are filed frequently. (You always wanted to play Sherlock Holmes, right?) Also, keep in mind the number of premature deaths, car accidents, divorces, and so on. These factors tell you a lot about the history of the neighborhood, as well as its current standing and how living in the area influences you energetically. The lives of families in surrounding homes are powerful factors and indicators of the kind of energy circulating in the neighborhood. A sign of upheaval in a neighborhood is that many homes in the area have recently been sold. Check the institutions in the area; the presence of a graveyard, funeral home, or hospital can symbolize negative energy. (I explain the effects of these institutions in the later "Investigating and Curing Potential Nearby Negatives" section.)

Noticing how street energy charges your home

Your residential street is one of the main exterior sources of energy for your property, home, and life. Streets are like arteries of a city that conduct the connecting energies of a society by funneling traffic and chi to and from the individual neighborhoods and homes. In American society, 90 percent of the population lives in metropolitan areas; consequently, the homes receive a good deal of their chi from the street.

Of course, the most important street is the one leading directly to your residence. The nature and power of the flow of energy (in this case, traffic) on your street is a prime indicator of whether your home is energetically well fed. Your street feeds the mouth of your driveway and front walk, your driveway and front walk feed your front door, and your front door feeds chi into the entryway and hallways of the body of your home.

Enjoying the ideal street situation

From the Feng Shui point of view, the ideal residential street situation is one that features brisk, lively, creative energy. The general feeling should be cheerful and uplifting. The overall energetic quality of the street leading to your home shouldn't be too active or too still; rather, it should be just right (call it the Goldilocks factor). Too little energy coming to your home from the street can mean an energy deficit, which is detrimental to your finances and even your physical health. On the other hand, excessive street energy (also known as *rushing chi*) tends to bring chaos and disruption into your life and result in negative consequences. Luckily, you can counteract any of these conditions with the Feng Shui cures in the next section.

Curing street problems

If you live at a T-intersection, on a cul-de-sac, on a sloping or one-way street, or on a dead-end road, you and your home may suffer negative effects. To transform negative energy into positive energy, perform one of the cures I describe in the next sections (and check out Figure 7-1).

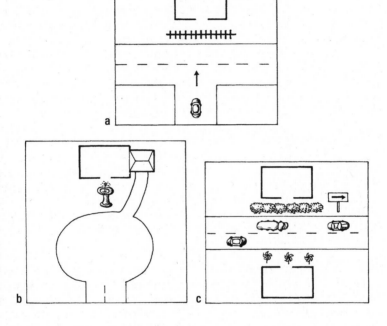

Figure 7-1:
Cures for T-intersections (a), cul-de-sacs (b), and one-way streets (c).

Escaping the dreaded T-intersection

If you live on a T-intersection where a street ends at your property (refer to Figure 7-1a) and the oncoming traffic heads directly toward your home, the energy bombarding your home is dangerous because it has rushing or attacking qualities. This onrushing energy can take the form of approaching vehicles, which occasionally run into this type of home!

The energy at T-intersections moves too fast and too forcefully for the well-being of the occupants. Over time, life in a T-intersection home can progressively deteriorate. The continuous effects of the street's chi crashing into the home can wreak havoc on the residents' lives, resulting in everything from subtle feelings of depression, paranoia, and being attacked to more serious psychological effects, and even accidents, sickness, or death. Also, the home can become harder to maintain.

You can cure the effects of rushing chi at a T-intersection by planting a tall hedge across the front line of the property to protect your home or building a fence in the same location (refer to Figure 7-1a). If you can't perform either cure, or if you need extra curing energy, hang a wind chime over the front door to the home to disperse the onrushing chi, place a Ba-Gua mirror over the front door for protection, or both. (I describe what a Ba-Gua mirror looks like later in this chapter.)

The same problems and solutions apply to a home located at a Y-intersection.

One of my clients moved into a new home, which happened to face a T-intersection. The unfortunate effects of the location were compounded by the fact that the road leading toward the home came down a steep incline, intensifying the onrushing traffic energy. The saving grace was a large tree that stood at the curb between the street and the front door. Usually, a tree directly in line with the front door is a no-no, but in this case, the tree was an excellent energetic and literal buffering agent for the attacking chi of the street. I prescribed a supplemental cure, and my client hung a metal wind chime in the tree, directly between the center of the road and her front door. The ringing sound of the chime helped diffuse the oncoming chi and provided safety and protection. Located in the Career Area of her property (the front-center section, as I explain in the later "Using Color to Empower the Life Areas of Your Property" section), the chime also activated the career energy of the household. Shortly after implementing this cure, my client's financial picture improved. She felt stronger and healthier, her husband's business took an upward turn, and they bought a new car that they'd wanted for some time.

Moving energy through a cul-de-sac

Cul-de-sac streets imply stagnation and a lack of energy. Because cul-de-sacs don't provide an outlet for traffic to flow through or past the home (as you can see in Figure 7-1b), much less energy flows to homes built on a cul-de-sac than to ones built on a typical street. Therefore, cul-de-sacs and their homes face dead or stuck energy and risk becoming low on vital chi. Life effects that come from living on a cul-de-sac include reduced physical vitality and difficulty receiving opportunities. Cul-de-sac residents can also find it difficult to move forward and make positive life changes.

Energetic cures for a cul-de-sac home counteract this stagnation by activating or awakening the chi. To wake up chi flow in a cul-de-sac, add motion, color, and activity (preferably in the front yard) to stimulate incoming chi and invite opportunities and money into your life.

A moving water cure with a strong upward spray is a great antidote to stagnation and lethargy. Placing a fountain on your property is a good way to encourage flow, activity, and abundance in your life. Fountain cures stimulate income and connections with new and old friends in addition to protecting the property. The best location for a fountain on a cul-de-sac home's property is near the mouth of the driveway (refer to Figure 7-1b). This position stimulates chi to enter the entire property. Alternate placements for the fountain include the center of the yard near the front of the home and near the front door.

Two additional ways to compensate for a cul-de-sac are to use color and motion to stimulate energy at the property entrance. A flagpole bearing a colorful flag or a bright windsock placed near the mouth of the driveway is a good solution for this situation.

One of my clients, the CEO of a technology company, moved into a new dream home. The home was great in most aspects, but it was located on a cul-de-sac. To keep his family and personal chi moving in this new location, the owner placed an energetic outdoor fountain near the front door of the home. I recommended that he orient the water flow toward the front door to invite cash flow into the home (instead of away from the door or away from the property, which would cause wealth to leave the family). Needless to say, he's doing booming business.

Slowing the energy of sloping and one-way streets

Living on a sloping or one-way street can create two energetic problems:

- ✔ Energy can pass through the street too rapidly to enter and nourish the property, thereby depriving the home's residents of desperately needed chi.

- ✔ The rapidly flowing chi can rob or strip away vital energy from your yard and life, causing your career, opportunities, and health to suffer.

Because the front of your lot (the part nearest the street) corresponds to the Life Areas of Helpful People, Career, and Knowledge (as I note in Chapter 3), rushing street energy can create unfortunate results in these areas. The solution is to slow down the street energy at your property and absorb some of its force for your own benefit. For an easy cure, you can plant bushes along the front property line (refer to Figure 7-1c to see this cure applied).

Another cure that works wonders for slowing the chi of a sloping or one-way street is a strong exterior fountain. You can place it in the Career Area of your property or near the mouth of your driveway to both counteract and utilize the rushing chi of the street. Yet another excellent solution involves using mobile cures, such as windsocks, pinwheels, or whirligigs. Apply these solutions along the front line of your property (at the street). The moving energy of these cures beneficially uses up the rushing chi of the street by simultaneously absorbing it for the property's benefit and preventing the street from pulling energy away from the lot.

The owners of an outerwear wholesale company once found themselves in a puzzling situation. They couldn't decide whether to move their business to another location and rent out their existing office and warehouse, sell the business, or just retire and head to Fiji. They preferred to rent out the building, but they couldn't find any takers. When I inspected the exterior of the property, I noticed their Feng Shui problem immediately: The building was located on a busy highway just outside of town, and the traffic on this highway consisted of huge, fast-moving trucks that zoomed by throughout the day. The diagnosis was clear — the rushing chi of the trucks was pulling energy away from the front of the building, damaging their Helpful People, Career, and Knowledge Areas. I suggested they hang colorful windsocks. They already had several tall light poles in front of the business, so hanging an odd number of large windsocks on the poles was easy. (According to Feng Shui beliefs, odd numbers of cure items, such as 1, 3, 5, and 7, can hold more curing power than even numbers, such as 2, 4, 6, and 8.) Not long after hanging the windsocks, the partners received a call from a company that had passed on renting their building months prior. They were interested in the property and wanted to move in immediately. Now the partners' path was clear, and they could move to a new location with relief. Chalk up another windsock victory!

Living on a dead-end street

A dead-end street receives even less inflow of energy than a cul-de-sac (I cover these earlier in this chapter). Hence the name dead-end, meaning the street is dead energetically, and you're at the end. Now I ask you, is this image the metaphor you want running your life?

The main problem with dead ends is that — by definition — no energy can flow through them. Because no traffic can pass, the energy is lower and less active, creating stagnation and dullness. The lives of residents living in homes on dead-end streets are often lower in energy, wealth, and opportunities. Getting to work in the morning and succeeding in life can be more difficult.

Awakening and enlivening the energy of the lot is vital to transforming the energy of a dead-end home. You can start by cutting back all overgrown bushes and vegetation. Make sure all outdoor lights are working. Keep your yard and street clean of debris and old belongings, including any junk cars, spare bulldozers, and dismantled 747s.

To attract and create a new flow of positive energy, do your best to enliven, energize, and awaken your property with sound, movement, color, and life. Here are some tips:

✔ Use energy activators such as windmills and windsocks, which feature motion and color.

> ✔ Hang wind chimes to activate and awaken the area to create more energy and movement in your environment and life.
>
> ✔ Install bird feeders to attract the lively energy of fine-feathered, musical friends. In Feng Shui, lovebirds and songbirds bring opportunities and messages that create new activity, movement, and harmony in your life.

Investigating and Curing Potential Nearby Negatives

Another way to determine the energy level of your environment is to pay attention to certain institutions that, if located near your home, can have negative effects on you and your family. Among other things, they include cemeteries, hospitals, police and fire stations, and schools.

The presence of these institutions, which I refer to as *nearby negatives,* can make it harder to maintain your health, career, marriage, and family. I offer more insight on nearby negatives, as well as cures to combat their negative energetic effects, in the sections that follow.

A negative element located across the street, next door, or directly behind your home is the most detrimental situation. One located on the same block can affect you with nearly as strong an impact. The next level out is a building that's visible from your home or yard on a regular basis. When in doubt (which is always a feeling you should listen to and address), perform a cure to feel safer and more protected.

Understanding types of nearby negatives

All the institutions I mention in the following sections are important and have a rightful place in society. They aren't bad or evil; they simply aren't necessarily temples of cheer, elation, celebration, and affirmation of life. Feng Shui teaches that these institutions can have unwanted effects on residents living near them. A prudent student of Feng Shui realizes that events and buildings near his or her home must inevitably influence his or her home, for better or worse.

Cemeteries and funeral homes

Cemeteries are places where dead people are buried. Lots of them. Feng Shui says that disembodied spirits can wander in graveyards and sometimes haunt nearby homes and their residents. If the spirits are unhappy, mischievous, or even malicious, they can cause no end of trouble for your home's occupants. Health problems, as well as mental anguish, can plague those living near cemeteries.

Even if no ghosts or spirits are haunting the home, living close to a cemetery can cause depression. The very *yin* (depressing and low) energy of a cemetery continuously affects the subconscious mind and exerts a cumulative effect. Funeral homes and mortuaries give off similar vibrations because they feature the energies of death, grieving, and sorrow.

Hospitals and convalescent centers

Hospitals, though important institutions, can negatively affect the health of the people living nearby due to the continuous stream of sickness, death, emergency, suffering, and grief that passes through them and resides within them. Similarly, convalescent centers can feature the energy of sickness, depression, and loneliness.

Police and fire stations

Police stations and fire stations can seem advantageous, and some people find living next to them exciting. Yet police and fire stations can stimulate the energies of emergency, alarm, and fear. Police stations especially can radiate the negative vibes of criminals, crime, and suspiciousness. (Fire stations, on the other hand, mainly feature the energy of alarm.) Although you may feel more secure — on the surface — living near these places, their energy never rests. As a result, you may find resting and relaxing difficult in your home, and you may always feel on edge waiting for the next emergency alarm to go off.

Schools and churches

A school can influence your home positively or negatively. The influence depends on the type of energy found at the particular school and whether you like the generally excited, happy, and hyper energy of children.

A church carries negative energy similar to that of a funeral home only if it holds funerals, memorials, or wakes on-site. If it doesn't hold these services on its premises, living near one generally isn't a negative influence. And if a church features numerous weddings, it can positively influence your home in a big way.

Performing cures for nearby negatives

Feng Shui offers cures for alleviating the unfortunate effects of nearby negatives. Thanks to Feng Shui, you can still live near one of these institutions and enjoy happiness, peace, and prosperity.

If you live by a nearby negative, you may choose to perform a cure for the protection of your home and family, particularly if you've experienced a run of bad luck since moving into your home. Remember that whatever's happening to your lot and home (whether known or unknown) has a simultaneous and corresponding effect on you and your family. These results occur in the physical, mental, emotional, and spiritual realms — not to mention your health, wealth, and relationships. You can reap great benefits by observing these things and taking action where needed to alter and improve your environment and your life.

A good all-around protection and blessing cure to counteract nearby negatives is to place a Ba-Gua mirror on the outside of the home, above the front door and facing outward. A *Ba-Gua mirror* is octagon shaped, framed in wood, and measures about 4 to 6 inches across. The Ba-Gua trigrams are marked around the outside with a round mirror in the center (see Figure 7-2). The Ba-Gua mirror is an easy and inexpensive protection method; an even stronger variation of this mirror uses a convex mirror (which curves outward) rather than a flat one. You can find a source for good Ba-Gua mirrors in the appendix.

Figure 7-2:
A Ba-Gua
mirror.

Another cure option for nearby negatives is to hang a set of five symbolic red firecrackers above the front door on the inside of the home. The firecrackers ward off negative people, energy, and events. I recommend the Yun Lin Temple as the source for this symbolic cure tool.

One of the most powerful Feng Shui cures for cleansing energy and protecting your home and family is the Rice Blessing (also called the Exterior Chi Adjustment). This blessing is designed to remove negative chi, reverse bad luck, and generally create a new start in life. I detail this blessing ceremony in Chapter 21.

Eliminating Home and Lot Problems

Nearby negatives (see the previous related sections) aren't the only factors that can affect your home and property. The following sections detail additional important home and property conditions you should be aware of. Check these situations to see whether they apply to your life.

Too close for comfort

If your home is positioned too close to another building, especially a taller one, you may experience feelings of oppression and victimization. I recommend curing this situation by hanging a Ba-Gua mirror on the wall of your home nearest the larger building or on the side of the roof closest to the other structure (see Figure 7-3). Regardless of where you place it, the mirror should face the opposing building. Hanging the mirror can relieve feelings of oppression and pressure and provide newfound freedom and ease. With this cure, as with all the cures you do, be sure to apply the Three Secrets Reinforcement and powerfully visualize your desired results (I cover reinforcement and visualization methods in Chapter 6).

An even stronger Ba-Gua mirror for this situation is one that features a concave (inward-curving) mirror in the center.

Figure 7-3:
Oppressed home with Ba-Gua mirror cure on roof.

Whole lotta shakin' goin' on

A major disturbing element close to the home structure itself, such as a main thoroughfare street or freeway, creates turbulence and chaotic energy. The continuous motion of cars and people passing by creates subtle (or profound) shakes, rattles, and rolls, which translate into aggravation and unease. The rushing sounds and intense energy tend to upset the sleep, moods, and psychological balance of the residents. If the disturbing element is a train track, subway, or freeway overpass, the problem can be greatly intensified depending on the volume of the traffic. Life consequences range from lack of rest and health issues to clashing arguments, unnecessary accidents, and frequent absences from the home.

You can counteract this situation by creating a visual block. Try planting a tree (or trees) or tall shrubs that can hide the negative element and provide energetic protection for the home. If the problem is a nearby train or street, a good cure is to place multiple pinwheels or windmills near the offending element (as shown in Figure 7-4), which disperse the chaotic chi and create a peaceful antidote to the noise and confusion. You can also cure this situation by attaching colorful flags to one or more flagpoles (the taller the better) near the disturbing element.

Figure 7-4:
Train near home with windmill cures.

Problematic neighbors

If your neighbors are loud, antagonistic, dangerous, or otherwise bothersome, Feng Shui offers some simple solutions to help you protect yourself.

✔ Consider planting a row of hedges between your home and your neighbor's home. This cure buffers the problem neighbor's energy and even helps bring peace into the situation.

✔ Hang a melodious, soft-sounding wind chime at the property line between your home and your neighbor's. The sound of the chime helps disperse conflicting and aggressive feelings, replacing them with a melody of harmony and balance. If that doesn't work, sign the entire family up for karate lessons!

If a situation is particularly intense and calls for strong help, well-placed mirrors can be effective. A mirror positioned on a fence or on the side of your home and facing toward your home can create an energetic boundary of protection and safety for you and your family. (Remember that the back side of the mirror should be toward your neighbor.) The larger the mirror, the better the cure. If even more oomph is needed, you can use a Ba-Gua mirror and place it so it's facing toward the neighbor's home; I introduce you to Ba-Gua mirrors in the earlier "Performing cures for nearby negatives" section.

As usual with Feng Shui, be sure to employ a mirror cure in a spirit of compassion and desire for mutual harmony, never with the intention of malice or returning negative energy to the other party. The mirror's purpose is to create safety and ease for your household, not to do something to or against your neighbor.

Sitting Pretty: Ideal and Not-So-Ideal Home Positioning

An ideally positioned home (like the one in Figure 7-5) is set up for good fortune thanks to its balanced and protected location. The idealized home position sits on a regularly shaped, symmetrical lot and has all of the following characteristics:

✔ It's located in the center third of the lot (from front to back) and the middle of the lot (from left to right).

✔ It's even with the road or above the road.

✔ There's flat land or upward-sloping land behind the home.

Figure 7-5:
Ideal home
position in
center of lot,
with
protective
hill behind.

The three thirds of the lot from front to back energetically represent the following:

- ✔ **The front third symbolizes planting or beginning.** This area is where opportunities and energy begin, germinate, and sprout.

- ✔ **The middle third represents growing.** This is where situations develop, progress, and begin to mature.

- ✔ **The rear third of the lot symbolizes harvest, cultivation, and completion.** Wealth is symbolically and energetically stored in this general area of the property.

The sections that follow delve further into home positioning and how to cure problems caused by less-than-ideal positioning.

Diagnosing and treating problems with your home's location on the lot

The following deviations from the ideal lot site can create obstacles and life problems:

✔ **If your home is in the front third of the lot, it may sit too close to the street and be vulnerable.** Plant a large tree or place lights in the back and sides of the yard to balance the lot's energy, as shown in Figure 7-6.

✔ **If your home is located in the back third of the lot, it sits too far from the street and, therefore, lacks incoming energy.** In addition, the area behind the home is symbolically where the money of the family is stored. A home in this position doesn't have a large space between it and the rear property line; this small or nonexistent area for wealth can negatively influence the finances of the household. One balancing cure you can try is placing a tree or light in the front of the property. (The same cure can apply if the home is too close to either side of the lot. Simply place a light on the side opposite the home, pointed at the roof.)

Figure 7-6:
Home too
close to
front of lot,
with light
cures.

Positioning your home topographically

A key factor affecting the position of a home is the contour of the land on which the home sits. The first general principle is that a home shouldn't be placed too high or too low.

✔ If your home is positioned on the pinnacle of a hill with steep sides, your family may experience danger or isolation. In this position (the top), the only way to go is down, and the home's residents may find plenty of volunteers to push them off their perch.

✔ If your home is in a very low area, such as the bottom of a valley or the base of a very high, steep hill, you can experience negative energetic effects, including depression, lack of energy, and failure to vigorously pursue your goals. Dismal spirits tend to gravitate to such places and can make prospering difficult.

The second general principle highlights the importance of the home's backing. The backing or shield behind the home represents support and protection for the home's occupants. The ideal backing includes a hill behind the home, which keeps invaders from approaching you unawares. Land that slopes upward behind the home can also help hold wealth for the occupants. The space between the home and the hill is the wealth pocket, where money energy can pool and remain.

Table 7-1 rates four common home positions.

Table 7-1	Influence of Home Position on Occupants
Home Position	*Life Influence*
On a flat piece of land	Neutral
On a gently rising slope	Good, offers protection
On a flat area with rising land or a hill behind	Very good, increases protection and wealth
Land slopes away behind the home	Poor, decreases wealth and energy

Living high up or down low from the road

The general Feng Shui rule states that a home is better positioned above the road than below it because this location helps provide the all-important Commanding Position for the home. (Head to Chapter 2 for the nitty-gritty on the Commanding Position principle.)

The best cure for land that slopes down behind a home is a bright light mounted on a tall pole or tree behind the home (the higher the better; as high as the roof is best). The light should shine at the roof of the home (see Figure 7-7a). The energy of this cure keeps precious chi from rolling away down the hill, uplifts the chi in the back of the property, and energetically fills in the missing land. The result is better wealth and health for the home's occupants.

If you live in a home that's located below the road, you may find your career and other aspects of life blocked by various obstacles. Rising each day to go to work may require extra effort. Also, you may subconsciously feel below the action — sensing that others are carrying on at a higher level than you — making your life unnecessarily difficult.

The cure for home-below-the-road syndrome is to place a bright light behind the home, shining up toward the roof (see Figure 7-7b). You can also uplift the home by placing a flagpole, antenna, or weathervane on the roof to raise the height of the home above the road. Or you can install bright, upward-shining lights on top of the home to uplift the energy of the home and improve your overall situation. (*Note:* This cure is especially powerful if you put an upward-shining light on each corner of the roof. The lights don't need to be on at all times, but they must be in good working condition to be effective.)

In addition, you can also energize the driveway to symbolically reach the street easier. Line the sides of the drive with lights, colorful flags, or windsocks. The energy of light and motion make it easier for you to get up to the street, an important factor for career success.

a

Figure 7-7:
Land sloping away from home with cure (a) and home below road with cure (b).

b

Diffusing projecting roof ridges

A neighbor's roof ridge pointing toward the front of your home, and in particular toward your front door, can project piercing energy — a situation that can bode ill for your future. Note that by *roof ridges* I mean any protruding corners or peaks of the roof. The most concerning roof ridge from a Feng Shui standpoint is an apex corner of a roof pointed at your home, but be on the lookout for other types as well.

One practical solution for roof ridges is to hang a wind chime between your front door and the neighbor's roof ridge. Use a red ribbon or cord cut to a multiple of 9 inches in length to hang the chime and make sure the chime is made of metal and has a pleasant, ringing sound. The power of sound helps disperse the invisible but harmful poison arrows of energy (I tell you all about poison arrows and how to cure them in the next section).

For particularly threatening circumstances, center a Ba-Gua mirror featuring a convex (rather than flat) central mirror above your front door on the outside of your home (or on the side facing the offending element), as shown in Figure 7-8. The mirror protects you not only from the roof ridge but also from other negative persons, events, and threats. It allows only positive and helpful energies to enter your home. (See the earlier "Performing cures for nearby negatives" section for more information on this powerful Feng Shui cure tool.)

Figure 7-8: Neighbor's projecting roof ridge with Ba-Gua mirror cure over door.

Curing poison arrows

A *poison arrow,* also known as a *secret arrow, piercing arrow,* or *heart-piercing chi,* is generated by sharp points or edges directed at your home, particularly at key spots such as the front door, bed, or stove. The points can be generated by elements such as roof ridges; the corners of homes or other buildings; large nearby rocks; satellite dishes, protruding wall corners; and other sharp, pointed features. Regardless of what's generating a poison arrow, it should be remedied as soon as possible.

Diagnosing poison arrows is a matter of judgment and experience, but in general, the larger, pointed roof ridges of nearby homes or other structures aimed at your home are particularly potent. Not surprisingly, the energy of poison arrows is penetrating and, according to Feng Shui, can have negative life consequences, such as accidents or unexpected misfortunes. The cure includes removing the offending item, if possible, or blocking the arrow point. You can plant a tree in front of a neighbor's projecting corner, place a potted plant inside the home covering an interior offending arrow point, or hang a decorative curtain in front of an interior protruding corner.

One key cure for an exterior poison arrow is to place a Ba-Gua mirror above your front door to deflect the poison arrow (and any other forms of bad luck elements) away from the area. Some Feng Shui enthusiasts place a Ba-Gua mirror over the front door even if they don't see any poison arrows, just on the off chance that they may have missed some.

Another cure for exterior poison arrows is to hang a wind chime in line with an offending arrow to deflect and disperse its negative energy. Or you can mount a weathervane in the path of the area with the vane pointed toward the poison arrow; one arrow energetically neutralizes the other. You can also employ a *gazing ball* (a mirrored sphere about 12 to 14 inches in diameter), which also reflects the negative force away. Search the Internet for gazing ball sources.

Check the bed and the stove to ensure they aren't threatened by interior poison arrows. Start by lying on the bed and taking a look around. Notice any sharp corners that point toward the bed, like the corner of a wall, sculptures, or the edges of large furniture; any of these objects may create poison arrows that negatively influence the sleeper. The best solution is to remove or rearrange the offending item so the corner no longer points toward the bed. For items you can't move, such as a wall, you can use either the curtain or wind chime solution mentioned earlier.

Enlivening Your Lot with Healthy Trees and Plants

Healthy vegetation is important because it provides green color, oxygen, and vitality to both outdoor and indoor environments. The color green exerts a positive influence on the psyche, creating hope, growth, and new life. Adding healthy plants— especially bamboo— and trees to your home and yard is one of the easiest ways to increase the living energy you enjoy daily. This cure can positively affect your health, moods, and actions. I reveal how to get the most positive benefit out of bamboo and trees in the next sections.

Trees in particular provide beauty and privacy. They can also serve as effective traffic screens, privacy shields, and air-pollution cleaners. However, you don't want to completely screen the front of your home from the street (except in situations such as the T-intersection covered earlier in this chapter). Doing so can block vital energy from coming to you and can cause stagnation and frustration.

On the other hand, you don't want a barren yard because this symbolizes a lack of growth, attention, and stability. A California client applied some Feng Shui cures on her own to her home and noticed significant life improvements. However, her husband had been locked into a dismal night shift at his job for several years. When she came to me for advice, I pointed out that she had removed all the flowers in the Career Area of her front yard, leaving it barren. She quickly replenished the space with healthy, flowering plants. Not long after this, her husband was offered a new work shift, which allowed them to spend more time together.

Introducing bamboo, the all-purpose plant

Bamboo is such an important and versatile plant (it's really an all-purpose Feng Shui cure item) that it deserves its own section. In Chinese culture, bamboo symbolizes strength, peace, adaptability, and safety; in fact, the Chinese believe the music from a bamboo flute can bring peace to a society. Bamboo symbolizes the marriage of yin and yang energies with its strong, hard exterior (yang) and its hollow interior and pliable nature (yin.) Another way bamboo represents positive influences is that it has great strength (enough to sustain heights of more than 100 feet), yet it's flexible enough to dance in beautiful harmony with the strongest winds. Bamboo also has the power to raise and uplift chi, which is why it's often used to ward off unwanted energies and negate the effects of negative chi.

You can use bamboo in a variety of settings to uplift and harmonize parts of your home or life.

- ✔ Bamboo can create safety around the perimeter of any property, generating a living barrier between you and the outside world. It's also a beautifying outdoor element.

- ✔ Inside the home, bamboo adds life and sophistication to any room and can be a cure for added life energy and protection for any Life Area of your home's Octagon. For example, if you need a boost in your family life, a simple and easy fix is to put a potted bamboo plant in the Family Area of your home, or in a common area such as the living room or family room.

One factor to keep in mind when selecting among the hundreds of bamboo varieties is that you can purchase either "running" *(pachymorph)* or "clumping" *(leptomorph)* species of bamboo. Your local horticulturists and nursery experts can guide you in your selection, but you should know the following:

✔ The running type of bamboo can rapidly expand its growth area on its own and spread across your yard unbidden, so unless you want lots (and I mean *lots*) of bamboo, you need to contain it with a hard plastic bamboo barrier.

✔ The clumping type of bamboo stays confined to a small area, so a containment barrier is unnecessary.

Utilizing positive tree energies

Table 7-2 lists the Feng Shui effects of some specifically beneficial trees. Plant these trees to enhance their special qualities in your life.

Table 7-2	Trees and Their Energetic Effects
Tree Types	*Positive Effects*
Apple	Safety
Banana palm	Scholarly ambitions
Olive	Peace
Orange	Good luck
Peach, plum	Compassion
Pear	Sweetness
Persimmon	Joy, luck in business, good start for new endeavor
Pine	Resilience, integrity, dignity, longevity
Pomegranate	Fecundity, fertility
Willow (only good in front)	Gracefulness, scholarly atmosphere

Employing helpful tree-selecting hints

When selecting trees, keep these hints in mind:

- ✔ Trees with umbrella-shaped canopies are a positive influence. They provide you with a symbolic covering of protection and safety.

- ✔ Evergreen trees are better than deciduous trees, whose leaves fall in autumn and stay bare all winter. (Of course, deciduous trees are better than no trees at all!)

- ✔ Upward-reaching trees are better than downward-reaching ones, such as weeping willows.

- ✔ Trees featuring flowers and fruits are more beneficial than those bearing no fruits or flowers.

Avoiding negative tree situations

Trees uplift the energy of the Earth, bringing vitality and life to a space. They also provide symbolic and energetic protection against evil energy or bad influences (both physical and nonmaterial) in the neighborhood. Planted in the wrong place, however, trees can have unintended negative effects. For best results, follow these tree rules:

- ✔ **Avoid mulberry trees in the front yard.** The Chinese believe planting a mulberry tree in this location may cause a death in the home. Also, because mulberry leaves are fed to hungry silkworms, your property and career can be chewed up.

- ✔ **Steer clear of weeping willow trees in the backyard.** This tree symbolizes weeping, parting, slipping away, and downward-flowing energy. As a result, occupants of the home may leave, lose money, or worse. (I leave it to your imagination.)

- ✔ **Avoid planting trees and bushes (including rosebushes and cacti) that contain thorns near a main entrance or on the pathway to your front door.** If you don't, you may engender needless conflicts and aggravation.

- ✔ **Try not to plant trees directly in front of the front door.** A tree in this location blocks the door, which can energetically harm every part of your life. (See the great remedy for this pesky problem in Chapter 9.)

- ✔ **Tend to barren or stripped trees by either healing or removing them.** The subconscious influences of these decaying trees on your psyche can result in sickness or general failing health.

Curing dead or dying trees

A dead tree near the front of the home symbolizes death or decay for the household, so replace any dead trees with new, healthy ones. If a dead tree is impractical to uproot, wrap a green artificial vine around the tree trunk, starting at the ground and circling upward to at least as high as the tallest member of the household. A good additional step is to plant a healthy new tree or bush nearby.

If a tree is alive but dying, perform this cure to offset the negative energy:

1. **Mix a bowl of rice with 99 drops of high-proof liquor and one packet (about ¼ teaspoon) of cinnabar powder.**

   Be sure to follow the cinnabar recommendations in Chapter 21.

2. **As you mix these ingredients together, repeat a prayer or mantra of your choice nine times.**

3. **Sprinkle the mixture on the ground around the entire tree.**

4. **Sprinkle the mixture from the tree all the way up to your front door.**

5. **Perform the Three Secrets Reinforcement and visualize new health and life for all in your household.**

   I tell you all about the Three Secrets Reinforcement in Chapter 6.

Using Color to Empower the Life Areas of Your Property

An effective and enjoyable way of empowering exterior areas of your property is to use color in the landscaping of your yard. As a first step, apply the Octagon mapping method to your property (flip to Chapter 3 for details on the Octagon.) Then apply plants or shrubs featuring the appropriate colors for the Octagon Life Areas that you want to empower. Table 7-3 tells you which colors to use to empower each Life Area; to determine the part of the lot in question, orient from the front of the lot.

Table 7-3	Using Color in the Yard to Empower Life Areas		
Part of Lot	*Octagon Life Area*	*Color Options*	*Improves, Aids, or Empowers Your . . .*
Right front	Helpful People	White, gray, black	Benefactors, travel helpers, networking
Front center	Career	Black, dark blue	Connections, career
Front left	Knowledge	Black, blue, green	Learning, spiritual and personal growth

(continued)

Table 7-3 (continued)

Part of Lot	Octagon Life Area	Color Options	Improves, Aids, or Empowers Your . . .
Center left	Family	Green, blue, blue-green	Immediate family relations, community
Back left	Wealth	Green, blue, purple, red	Money, prosperity, abundance
Back center	Fame	Red	Reputation, vision for the future
Back right	Marriage	Pink, red, white	Marriage, key partner in home or business
Right center	Children	White	Children, creative projects
Center	Health	Yellow, orange, earth tones	Physical, mental, and emotional health; all parts of life

Engaging the Power of Water

In Feng Shui, water has two separate aspects: dynamic (moving) and still. Each aspect holds a different energy, activity, and meaning, as you discover in the following sections.

Moving water brings flow

Flowing water represents flowing money, so water cures are excellent for improving your cash flow and financial circumstances. Moving water also represents social connections. Therefore, adding flowing water to your environment can improve the amount and quality of your personal friendships as well as business contacts and networking connections. Streams, rivers, fountains, and waterfalls all create dynamic water. I help you figure out where and where not to place moving water on your property in the sections that follow.

Choosing good spots for moving water

Fountains and waterfalls help humidify the air and create beneficial psychological effects. They release negative ions and add soothing white noise to a space. They also make excellent additions to your landscape and can be beneficial in the following locations:

- **Near the entrance of the driveway:** Moving water here can stimulate a greater inflow of wealth and energy.

- **Near the front entrance of the home:** This position is one of the all-time best for moving water cures, creating a host of life benefits.

You can also choose a spot based on the Octagon as it applies to your property.

- **The Career Area (front-center sector of the lot):** Boosts your chances of success in your career because the natural location for Water is in the Career Area of the Octagon, as I explain in Chapter 5.

- **The Knowledge Area (front-left sector):** Helps create fresh, clear thoughts.

- **The Family Area (center-left sector):** Increases family harmony and flow.

- **The Wealth Area (back-left sector):** Attracts additional money.

- **The Children Area (center-right sector):** Stimulates increased creativity.

- **The Helpful People Area (front-right sector):** Invites more folks to your aid — you can never have too many beneficial friends and helpers!

 One of my consultations involved the owners of an office furniture firm whose business was experiencing a slow period. They applied the power of flowing water to their business and received amazing results. Their cure was to place a large fountain outside the main door of the business. Shortly thereafter, the pace of the business quickened. New sales increased so rapidly that they soon had to hire new staff to handle the incoming business.

Avoiding bad spots for moving water

According to the Octagon as it applies to your property, two spots to avoid placing moving water in are

- **The Fame Area (back-center sector of the lot):** Water features, whether still or moving, in this Life Area can cause damage to one's reputation and name.

- **The Marriage Area (back-right sector):** Fountains in this Area can cause excess emotion in the primary partner relationship. If you have a water feature in this Area, you can apply a cure by placing healthy potted plants near the water feature.

The soothing and clarifying effects of still water

Still water has dual connotations: One is increased wisdom and knowledge; the other is stored or contained wealth. Still water brings peace and serenity, and if clear, depth and clarity of mind. Still water is found in ponds, lakes, and both natural and artificial pools (including swimming pools).

Still water features should be kept as clear and clean as possible. Stagnant, cloudy, or debris-filled water creates negative energy in any Octagon Area (as well as the corresponding Life Area) of the property, which promotes confusion, unnecessary life entanglements, and shady dealings with money. If your property contains muddy water, get it cleaned up as soon as possible.

Still water features are beneficial in any Life Area of the property, except for the Fame and Marriage Areas of the Octagon. Precautions are the same as for moving water features in either Area (see the preceding section).

Positioning Outbuildings

The location of outbuildings is another important part of your exterior Feng Shui. An *outbuilding* is any structure on the property that isn't attached to the home, such as a tool, garden, or storage shed; a green house; a guesthouse; or a detached garage. Outbuildings represent added weight, significance, and value on the property. They also reflect additional growth and expansion on the property and in their corresponding Life Areas. (For details on which parts of your property influence which aspects of your life, turn to Chapter 3; for a quick reference, see the earlier "Using Color to Empower the Life Areas of Your Property" section.)

A storage shed in the Wealth Area of your property symbolizes increased money in your future. Another positive outbuilding location is a detached garage in the Children Area (as long as the garage is near the edge of the property and not right next to the home). This outbuilding can mean that another curtain-climber (also known as a child) may join the household.

My clients erected a children's playhouse on the Family Area of the property and then placed a tool shed on the Children's Area part of the lot. They soon found themselves in the somewhat unusual (and enjoyable) position of owning a second home 30 minutes from their main residence. This home is closer to the beach, and they enjoy meeting their relatives (the Family Area influence) and playing with their kids (the Children Area influence) at the new home. Of course, your mileage may vary.

One more idea: An open gazebo can be an excellent positive addition to your property — just be sure that you site it away from your home. If it's too close to your home, it may unduly "crowd" the structure and energetically encroach on its space, causing negative life effects. I recommend using a gazebo that's open on all sides (as opposed to a closed one). An octagonal gazebo is particularly potent, especially when placed in the back of the property, behind the home. The Wealth Area is an excellent location for this beneficial structure (see Figure 7-9). Enliven this cure even more by hanging a musical, clear-sounding wind chime in the gazebo's center.

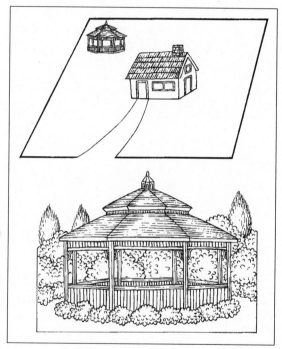

Figure 7-9:
Octagonal gazebo in Wealth corner of lot.

The following sections present specific outbuilding situations that can create negative results, as well as helpful cures for each one.

Who's that sneaking 'round my back door?

An outbuilding can be negative if located in the Marriage Area of the yard (the back-right sector). This building placement indicates that one spouse (or both) can start a separate relationship or even a separate household on the side. A cure for avoiding this unhappy event is to mount a spotlight on the outbuilding. Make sure it shines at the main house, ideally at the roof, to energetically connect the two buildings. The light doesn't need to shine at all times, but it should be in good working condition. Installing this light can transform the negative situation into a positive image of energetically-connected-yet-independent structures, and the marriage can prosper and flourish.

Stuffed shed syndrome

Buildings on your lot that are run down or in disrepair (or lovingly stuffed to the gills with your all-important junk) can quickly become a negative force on your lot. Simply keep your outbuildings shipshape, tidy, and shiny to avoid any negativity.

Honey, I shrunk the view

When a building blocks your view of the street or a good portion of the view from a bedroom, living room, or kitchen window, moving it to a better spot on the property can free up your vision of the future. If moving the building is impractical, you can hang a wind chime between the building and the window to disperse the building's blocking influence.

What's so draining?

Drains on the property are an important aspect; improperly located, they can be, well, draining. Drains can pull down energy and water, both of which symbolize money, and cause it to vanish to who knows where. Therefore, a visible drain can represent loss of wealth. If your lot contains a visible exterior drain, you can place a lively new potted plant on top of the drain.

If the drain is close to (or in a straight line with) your home's front door, the problem is even worse. An advanced solution for an auspiciously located exterior drain is to apply the special cinnabar and liquor cure given in the earlier "Curing dead or dying trees" section.

Chapter 8

Making the Most of Your Lot and Home Shape

"We shape our buildings; thereafter, they shape us."

— Winston Churchill

Throughout the ages, people have been fascinated with the creation and meaning of geometric shapes. Feng Shui looks at these aspects of different shapes as well as the influence they exert upon people. In fact, shape is one of the most influential factors in Feng Shui. The shapes of your personal environments — including the outlines of your home and lot (top-down view), the elevation of your home (side views), and the contours of the land — affect you both energetically and physically.

Whether positive or negative, the shapes of your home and lot determine how the energies flow within your personal living environment. They also strongly influence your immediate experience and your long-term destiny. Having a perfectly shaped home and an irregularly shaped lot (or vice versa) can enhance certain aspects of your life and hinder others. (Frodo the Hobbit lived in an irregularly shaped home and lot, which he never fixed with Feng Shui, and look what happened to him!) The skill of Feng Shui is to discern which areas may be holding you back energetically so you can adjust them.

This chapter examines the nature and effects of various shapes to assess their impact on your career, relationships, prosperity, and other key parts of your life. Read on to find out how to distinguish positive and negative shapes and create effective cures for your particular situation.

Discovering What Shapes Mean to You

Some of the most important Feng Shui factors in your environment are the shapes of your lot and your home. These shapes help determine the boundaries of your space and influence several Feng Shui characteristics, including placement and orientation. Room shapes and sizes also affect your *chi* (life-force energy) and the energy flows in your home.

The overall shapes of your lot and home influence a variety of factors related to quality of life, such as health and well-being, good or bad fortune, and so on. The shapes you inhabit mold your actions, feelings, and daily life path. They determine energy flow and represent important symbology that affects your personal energies.

According to the Theory of Relative Positioning (see Chapter 2), defects in the shape of your home affect you more than defects in the shape of your lot.

If you're an apartment dweller, then according to the Theory of Relative Positioning, the shape of your individual apartment is more important than the shape of the apartment building and of the lot on which it stands. (However, these factors still influence the lives of the tenants in the building.) Also, you can energetically alter the shape of your apartment with Feng Shui, which is something you can't do with an entire apartment building and its lot — unless of course you own them. Flip to Chapter 16 for details on applying Feng Shui to your apartment.

Enjoying Balance: The Positive Effects of Symmetrical Shapes

In Feng Shui terms, symmetrical shapes are the most favorable for homes and lots. Symmetrical shapes include squares, rectangles, circles, and octagons. These shapes, which I delve into in the following sections, all promote even, balanced, harmonious living. Because everything in your environment corresponds to your body and mind, the positive qualities of these shapes have similar effects on you — although if you live on a triangular lot, you won't end up looking like a pyramid. Circular and octagonal homes and lots are rare (they're difficult to find and build); square or rectangular lots and home shapes are generally more available and more favorable.

Admittedly, many uneven or asymmetrical shapes can be interesting to look at, visit, and design. An asymmetrical shape is initially more arresting to the eye than a regular, balanced shape. Unfortunately, the problems with unbalanced shapes come not from looking at them but from living in them. Over time, the imbalance of the shape tends to produce an imbalance in the physical and mental well-being and life circumstances of the residents.

In terms of shape, the Feng Shui truth is that interesting or unusual isn't necessarily better; in fact, it's often worse. An ancient Chinese curse that says "may you live in interesting times" can be paraphrased in Feng Shui as "may you dwell in interesting shapes." Unbalanced and irregular shapes can result in unbalanced and problematic lives.

Living foursquare: Squares and rectangles

A square represents a solid, even, stable existence. A rectangle shares the same basic energy, but if a rectangle is much longer in one direction, the main entry to the home or lot is best located on one of the short sides of the rectangle. If the entry sits on one of the long sides, the energy can quickly exit the structure without nourishing it, leading to a loss of good fortune for the residents. (***Note:*** The main entry of the lot is the mouth of the driveway; the main entry of the home is the front door.)

Before you celebrate the wonderful fortune of having a square or rectangular home or lot, make sure your lot or home is a true square or rectangle and not an impostor. A true square or rectangle has only four flat, even sides and four 90-degree corners, with no indentations, protrusions, or slants.

If your home or lot isn't a perfect square or rectangle, the irregularities can be either helping or hindering you. Read on in this chapter to determine whether your shape features projections (which are generally favorable) or missing areas (these aren't so good) and trust that Feng Shui always provides a cure for enhancing the positive and countering the negative.

Round and round: Circles and octagons

Round shapes denote unity, wholeness, and balance. A circle has a pleasing symmetry that's good for life in general. Octagonal shapes are powerful, strong, and lucky, and they have a special association with the Feng Shui Octagon that I describe in Chapter 3. Round and octagonal homes reflect the positive aspect of having a strong, whole shape, but often their interiors have many irregularly shaped rooms.

Defining Projections and Missing Areas

When you place the Feng Shui Octagon (described in Chapter 3) on any symmetrical shape, all the Life Areas of the Octagon are somewhat evenly represented, indicating balance and harmony. However, if one or more sides of your home or lot shape aren't completely even (say your shape isn't four completely flat sides with four 90-degree angles in the corners), you may have either a projection or a missing area in one or more corresponding Life Areas. (I address elements inside the home that can affect the Life Areas in Part III.)

Hey, are you projecting?

Projections expand the space in the home or lot and allow more chi to circulate, resulting in better fortune in the corresponding part of your life. For example, a projection in the Wealth Area of your home can positively influence your financial situation.

Oops! My areas are missing!

A *missing area* means proportionally less space for the all-important chi to circulate or reside in any particular part of your home or lot shape. This situation bodes ill for the corresponding part of your life. For example, a missing area in the Helpful People Area of your lot shape may explain why your network of supportive helpers and friends has shrunk since moving into your current residence. Similarly, a missing area in the Marriage Area can contribute to marital troubles or romance problems. (Inviting a new paramour for a romantic evening in a missing area in your home is the Feng Shui version of taking a candlelight cruise into the Bermuda Triangle.)

Locating Projections and Missing Areas

Before you can enhance the positive influence of a projection or cure the negative influence of a missing area, you need to know where the projections and missing areas are located in the shape of your home and lot. You may be able to figure out whether the sides of your home and lot contain projections or missing areas simply by comparing your diagrams to the illustrations given in this chapter.

If that doesn't work, try the following easy steps, which help you analyze your home and lot shapes to see how they may be helping or hurting you:

1. **Obtain or create scale drawings of your home and lot plan.**

   You can measure the home and lot yourself and draw it on graph paper, or you can use the architect's drawings, blueprints, or plot maps. If the measurements are given on the drawings, that can speed up the process. (The quick-and-dirty version of the following process is to measure the distances by walking them off evenly. Estimate 3 feet for each step you take.)

2. **If any side of the home or lot is completely flat and even, with no variations at all, the side has no missing areas or projections.**

3. **Apply either the 50 Percent Rule or the 33 Percent Rule to any side that isn't completely flat.**

   If you have either an apparent missing area or projection in the center section of a wall, apply the 33 Percent Rule to that side. If you have a missing area or projection at the left or right end of a wall's side, apply the 50 Percent Rule. I explain both rules in the sections that follow.

If a side of a wall is more complex than what's presented in the following sections, you may need a Feng Shui professional (turn to Chapter 24 for help finding one), or you may choose to apply the Feng Shui Octagon room by room instead of to the entire home.

One projection or missing area by itself never tells the entire story of that Life Area. You need to take a look at all Feng Shui factors holistically.

Using the 50 Percent Rule: Remembering the importance of "less than half"

The *50 Percent Rule* says that if a portion of a wall that seems to be either missing or projecting is less than half the length of the side, then you have a missing area or projection. On your scale drawing of your home's floor plan, measure the entire length of the side in question with a ruler. Say the length is 6 inches on paper with a 1-inch-to-5-feet ratio; that means the side is 30 feet long in real life. The following guidelines show you how to use the 50 Percent Rule (the key concept to grasp is "less than half"):

- ✔ If the part of the home or lot side that appears to be sticking out is less than half the length of the entire side (3 inches, or 15 feet, in this example), call it a projection (see Figure 8-1a). Projections enhance the Octagon Life Area in which they're located, so hand out those celebratory cigars and then continue reading.

- ✔ If the part of the side of the home or lot that appears to be indented is less than half the length of the entire side (still 3 inches, or 15 feet, in this example), call it a missing area (see Figure 8-1b). This isn't quite so good, but don't panic; I provide cures for this situation in the later "Curing Missing Areas" section.

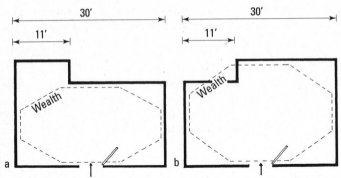

Figure 8-1:
Using the
50 Percent
Rule to
identify
projections
and missing
areas.

Here's an easier way to look at applying the 50 Percent Rule:

- ✔ If the part of the side that appears to be indented or missing is more than half the length of the entire length of its side (in this case, 3 inches or 15 feet), then you don't have a missing area. The part of the wall that appears to be sticking out is actually a projection. Whew! (Refer to Figure 8-1a.)

- ✔ If the part of the home or lot side that appears to be indented or missing (not sticking out) is less than half of the entire length of its side (in this case, 3 inches or 15 feet), then it truly is a missing area. (Refer to Figure 8-1b.)

Using the 33 Percent Rule

The *33 Percent Rule* consists of two parts. If the side of the home or lot in question appears U-shaped, or if it has a part on either end sticking out with an area that looks like it may be missing between them, apply Part 1 of the 33 Percent Rule, which calls for you to determine whether you have two projections or one missing area. On the other hand, if the side in question has what looks like a part sticking out in the center, apply Part 2 of the 33 Percent Rule to determine whether you have a projection in the center or a missing area on each end. The next sections break down the details of the two parts to the 33 Percent Rule.

Part 1: Assessing possible end projections

To assess whether you have two projections or one missing area, you need to either measure the entire length of the side or read the length from your accurate diagram. Using Figure 8-2, say you're working with the back side of the home or lot, which features the Wealth, Fame, and Marriage Areas. Say the length of the side is 6 inches on paper (30 feet in actual distance). Your eagle eye notices an indented spot in the center of the side (around the Fame

Area), which looks like it may be missing. Now you can determine which of the following measurements describes the indented space:

- ✔ **The spot that appears indented is more than 33 percent of the total length of its side (see Figure 8-2a).** If your indented spot meets this description, you don't have a missing area. Instead, you have two projections, one on each end with each reflecting a positive influence in its corresponding Life Area. If you want, you can perform the Three Secrets Reinforcement for these projections to further enhance their positive influence. (See Chapter 6 for information on the Three Secrets Reinforcement.)

- ✔ **The spot that appears indented is less than 33 percent of the total length of its side (see Figure 8-2b).** If your indented spot fits this description, you officially have a missing area. In this case, the missing area is in the Fame Area of your home or lot's Octagon. You may want to perform a cure to fix this missing area. (I describe cures for missing areas later in this chapter.)

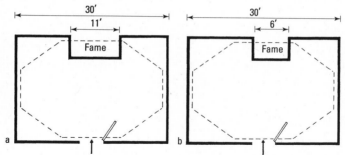

Figure 8-2: Spotting projections and missing areas by using the 33 Percent Rule, Part 1.

Part 2: Assessing a possible center projection

When you have a section extending out in the middle or near the middle of the side of a wall or lot, your mission is to discover whether you have an actual projection in the center or two missing areas (one on each end). To determine which of these two conditions is the case, apply the 33 Percent Rule, Part 2, to the side.

As in the preceding section, measure the entire length of the side or read the length from your accurate diagram. (For consistency's sake, I'm going to continue using the back side of the home or lot for this example, but the same principle holds when working with any of the four sides.) Look at Figure 8-3, which shows the Wealth, Fame, and Marriage Areas. The total length of the side is 6 inches on paper (30 feet in actual distance). What you're trying to determine is whether the central part that may be a projection measures more or less than 33 percent of the total length of the side. Here's what you may find:

✔ **The part that appears to project is more than 33 percent of the total length of its side (see Figure 8-3a).** Using the example, if the projected space is longer than 2 inches on the diagram (10 feet in actual distance), you don't have a projection. Instead, the wall features two missing areas, one on each side, each reflecting a negative influence in its corresponding Life Area. In this case, the shape features missing areas in the Life Areas of Wealth and Marriage; you can choose to perform cures for each Area.

✔ **The part that appears to project measures less than 33 percent of the total length of its side (see Figure 8-3b).** Continuing with the preceding example, if the part that's projecting out is less than 2 inches (10 feet) on the diagram, you have a projection, which means positive influences for that Life Area. In this case, the projection and corresponding positive influence is in the Fame Area. To further enhance this projection's positive influence, perform the Three Secrets Reinforcement. (Flip to Chapter 6 for Reinforcement info.)

Figure 8-3:
Using the
33 Percent
Rule, Part 2,
to identify
projections
and missing
areas.

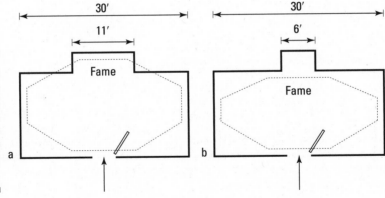

What if the part in question is exactly one-third the length of the side of the wall? In this case, you have to make a judgment call. However, I can tell you that the default approach is always this: When in doubt, cure it out. (It's better to be safe than sorry.)

Enhancing the Benefits of Projections

Because a projection helps its corresponding Life Area, you don't *need* to change anything, but you *can* do something to enhance the benefits of the projection: Turn the benefits into a cure by using the Three Secrets Reinforcement.

This method applies equally to projections in any Life Area, but — for the sake of providing an example — say you have a projection in the Family

Area of your home or lot, and your family life is great. Why mess with a good thing? Well, could it hurt if things got a little bit better? Certainly not. To increase the beneficial influence of the projection in the Family Area, perform the Three Secrets Reinforcement for this Area. The Three Secrets Reinforcement, typically performed right before or after you apply the physical portion of a Feng Shui cure, activates the invisible powers of the cure (including intention, motivation, and visualization). In this case, the positive physical element (the projecting part of the shape) is already in place. The Three Secrets Reinforcement simply magnifies the positive effects of the projection. For details on how to perform the Reinforcement, see Chapter 6.

Curing Missing Areas

A missing area in your home or lot can create problems and hold you back from fulfilling your potential in the corresponding Life Area of your Feng Shui Octagon. For example, a missing area in the Children Area of your lot or home can contribute to one or more of the following effects, depending on your particular life circumstances:

- Problems conceiving or bearing children
- Health difficulties with the children in your household
- Behavior problems or issues with education and schoolwork

Similar types of problems can ensue in any Life Area affected by a missing area. So the important question is this: What can I do right now to minimize or counterbalance any negative effects and to positively influence my situation in a particular Life Area?

I recommend two cure options for missing areas in homes: interior (inside the home) cures and exterior (outside the home) cures; use the ones that work best for your overall situation. (***Note:*** You rarely need to perform an interior cure *and* an exterior cure for the same missing area — unless of course you feel the need to go for the strongest possible effect.) I cover cures for missing areas in homes as well as lots in the next sections.

Exterior solutions for missing home areas

The exterior cure for a missing area symbolically and energetically completes the area that's missing. You determine the spot where the corner would be if the home were complete and then activate this point with your cure. By placing your cure here, you energetically help to fill in the whole space. After you restore energy to the structure and, more importantly, to the Life Area in need, you're off and running.

Perform one or more of the following cures to activate a missing area:

- ✔ **Place a bright light on a tall pole at the indicated corner.** The taller the light, the better — although a light of any height is better than no light at all. The light should point toward the home (generally at a 45-degree angle) and shine at the roof if at all possible. The chi of the light helps fill in the missing area, creating energy where a void once reigned.

  The light doesn't need to shine all the time, especially if it can bother your neighbors. (Bothering neighbors is generally bad Feng Shui!) But the light does need to be in good working order for the cure to be effective.

- ✔ **Place a flagpole rather than a light at the indicated corner.** This cure serves to uplift the chi and complete the area. If you so choose, you can use a flag with the colors of the associated Life Area for extra oomph. (See Chapter 3 for Life Area color details.) Otherwise, a green flag is generally effective; green symbolizes life, healing, and energy.

- ✔ **Position a smooth and heavy rock, boulder, or statue at the corner.** The object's heft and solidity bring energetic weight to the area, filling the gap (see Figure 8-4). Size does matter here, and bigger is generally better. A 5-pound rock or 6-inch statue won't do the job, though you don't need to reproduce Stonehenge or the Statue of Liberty in your backyard.

- ✔ **Plant a healthy tree, a large plant (or bush), or flowers that are the color of the missing Life Area at the corner spot.** For example, planting white flowers in the Children Area can do the trick.

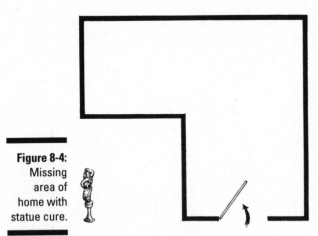

Figure 8-4:
Missing area of home with statue cure.

You can mix and match any of the previous solutions and apply more than one at the same time for an additional punch. If a large stone statue at the corner area combined with a patch of appropriately colored flowers suits your fancy, feel free.

Interior solutions for missing home areas

You can choose from two main options for correcting a missing area inside the home:

- ✔ **Remodel the home and fill in the missing area.** Although this cure can be incredibly effective, unless you're a professional contractor with lots of free time or you have piles of cash to spare, remodeling may not be the most practical option. Plus, remodeling tends to disrupt the household, can take two to three times longer than planned, and can cost 20 to 30 percent more than you budgeted for.

- ✔ **Perform a Feng Shui cure.** This is the easier, faster, and cheaper alternative to structural modification. Energy solutions are quite effective even though you haven't moved any of the walls in the home.

Fortunately, you can choose from several effective interior cures (see Figure 8-5):

- ✔ **Line one wall or both walls with sizeable mirrors (floor to ceiling is best) to energetically expand the area to make up for the defect.** One wall is okay, but two walls are even better. See Chapter 4 for important mirror tips.

- ✔ **Hang a wind chime or large faceted crystal sphere (2 inches in diameter or larger) right at the interior corner in question.** As with virtually all cures that involve hanging an item, use a red ribbon cut to a multiple of 9 inches in length for the greatest results.

- ✔ **Position an odd number of healthy new green plants along the two walls of the missing area.** Odd numbers are a bit stronger than even numbers, and the vital, living chi of the plants attracts energy to the space and energizes the missing area.

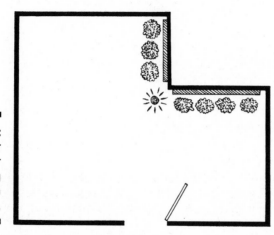

Figure 8-5:
Interior
cures for
missing
areas of a
home.

If you live in an apartment, you likely can't get permission to apply an exterior cure for a missing area inside your apartment. If the apartment is higher than the ground floor, the missing area is floating somewhere in space, which means an interior cure is just the thing for you.

Cures for missing lot areas

A missing area of the lot is a little trickier to cure because you can't get outside the lot to put something at the missing corner. After all, the exact corner spot is part of someone else's lot. Fortunately, you can fix this problem in several ways:

- ✔ **Place a bright spotlight or a flag on a tall pole at the corner of the missing area.** If you opt for the light, it should ideally shine at the roof of the home. If you opt for the flag, you can use a green one or one in the color of the Life Area you're improving (see Chapter 3 for the scoop on the colors of different Life Areas). The taller the flagpole, the stronger the cure. The added light chi or the color and motion of the flag energetically compensates for the missing space of the lot.

- ✔ **Install three lights or flagpoles, one at each of the three corners.** This cure is a stronger version of the one in the previous example (see Figure 8-6); it helps energetically compensate for the missing space of the lot. (It also gives you security protection at night.) Just be sure to shine the lights toward the home.

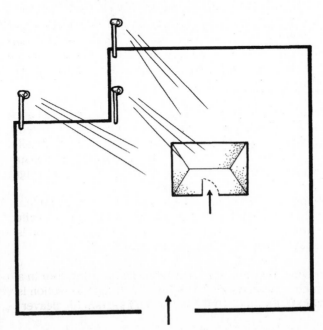

Figure 8-6:
Missing lot area with light cures.

✔ **Plant healthy green plants or a lively hedge along the perimeter of the missing area to put living chi in the area.** This cure uses the power of living energy to compensate for the missing area and jazzes up the corresponding Life Area. For extra credit, plant flowers of the color associated with the Life Area you're looking to cure.

Fruit- and/or flower-bearing plants generate even stronger Feng Shui cures. The living energy of the plants adds needed chi to the space by replacing what's missing and boosting your energy quotient in the Life Area.

Fixing Irregular Home and Lot Shapes

The reality is that most people don't live in perfectly symmetrical homes or on perfectly symmetrical lots. If your home or lot fits one of the following descriptions, you can balance the shape with the proper cure.

L-shaped and boot-shaped homes

An L-shaped home (or lot) is missing one-fourth of its area. This shape can negatively affect one Life Area of the Feng Shui Octagon (see Chapter 3) greatly and the three other Life Areas to a lesser degree.

The suggested exterior cure for an L-shaped home is to place a tall spotlight or flagpole — the taller the better — where the corner would be if the home were a complete shape (note that the spotlight should shine toward the roof of the home). This cure serves to balance and complete the shape of the home and provides the area with additional energy. You can also place a water feature (such as a fountain or pond) at the location where the corner would be if the home were complete.

If you live in an L-shaped apartment or for some reason can't apply an exterior cure to your L-shaped home, interior cures can provide a remedy. Placing mirrors at points along the walls of the missing area energetically completes it. In addition, you can place a bright light or a faceted crystal sphere at the interior missing corner point to strengthen the area (refer to Figure 8-5).

The boot shape, similar to the L-shape, can also cause trouble. A door, bed, or stove located at the ball or toe of the boot can negatively affect your health, relationships, and finances. The cure for this situation is to move the door, bed, or stove away from the danger zone.

Note that moving the door means creating a new front door in a better position, which isn't an easy cure. If implementing this option isn't possible, try the mirror solution I describe in the next section on cleaver shapes. The mirror pulls the door, bed, or stove away from the ball of the foot to relieve the pressure. A good exterior cure to balance the boot shape is to place a pool of water (such as a fountain, pond, or actual swimming pool) at the point where the corner would be complete (see Figure 8-7a).

Cleaver home shapes

A home shaped like a Chinese cleaver (see Figure 8-7b) can have unfortunate effects if the stove, the front door, or the bed is placed along the blade's cutting edge. This placement can contribute to fortunes being cut, or even actual lacerations of the body by physical accidents or surgery. To apply a cure for this situation, you can

✔ **Move the stove, bed, or front door away from the cutting edge.** For example, in the bedroom, you can move the bed from the cutting wall to another wall.

✔ **Place a mirror in line with the stove, door, or bed.** The mirror pulls the stove away from the cleaver's sharp edge. This solution counteracts the negative effects of the unfortunate placement.

One cure for a cleaver-shaped home — though it involves remodeling — is to place the main entrance in the end of the cleaver's handle. This way, you maximize active energy and use the cleaver shape to your advantage.

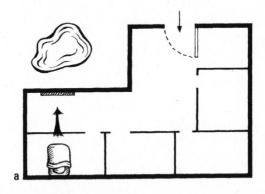

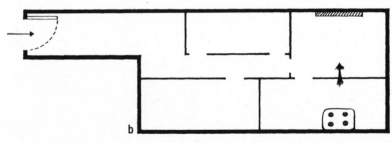

Figure 8-7: Boot-shaped home (a) and cleaver-shaped home (b), with cures.

Dustpan and money purse lot shapes

Your cleaning habits aside, you may be energetically living in a dustpan if your home or lot is shaped like Figure 8-8a. The dustpan shape can attract chaotic or negative energy. The money purse shape shown in Figure 8-8b is far better for attracting money to the site. Of these two shapes, a money purse is preferable to a dustpan, but balance is awkward for both shapes because each shape has two slanted sides.

One cure for a dustpan lot is to change the entrance to the other side so the shape resembles the money purse. This way, although the front of the lot is pinched, the back of the lot is wider and symbolically holds wealth energy. If moving the entrance isn't feasible, you can place spotlights or flagpoles featuring green flags (for either solution, taller is better) in the corners, as shown in Figures 8-8c and 8-8d.

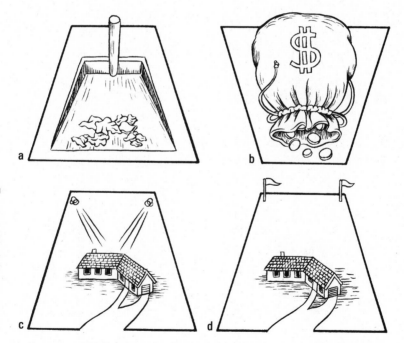

Figure 8-8:
Dustpan (a) and money purse (b) lot shapes, with cures for dustpan shape (c, d).

To further empower the money purse shape, place lights in the front lot corners, shining toward the home.

Triangular home and lot shapes

Triangle shapes, although great for pyramids (except for the curses), are lousy for homes and lots. The sharp corners and angled sides promote conflicts and accidents in the household. The house orientation shown in Figure 8-9a is negative because the path away from the front door leads to a vanishing point in the lot, foreboding a diminishing future. If your house and lot have this shape, you can choose from the following effective cures:

- ✓ **Place cures in each corner of the triangle.** Cure items you can use include plants, bushes, and trees.

- ✓ **Place a bright-shining light inward or a flag on a tall pole at the vanishing point.** See an example of the flagpole cure in Figure 8-9a.

- ✓ **Place flagpoles in each of the three corners.** The most effective flagpoles are tall ones bearing green flags.

Reinforce your cure placements by using the Three Secrets Reinforcement to receive maximum effects from your solutions. (I explain how to perform the Three Secrets Reinforcement in Chapter 6.)

Angled lot side

If one side of your lot is angled, unbalanced living can result. You can cure this situation by planting healthy plants or bushes along the angled side, infusing the space with healthy, living chi (see Figure 8-9b).

Figure 8-9: Triangular (a) and angled (b) lot shapes and cures.

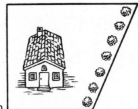

Multicornered and other oddly shaped lots

An odd number of corners may be a negative condition for a lot or house because they can promote confusion and imbalance. A recommended cure for imbalanced shapes is to place spotlights or green flags on flagpoles at each corner of the lot or house exterior. This cure balances the energy of the lot, promoting harmony, cohesion, and forward progress for the residents.

Chapter 9

Open Sesame! Creating a Welcoming Entry

The entryway of your home is responsible for the first energetic and sensory impression that you receive from your home — and that first impression is important. This chapter helps you create the best possible first impression and channel the utmost energy and good feeling into your home. The payoff? Desired improvements in vital parts of your life.

Recognizing the Importance of the Front Door and Foyer

Feng Shui considers the front door and entry to be the most important points in your home environment. The approach and entry determine the amount and quality of energy that flows into the home as well as whether this energy nourishes or depletes the home, thereby helping or hindering the aspirations of the residents. A smooth, grand, open entry and approach supports free-flowing prosperity and vitality. Conversely, a convoluted or difficult approach can create corresponding unpleasant effects in various parts of your life.

The front door is the first and foremost of the three Life Pillars, a concept I introduce in Chapter 2. The Life Pillars provide fundamental energies to the home and its residents, so focusing your attention on the condition of your front door is very beneficial. Imagine going through life with your jaw wired shut — now you have an idea of the problems you can encounter if the main door is blocked.

The energy of the entry is mediated by the approach to the door, the entryway itself, the physical door and doorway, and the first room or thing you see upon stepping inside. The front door, the controlling point of the home's energy, is a crucial fulcrum point. Seemingly minor flaws at your front door can affect you quite negatively, whereas improvements made at the entry can significantly affect your life in positive ways. To paraphrase an old saying, "when it's good, it's very good, but when it's bad, it's very bad."

Your entryway should be open, inviting, and attractive. It should also look and feel positive. As you clear your entryway of energy blocks and positively activate its chi, you may notice more energy flowing into your life, obstacles melting, and opportunities knocking on your door (in more ways than one). An entryway that's gloomy, dark, overrun, or difficult to approach has subtle, and in some cases profound, negative effects on your life, including diminished opportunities, constriction of your cash flow, and difficulties in making important contacts.

If you think of your home as a body, you can consider your front door to be the mouth — the point where energy enters to nourish the body. Of course, additional energy comes in through the other doors and the windows, and some natural energy enters through the walls, floors, and roof. But the major source of energy in a home is the *Mouth of Chi,* your front door. If the Mouth of Chi is physically or energetically blocked, the home is metaphorically starved and suffocated, which creates problems in your life.

No matter how fabulous the interior of your home seems, if the approach, entryway, and/or front door are problematic, you can see corresponding life effects. What's more, if the only place in your home you improve is the entry, you're still way ahead of the game. Something good, perhaps very good, may come of your improved door situation. Try it and see. (If you need further encouragement, consider that the fixes are quite easy compared to the inconveniences an improper entry can generate.)

Dealing with Driveway Issues

When energy flows freely onto your property and into your home, your life flows smoothly and easily. Your driveway is a key source of energy and societal chi — connections, money, and helpful people — for your property and home, and by extension, you. Your home is also fed energy by the front walkway. (If your home doesn't have a driveway, the main source of outdoor energy flowing into the property is the front walkway.) If you live in an apartment, the ease and accessibility of the path you take from the outside to reach the front door of your apartment serves a similar function.

In the following sections, I give you the ideal driveway conditions as well as common driveway problems. I also help you cure your drive if you have any of these problems.

Positive driveway conditions

The best type of driveway is one that's flat or that slopes gently upward and is slightly winding instead of being arrow straight or convoluted (although a short, straight drive leading to the garage, like the type found in many homes, isn't negative). The driveway should have a smooth surface, and it shouldn't be bumpy or difficult to navigate. Also, the home and front door should be clearly visible from the front entrance to the property (the beginning of the driveway at the street), and the sights you see when driving up to the home should either be uplifting or inspire positive feelings.

Problematic driveway conditions and their solutions

Problematic driveways include steep drives, blind drives, shared drives, and driveways that face a neighbor's drive that's wider or goes down. (Alas, not all architects and construction contractors are fully Feng Shui savvy — yet.) So in the sections that follow, consider a few common problematic driveway scenarios and their Feng Shui implications and cures.

A steep drive going down or going up

If your driveway goes steeply downward from the street, your home is probably below the road. In this situation, leaving the home, whether for occasional errands or for work each day, is difficult because you tend to strain to climb upward and out in order to leave the property. This situation can generate career difficulties — not to mention the practical problems of leaving the driveway itself.

A cure is to place your trusty energy generators along the drive to help move energy up to the street (see Figure 9-1). Energy generators include lights, windsocks, and wind chimes. These cures also help protect the home from excess energy that can roll down the driveway and affect the home.

Being above the road is generally better than being below it. However, a home sitting high above the road can feature a steep driveway leading up to it, which fosters two kinds of problems:

✔ Energy has a hard time getting up the driveway to the home, making it physically hard for people and energetically hard for money to reach you.

✔ Whatever energy (money and people) does make it to the home has an easy time rolling back down the drive and being lost.

Figure 9-1:
Steep drive
leading
down to
home below
road, with
light cures.

A good cure for a driveway that descends sharply from the home down to the street is to place bright lights on each side of the drive where it meets the street. Another cure for a steep drive going up to a home is the same as the cure for a steep, descending one: Activate the driveway with windsocks or use other mobile cure items to stimulate energy (I fill you in on mobile cure items in Chapter 4).

Note: The solutions in this section are specifically for curing driveway issues. Flip to Chapter 7 to find cures for a home situated below the road.

A blind drive

In Feng Shui, a recurring principle is to be able to see what's coming toward you in life. A *blind drive* prevents you from seeing who or what's approaching both at home and as you leave the site, and this constraint creates a psychological blind spot as well as physical security issues.

For a good cure, place a large, convex mirror (the larger the better) near the end of the drive so you can see the approaching street traffic as you come down the driveway. If this mirror also allows you to see the street from your home, that's even better.

You may need one mirror on each side of the blind drive to see the traffic coming from both directions.

A problematic neighbor's drive

A neighbor's driveway directly across from yours can affect you negatively if the mouth of the driveway is wider than your drive or if it slopes down and away. In both cases, the opposing drive can steal part of your home's energy supply.

The solution for both opposing drive situations is to mount a large, convex mirror at the mouth of your driveway, above your garage door, or at another position that's in line with the opposing drive in order to reverse the effect of the larger or downward-sloping opposite driveway and pull needed chi back into your property. A 24- to 36-inch mirror works well, but a larger one may be even more effective. Regardless, this mirror must face toward the mouth of the neighbor's drive.

A shared drive

A *shared driveway* is one that's used by more than one residence or one that leads to your home and also splits off to go to another home. If you share your driveway with one or more residences, this situation can affect your site by reducing its share of incoming energy.

If you share a driveway with a neighbor, you can mount a bright light on a pole (the taller the better) at the place where the neighbor's drive splits off from yours. The light marks an energetic division between the two driveways and helps prevent the loss of chi (which translates to money, opportunities, health, and more) from your home and life.

If you put lights on both sides of your drive at the splitting point, the cure is even stronger.

Clearing the Way to the Front Door for Natural Chi

Your home insulates you from the external chi of nature, which your body continuously needs, so one purpose of Feng Shui cures is to overcome this unfortunate liability by inviting more of this vital natural energy into your home. I describe some of your options in the next sections.

Throughout this book, I use the terms *front door* and *Mouth of Chi* interchangeably. They both refer to the same place: the original, designed, front entry to the home. Each residence has only one main door (even if you rarely or never enter through it); all other doors are secondary, whether side, back, garage, or patio. The only way the front door ceases to be the main door is if you remove it completely, finish the wall, and make another door the front door — something I rarely recommend. Consult a Feng Shui practitioner before moving a front door (see Chapter 24 for details on finding a professional).

Solving the hidden front door dilemma

Generally, the front door should be visible from the street for maximum energy flow. *Hidden front door* is a Feng Shui term describing a front door that can't be seen from the street, is recessed, is dark or in shadow, directly faces a hill, or is somehow obscured or obstructed from the flow.

If you have a hidden front door, you may find that moving ahead, receiving opportunities or income, and even selling your home can be difficult. From the opposite point of view, if you can't see the street from your front door, your career can be energetically hindered, whether you work at home or outside of it. (*Note:* I apply this principle somewhat differently if you live on a large estate where the home is a long distance from the main street. In this case, ideally the main drive is visible from the front door and the front door is visible from the drive.)

Following are two cures for hidden front door problems:

✔ If possible, mount a convex safety mirror (the kind used on parking ramps to help drivers see around corners) that allows you to see the door when approaching the home and to clearly see the street from the front door (check out Figure 9-2a).

The larger the mirror, the stronger the cure. If the mirror is too small or incorrectly angled to allow you to see the approach clearly, the cure won't be highly effective. I recommend using a mirror that's at least 24 inches in diameter, although larger is better.

✔ Line the path from the street to your door with lights or plants (see Figure 9-2b). This cure guides the chi right up to your door.

Curing common outdoor stairway dilemmas

Stairways leading to the front door, whether short or long, are an important aspect of your entryway. Reading the energy of your stairway is easy with your Feng Shui thinking (and feeling) cap on. If humans can flow easily and freely up and down the stairs, so can energy and income. The ideal entry stairway is wide and easy to ascend, not too long or too steep, and free of sharp turns. The stairway is stable, with complete *risers* (the vertical parts connecting stairs) and a solid handrail.

Following are some common entry stairway problems and their Feng Shui solutions. (For the scoop on stairways inside your home, see Chapter 14.)

Figure 9-2:
Hidden front
doors with
convex
mirror and
light cures.

a   b

A long stairway

A stairway that's a long trip up to the front door can have definite energetic liabilities. This type of stairway is common to second floor apartments or duplexes accessed by exterior stairs. Such a stairway makes it difficult for energy, income, and you to get to your front door (kind of like salmon swimming upstream). Steep stairways can also make opportunities more difficult to come by. The energetic effects may include difficulty resting or getting home. You may also end up away from home more than you desire to be.

If the average person who visits you gets a bit winded climbing to your door, your stairs are probably too long. Curing them can counteract and improve the negative factors, even though your stairs may still give everyone a good aerobic workout. The suggested cure for a long staircase is to wrap a realistic-looking artificial green vine around the stair rail from the bottom all the way up to the top. (If the staircase has no rail, I recommend installing a good one. For further details, see the "A rickety banister" section later in this chapter.) The lively green energy of the vine adds health and vigor, compensating for the long journey upward.

An alternate (or even additional) cure for a long stairway is to run small holiday lights or rope (white is good; multicolored is better) along the same path. The lights guide the energy up the long stairway, feeding the front door. (Light represents the energy of attraction as well as radiant energy.)

Missing risers

Your toe points to each riser with every step unless the riser is missing or broken. A stairwell with missing risers potentially promotes the loss of income and life energy (chi) to the home and its residents. As energy ascends the stairs, it slips through the riser gaps like water through a leaky bucket, equaling less mojo for you. Because your feet are energetically connected to your career, missing risers can trip you up, both physically and in your life's work. On a practical note, missing risers are also a safety issue. Twisted, sprained, or broken ankles and feet are bad personal Feng Shui. (Plus, they hurt.)

Curing a tree or post in front of the front door

A tree growing in a direct line with the front door can promote bad luck because it obstructs the path to the door. An obstructed path can block income and inhibit career success. This tree or post can also jeopardize the front door — and consequently all life factors — by acting as a direct threatening element. The following solution from Chinese folklore allows you to transform this bad luck to good, without chopping down the tree or removing the post.

1. **Buy a new, unused ink pen and a piece of red writing paper.**

   Most office supply stores sell red paper.

2. **Cut a circular piece from the red sheet of paper.**

3. **With the pen, write the following four words without a single pause on the red circle: "Raise head, see happiness."**

4. **Attach the paper to the tree trunk or post at the eye level (or higher) of the tallest person in the home.**

5. **Reinforce this cure with the Three Secrets Reinforcement.**

   I fill you in on the Three Secrets Reinforcement in Chapter 6.

As you write the words and perform the Three Secrets Reinforcement, visualize the god or deity of your religion shining light on the words you've written. If you're an atheist, visualize sunlight or universal light or energy positively affecting the words.

Note: Another solution is to place a melodic metal wind chime over the front door to deflect negative effects from the tree, as pictured here.

The cure for missing risers is straightforward and usually involves a carpenter or handyman: Physically fill in or replace missing risers in your stairway. After completing this task, you're likely going to feel more solid and complete in life as well as every time you ascend or descend the stairs. This feeling creates beneficial energetic effects that flow directly into your practical life.

A stairway with a turn

A right-angle turn on a front door stairway often creates an energy block, robbing you and your home of vital chi. If an actual robber stood at your door and snagged your wallet every time you passed by, you'd do something about it pretty darned quick! Yet most people allow these Feng Shui robbers to reduce their vital energy day after day, rarely doing a thing about it.

An excellent cure for a right-angle stairway is to place a healthy potted plant on the landing at the turn. The living chi of the plant nullifies the negative influence of the turn, attracts chi, and boosts the energy on its way to the door. Be careful that the plant doesn't block the way, though. If it does, you've simply compounded one problem with another.

My clients Sam and Maureen had a narrow exterior stair leading to their front door that featured a 90-degree turn, and both were unhappy in their professions. They replaced the existing staircase with a much wider, more open, and completely straightforward one. Coincidentally — not! — Sam started a new and much happier career as a designer and consultant not long afterward. Maureen remarked on how much freer and more expansive the new stairway made them feel (she has since embarked on her dream career as well). Although this cure is virtually the only noticeable change the couple made, their friends rave about how much more open, pleasant, and inviting the home now feels. Sam and Maureen also feel energetically connected to their front yard for the first time.

A rickety banister

A problem banister (one that gives when you grab it) creates unsafe feelings and a lack of control in life. It may also cause subconscious uncertainties to creep into your mind for no apparent reason. The remedy is easy: Repair a rickety banister or install a good, solid handrail that supports you completely when you hold it.

Dealing with pesky approach issues

The following barriers and impediments to a smooth entry are physical and energetic stumbling blocks in your life path. The more these obstructions exist on the path into your home, the more your liabilities are compounded. Fixing them removes obstacles from your life's path, quells frustrations, and generally makes life an easier game to play.

Multiple gates, barriers, porches, and doors

Having to go through multiple gates, barriers, porches, and doors can produce frustration, mental blocks, a lack of energy, and feelings of being stopped in life. Cures include removing some of the barriers and hanging wind chimes or faceted crystal spheres (I cover these items in Chapter 4) between the doors and gates. When performing such cures, be sure to visualize abundant energy and finances flowing into your life as you apply the Three Secrets Reinforcement (see Chapter 6 for details on this).

No walkway from your front door to the street

Often the garage projects out from the home and blocks the front door, and in many contemporary homes, the path to the front door connects to the driveway rather than to the street (or the sidewalk next to the street). The potential Feng Shui problem in this case is that you may receive less income and have fewer helpful friends in your life than you deserve — all because the front door feeds from the driveway and not the street. The driveway is a secondary energy source for the front walk and front door; it carries less incoming chi than the street. (See Figure 9-3 for an example of this situation and the appropriate cure.)

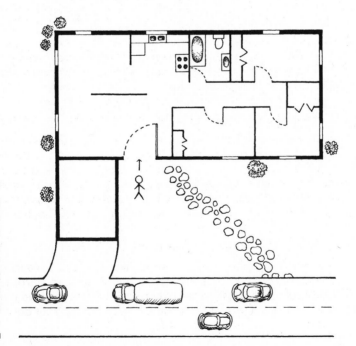

Figure 9-3:
Walkway cure for no path from front door to street or garage blocking front door.

The expensive cure for this problem is to build a new sidewalk from your front door to the street. If you're up for it, go for it. Several of my clients are now happily enjoying better incomes and careers after applying this new sidewalk cure. If not, you can use the walkway and chime cures I present in the next section.

A projecting garage that blocks the front door

A projecting garage that blocks the front door is a common situation that creates at least two problems:

- ✔ The structure of the home is unbalanced, usually in some form of an L-shape.
- ✔ The garage hides the front door from view on at least one side of the home.

I recommend these two cures:

- ✔ Build a second stone walkway to the street (refer to Figure 9-3) leading away from the garage — from the front door to the street. If your garage projects out, this cure has the important effect of balancing the home shape. Whether or not your garage projects, the new pathway has the additional benefit of bringing new (and more!) chi to your front door.
- ✔ Place a wind chime either along the side of the garage or near the front door to attract more chi into your home. (Turn to Chapter 4 for important wind chime tips.) Note that this cure is more practical but slightly less powerful than the preceding one.

A narrow, overgrown, or tunnel-like pathway to the front door

A narrow, overgrown, or tunnel-like pathway to your front door restricts your energy, making it harder literally and figuratively for you and the home to breathe. Ideally, your entry path should be at least as wide as the front door. Better still, have it wide enough for two people to walk side by side. Cures include widening the path and cutting back bushes and hedges to open the way. Also, make sure the path is well lit, clear, clean, and bright.

A recessed front door from the front line of the home

Less income and fewer career opportunities are the result of a front door that's recessed from the front line of the home. To cure this problem, either brighten the exterior with powerful lights or place a brass wind chime by the entryway. Doing so activates the energy around the front door to attract more of the good things you want in life.

Obstacles on the path to the entrance, near the front door, or on the porch close to the door

Obstacles such as bikes, boxes, trash, skateboards, and buckets may be on the path to the entrance, near the front door, or on the porch close to the door. The results of such scenarios include frustration, confusion, and finding it easy to figuratively stumble in your life (much like physically stumbling over all the debris). The simple cure is to remove the obstructing junk and clean up the path or porch.

Decay or disrepair at the entrance

Decay and disrepair in and around the home can relate to decay in one's life circumstances. They can bring you down and make winning in life much harder. These signs, which are especially negative when located near the front door, include burnt-out or missing light bulbs, broken light fixtures, a broken or missing doorbell, cobwebs around the entrance, wasps nesting near the door, and a 4-foot-long pickaxe stuck in the front door. (Just take a look; you'll know it when you see it.) The cure? Fix, clean, replace, and repair.

Making the Most of the Mouth of Chi

The front door serves as the mouth of the home. Like your physical mouth, it takes in the sustenance that nourishes the home: chi or energy. If the mouth has trouble, you have trouble. "Health begins with the mouth," goes an old saying. The same is true in Feng Shui. The health of the home (and the fortunes of the inhabitants) begins with the front door and entry.

In the sections that follow, I describe the ideal front door, provide cures for front door dilemmas, and point out some lucky front door colors.

Knowing the principles of the ideal front door

An ideal front door adheres to three key principles:

- ✔ **It's well illuminated.** Your front door should be well lit and free of shadows and darkness. Good lighting at the entrance is a good energy principle for the door and the home.

- ✔ **It's bright and clear.** The door, the approach, and the entryway should be cheerful, lively, and uplifting. Ideally, your front door invokes a pleasant, happy feeling and attitude. The front doorway should also be free of obstacles and obstructions to chi and people entering.

✔ **It's proportional to the size of the front of the home.** The front door shouldn't be too large or too small compared to the front facade of the home.

- A door that's too small proportionally can't attract sufficient chi for the residents and can diminish their social stature.

- A door that appears too large for the home projects a boastful attitude and engenders subconscious dislike from your neighbors.

Solving front door problems

The following deviations from the ideal front door condition can be cured with properly applied energetic remedies. So carefully check the Feng Shui of your front door and make as many improvements as you can.

Squeaky door hinges

The Chinese say that "squeaky doors bring hungry ghosts," meaning a door with squeaking hinges attracts real or imagined spooks. At the very least, a squeaking door is subliminally scary, which is possibly why it's the most common sound effect in scary movies. The cure? Apply WD-40 generously. I'm amazed by how many of my clients fail to notice their squeaky doors until I point out the noise. (Only then do they recall that "it's been that way for years.")

The seemingly small cure of oiling a squeaky hinge can make a big difference for all doors, including front doors, side doors, bedroom doors, closet doors, and cabinet doors.

A window in the door

The front door protects your home. The ideal front door is therefore solid and without windows. Front doors with windows in them are energetically, not to mention physically, weaker. They can be easily broken into and thus create vulnerabilities in your home's energy field.

The best cure is to install a new, solid door (one without any windows or openings, although a peephole is fine). A budget-wise solution until you can swing a new door (pun intended!) is to cover the window with a cloth, blind, or curtain that matches the color of the door, making the door look complete from the street. (If you prefer, you can use the Feng Shui power color of red instead.) Even if you rely on this window for light, a solid door is still energetically better for your home and for you. Besides, you can always put additional lights in the entryway as needed. As you perform either cure, visualize protection and solidity and reinforce the cure with the Three Secrets Reinforcement (see Chapter 6). ***Note:*** Having a craftsman create a solid piece of wood to fill the door opening may cost as much or more than simply getting a new door or performing the budget-friendly cure — and it's likely to be less effective in the long run.

A writer client of mine, whose home featured an elegant glass front door, reluctantly installed a new, solid door as a cure. She enthusiastically reported that after closing the new door for the first time, she proceeded directly to her writing room and that day completed the novel she'd been struggling to finish for several months. Feng Shui results don't *always* happen this quickly, but many times they do.

Regardless of the type of front door you have, you can reduce vulnerability in your life and career by covering *sidelight windows* (those tall, narrow windows flanking the front door) with miniblinds or curtains.

The door swings closed or drifts open by itself

An open front door should stand where you put it. A front door that swings closed automatically shuts out money and keeps people from coming to you, and a door that drifts open on its own allows energy to leak out of the home and invites unwanted people in. The cure for both types of front doors is the same: Get a carpenter to rehang or replumb the door so that it stands still wherever you place it.

The door doesn't fit right in the doorframe and/or is loose on its hinges

This awkward door situation creates confusion, mental blocks, and aggravation (not to mention unneeded teeth and mouth issues). The cure is to hire a finish carpenter or door-hanging expert. The door may need to be reframed, replaced, or both.

One of my clients had a strong career and beautiful home but was perplexed by her lack of a meaningful relationship. Her home featured a door and frame combination that didn't fit correctly. (The door had been planed and shaved several times in partial attempts to make it fit.) After the consultation, she hired a craftsman to install a new, proper door and redo the doorframe. (She also, of course, reinforced this cure by using the Three Secrets Reinforcement I tell you about in Chapter 6.) To her pleasant surprise (but not to mine!), shortly after performing the cure, she happily moved to an even nicer home with a new partner.

The door doesn't close, latch, or stay closed on the first attempt, or the latch sticks on the strike plate

A front door that fails to close, latch, or stay closed on the first attempt or a latch that sticks on the strike plate creates subtle life blocks, making it difficult to complete things and keep them complete. Seemingly finalized deals can tend to pop out of completion or come undone. To cure such a situation, replace or repair the strike plate and/or latch.

Dead/unused locks are still on the door, or the door handle is loose

When unused or broken locks are still on the door, or when the door handle is loose, you may experience difficulty getting a grip in life, have weak energy, or hang on to old and useless things in life. The cure? Repair the door handle and remove or replace outmoded lock fixtures, making sure to visually fill in and seal any resulting holes in the door.

The door scrapes on the floor

A scraping door obstructs or drags on your income and freedom. The ideal door swings freely at least 90 degrees without hindrances. This principle holds true even if what scrapes on the floor is the insulator strip on the bottom of the door (which is there to keep cold air out). Because most thresholds sit an inch above floor level, the rubber insulation strip shouldn't scrape on your carpet or foyer floor. Plane or shave the bottom of the door to cure this problem so that the door swings freely.

The door is broken, worn, warped, or dilapidated, or the paint is peeling

Here's the skinny: Dilapidated doors symbolize dilapidated lives. The front door represents the home, and the home represents your life. Ergo, a worn-out front door can energetically influence you to feel (and possibly become) worn-out as well. Sound attractive? No? I didn't think so. Replacing an old door can easily cure this situation.

Changing your luck with front door colors

Door colors on many homes are white or a color that matches the home. These color choices are generally fine. However, you can boost your front door chi by painting the door a particular color. The colors with the strongest energetic effects include

- ✔ **Bright red:** This classic Feng Shui door color is said to confer power, protection, luck, and a sense of royalty to the home and its occupants. This cure is known in Feng Shui circles as *the lucky red door.* Painting your front door a bright shade of red is a great all-around cure for boosting your home's energy.

- ✔ **Green:** This color is another excellent choice because it symbolizes life, health, and money.

- ✔ **Black:** Black is a fine color for a front door and is especially good if your front door is in the center, which represents career. Black symbolizes water, which equals money. Enough said.

Moving On In: Mastering Interior Entryway Problems and Solutions

If energy flows from your front door through your home without obstructions or blocks, the chi of your entire home is fed and nourished, which promotes positive life results. If your energy is obstructed, problems may occur in the areas of career and physical and mental health. Some of these problems can occur right at the front entryway. I detail the solutions in the following sections.

An upward-leading interior stairway that faces the front door

An interior stairway leading directly to both an upper floor and the front door signifies money rolling out of the home, as well as unfortunate outcomes in many parts of your life. The gravity force coming down the stairs pushes incoming chi back out the front door, symbolizing loss of wealth or income. The steeper, taller, and closer the stairway, the more intense the effect, but even a small upward-leading staircase can bring problems. (See the nearby sidebar "Too close for comfort? Measuring the distance from your front door to the stairs" for important information on the proximity of a stairway and the front door.)

Because remodeling the stairs is sometimes impractical, an energetic solution is more pragmatic. Place either a faceted crystal sphere (see Figure 9-4) or a pleasant-sounding wind chime halfway between the front door and the base of the stairs. Hang either item on a red ribbon cut to a multiple of 9 inches in length. This cure redirects the stairway's descending chi into the home instead of letting it escape out the door or repel vital inflowing chi.

An especially large stairway may benefit from a larger cure, such as a bright, leaded-glass, crystal chandelier, which can be even more effective than a single crystal sphere. (Although you can affix a single faceted crystal sphere to the bottom of the chandelier for good measure in order to increase the effect.)

A downward-leading interior stairway that's directly in line with the front door

When an interior stairway descends to a lower floor directly in the forward path of the front entry, the effects can be just as severe as those resulting from an upward-leading interior stairway (see the preceding section). In Feng Shui terms, a downward-leading interior stairway that's less than 12 feet from the front door symbolizes a decline in life fortunes; it can lead to accidents and falls, significant career problems, and other issues that can occur suddenly and without warning.

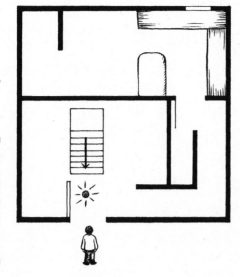

Figure 9-4:
Upward-
leading
stairway
facing the
front door,
with cure.

To assess the need for a cure in this situation, determine the distance from the stairway to the front door (I explain the importance of the distance between an interior stairway and the front door in the nearby sidebar). If a cure is needed, hang a faceted crystal sphere (or a wind chime or leaded-glass crystal light fixture) from the ceiling midway between the door and stairs.

A mandarin duck stairway

A main entry that opens directly onto a stairway landing, requiring you to go up one stairway or down another to proceed into the home, features a *mandarin duck stairway*. This situation combines the features of the two stairway problems detailed in the previous two sections. Under its influence, one partner in the marriage may go up in life while the other goes down; one may enjoy career success while the other struggles; or their life-paths may diverge, leading to separation or divorce. (The unusual name stems from the Chinese custom of having a special dish — mandarin duck — at the wedding banquet. Apparently the staircase looks similar to the roasted duck at the feast.)

To cure this type of stairway, place a plant at the juncture of the two staircases. Another effective addition (or alternative cure) is to wrap a realistic-looking green silk ivy vine (see Figure 9-5) around the banister of the stairway from bottom to top, imparting life and green energy to the stairway and counteracting its negative effects.

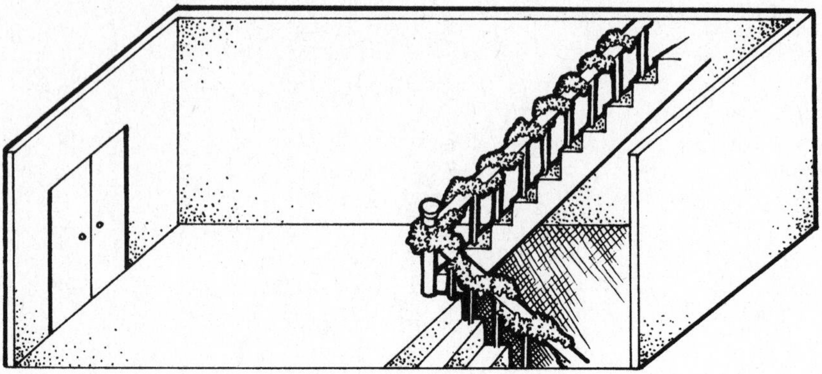

Figure 9-5:
Mandarin
duck
stairway
with ivy
cure.

A split view upon entering

You have a split view upon entering when a close wall blocks half of your field of vision but you can see much farther into the home with the other half of your field of vision. One negative effect of this feature is a physical dissonance between your left eye and right eye and between your left brain and right brain. A perceptual rift occurs when this sight continuously greets you upon entering your home. Repeated viewing can subconsciously stimulate anxiety, stress, schizophrenic tendencies, and other psychological problems, leading to bad decisions and even accidents.

The cure for a split view is to place a mirror on the partially blocking wall to balance the view and restore harmony to the entrance. Check out Figure 9-6 for an illustration of this solution.

Figure 9-6:
Split view
upon
entering,
with mirror
cure.

Too close for comfort? Measuring the distance from your front door to the stairs

How close can an interior stairway be to the front door before it becomes a Feng Shui problem that may wreak havoc on your life, wealth, and career? Inquiring Feng Shui minds want to know! Grandmaster Lin Yun's Feng Shui school teaches that residents should be on alert if they have a stairway that's closer to their front door than twice the height of the tallest family member. Based on this principle, I've developed a rough guideline of approximately 12 to 13 feet as the distance in question. When in doubt, grab a tape measure and start measuring both the height of your tallest family members and the dimensions of your front entryway.

Note: Even with this handy guideline, the final analysis of whether or not a cure is necessary is a judgment call based on the overall condition of the front entry. For example, if you have an enormous upward-leading stairway that sits, say, 13.5 feet from your door (in other words, just a little farther than the distance given in the guideline), a cure is definitely in order. When in doubt, it may pay dividends to speak with a qualified Feng Shui consultant for clarification of this or any other Feng Shui matter. (Refer to Chapter 24 for tips on finding and working with a Feng Shui professional.)

Being Aware of Continual First Impressions

Feng Shui theory emphasizes the importance of first impressions, including the view of your home from the street and of the street from your front door. In fact, these first impressions are also continual impressions.

The first thing you see as you enter a home is a crucial first impression that sets the tone for your entire experience in the home (and for much of your life experience). A positive first entry impression creates uplifted spirits, hope, and positive expectations. A negative first entry impression, like an unpleasant smell encountered when entering a restaurant, sets up lowered expectations. Such a continual first impression over time can make you a truly unhappy camper. The next sections reveal how to ensure your home gives off good first (and continual) impressions.

Examining features of the ideal entrance

The ideal entrance welcomes you in, greeting you with pleasant, uplifting sights, feelings, sounds, or smells. It makes you feel comfortable, peaceful, and at home. A wide, spacious, and bright interior entryway gives you ample room to move forward and makes you want to move forward. You can easily see a place to sit or rest; at the very least you can see something pleasant and attractive ahead. An ideal entryway promotes career success and harmony at home as well as a positive attitude and a clear spirit.

A less-than-ideal entryway is correspondingly less positive, or at worst, negative. If the first impression of the entryway is one of a dark, cramped, blocked, or unpleasant space, the effect can take its toll on you over time.

The first impression principle has two important factors:

✔ The first room you enter (or if you enter into a foyer or entry hall, the first room you see or approach as you proceed into the home) affects your psychology and physical health.

✔ The very first item or object your eye is attracted to as you enter the residence specifically affects your psyche, so carefully check out this aspect of your entrance.

I detail the implications of both of these factors in the following sections.

Positive rooms to enter from the front door

An ideal front door entrance leads into a foyer, entry hall, living room, den, family room, study, or library. When located near the front door, any of these rooms has either a neutral or positive energy, with corresponding life effects (unless of course the room is an energetic disaster area). Be aware, though, that negative factors such as problematic furniture arrangements may counteract the positive effects of the location of one of these rooms. (See Chapter 13 for more information on these spaces.) Following are the specific qualities and effects of these positive rooms, broken down by room:

✔ **Foyer or entry hall:** This room is generally good and fine at the entrance.

✔ **Living room:** Seeing a comfortable place to sit down as your first impression provides a feeling of rest and relaxation.

✔ **Den or family room:** These rooms create a similar effect as a living room, inducing a sense of relaxation and comfort.

✔ **Study or library:** A study or library imbues an environment with an aura of learning, intelligence, knowledge, and studiousness that positively influences all residents of the home.

Negative rooms to enter immediately from the front door

According to Feng Shui principles, unfavorable rooms to enter (or even see) directly and immediately from the front door are the kitchen, bathroom, bedroom, or dining room. Particular features of each of these rooms, when visible from the front door as I show here, become significant Feng Shui issues. The following list details potential negative effects of each room and provides cures for each situation:

✔ **Kitchen:** The kitchen serves as a direct route to health and eating issues. If entered from the front door, issues may include digestion problems and binge eating. Cure this negative kitchen placement by hanging a wind chime or faceted crystal sphere between the front door and the kitchen.

If the stove is visible from the front door, the negative effects can be much more severe and may include impaired finances, accidents and severe health challenges. For this situation, install a cure that blocks the view of the stove from the door. Options include

- Installing a door (if there's a convenient doorway in the path)
- Hanging a curtain (regular or bamboo)
- Installing a screen or divider
- Strategically placing one or more large potted plants

If none of these cures work in the space, opt for hanging a wind chime halfway between the front door and the stove, over the cook's position at the stove, or in both spots.

✔ **Bathroom:** A view of the bathroom from the front door isn't an ideal first impression. It can have psychological, physiological, and financial draining effects, especially if the toilet is visible. Water symbolizes money, and a visible toilet in this position represents flushing energy and money out of your life.

The most basic cure is to keep the bathroom door closed at all times. Doing so helps reduce unneeded energy drainage from the household. An additional cure involves hanging a high-quality, full-length, full-width mirror on the outside of the bathroom door to help remove the bathroom from the flow of energy. To be effective, this mirror cure requires that the bathroom door be kept closed. (Turn to Chapters 10 and 13 for more information on bathrooms.)

If family members don't cooperate in keeping the bathroom door closed, you can install inexpensive spring hinges on this door.

✔ **Bedroom:** If your bedroom is visible from your front door, you may find yourself feeling lazy, frequently tired, and not wanting to work. To cure this situation, hang a wind chime halfway between the door and your bed.

If the master bed is even partially visible from the front door, the problem is worse. Relationships can be negatively affected and residents can experience instability in life and threats to their security. The cures for this Feng Shui faux pas are the same as those given for the stove-visible-from-the-door problem. (Flip to Chapter 11 for more Feng Shui principles to apply to bedrooms.)

✔ **Dining room:** A visible dining room can negatively affect your eating habits and personal energy. Hang a faceted crystal sphere between the front door and the entrance to the dining room for a cure. A dining table that's directly visible from the front door creates a lack of ease and can result in eating issues. This lack of ease may also encourage guests to eat and run instead of spending quality time with you.

Entering regularly other than through the front door

Using a garage door as a regular entry can negatively affect your life, depending on the conditions in the garage. A garage that's cold, unpleasant, or obstructed, or one that has unpleasant smells, creates corresponding effects in your life. If the garage door leads directly into the kitchen, a double problem exists. Fumes and noxious chi from the garage follow you into the kitchen and can negatively affect the kitchen's energy and, in turn, the food and your health.

To perform a cure, you can always park outside and use the front door to enter your home. Doing so gives you the added benefit of creating a calmer and more peaceful home because you're no longer bringing a loud, powerful, 3,000-pound beast (your car or truck) into your home every day. If this cure isn't feasible for you, use a red ribbon cut to a multiple of 9 inches in length to hang a pleasant-sounding wind chime from the ceiling in the garage, directly in front of the entryway to the home. The sound of the chime can act as an energy filter, helping to disperse the negative chi from the garage.

Note: If you regularly enter a laundry room on your way into your home, I recommend keeping the laundry room as clean and tidy as you can to eliminate possible negative health effects.

Handling two separate doors on the front of the home

Two separate doors on the front of a home are a major source of confusion. A second door detracts energetically from the main entry and can cause career blocks, confusion, and other difficulties. To cure this situation, use the originally intended front door for entering and exiting, if possible. Mark the chosen front door with the house number and place plants on both sides of it to attract energy. Hide the second door with a large potted plant and don't use that door more than a few times a year (just to keep it functional).

Good things to see when entering a home

A view of books first thing upon entering a home fosters excellent school performance and increased intelligence. Also beneficial are positive images; scenes of nature or waterscapes; and paintings or photos of peaceful, uplifting subjects. Additional positive first impression objects are flowers, plants, and aquariums because energies of life in the space give positive input to your life energies.

Part III

Feathering the Nest: Nurturing and Nourishing Indoor Spaces

The 5th Wave — By Rich Tennant

While practicing Feng Shui in a kitchen, Dwayne, the refrigerator repairman, causes a disharmonious event within the area of his attire.

In this part . . .

This part is bulging with incredibly easy-to-follow yet highly effective ways to cure problem areas in your home's layout and in individual rooms. In it, I reveal the most desirable arrangements for each part of your home and how to fix problems that may crop up. For each feature, I supply you with practical solutions that crank up the energy of your space and help you create dramatically improved peace, satisfaction, and harmony.

I also discuss career Feng Shui in this part. Practicing Feng Shui in your office helps you balance your energy, manage your workload, and move up in your career. It can also help you bring in more cash.

Chapter 10

Reinventing Your Home's Layout

In this chapter, you examine each part of your home, as well as your home's basic structure, in Feng Shui terms. You discover what each part of your home represents, how each part influences you, how different parts relate to one another, and whether they're compatible with one another. I also show you how to analyze your floor plan and make necessary Feng Shui changes, explain the difference between the front and back halves of your home (and note what fits best in each half), and help you analyze the center of your home.

The center of your home is a very important space energetically; it's the nucleus that holds everything together. Your home's center chi especially influences your health and connects to all other parts of your life.

Looking at Your Home: Front and Back

An easy way to analyze your floor plan in terms of Feng Shui is to consider the front half and the back half of your home separately. For this exercise, you need a floor plan of your home, drawn to scale. On your plan, measure the length of the home from front to back. Then draw a line across the floor plan from left to right at the midpoint, dividing the home into front and back halves. For example, if your home measures 6 inches from front to back, draw a line dividing the home in half at the 3-inch midpoint (see Figure 10-1).

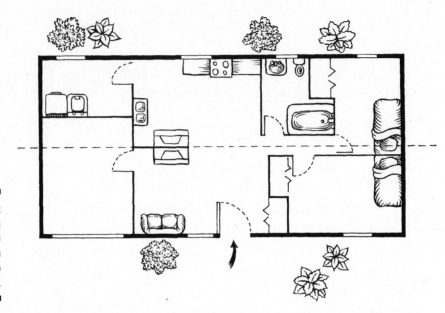

Figure 10-1:
Dividing your home in half from front to back.

The front door, found on the front side of your home, is your orientation point. Whatever's in front of the midline is in the *front half* of the home; whatever's behind the line is within the *back half* of the home. The following sections show you which rooms are best located in the front half of your home and which are best situated in the back half.

Good rooms for the front

The energy of your home enters at the front of the home through the front door. This part of the home involves movement, career, social life, and connecting with the outer world. The front half is the *yang,* or active, part of the home. The living room, family room, and den are good rooms to have located in the front of the home; their proximity to the front door enhances both your social life and family gatherings. However, these rooms are fine to have in the back of the home as well. Other rooms that are well suited in the front area include the following:

- **Office:** A home office that's close to the street can assist your career and business and help keep the office energies separate from the rest of the home.

- **Guest bedroom:** If the guest bedroom is in the front of your home, your guests won't overstay their welcome. (If the guest bedroom is in the back, they may still be there!)

✔ **Child's bedroom:** Putting an older child's bedroom in the front of the home can help him or her become independent, if that is needed change.

Good rooms for the back

The back half of the home is more naturally the *yin,* or quiet and receptive, environment; it's ideally suited for privacy, rest, serenity, and connecting with the family. Nourishing activities such as rest, relaxation, and preparing and eating food ideally occur in this half.

Pay close attention to the positions of your master bedroom, kitchen, and dining room. Ideally, these rooms should be located in the back half of the home. The closer the master bedroom or the kitchen is to your front door, the more life problems you're likely to experience.

✔ A master bedroom positioned too close to the front door can create marital disharmony, which may result in separation or divorce.

✔ A kitchen placed near the front door threatens your health and finances and may cause money to exit the home.

✔ A dining room close to the front door can lead to eating issues or other health problems.

The next sections provide a few simple cures to counteract negative effects if these rooms are located in the front of your home.

Note: If the master bed or stove sits in front of the front line of the home, then according to Feng Shui, it's located outside of the home. (The *front line* of the home is a left-to-right line drawn on your floor plan that contains the front door.) In this case, the problems mentioned in the following sections are magnified, and the cures given are even more vital.

Master bedroom

The ideal location of the master bedroom is as far back as possible from (and cater-corner to) the front door. If the bed sits in the front of the home, sleep can be disturbed, and the marriage can suffer.

You can cure the negative effects of a master bedroom located in the front of your home by placing a sizable mirror (at least the width of the bed, if possible; larger is even better) directly in line with the bed. Ideally, this mirror is in the same room as the bed and is positioned farther back in the home than the bed. The mirror symbolically and energetically pulls the bed to a better position — the rear of the home (see Figure 10-2 for an example). Just make sure the top of the mirror is higher than the top of the tallest resident's head.

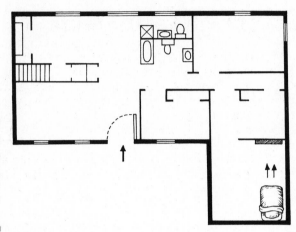

Figure 10-2:
Mirror cure
for bed (or
stove) in the
front of the
home.

Kitchen

A kitchen in the front half of the home is a Feng Shui liability, and a kitchen that's easily visible or accessible from the front door has the worst effects. Why? Because the stove's energy is easily disturbed and energetically overwhelmed by the active, stimulating energies of the front — a situation that can lead to loss of money, health problems, or even sudden negative events.

To cure this situation, perform the mirror cure I mention in the preceding section (refer to Figure 10-2) to energetically pull the stove farther back in the home. If that's not feasible, cut a red ribbon to a multiple of 9 inches in length and hang a faceted crystal sphere from it over the stove.

Dining room

A dining room in the front half of the home can generate problems, though of a lesser and more social nature than those caused by a master bedroom or kitchen in the front half of the home. Visitors may tend to eat lots of food and quickly leave or stay too long.

To cure a front dining room, hang a large faceted crystal sphere (at least 2 inches in diameter) from a red ribbon above the dining room table. Note that the ribbon should be cut to a multiple of 9 inches in length.

Finding the Center of Your Home

The most important part of your home after the front door is the center. This is the solar plexus of the home where chi is stored. The energy here dramatically influences your health and radiates out into every part of your life. All action and energy pass through and depend on the center of your home, like the hub of a wheel. This principle holds true even if you rarely spend time in the center — even if it's a closet.

In the following sections, I describe the center's importance and ideal energy condition, explain what works best in the center, and show you how to cure problematic rooms in this part of your home.

Recognizing the importance of the center

The following four characteristics make the center stand out from all the other parts of the home:

- **The center energetically connects to and interrelates with all other parts of the home.** The center affects and is affected by every area.

- **The center affects your health and well-being.** Good health and physical vitality allow you to achieve your fullest potential. If your health suffers, every part of your life suffers as well. To keep your life in balance, take a look at the center of your home.

- **The center affects every aspect of your life.** If you want to create overall life improvement, start at the center. Cures performed in the center spread energy outward to other areas. By the same token, if your home needs lots of Feng Shui work but multiple cures are beyond your budget, a single effective cure in the center can help you turn things around.

- **The center of the home can even make you centered.** Are you at your wit's end? A cure in the center can help put things right by getting you centered.

Knowing the ideal energy condition of the center

Ideally, the center of the home should be open, airy, free, bright, uplifting, and pleasant. It should never be stuffy, dark, cramped, dull, or oppressive. The best room for the center is a living room, family room, den, or study.

Figuring out what's good in the center

Because the center of the home connects to all aspects of your life, performing cures in the center can energize you and create various positive life benefits. The following cures can help enhance the center's effects on your life in multiple ways:

- ✔ **Attract vital energy with plants.** Placing fresh, healthy green plants in the center of the home is a great all-around life cure. One plant is good, but two or three (or more) is better.

   Odd (or yang) numbers are inherently more active than even (or yin) numbers. So an odd number of plants (three, five, seven, and so on) can create more activity and change than an even number.

- ✔ **Display the color of health.** Yellow is the color of health. For an excellent cure, place yellow objects in your home's center or paint the walls in the area shades of yellow or gold. (See Chapter 15 for more details on color.)

- ✔ **Apply a special life cure.** If you're experiencing problems and really need relief, you can perform the all-purpose "save me!" cure. Using a red ribbon cut to a multiple of 9 inches in length, hang a faceted crystal sphere in the center of your home.

Curing troublesome central areas

Three types of rooms create problems in the center: bathrooms, bedrooms, and kitchens.

- ✔ A bathroom drains the vital energy of the center, harming everything at once.

- ✔ A bedroom in the center poses a problem because the powerful energies of the center threaten the peace and safety of the bed.

- ✔ A kitchen in the center is problematic because the strong, fiery chi of the stove adds too much intensity to the already highly active center area, posing health risks.

A spiral staircase in the center of a home is also a problem. Spiral stairs positioned in the center can lead to a downfall in health or any other part of life.

If building a fully compatible Feng Shui dream home isn't an option for you, check out the easy-to-follow cures I present in the next sections for help calming pesky negative energies in your home's center.

A bathroom

According to Feng Shui, a bathroom in the center of the home can bring about multiple adverse life effects. Bathrooms symbolize draining and loss — energy going down the drain. So a central bathroom can generate negative health, loss of money, and general life troubles. It's no coincidence that the phrase "taking a bath" is used to describe financial catastrophe.

For this situation, I suggest you apply two cures, one for the exterior and one for the interior of the bathroom.

- ✔ **Exterior cure:** Add a full-length mirror on the outside of the door (see Chapter 13 for details) and keep the door closed.

- ✔ **Interior cure:** Fully mirror all four interior walls of the bathroom. The four-mirrored-walls solution powerfully transforms the negative influence of a central bathroom. (An added bonus? You'll never feel lonely on the toilet again!) As with all cures, strongly visualize your desired life results materializing while you perform this cure.

  If mirroring the walls isn't possible, an alternate cure is to hang four bamboo Feng Shui flutes in the bathroom. Hang the flutes vertically, one in each corner of the bathroom. (Turn to the appendix for a good flute source.)

Make sure the short sections of your flutes are pointing toward the floor and the longer sections are nearer to the ceiling. The top of each flute should hang at the eye level (or higher) of the tallest person in the home. (Flip to Chapter 4 for flute tips.)

A master bedroom

A master bedroom in the center of the home can cause havoc and confusion. The center's active, vital energies can disturb your sleep, peace of mind, marriage, and wealth. The mirror solution, shown in Figure 10-2, restores the balance of a centrally positioned master bedroom. Simply place the mirror in the room (farther toward the back of the house than the bed is), and visualize the bed pulled back to a safe position. (***Note:*** Children's bedrooms are also unadvised in the center of the home; you can apply the same cure.)

If you can't perform the mirror cure, hang a wind chime in the center of the bedroom to calm and harmonize the room's energy. This cure is slightly less powerful than the mirror cure, yet it still substantially improves the situation.

A kitchen

A kitchen located in the center of the home creates vulnerability to accidents, major health problems, or even fires in the home. The mirror cure works wonders in this situation (refer to Figure 10-2). For an alternative cure, hang a large faceted crystal sphere (2 inches or larger in diameter) above the cook's standing position at the stove or in the center of the kitchen. The sphere harmonizes and balances the chi of the stove and the center, promoting better luck and health. Also make sure the rest of the kitchen follows Feng Shui principles; I share these in Chapter 12.

A spiral staircase

A spiral staircase acts like a corkscrew boring down into the Earth. Downward-spiraling energy in the center of your home can provoke a downward trend in your finances, health, and life fortunes. The antidote is to create upward, rising chi, so an appropriate cure is one that draws energy upward. I recommend these two solutions (apply both of them at once for a double whammy of a cure):

- ✔ Wrap a realistic-looking green silk vine around the banister from the bottom to the top.
- ✔ Hang a faceted crystal sphere from the ceiling above the center of the staircase using a red ribbon cut to a multiple of 9 inches in length.

Head to Chapter 14 for additional staircase principles and cures.

Addressing Neighboring Rooms

The two most vital rooms in a home are the master bedroom and the kitchen. Not to downplay the importance of your kids' rooms, but the master bedroom empowers the parents who literally and energetically feed the children. Therefore, the location of these two rooms affects the overall life and fortune of the home's occupants.

The bedroom and kitchen contain the all-important bed and stove, which create, nurture, and give life to the household. Ideally, the kitchen and master bedroom shouldn't be located near each other because the energies of the bed and stove can conflict if they're too close. If the bed and stove are positioned back-to-back on a common wall, or if the doors of these two rooms directly face each other, your marriage and/or health can suffer.

In addition, neither the bed nor the stove should sit near a toilet. Conflicts involving any combination of these three features can lead to serious problems in the corresponding Life Areas of the Feng Shui Octagon (see Chapter 3 for details on the Life Areas and the Octagon). If these scenarios define your home environment, apply the cures in the sections that follow and be sure to check out Chapters 11, 12, and 13 to make sure the affected spaces completely align with Feng Shui principles.

Toilet/stove and toilet/bed wall connections

A toilet shouldn't be positioned directly back-to-back on a common wall with a stove or a bed because the repetitive influence of the toilet flushing sucks life-force energy from either one.

- ✔ Potential toilet/stove consequences range from digestive problems to loss of wealth to serious illness or accidents.

- ✔ Toilet/bed consequences include not only these problems but also the possibility of divorce or even loss of life. (If the sink sits on the wall behind the bed, the same problems may arise, though not as severe.)

To cure the toilet/stove situation, install a mirror on the kitchen wall behind the stove. Make sure the mirror is the same width as the stove and that it extends from the floor to at least the top of the stove or up to the bottom of the cabinet above the stove. Also, check that the reflective surface of the mirror is facing the stove.

For the toilet/bed situation, place a mirror on the wall behind the bed, running from the floor to at least the top of the headboard (see Figure 10-3). The mirror width should equal the width of the bed, and the shiny side should face the bed. If you don't have a headboard, the mirror can come up to the top of the mattress. When you perform this cure visualize peace, safety, and good health in order to maximize results.

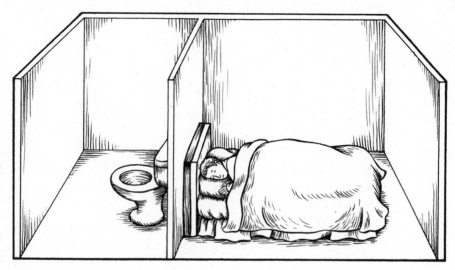

Figure 10-3:
Cure for bed and toilet on a common wall.

A toilet located on the floor above and directly over a bed or stove can also mean potential disaster. (Take a moment to visualize a toilet flushing in either scenario and it becomes obvious.) To cure this situation, fix a small, round mirror on the ceiling above the sleepers' heads or above the stove and directly under the toilet, with the shiny side facing down. An alternative or additional cure is to hang a faceted crystal sphere and/or a metal wind chime from a red ribbon (cut to a multiple of 9 inches in length) directly over the sleepers' heads or over the cooktop.

Note: In an apartment building, a toilet located on the floor directly above your bed or stove causes the same negative effects, even if the toilet is located in another apartment. I recommend applying the previous toilet cures to this situation.

Stove/bed wall connection

If the stove and bed are directly back-to-back on a common wall, the potential problems are similar to the ones I describe in the preceding section. The solution is virtually the same: Install a mirror behind the bed with the reflective side facing the bed.

Curing Opposing Doors

Doorways of any two of these rooms — the kitchen, master bedroom, and bathroom — shouldn't face each other. You also have an issue if your front door is in line with your back door. The sections that follow explain the potential pitfalls and cures for incompatible doors.

A bathroom door opposite the master bedroom door or kitchen door

A bathroom door across from the bedroom door or kitchen entryway can stimulate stomach and intestinal problems. It can also result in depressed or negative states of mind. The situation worsens if the bathroom door is inside the kitchen or bedroom, or if the bathroom door facing the kitchen is larger than the kitchen door. And if you can see the toilet from either the cook's standing position or the bed, watch out!

For any of these situations, you can apply the following cure package:

✓ **Always keep the bathroom door closed.** This one's easy, basic, and foolproof.

✓ **Install a full-length mirror on the outside of the bathroom door.** This cure works only if you keep the bathroom door closed.

✓ **Hang a faceted crystal sphere midway between the two opposing doors.** Hang it from a ribbon that has been cut in 9-inch increments.

Bathrooms inside of bedrooms have their own Feng Shui issues; I cover bathroom/bedroom situations in Chapter 11.

A kitchen door opposite a bedroom door

Potential problems abound when the kitchen door directly opposes the bedroom door. Because you must always head toward the kitchen as you leave the bedroom, the sight of the kitchen influences you to overeat. Consequences include weight gain and digestive problems. Also, the fiery chi of the stove can overheat the marriage or relationship, creating arguments and discord. If you can see the stove from the bedroom, the problems get worse.

You can disperse these conflicting energies by hanging a wind chime halfway between the bed and the stove. The healing sounds and energy of the wind chime diffuse and harmonize the energies, creating peace and abundance. As an alternative cure, you can place new and healthy green plants on either side of the doorway.

The back door in line with the front door

Another troublesome Feng Shui situation arises when your home's back door sits in line with its front door. The situation exists when the back door is visible from the front door and in its direct path. Why? Because the front door is the energetic mouth of the home, called the *Mouth of Chi* (see Chapter 9 for more). For good energy flow, the vital, natural energy needs to enter through the front door and circulate throughout the home. If the back door sits directly in line with the front door, this vital energy can exit straight out, resulting in a significant loss of household income, wealth, health, and more.

Remedies for this situation include placing a screen or other object between the two doors to visually block the path between them, if practicality and your floor plan permit. If they don't, you can hang a wind chime halfway between the two doors. As an alternative to the wind chime, you can hang a faceted crystal sphere in the same location to diffuse the chi of the front door throughout the home and prevent its needless and harmful loss (see Figure 10-4).

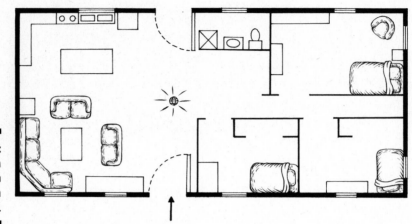

Figure 10-4:
Cure for a
back door in
line with a
front door.

Chapter 11

Maximizing Results in the Bedroom

This chapter covers the second Life Pillar — the all-important master bed — and its surroundings — the master bedroom. The bed exists as a foundation for rest, health, and relationships or marriage. In this chapter, I present a wealth of principles and pointers that, when you apply them correctly, can lead to tangible and powerful improvements in many parts of your life. (For an overview of the Life Pillars, see Chapter 2.) This chapter sets forth the ideal Feng Shui conditions for the bedroom, explains how deviating from these ideals can create life problems, and gives you practical solutions for curing the deviations.

The master bedroom — the most critical room in the home — nourishes the chi of the adults. And the energy of the adults, in turn, feeds the children. If the chi of the adults suffers, so can the energy of the children. This situation makes the condition of the master bedroom important for the welfare of everyone in the home.

Note: You can apply many of the principles in this chapter to other bedrooms besides the master one. For information on children's bedrooms specifically, turn to Chapter 13.

Putting Your Bed in the Commanding Position with Four Important Principles

Feng Shui involves many principles for the *auspicious* (favorable) positioning of your bed. To take advantage of as many of them as you can, use common sense along with the conditions of your individual room to make the best choices possible. In the following sections, I explain the four principles that make up the Commanding Position concept (introduced in Chapter 2) for bed placement. This principle shows you how to achieve the most powerful bed position according to Grandmaster Lin Yun's Feng Shui school. If you see that your bed position doesn't meet all four criteria, don't panic. Just keep reading. I show you cures you can implement to dramatically enhance your health, wealth, and love life.

Note: The Commanding Position concept states that the position of the bed relative to the bedroom door rates more importantly than the compass direction the bed faces. So you don't have to consider whether your bed faces east, west, north, or south. (Grandmaster Lin Yun's Feng Shui school doesn't use compass directions at all, but it does respect and honor this method.) Simply position the bed according to the way it best relates to the other main feature of the room — the door.

Whenever you alter the bed or its position, always handle the bed softly, gently, carefully, and respectfully. Banging or harshly disturbing your bed while moving it can create intense negative chi for the occupants of the bed, which can in turn lead to possible fights in the family. This commotion proves particularly harmful if the sleeper is a pregnant woman. For optimal health of both the mother and the unborn baby, don't move the bed at all during the pregnancy.

Commanding Position Principle One: Situating the bed far from the door

The first Commanding Position principle holds that the bed should sit as far from the bedroom door as possible (see Figure 11-1 for examples). The farther your bed sits from the door, the more control you can feel over your space and your life. You aren't startled as easily, and you have plenty of time to prepare for events as they unfold.

- ✔ If the door is on the left, the best position for the bed is the far-right corner of the room.

- ✔ If the door is on the right, the best bed location is the far-left corner of the room.

- ✔ If the door is centered, the best spot for the bed is either the far-right or far-left corner of the room.

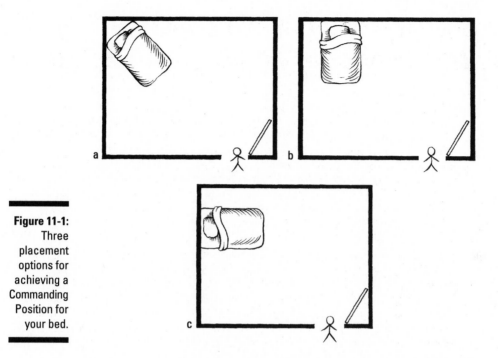

Figure 11-1:
Three placement options for achieving a Commanding Position for your bed.

Commanding Position Principle Two: Widening the sleeper's scope of vision

The second Commanding Position principle asserts that the bed position should allow the sleeper the widest possible scope of vision in the room. A diminished range of sight can restrict the sleeper's chi and life vision.

The larger the space in front of your bed, the more your life expands, breathes, and improves. For this reason, Feng Shui cautions against placing the foot of the bed against a wall, which can block your career and cause foot and ankle problems. As for placing the side of your bed directly against a side wall, although this isn't a negative factor, some people find greater freedom in life if they can enter or leave the bed from either side (others feel more secure with a little space between the wall and the side of the bed).

Commanding Position Principle Three: Ensuring bedroom door visibility

The third Commanding Position principle states that you should be able to clearly see the bedroom door from the bed. This concept means that when lying on your back in bed — that is, in the center of the bed if you sleep alone or on your side of the bed if you sleep with a partner — you can open your eyes and immediately see the door of the room without repositioning your body. If you have to perform gymnastics or create new yoga positions to see who or what is coming in the door, your bed position doesn't meet this principle.

Not being able to see who's approaching can keep you uncertain and on edge. Even if you think you're accustomed to not seeing the door, you likely still experience ongoing subconscious stress, which can create imbalance and frustration. The possibility of always being startled can keep you on edge. Over time, this continual tension and unrest can cause an imbalance in the nervous system. Results can include nervous problems (think Uncle Fester from *The Addams Family*), arrhythmia, and heart palpitations. In addition, constantly twisting around to see who's approaching you can cause neck and spinal problems in the long run.

If your bed position doesn't allow you to see the bedroom door and you can't move the bed to get a better view, place a sizable mirror opposite the bed. For this cure to be effective, the mirror must allow you to clearly see the door's reflection and anyone standing in the doorway while you're lying in bed (see Figure 11-2c, later in this chapter, for a depiction of this cure). If you need to angle the mirror to show the door, you may choose a standing mirror that's angled to the appropriate position.

Commanding Position Principle Four: Keeping the bed out of the door's path

The fourth Commanding Position principle holds that the bed shouldn't sit in the direct line of the path of the doorway. If your bed does sit fully or partially in the direct line of the door, the chi of the door runs over the bed, which can create physical problems with the associated body parts.

Putting all the principles together

To sum up the Commanding Position concept — as it relates to your bed, that is — the farther you sleep from the door and the more of the room you see while in bed, the more you can feel in control of your environment and, therefore, your life. Seeing the door to your bedroom symbolizes that you know what life is bringing and feel prepared to deal with whatever comes. You're in command, and the results manifest themselves positively in many parts of your life.

Note: As always when you perform Feng Shui, you achieve best results when you observe all the relevant factors and consider them as a whole. You derive the optimal situation not only by achieving the Commanding Position for your bed but also by doing so in the context of all the other bedroom Feng Shui tips you find in this chapter.

When following the Commanding Position principle, you can choose from three alternatives for good bed placement. (Refer to Figure 11-1.)

✔ Position 11-1a (the bed angled in the corner) is the strongest choice of all because it gains support from two walls rather than one. If you choose this position, I recommend that your bed feature a solid headboard (see the later "Improving the Power of Your Bed" section for more on this concept). Make sure the corners of the bed firmly touch the walls.

You can strengthen this bed position even further by placing a plant and a light behind the headboard. A real or artificial plant works for this cure. As for the light, it should be in good working order, but it doesn't need to be on at all times.

✔ Positions 11-1b (bed against the upper wall of the room) and 11-1c (bed against the left wall of the room) are both excellent; just be sure, if possible, to leave enough room on the side closest to the wall for your partner (or yourself) to get into bed.

Exploring Additional Bed Positioning Secrets

Before considering other options, I always recommend that your master bed be placed in a position that conforms to the Commanding Position guidelines I outline earlier in this chapter. If you can't move your bed to a better position, check out the following cures, which can help your bed position and can even improve your relationship, health, and wealth.

Use your common sense to do the best you can in your situation. Often, following every Feng Shui pointer at once proves impossible; the trick is to adhere to as many of them as you can.

Recruiting the power of the mountain

Positioning the head of your bed against a solid wall — your symbolic mountain — provides you with a strong sense of support, safety, and protection. (Figure 11-1a, earlier in this chapter, follows this principle because the two top corners of the bed touch the walls.) If the head of the bed stands free in the room (not against any wall), your life and career tend to lack support. This position — for either the parents' or the children's bed — can also influence the children to do poorly in school and, in general, not receive strong parental support.

The easiest cure for recruiting the power of the mountain is to push the head of the bed against a wall. If your bed already sits on a wall, check to see whether it physically touches the wall. You don't want any space between the headboard and the wall; even a 1-inch gap can reduce your security, cause mental strain, and negatively affect your dreams and sleep.

Ideally, you shouldn't position the head of your bed against a window. The opening in the wall weakens the support of the mountain and can create health-challenging drafts during sleep. If a window must be positioned over the bed, cover the window with a drape or curtain. The best curtain gives you the visual illusion of a solid wall. For added strength, hang a faceted crystal sphere in the window.

If a door stands behind your bed, the problem is significantly worsened. The best solution is to move the bed away from the door (if, of course, you can find a better position). If that isn't possible, cover the door and hang a wind chime over the head of the bed to disperse and diffuse any harmful chi coming from the door.

Addressing a bed in the path of the door

If the straight-ahead path of any doorway in your bedroom — particularly the main door to the room — runs across the bed, you can encounter physical problems in the body parts in which the energy path crosses (see Figure 11-2b in the next section.) For example, if the energy runs directly across your heart and stomach, you can experience digestive problems or even heart conditions.

The worst version of this problem occurs if your feet or head point straight out the door (see Figure 11-2a in the next section). In this position, you lie in the "coffin ready to be carried out" bed position, a colorful Feng Shui metaphor that alerts you to the dangers of this placement.

To cure this situation, move the bed to the optimal Commanding Position in your room. If doing so is impossible, hang a metal wind chime halfway between the door and the bed. The sound of the chime deflects the onrushing chi of the door and creates safety and relief. Another option is to hang a large faceted crystal sphere (50 millimeters in diameter or larger) by itself or in combination with the wind chime.

Selecting cures for problematic bed situations

The best way to cure problematic bed positioning is simply to place your bed in the Commanding Position, as I explain earlier in this chapter. But what if this cure isn't reasonable? Maybe the builder of your home forgot to cooperate with your Feng Shui goals, and you want to make the best of what's available. The following three situations, shown in Figure 11-2, give you a good idea of common bed-positioning problems along with cures for each one.

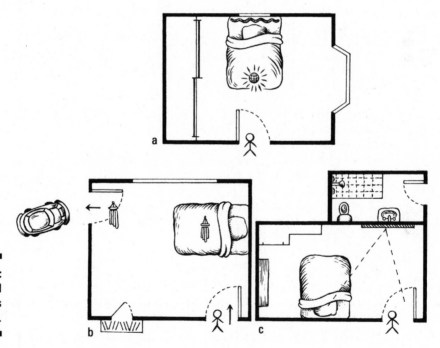

Figure 11-2: Problem bed positions with cures.

Curing the coffin position

Figure 11-2a shows you how to perform cures to make a tough bed position better. In this situation, the bed lies in the dreaded coffin position. The incoming energy from the door can create health problems along the midline of the body and can split the relationship. Moving the bed significantly is difficult because of the closet door on the left as well as the large bay window on the right.

I recommend hanging a faceted crystal sphere over the foot of the bed to disperse the oncoming energy from the door to protect the sleeper. Then hang a solid curtain over the smaller window behind the bed. The curtain makes the wall more solid and gives more support to the sleeper.

Fixing the exterior door

In Figure 11-2b, the outside door and huge window make it impossible to place the bed in the Commanding Position (the upper-left corner of the room). Also, the location of the door in the Wealth Area (see Chapter 3 for details on this and other Life Areas of the Feng Shui Octagon) implies the possible loss of money. The situation worsens because a car parked right outside threatens the bed and sleeper. (Also, the closet prevents the bed from being placed in the lower-left corner of the room.) The outside door can be cured with a wind chime; the sound of the chime disperses the attacking chi and helps retain the wealth energy within the room.

However, this bed position involves another problem: The energy from the bedroom door runs right across the sleeper's body and can create health problems in the torso (heart, stomach, and so on). Hang a wind chime or faceted crystal sphere halfway between the bedroom door and the bed (or over the bed) to cure this problem, or place a bamboo Feng Shui flute (see Chapter 4 for more on this cure item) over the door on the inside wall.

Showing me the door!

Figure 11-2c details another tough bed situation. Built-in furniture on the left side of the room prevents placing the bed in the ideal position — along the left wall. The bed can't be placed on the top bedroom wall (the uppermost one in the diagram) because this position shares a wall with the toilet and sink. The remaining available position is on the bottom wall of the room, which makes the door invisible to the sleeper. The cure for this situation is simple and effective: Place a mirror on the wall across from the sleeper so the door is visible from the bed.

Quick tips for helping your bedroom problems

Check out the following methods for improving your bedroom and your life:

✔ **Fixing clashing doors:** If one door hits another door in the bedroom, arguments can ensue. Cure this situation by hanging bright-red drapery tassels from each knob on the clashing sides of the doors.

✔ **Curing a slanted ceiling in the bedroom or a beam over the bed:** This situation can bring insomnia and unfortunate mental and physical pressures to the bed's occupants. Cure it by hanging a faceted crystal sphere from the slanted ceiling or beam. Be sure to hang the crystal from a red ribbon cut to a multiple of 9 inches in length. (Flip to Chapter 14 for additional ceiling and beam cures.)

For information on colors and lighting in the bedroom, check out Chapter 15.

Recognizing the Critical Importance of a Good Bed

In addition to the bed position and the ways in which the master bedroom's features relate to the bed, the nature and condition of the bed itself is also vital, as you find out in the following sections.

New versus used beds

For positive Feng Shui of the bed, the first criterion is the energetic condition and origin of the bed itself. A new bed contains fresh, unblemished energy that supports health and vitality. A used bed (one that comes from someone else and not new from a store) can be a strong recipe for experiencing sexual problems, a lack of energy, and mysterious illnesses. This principle encompasses all parts of the bed: the mattress, the box spring, and the frame. And it applies even if you sleep on an antique bed that you really love and don't want to part with.

In a used bed, previous owners leave subtle energetic impressions; the bed can retain emotions, events, sexual energy, and sickness. So Feng Shui offers one word of advice about sleeping on a used bed: Don't. If you currently sleep on a used bed, I recommend getting a new one. The worst bed to inherit is one that belonged to someone who just passed over to the next plane — and I don't mean airplane. If getting a new bed is impossible right now, you can improve the situation by performing the Citrus Water Blessing ceremony on the bed in the meantime (see Chapter 21 for details on this cure).

Good times to get a new bed

Feng Shui advises that you consider getting a new bed, including the frame, mattress, box spring, and bedding (sheets, pillows, pillowcases, and so on) when any of the following events occur:

- ✔ **The person you share the bed with dies:** A new bed can help you cope and keep you from living in the past.

- ✔ **A relationship ends:** Getting a new bed helps clear the old energy and bring in the new.

- ✔ **Anyone using the bed experiences a major sickness:** A new bed supports your health and protects you from illness.

- ✔ **You move into a new home:** This cure puts old energy behind you if making a fresh start is important to you.

✔ **You get married:** In this situation, the new bed symbolizes a fresh and powerful new start.

✔ **Someone steals your bed:** This one's a real no-brainer.

If you can't afford a new bed, a substitute option is to change the mattress or even just the bedding.

Types of beds

You can fix a myriad of Feng Shui glitches in the following bed situations:

✔ **King-sized beds:** A king-sized bed can induce a split in the marriage or partnership if the box spring of the bed comes in two pieces. The separate pieces create a physical division within the bed — an energetic inducement for one partner to saddle up and flee the scene. The secret cure for this situation is to place a bright-red cloth that's the full size of the bed between the mattress and the box spring.

✔ **Storing things under the bed:** Stuff stored under the bed can stifle your creativity and induce blocks and stagnation in your energy. Not exactly a barrel of laughs (or monkeys). Large piles of stuff under the bed can also energetically hamper you if you're trying to conceive. The cure is simple: Get the stuff out!

✔ **Beds with drawers:** Beds with drawers underneath the sleepers can confuse all parties involved. One cure is simply to leave the drawers empty. If you must use them, put only items concerning the bed and sleep inside, such as blankets, sheets, and pajamas. Books, guns and ammo, tax records, and other unrelated items (think hot photos of ex-lovers, divorce documents, pints of whisky) definitely aren't recommended.

✔ **Too-high or too-low beds:** A bed that's positioned too high or too low can throw off your energy patterns. If the bed sits too high to get into easily, it can block your chances of attracting a mate. I once had a client who positioned her bed so high that she had to use a small stepladder to get into the bed. Her complaint was that she couldn't find a relationship; I explained that it was because of the small population of pole-vaulters in her town. When she started sleeping on a bed of a more reasonable height, she rested easier and found more prospects in her romantic life.

On the other hand, a bed sitting on the floor (or only a few inches off the floor) can symbolically keep you low in life, making receiving and keeping money more difficult. A bed that stands on actual feet supports you better energetically than one that sits on the floor.

✔ **Metal-frame beds:** A metal-frame bed can surround your body with a distorting magnetic field while you sleep. Wood frames, if possible, work better. Beds made from metal tubing (and mattresses and box springs containing metal coils) can create an unwelcome magnetic field around the body and don't have the insulating quality of wood.

✔ **Beds with built-in entertainment units or bookshelves:** Beds with built-in entertainment units, bookshelves behind the sleeper, and other kinds of large, multipiece bed units aren't recommended. Huge and heavy, these beds typically tower over the sleeper, and their shelves and cubby spaces can hold many sleep-stealing distractions. Many of these units leave an open space behind the sleeper's head — as with bookshelves behind the head of the bed — which can lead to insomnia, fitful sleep, or negative dreams. The best situation occurs when the sleeper's head lies next to the wall or headboard.

✔ **Beds that have something rising above the foot of the bed:** Ideally, your bed should hold nothing above the mattress's surface at your feet — this principle includes chests, plants, and other items. Anything that rises above the foot of the bed blocks you and your progress. For example:

  • A bed with a footboard rising above the top of the mattress can block your travel and hamper your career and future.

  • If the footboard is in the form of bars (such as the footrails on a brass bed), this can foreshadow legal troubles or even jail time (or, at the least, a fondness for really large tattoos.)

  • Sleigh beds have two issues at once: a headboard and footboard that curve toward the sleeper as well as a footboard that rises high above the mattress. This entire setup can create compression on the sleeper, causing partners to feel trapped and making one or both partners want to leave.

To cure something rising above the foot of the bed, you can either buy a new bed or replace the too-high footboard with one that's even with or lower than the top of the mattress. However, you can attract bad luck by unduly disturbing the tranquility of the bed through hammering, sawing, or using power tools on a footboard (or any other part of the bed) that's still attached to the bed. Gently remove the piece to be modified, have it corrected (or replaced, ideally), and then gently put the piece back in place.

✔ **Folding beds:** These beds include Murphy beds (which fold up into cabinets), sleeper sofas (where the bed folds out from the couch), and pull-down beds (the kind that fold up into the wall when not in use). All folding beds make the sleeper feel temporary, ungrounded, and not at home — even if left down all the time. (One plus for having a Murphy bed in your guest bedroom? It helps ensure guests don't overstay their welcome — especially if you accidentally fold it into the wall while they sleep!) The cure for folding beds is pretty straightforward: Replace them with a regular bed that has positive Feng Shui aspects.

✔ **Waterbeds:** A waterbed provides anything but a firm foundation for life, sleep, and success. The swaying and rocking motion may be comfortable, but you sacrifice security, groundedness, and career stability. The fix for this situation is simple: Get a solid bed.

Improving the Power of Your Bed

All aspects of your bed affect your chi, which is why the following tips give you additional areas that you can improve for greater health and comfort:

✔ **Use a strong headboard to help your career, marriage, and overall stability.** A headboard on the bed can help make you stronger in general and promote growth in your career and solidity in your relationship. The headboard should attach firmly to the bed (meaning when you grab the headboard and try to wiggle it with your hand, it shouldn't move). A headboard that feels loose or, worse, is separate from the bed (that is, one that stands on the floor behind the bed) weakens the occupants.

The best type of headboard is solid — made of one piece without major gaps or holes. The worst headboard is made of bars, which symbolically look like prison bars and can lead to legal trouble; the cure for this type of headboard is to replace it with a solid version. If you can't replace the bars right away, a great curing method is to wrap them with realistic-looking green silk vines. The positive symbology of new life energy helps negate the negative symbology of the bars.

✔ **Color your bed for vitality.** Your bedsheets and/or blanket colors can help you create specific results based on your intentions. For instance, pink and peach sheets attract love and romance, and red sheets spark passion and sizzle — but take them off if things get too hot to handle! Green sheets are good for health, healing, money, and new growth. Yellow represents another great healing color for bedsheets. (Try to avoid very dark or black bedsheets.)

✔ **Avoid sweeping underneath when trying to conceive.** Chinese energetic theory holds that as a woman attempts to conceive, the energy representing the new baby first coalesces underneath the bed. When the conditions are right, the fetal energy moves up into the woman's body, and she becomes pregnant. Therefore, the stability and security of and around the bed are paramount. Folklore beliefs hold that sweeping or cleaning under the bed while trying to conceive can help prevent conception. Also, avoid beds on wheels that can easily move around. If you have this type of bed, you have three options: Get a new bed before the pregnancy (this option is probably the best), replace the wheels with fixed feet, or adjust the wheels so they don't move.

Placing Your Master Bedroom in a Powerful Position

The welfare of the entire household rests in large part on the placement, condition, and energy of the master bedroom. Consequently, you need to consider the location of this bedroom in your floor plan. The following sections help you get the process started, but be sure to check out Chapter 10 for additional key issues regarding bedroom placement in the home.

Recognizing ideal bedroom location using the Commanding Position

The ideal placement of the master bedroom is in the Commanding Position of the home (head to Chapter 2 for an introduction to the Commanding Position). This principle says that the best place for the bedroom is at the back of the home and as far from the front door as possible. The front half of the home is less favorable for the bedroom because this area is closer to the active energy of the street. The back half of the home is generally quieter, more peaceful, and (most importantly) better protected.

Commanding Position areas of the home usually lie cater-cornered to the front door of the home. When assessing the following door positions, you orient from outside the front of your home looking inward (look to Figure 11-3 for a visual of the Commanding Position areas of the home for best bedroom placement):

- For a front door on the left, the Commanding Position lies in the back right.

- For a front door on the right, the Commanding Position sits in the back left.

- For a center door, the Commanding Position is either to the back left or back right.

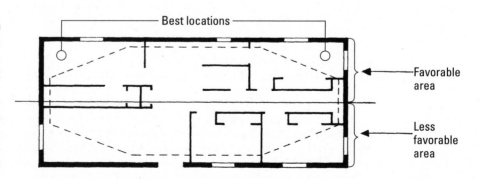

Figure 11-3: Commanding Position areas for the bedroom within the home floor plan.

Rescuing a bedroom over the garage

An increasing number of people sleep in master bedrooms that are located over the garage. This is an unfortunate Feng Shui placement for several reasons. For one, 80 percent of modern garages are located toward the front of the home, which automatically places this type of master bedroom in an undesirable location. Moreover, this location separates the bedroom from the vital grounding energy of the Earth and leaves you sleeping over an energetically colder, emptier space. The garage feels colder, messier, and less friendly than the rest of the home, and it drains chi and warmth from the bedroom.

Another negative influence is the car within the garage. The chaotic, noisy energy of the car tends to disturb the tranquility of the bedroom; in addition, exhaust fumes inevitably find their way up into the bedroom and can negatively affect the respiratory systems, as well as the overall health, of the occupants.

One cure for this situation is to move to another bedroom, although I recommend you undertake this cure only if you can properly assess all the bedroom options in your home according to Feng Shui principles. An alternate solution involves using the symbolic energy of trees to help ground and stabilize the energy of the room. Under the bedroom and inside the garage (preferably, but not necessarily, under the bed), paint a large tree with brown roots that appear to go down onto the garage floor and a large powerful trunk that rises up the garage wall. The branches of the tree should bear a multitude of healthy green leaves and extend far up onto the garage ceiling, where they can flourish into an abundance of fruits and flowers (see Figure 11-4 for an example).

You can perform a variation of this cure by decorating the bedroom with the same colors as the tree. Paint the walls of the bedroom healthy shades of green and install carpet or flooring in brown or earth tones. Also, have the upper parts of your walls and your ceiling feature many flowers and fruits in multiple friendly colors.

For an alternative or additional cure to the previous methods, you can place lively green plants in the bedroom to stimulate more nourishing, living chi.

Protecting a bedroom threatened by a car

Cars that pull into an attached garage (or park directly outside of the home) and point toward the bed on the other side of the wall may energetically threaten the health and welfare of the sleepers. Over time, the continuous possibility that the car may come through the wall and harm the sleeper can negatively affect the sleeper's energy. One of my client's teenage daughters inadvertently drove the family car through the garage wall into the home. (A quick thinker, she claimed to be starting some impromptu remodeling!) If the bedroom had been located on the other side of the wall, an expensive accident may have otherwise resulted in a tragedy.

To protect yourself in this situation, you can choose from two cure options:

- ✔ **Hang a large mirror facing into the room on the bedroom wall that's nearest the offending car.** The mirror expands the bedroom and symbolically pushes the wall and car far away.
- ✔ **Hang a metal wind chime in the garage between the front of the car and the common wall.** The chime diffuses the chi of the car and reduces the subconscious threat to the sleeper.

Figure 11-4:
Tree-painted-on-wall cure for a bedroom over a garage.

Considering Your Bedroom's Shape and Layout

The best shapes for bedrooms are squares or rectangles. If your bedroom is irregularly or oddly shaped, consult Chapter 8 for the appropriate cures. The next sections deal with issues that affect the shape and layout of your bedroom.

Positioning the Octagon

The Octagon is a basic Feng Shui mapping tool, which I explain in Chapter 3. It shows you which parts of your bedroom constitute each of its nine Life Areas. Apply the Octagon to your master bedroom the same way you apply it to your yard or home. (See Figure 11-5 for a reference.)

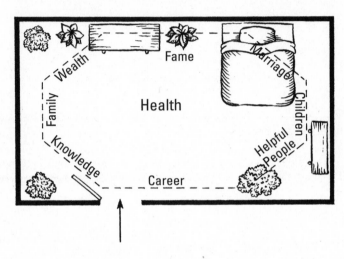

Figure 11-5:
Feng Shui Octagon placed on the bedroom to show the nine Life Areas.

After you position the Octagon, you can analyze your bedroom to determine the situation of each of the Life Areas. Then you can use the cures and principles within this chapter to correct any defects you find. For example, if you have a missing area in the Marriage Area of your bedroom, your marriage can experience unnecessary stresses and problems. To improve your marriage, you can perform a cure by hanging a mirror to expand the Marriage Area.

Dealing with doors and windows

The ideal master bedroom contains only one door (excluding closet doors); this door is the main entrance to the room. Multiple doors or doorways mean additional energy flows in the room, which can distract you from rest and increase your vulnerability. These extra doors can also leak vital energy from the bedroom; consequently, they can drain your health and your money and also harm your relationship. I give you cures for extra doors in the bedroom in the sections that follow.

Note: Windows provide needed natural light, but if they're located too close to the bed, they can be an energetic security issue and cause unhealthy drafts for the sleepers. If a window is positioned near your bed, you can hang a faceted crystal sphere in it to diffuse the excess energy flows.

Curing a bathroom door in the bedroom

A bathroom door in the bedroom is a prime opportunity for you to experience energy loss in both your health and marriage (with opportunities like this one, who needs a crisis?). I recommend keeping the bathroom door closed and hanging a full-length mirror on the outside of the bathroom door. In addition, I suggest you check out the other bathroom cures I present in Chapter 13 to transform this critical Feng Shui situation.

Checking an outside door in the bedroom

An outside door in the bedroom symbolizes the frequent absence of one partner from the home as well as the possibility of divorce and loss of money. A door featuring windows only aggravates the situation; French doors are especially problematic. You can improve these doors in terms of Feng Shui by replacing them with solid ones and using them less often. If the door into the bedroom leads straight to an outside door, money and marriage partners can quickly leave the site.

To cure any outside door in the bedroom, hang a brass wind chime (with a sound you like) in front of the door. Also, use the door as infrequently as possible.

Curing multiple layout issues

This section demonstrates how you can apply cures to the entire bedroom at once. Figure 11-6 shows two examples of bedroom layouts that feature multiple Feng Shui problems. I've purposefully chosen rooms with several issues to demonstrate how multiple cures can work together in a room.

Figure 11-6: Problematic bedroom layouts with cures.

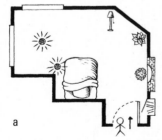
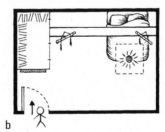

a   b

You don't necessarily need to perform all the cures in this section to have good Feng Shui in your bedroom. Some rooms have great Feng Shui without adding any cures. The key is to be practical: Apply the cures that fit your needs.

Curing an oddly shaped bedroom

The following list describes the problems of oddly and irregularly shaped bedrooms as well as practical cures for remedying each situation (refer to Figure 11-6a):

- **An oddly shaped room:** This room shape can create confusion and stagnation, sleeping issues, and marriage problems. To cure the odd shape, you can hang a faceted crystal sphere or wind chime from the center of the room.

- **An angled wall in the Marriage Area:** This problem can provoke arguments. Cure this situation by putting a light on one end of the angled wall and a plant on the other. (See Chapter 14 for more specifics on angled walls.)

- **A pointed wall corner that juts toward the bed:** This condition can project threatening, arrowlike energy at any part of the body it points toward — in this case, the legs and feet of the sleepers. To cure it, hang a faceted crystal sphere directly in front of the projecting corner.

- **A large window on the left wall and an exterior sliding glass door on the top wall:** This situation can cause excess chi to enter and leave the room, which can create an energetic lack of safety and protection for the sleepers. To harmonize these energy flows, hang a faceted crystal sphere at the midpoint between the window and exterior door. (Note that in Figure 11-6a, the sliding glass door is on the top wall.)

- **A fireplace in the bedroom:** The heat from a fireplace can burn up the energy of the marriage, leading to exhaustion and strain. One easy solution is to refrain from having fires in the fireplace. You can also place a potted plant or plants in front of the fireplace to cover the opening. (Flip to Chapter 14 for more on curing fireplaces.)

- **A closet door that hits the main door of the room:** Clashing doors (two doors that hit each other) can lead to arguments and personality clashes among the occupants. To cure this problem, hang two bright-red drapery tassels, one on each doorknob, on the common sides of the doors. (For more details on clashing doors, see Chapter 14.)

- **A narrow entrance into a bedroom:** This tight spot can harm your career and prospects. Cure this problem by hanging a wind chime over the entryway on the inside of the bedroom.

- **A door not visible from the sleeping position:** This situation makes succeeding in many aspects of life difficult. Cure it by installing a wall mirror or standing mirror across from the bed so you can clearly see the door from the bed. (I give you additional solutions for this situation in the earlier "Putting Your Bed in the Commanding Position with Four Important Principles" section.)

Curing a bedroom with a blocked entrance, skylight, or beam

The following bedroom positions make entry difficult and can create health challenges (refer to Figure 11-6b):

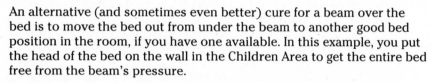

- ✔ **Blocked entrance:** The closet wall provides only a small area to move forward as you enter, making it difficult for energy and people to enter — and exit — the bedroom. Results can include blocked feelings in life, frequent absence from home (or sleeping alone for months on end), career failures, and difficulty finding a relationship. Cure this situation by placing a full-length mirror on the wall facing the doorway. This cure expands the entrance and draws additional energy into the room.

- ✔ **Beam over the bed:** A beam can cause constriction and pressure on the underlying portion of the sleepers' bodies (in this case, the heart). You can hang two bamboo Feng Shui flutes at 45-degree angles, one on either end of the beam. This cure relieves the pressure of the beam and creates better fortune in the Health and Marriage Life Areas. (Flip to Chapter 14 for more information on beams and Chapter 4 for the scoop on bamboo flutes.)

An alternative (and sometimes even better) cure for a beam over the bed is to move the bed out from under the beam to another good bed position in the room, if you have one available. In this example, you put the head of the bed on the wall in the Children Area to get the entire bed free from the beam's pressure.

- ✔ **Skylight over the bed:** A positive aspect of a skylight is that it adds light to a room. On the other hand, a skylight situated over the bed can threaten the sleeper. To cure this problem, hang a faceted crystal sphere from the skylight. For best results, hang the sphere from a ribbon cut to a multiple of 9 inches in length.

Resolving the master suite dilemma

Large, beautiful, and convenient for owners, master suites highlight a major trend in today's home market. Amenities of a master suite often include the availability of a large closet and a bathroom integrated with the bedroom. Unfortunately, a master suite can negatively affect the energy of its occupants in several ways:

- ✔ A very large master suite can cause disorientation, confusion, and conflicts among the partners. Also, a massive bedroom lacks coziness and tends to make its occupants feel lonely or despondent. (Some partners end up communicating with each other by cellphone from different parts of the room; others use smoke signals or tin cans joined with string.) Adding healthy plants to the space can make a large room feel more occupied and full of life.

✔ An irregular space (which is what many master suites create) is generally an unwanted, persistent puzzle for your subconscious. It causes confusion because the mind continuously attempts to make sense of its space. A room with multiple openings and odd shapes (refer to Figure 11-6a) is like living inside a mystery — determining where the room actually begins and ends is difficult. "So what?" you say. So you're more tired, cranky, and confused, I reply. Thankfully, you can give your mind a needed rest with appropriate Feng Shui!

✔ The opening to the bath area acts as a gaping hole in the room that inevitably draws precious energy away from the bed and is a draining influence on the entire room. The best cure for this situation is to place a curtain or door across the opening.

The most elaborate master suites (featuring multiple openings, doors to outside patios, and multilevel and/or slanted ceilings) are classic Feng Shui ordeals. These rooms can provoke multiple life problems and can make finding a good bed position quite a challenge. An overall good cure for a master suite is to hang a faceted crystal sphere from the center of the room to harmonize the disparate flows of energy. For a stronger cure, you can hang a high-quality, leaded-glass, crystal chandelier (as long as you don't hang it over the bed).

In the following list, I analyze the Feng Shui problems that can occur in master suites (see Figure 11-7 for a visual of the problems along with their cures):

✔ **The room features an outside door in the bedroom.** This situation can lead to problems in the relationship, including loss of the relationship, drainage of money in the household, or loss of health. The outside door also introduces excess chi into the room, which causes additional problems.

✔ **The path of energy from the main door to the exterior door runs across part of the bed.** In this case, it crosses the foot portion of the bed, which relates to your career. This condition can not only create challenges in your career but also foot and/or ankle vulnerabilities.

✔ **A huge opening in the room leads to the bath area.** This opening is directly across from the foot of the bed and can drain the sleepers' energies. The wet, draining energies of the bathroom, along with the gaping hole in the wall, can wreak havoc on the relationship and the couple's physical health.

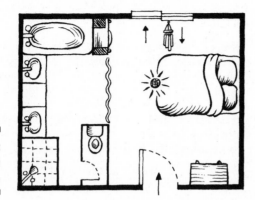

Figure 11-7:
Master suite
with cures.

A master suite with the previous three conditions often doesn't feature a Feng Shui–compliant bed placement. In Feng Shui, bed position is the most important bedroom factor; it provides a foundation for health, strength, and life success. Three of the walls in this room contain an opening or doorway, which makes them impractical for the bed. The right-hand wall is the only feasible alternative, but this position is a Feng Shui problem. You can apply the following cures to a master suite suffering from these conditions (refer to Figure 11-7):

✔ **Place a curtain across the opening to the bath area.** This visual barrier reduces the effects of the opening and completes the room, which helps stabilize and solidify the marriage and the couple's health. Attaching a door to this opening makes a stronger cure, but for some residents, a curtain is more feasible.

✔ **Hang a faceted crystal sphere in the center of the room.** This cure serves two purposes:

• A cure in the center is a good antidote to having multiple problems at once, and it can improve luck and fortune.

• The energy flowing from the main door to the exterior door meets the energy that comes from the bath opening toward the bed (and vice versa). At this critical juncture, the sphere in the center helps balance and calm the energies, thereby protecting the sleepers and harmonizing the entire room.

✔ **Hang a wind chime before the exterior door in the room.** The wind chime regulates the flow of energy in and out of the exterior door. This cure helps retain energy and life in the room, and it protects the sleepers.

Curing an empty door

The *empty door* is a Feng Shui concept representing a doorway, or any opening that looks like a doorway, that has no physical door. Empty-door conditions exist in several locations in modern homes, but they assume special importance in your master bedroom.

Doors represent many things in Feng Shui, but one particularly important connection is that doors represent "the self" or "the human." According to Feng Shui thought, when a physical door is missing in a space where you would or could find one, then correspondingly a "self" or "human" may be missing from the home situation, either currently or in the future.

Because the bedroom is the room of romance and partnership, which requires at least two to tango, an empty door can mean one or more parties is absent from the relationship. This can happen in various ways. For example, one or both partners may continuously work long hours, travel constantly, or be emotionally unavailable. Divorce and death can also enter the picture. An empty door in the bedroom can also hinder discovery of a new, stable relationship for those who are currently single and seeking a new partner. (Conversely, purposefully removing a door to end a current relationship and get rid of a problematic partner isn't recommended. Grandmaster Lin Yun's Feng Shui school teaches that Feng Shui methods must be used for positive purposes only at all times.)

Many master bedrooms have empty doors within the bedroom that are openings to hallways, closets, or bathrooms. Cure this situation as soon as possible by either installing a physical door in the opening or placing a bamboo or beaded curtain in the opening to create a virtual door (see Figure 11-8). If you go the curtain route, choose something that's pleasing to the eye; the length is up to you. Another option is to use a high-quality *noren* (a Japanese door curtain; search the Internet for sources) in this location.

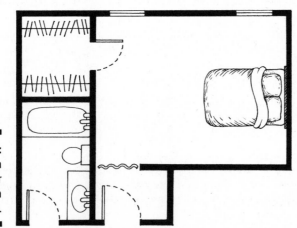

Figure 11-8:
Cure for an empty door in a bedroom.

TIP

Failing any of these options, you can hang a wind chime or faceted crystal sphere in the opening to diminish the empty door's negative influence on your relationship.

Enlivening the Entryway into the Bedroom

The entry into the bedroom should allow a clear, straightforward path into the room. This principle applies to the pathways outside and inside the bedroom door. If the entryway — on either side of the door — is small, dark, or blocked, you may experience health, relationship, and finance issues. The following cures can open up new prospects in your life and relationships:

- **Use a bright light to bring about good luck.** A bright light is always helpful outside (and inside) the entrance to the bedroom. In addition to brightening up a dark entryway, this cure helps bring good luck, which is never a bad idea.

- **Widen the narrow path.** If the entryway to the bedroom is narrow, you can hang two mirrors, one on each side of the entryway. This cure opens up energy flow into your life and stimulates creativity and lateral thinking. It can be effectively applied to the entryway either outside or inside the bedroom. Use the size of mirror that you can afford, but remember that the larger these mirrors are, the more effective and fast-acting the cure will be.

- **Make sure the door has a full swing.** The door to the bedroom should open a minimum of 90 degrees. Anything located behind the door, hanging on the back of the door, or hanging on the wall behind the door can cause a block in your life — even if the door doesn't technically hit the items. (This principle holds true even if the door can swing open a full 180 degrees.)

  If your bedroom door can't swing fully, simply remove the things that come between the back of your door and the wall. If the door is blocked by a wall and can't open 90 degrees, you can hang a wind chime just inside the door to help propel sufficient energy into the room.

- **Cure negatives seen when exiting the room.** Facing a close blocking wall or bathroom door upon exiting your bedroom may frustrate your opportunities and career.

  - If you walk out toward a blocking wall (around 3 feet is a rough guide), you can hang a convex mirror (the larger the better) directly ahead of you in plain sight, preferably at the eye level of the tallest person in the home. Or you can use a flat mirror that's as large as possible.

> • If you exit the bedroom toward a bathroom door (especially an open bathroom door), the effect worsens; problems can include loss of money and poor health. I recommend these cures: Place a full-length mirror on the bathroom door, keep the door shut, and hang a wind chime halfway between the two doors. (See Chapter 13 for additional cures you can implement inside the bathroom.)

Remembering the Purpose of the Bedroom

The bed should be the main focus of any bedroom. Nowadays, many people turn their bedrooms into small apartments with heaps o' conveniences. The bedroom now serves as a location for work, physical exercise (treadmill, anyone?), TV watching, storage, reading, and even eating area (think mini-refrigerator) — all in addition to serving as the place that's supposed to provide rest, rejuvenation, and intimacy in the relationship. You may as well fix your motorcycle and hold church services in the bedroom, too.

In this hectic environment, the quality of your sleep (and health) can take a real beating. The busier and more connected your daily life becomes, the more you need a safe haven from the clamor of the outside world. Bringing media in all of its wonderful forms (phone, TV, radio, Internet, alien civilizations) into your bedroom is indeed mentally stimulating and highly enjoyable, but it's exactly the opposite of the peace and calm you need for rejuvenation and high-quality rest.

Do your best to return the bedroom to its original, intended functions. In case you've forgotten, these functions are sleep and intimacy. (Try 'em out sometime. They're really great.) Let your other activities take place outside the bedroom, like in the living room and dining room, and watch your sleep and attitude improve remarkably and rapidly.

One way to convert your bedroom back to a place of rest is to keep the room dark at night. Studies indicate that the darker your room is at night, the greater the benefits of your sleep. So cover up some of those blinking lights (radio, smoke alarm, and so on) and invest in some darker shades for the windows to dramatically improve your rest.

For Feng Shui bedroom décor, remember the KISS formula (pun intended): Keep It Simple, Sweetheart. Multiple functions and purposes in a room tend to breed confusion, and this concept is particularly true of the bedroom. If you crave increased balance and vitality — as well as better sleep and more togetherness, romance, and passion in your relationship — I recommend the following quick and easy Feng Shui adjustments:

✔ **Get all phones and answering machines out of the bedroom.** Modern conveniences are great. The issue is how much technology and interruption your mind and body (not to mention significant other) can gracefully handle. If you can't rid the bedroom of all the phones, at the very least, unplug or turn off the phones at night.

✔ **Remove TVs, stereos, and entertainment centers.** The TV is relationship zapper numero uno in the bedroom. After all, late-night talk show hosts aren't exactly erotic mood enhancers. In addition, falling asleep while watching TV is a great way to turn into a zombie. Just keeping these culprits in the room detracts from one's rest, even if they're not turned on very often. If you can't handle this cure, you can cover the TV (or keep it in a closed cabinet) whenever it's not turned on.

✔ **Haul out bookshelves and piles of books, magazines, bills, and paper.** These items distract you from sleeping and keep your mind busy while you sleep. A few books or magazines (not giant piles of both) on your nightstand, however, are fine. Ideally, these publications are on relaxing and/or uplifting topics, not study manuals or heavy tomes from work.

✔ **Remove office equipment, computers, printers, and desks from the bedroom.** These critters offend for several reasons; they're noisy, they fill up the room, and they emit electromagnetic fields that can sap your energy. In addition, office items distract you from sleeping and from relating to your significant other.

✔ **Move electrical equipment away from your body in bed.** Because of the electromagnetic fields created by electronic devices, you should also move electric alarm clocks, radios, and all other electronic equipment at least 30 inches away from your body. Set up electric blankets to heat your bed before bedtime and then unplug and remove them before turning in for the night (don't just leave them off but in place).

✔ **Get the excess furniture out.** Large amounts of tall, heavy furniture can dominate the bedroom and can even make you feel energetically dominated, oppressed, or frightened. Likewise, excess furniture can stifle the energy of the bedroom and the people who sleep in it. Keep your bedroom simple to feel more balance, peace, and calm. Also, watch out for poison arrows, angles, and parts that jut out from furniture and point toward the bed. As I note in Chapter 7, poison arrows can negatively affect your health.

If your bedroom contains large or protruding pieces of furniture, do your best to rearrange or remove the offending items. If you can't, drape cloth in front of the angle or place a potted plant at a jutting corner to protect yourself.

Note: I'm not saying you can't have good Feng Shui if you don't follow all the previous tips. Just remember that a bedroom really exists for health, wealth, and relationship or marriage — then adjust your life accordingly as best you can.

If limited space forces you to keep multiple functions in one room (such as an office in the bedroom), you may benefit from sectioning off the nonsleeping portion of the room with a screen or room divider.

Chapter 12

Now You're Cookin': Feng Shui for Your Kitchen

In This Chapter

▶ Identifying the subtle energy of food

▶ Paying attention to kitchen layout and stove location

▶ Checking out the stove — the energy generator of the home

▶ Kicking kitchen problems to the curb

*F*eng Shui knowledge states that the energy flow in the kitchen greatly contributes to how food affects you. Food carries *chi* (life force energy) that enters your body when you eat. According to Chinese energy theory, the amount and quality of chi in your food rates more highly than the food's nutritional makeup. (Energy theory doesn't ignore vitamins, minerals, and nutrients, but it does look at a food's energetic qualities as the number one consideration.)

The stove — the third of the Life Pillars I present in Chapter 2 and the most important factor in the kitchen — is where the cook physically and energetically creates the food. Food universally symbolizes health and nourishment; however, the Chinese make a further connection by saying that food also relates to money. Feng Shui refers to the stove as the home's *energy generator,* the place where the energy of the cook, the food, and the fire meet to create sustenance for physical health and the strength to earn money. Therefore, Feng Shui masters carefully scrutinize the energy conditions of the stove and kitchen.

In this chapter, I show you the principles of ideal kitchen layout and stove positioning and provide simple adjustments that you can perform if your kitchen needs Feng Shui help. I also cover vital aspects of stove Feng Shui, including your stove's usage, quality, and condition, and I help you solve a variety of other kitchen problems.

Understanding the Energy of Food

The energy of food affects not only your health but also many other parts of your life. Two factors help determine the energy in food:

- **The food's origin:** The energy of food derives initially from the quality of the land and the way it was grown, harvested, and handled. You don't need a Feng Shui master to tell you that purchasing the highest-quality food available greatly benefits your health, vitality, and personal strength.

- **Preparation and cooking:** In particular, the energy state and mood of the cook while he or she cooks greatly affects the food's chi. If you've ever had a meal and later remarked to yourself that something in the food tasted off, it's likely that an unhappy cook made your meal. The clashing or moody feelings a cook experiences can transfer to your body and emotions through the food. In fact, you can get sick by eating food made by someone who's upset or sick while cooking.

Maximizing Kitchen Location, Layout, and Stove Placement

In the ideal Feng Shui floor plan, the kitchen location is in the back half of the home. Because this area is more protected, calm, and secure than the front of the home, locating the kitchen in this area protects the sensitive energies of the stove and fosters health and wealth.

The worst places for the kitchen are energetically outside the front door of the home and in the center of the home; these areas are more active energetically. If your kitchen is located in one of these spots, turn to Chapter 10 for further information and cures.

In the ideal kitchen layout, the cook can easily see the kitchen door while standing at the stove so he or she is never startled while cooking — a feeling that can enter the food and profoundly affect the eater. If your back currently faces the kitchen door while you cook, you're probably being startled — whether or not you're aware of it.

Here are two of the most important kitchen Feng Shui factors:

✔ **The relative energetic safety of the cook as he or she stands cooking at the stove:** The cook's standing position greatly determines the quality of chi he or she puts into the food. This position derives from the stove position itself.

✔ **The placement of the stove in the kitchen and the effect of the kitchen's energy on the stove:** At the stove, everything comes together to create nourishment and energy for the family. The energy that circulates in the kitchen affects the stove, so the position of the stove determines whether your raw ingredients are lovingly transformed into delicious meals for your enjoyment and health or whether they contribute to health issues and loss of money.

In the following sections, I describe guidelines and cures for your kitchen's layout and your stove's placement.

Recognizing the ideal kitchen layout

A good kitchen layout prevents energy from attacking the stove or the cook. The best layout affords the cook a powerful standing position and protects both the stove and the cook. In other words, there's no need to worry about the compass direction your stove faces; Grandmaster Lin Yun's Feng Shui school doesn't use compass directions, although this method is also a valid way of practicing Feng Shui.

Ideally, the cook should be able to see the kitchen doorway — and anyone approaching — while cooking without needing to turn around. Also, the energy from the main and secondary doors into the kitchen shouldn't flow directly (straight toward) the face of the stove, and the stove should be in balance with another kitchen feature: the refrigerator.

If practical, I recommend an island stove, like the one in Figure 12-1, behind which the cook can stand and observe the kitchen doorway. Of course, the vast majority of all American stoves sit against a wall, so in most homes, energy comes from the door toward the back or side (or both) of the cook. The best cure for this situation is the mirror-behind-the-stove cure (see the later "Seeing a kitchen door behind you" section for details).

Note: Even if you live and cook alone, you need to be able to see the door when you're cooking because the stove's position still affects your emotional, physical, and financial well-being. The energetic relationship between you and the energy generator of the home — your stove — is more important than whether you share your home with other people.

Figure 12-1: Powerful cooking position allowing the cook to see the kitchen door.

Positioning your stove for wealth and health

If any door into your kitchen isn't visible when you're at the stove, you can solve the problem with one of the solutions I present in the sections that follow.

Seeing a kitchen door behind you

A single door behind you is the simplest version of the stove/door problem. (Note that if the door points straight at the stove, an accident involving visible blood can occur in the home.) Because remodeling the kitchen is impractical for many people, here's an easier cure: Hang a mirror on the wall behind the stove. This cure provides an inexpensive way to see who's coming and effectively solves the issue of ensuring the cook's safety and protection.

The mirror should be at least as wide as the stove (although the wider it is, the better), and it should run from the top of the stove to above your head (or to where the extractor fan or hood begins). You can see this setup in Figure 12-2. When installing the mirror, make sure it gives the cook a clear view of the kitchen doorway, and visualize better physical health and increased income in order to achieve the best results. (See Chapter 6 for help with visualization.)

If your mirror is going to sit within a few inches of your stovetop, consider specifying heat-tempered glass when you acquire your mirror. If you don't, you might not end up with shards of glass in your food, but you'll probably have to buy a new mirror when the original mirror cracks from the heat.

A mountain behind a home provides energetic backing and protection; flip to Chapter 7 for basics on home positioning.

This home sits in an auspicious Commanding Position above the road, with a hill beyond and a stately path to the door. See Chapter 7 for details on home positioning.

A fountain at a home's entrance helps usher wealth energy into the home; check out Chapter 7 for details.

The living chi of koi in a water feature adds vibrant energy to a site;
see Chapter 7 for more about water features on properties.

An octagonal gazebo can boost the Wealth, Fame, and Marriage Life Areas of a property (as well as others); turn to Chapter 7 for more information.

A curving walk and bright, colorful flowers escort vital energy along a front path; see Chapter 9 for tips on creating a welcoming entry.

A red front door activates positive energy for a home's residents, as you find out in Chapter 9.

Expanding a home's entryway with a mirror invites beneficial exterior energy into the home. Flip to Chapter 9 for more about using Feng Shui in an entryway.

A pink-themed master bedroom stimulates love and romantic energies, as you discover in Chapter 11.

An island stove places the cook in a powerful and protected cooking position, stimulating wealth and safety for a home's residents. Chapter 12 has full details on kitchen Feng Shui.

An aquarium placed at a living room's entrance adds vitalizing life and color.
Check out Chapter 13 the scoop on living room Feng Shui.

A living room mirror nicely balances the energy of a fireplace; see Chapter 13

Bright colors, lights, and crystals combine for a luminous dining atmosphere; flip to Chapter 13 for more on dining room Feng Shui.

Blue is an excellent color for a child's bedroom; it stimulates both growth and intelligence. Chapter 13 has more about Feng Shui for kids' bedrooms.

A plant below a spiral staircase helps balance the stairway's energy. Check out Chapter 14 for more on using Feng Shui around stairs and other parts of your home.

A desk placed in the Commanding Position (as shown from the doorway) provides the owner with control of the room and stimulates his or her career. Turn to Chapter 17 for the scoop on office Feng Shui.

Figure 12-2:
Mirror
behind
stove
enabling the
cook to see
the door.

Depending on the design of your kitchen, a mirror directly behind the stove may not show you the door. Fortunately, there's still an easy fix. Just place a mirror (as large as you can find) on the wall to the side of the stove. One good option is to mirror the space between the countertop and the upper kitchen cabinets and run this mirror as far left and/or right as you can. In any case, ensure you can see the door in the mirror when you stand at the stove.

If your stove design (such as an all-in-one vertical unit featuring a built-in microwave) or other limitations prevent you from placing an effective mirror behind the stove, hang a pleasant-sounding metal wind chime from the ceiling halfway between the door and your standing position at the stove. The chime deflects the chi of the door away from the cook's back and ensures the protection and safety of the stove and the cook (see Figure 12-3). Or you can hang a faceted crystal sphere in the same location and to the same effect. Either way, for best results, hang the cure from a red ribbon cut to a multiple of 9 inches in length. For another alternative, you can angle a standing mirror on the counter next to the stove so you can see the doorway.

Curing a stove that's visible from the front door

Severe Feng Shui problems can result from seeing the stove as you enter the front door of the home. If you can see the stove through one or more angled doorways, the trouble can intensify (worst-case scenarios include violence and tragedy in the home). To cure this problem, install a door or hang a curtain to visually separate the stove and the front door. If a door or curtain doesn't work in your situation, you can strategically position one or two wind chimes or faceted crystal spheres along the path between the front door and the stove.

Figure 12-3:
Wind chime or faceted crystal sphere cure for a door behind the cook.

Curing multiple doorways and traffic pattern problems in the kitchen

When multiple doorways enter your kitchen, the picture becomes more complex. The following sections deal with the different doorway situations you may face.

A pass-through kitchen or doorways leading in front of the stove

When a walkway passes directly in front of the stove, constant traffic can pull away the stove's healthy chi. If the kitchen functions as a hallway, negative results can include fighting in the home and difficulty holding onto money. To cure this situation, hang wind chimes in the pathway. Place one between each door and the stove, as shown in Figure 12-4.

An outside door leading into the kitchen

If a door in the kitchen leads to the outdoors, threats to health, safety, and money are heightened. I recommend both of the following cures:

✔ Use the outside door less often to reduce the effects of outdoor chi on the kitchen and stove.

✔ Hang a special bamboo Feng Shui flute horizontally above the door frame of the exterior door on the kitchen side of the wall (see Figure 12-5). The flute brings peace and safety, an effective antidote to the door's threatening energy. Visualize these effects when you apply the cure (turn to Chapter 6 for the scoop on visualization).

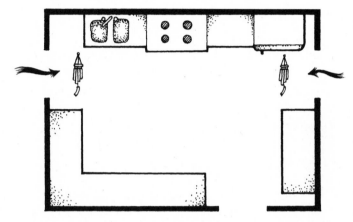

Figure 12-4:
Wind chime cures for a pass-through kitchen.

Figure 12-5:
Special bamboo flute over kitchen door that leads outside.

A garage door leading into the kitchen

A garage door that connects directly to the kitchen can carry noxious fumes and pollution directly into your food and body. Of course, if you don't park in the garage, you alleviate most of this problem. But if you do park in the garage, you can place multiple healthy plants in the kitchen to provide healthy chi. (*Note:* Certain plants such as Boston ferns and spider plants provide added benefits by purifying and cleansing the kitchen air.) I also recommend using the flute cure I detail in the preceding section.

Multiple doorways opening into the kitchen

If your kitchen has several doorways, excessive energy flowing into the room can cause chaos and confusion. I recommend applying the principle of curing the center: Hang a large faceted crystal sphere from the center of the kitchen. The crystal in the center balances the disparate energies that circulate in the kitchen, resulting in balance and calm. (Flip to Chapter 10 for more on the center.)

Looking at the Stove: Your Home's Energy Generator

The stove is the energy generator of the home; it provides the food that gives nourishment and vitality to the home's residents. Consequently, the quality and condition of the stove contribute to — or detract from — the chi of your home.

The stove not only affects your physical health, vitality, and stamina but also influences many other parts of your life. Chief among them is money. That's right. Your stove affects your wealth situation. A family's financial welfare depends more on the energetic status of the stove than on most other Feng Shui factors. Surprising? Read on — the chi of the stove also correlates to the following:

- ✔ The quality of your marriage and the degree of family harmony versus upheaval and disagreement in the home
- ✔ Your freedom from or involvement in lawsuits, legal trouble, or other major life entanglements
- ✔ Your level of personal safety, security, and protection versus danger, accidents, mishaps, surgeries, and other problems

As you can see from this list, the stove can greatly affect your well-being. Consequently, putting time and attention into the stove's chi can reap powerful rewards. Regardless of your status in life, you can improve your situation and prevent serious problems by adjusting the Feng Shui of your stove.

In the sections that follow, I touch on the choice between a new stove and a used stove, the importance of cleaning your stove, and the benefits of inspecting and fixing all the parts of your stove.

Which type of stove cooks food best?

For the energetics of food, the best-quality fire comes from cooking with wood or straw. In modern homes, most people generally cook at appliances, not hearths, so the choices are limited to gas, electric (including induction), and microwave (although new options are beginning to appear, including convection — or hot air — combined with electric, microwave, and other energies).

✔ Of the three common types of cooking, gas provides the best energy by far (note that this is an energetic analysis of stoves, not necessarily a scientific viewpoint). Gas stoves cook with real fire, which cooks food better and puts stronger chi into the food itself.

✔ Electric stoves don't produce fire, but they do cook the food with a hot electrical field, which creates at least two problems: low-quality food energy and possible exposure of the cook to a high level of electrical/electromagnetic fields. The human body isn't energetically compatible with these fields, which can prove debilitating over time. The same goes for toaster ovens and electric ovens.

✔ Microwaves are further down the line of poor quality because they create deep energetic problems in the food, which can disturb both your emotions and physical body — no matter what scientific experts say on the subject. For a helpful cure, lose the microwave or consider a healthier way to cook your food.

Choosing a new stove versus a used stove

The best stove is one you purchase new. A used stove inevitably retains the previous owner's energy and creates an energetic drag on your life and progress. Buying a brand-new stove when you move into a residence can give you a new start in health and wealth. If you can't afford a new stove, you can cure your existing one with a thorough physical cleaning, as explained in the following section.

For even more benefits, you can energetically cleanse the stove by performing the Citrus Water Blessing ceremony I describe in Chapter 21.

Improving the cleanliness of your stove

Take a look at your stove's cleanliness. Feng Shui says that a dirty stove makes you tired and depressed and makes it harder to earn money. Old food particles hold stale energy, which mixes with the chi of the new food you cook. The cure is simple: Clean your stove and keep it clean, especially the stovetop, which holds the burners. *Note:* In order to experience the full benefits, you should clean everything: the oven, the broiler, the front of the stove, the controls, and all the other areas.

You can also move the stove out from the wall and clean its sides, back, and bottom, as well as the walls behind and to the sides of it and the floor underneath it. You may be amazed at what you find, and you may be pleasantly surprised at how much better you feel when everything's spick-and-span.

Inspecting the condition and use of your stove burners

Burners are to a stove like the engine is to a race car — the most important part that makes everything run. I cover two important burner issues in the next sections.

Repairing broken burners

A broken (or poorly working) burner is like a car without one of its cylinders; the car may run, but you need repairs quickly if you want reliable transportation. The same holds true with your stove. If one or more burners don't work, this situation should top the list for your immediate attention.

The one and only cure: Fix defective burners. This cure includes fixing burners that technically work but show other problems, including the following:

✔ They don't light reliably, or they mysteriously go out on a regular basis.

✔ You need to use a match to light them because the pilot light is bad.

✔ The burner or grate is cracked or broken.

In San Diego, a therapist who invited me to do a Feng Shui consultation had kept a broken stove for several years. After I gave her the stove repair cure, her landlord not only fixed the stove (which had several other problems) but also approved a major remodeling and improvement of her home as well. Since applying this cure, she has enjoyed increased wealth, travel, and freedom.

Nonworking burners can directly affect your health as well as your finances. A Feng Shui colleague told me the story of a client who owned a large home containing three stoves, and he was consistently plagued by a mysterious stomach malady. Consulting with top-level doctors and nutritionists proved fruitless. During the Feng Shui consultation, however, the client revealed that two of the stoves in his home worked just fine but that the third one hadn't worked since he purchased the home. After repairing stove number three, the man's indigestion quickly cleared up.

Using all your burners for maximum earning power

Believe it or not, how you use your burners is important, regardless of whether you have a traditional gas stove or an electric one. The Feng Shui trick is to utilize all the burners regularly. Many people use only their front two burners, and the back two sit idle much of the time. Rotate your burner usage regularly so all the burners stay active. The stove's burners represent the wealth-generating potential of the home, but when they sit idle, wealth doesn't come as powerfully as it can.

Previously one of my clients had been able to acquire money pretty smoothly, but in the year or two before we met, she couldn't always make ends meet. When I visited her home, I asked her about how she used her stove. She told me that although all the burners worked, she mainly used the front two and left the other two idle most of the time. I encouraged her to perform the wealth cure of using all the burners on a regular basis. Shortly afterward, she reported to me that her money picture had improved considerably "and from such a small change." I informed her that activating her stove fully — that is, using all the burners on a regular basis — was actually a really big change in her energy even though it was a seemingly small thing.

Examining the overall functioning of your stove

Every component of your stove must work if you want to get the most benefits out of it. No part is too small. In addition to examining and fixing broken burners, you need to look at (and repair as needed) the following items:

- ✔ Knobs and switches
- ✔ Light fixtures and light bulbs
- ✔ Fans and hood assemblies (attached to or above the stove)
- ✔ Broiler elements
- ✔ Clocks and timers on the stove
- ✔ Oven door hinges
- ✔ Anything you can find on the stove that doesn't work as perfectly as it worked when the stove was new

Visualize improved income and life circumstances when fixing these components (see Chapter 6 for more on visualization).

Remodeling the kitchen: A good time to be careful

Because of the sensitivity and importance of the kitchen in all aspects of life, undertaking a kitchen remodeling job can bring misfortune to one's home unless the appropriate precautions are taken. I recommend the following two cures:

✔ Choose a good date and time to begin the job (see Chapter 23 for timing details).

✔ Perform the Rice Blessing (see Chapter 21) on the day you begin the project and then on the day the project is complete.

For a major residence change, however, you may want to consult a Feng Shui professional to ensure you receive the best outcome from the project; see Chapter 24 for pointers on finding a professional.

My Feng Shui colleagues and I often shake our heads in amazement at how effectively the stove-repair principle helps people get past sticky and drawn-out money problems. The success stories include legions (actually, large stadiums full) of people who simply repair their stoves and then receive new jobs, get over nagging health issues, or hear from someone who owes them money and has suddenly decided to pay up. Get the point?

Solving Miscellaneous Kitchen Problems

In the following sections, I list common kitchen Feng Shui problems along with simple solutions to ensure the best chi and good luck.

The kitchen is small

A large, spacious kitchen is favorable and portends wealth for the family, so you want to avoid a cramped or stifled feeling in this space. Mirrors are the best tools for expanding small kitchens. Add mirrors in as many places as possible so that when you enter the kitchen your small room now feels huge. In this case, more and bigger can definitely be better. (As Mae West, the patron goddess of feeling good, once said, "Too much of a good thing can be wonderful." I agree.)

Another option for expanding a small kitchen space is to hang a faceted crystal sphere from the center of the kitchen ceiling.

The stove is next to the refrigerator

If your stove is adjacent to the refrigerator, you can have an energy conflict between the cold energy of the refrigerator and the hot energy of the stove.

This placement can cause health and wealth problems. Here are several good cures for this problem:

- ✔ Mirror the side of the refrigerator next to the stove; this mirror should face the stove. The mirror energetically expands the stove area, symbolically moving the refrigerator away.

- ✔ Hang a wind chime or faceted crystal sphere between the stove and refrigerator to create energetic balance.

- ✔ Place small potted plants on the counter as an energetic buffer. (This cure works best if you have a small amount of counter space between the stove and refrigerator.)

A window is over the stove

A window positioned above the stove creates a negative Feng Shui situation. However, the situation worsens dramatically when the cook sees one of the following through the window: bars, a grid, grating, a trellis with a crosshatched pattern, or a blocking wall. This arrangement can lead to family problems, exhaustion, legal problems, anemia, and blood diseases.

The cure for this scenario is to remove the offending symbolic feature. If you can't remove the culprit, you can plant ivy on it to add the color green, which represents the energy of life (you can also use artificial silk ivy). Or you can hang a faceted crystal sphere in the window in order to expand your view and disperse the negative chi.

A toilet or bed is located directly behind the stove on a common wall

If your home's layout features a toilet or a bed on the opposite side of the wall from the stove, your cure options depend on your specific situation.

- ✔ For the toilet/stove combo, hang a mirror behind the stove that's the same width and height as the stove. The shiny side of the mirror should face the stove.

- ✔ For the stove/bed situation, hang a mirror on the bedroom side, behind the bed. The mirror should be the width of the bed and run from the floor to the top of the headboard (or mattress if you have no headboard). Make sure the shiny side of the mirror faces the bed.

See Chapter 10 for additional cures for these scenarios.

The kitchen is dimly or harshly lit and dark in color

The light level in your kitchen helps determine your mood and finances. Generally, bright light in the kitchen is better than dim light, but harsh light is negative. Similarly, incandescent lights are better than fluorescent ones. An easy light cure is to place small lamps on your kitchen counters to add cheer to dark corners.

The best color for kitchens is white; try to avoid dark colors in the kitchen. (Flip to Chapter 15 for expanded information on these factors.)

Knives are visible in the kitchen

Visible knives in the kitchen symbolize accidents, especially cut fingers. This situation requires a simple cure: Keep your knives in drawers instead of displaying them in plain sight. You can use a block if you prefer, but the drawer option is probably even better.

The stove is outside the front door

What exactly does it mean to have your stove "outside the front door"? This situation occurs when your stove is located in a space that's in front of the wall containing the front door. Having the stove outside the front door can result in money leaving the home and other problems. This situation is one that you'll most likely want to remedy. The cure is to symbolically bring the stove back into the home with a strategically placed mirror; see Chapter 10 for specific information on this situation and its cures.

Don't bang, bang, bang on the stove!

Be careful not to forcefully bang your cooking implements down onto the stove surface. Banging pots and pans (or anything else) on the stove can disrupt the energy being produced in the home and negatively affect all household members, causing arguments and bickering. I also recommend being gentle and cautious when you move the stove or repair it so you don't bang on it accidentally.

Chapter 13

Home Is Where the "Shui" Is: Enhancing Your Family Areas

*I*n this chapter, you discover how to apply Feng Shui to enhance the energy and beneficial effects of the family areas of your home. From the living room to the garage, each part of your home has an ongoing effect on your personal progress and emotional state. Read on to find out ways to keep the positive energy circulating in your home.

The Living Room, Family Room, and Den

The living room exists for relaxation, guest reception, and social interaction. If a living room is visible from the front door and/or the front hall or entryway, peace and comfort greet the weary residents as they arrive home. Therefore, a living room situated in the front of the home is positive. However, living rooms also fit well in other areas of the home, like in the center of the home. (*Note:* Family rooms and dens serve as informal, secondary living rooms for the family and intimate guests, which is why the Feng Shui principles that apply to your living room also apply to your family room and den.)

Sitting and conversing are the main social activities that occur in living rooms. The best seating positions for these rooms ideally afford both the guests and the residents clear views of the main door into the room. This arrangement makes everyone feel safe and comfortable. Figures 13-1a and 13-1b show examples of positive furniture placement.

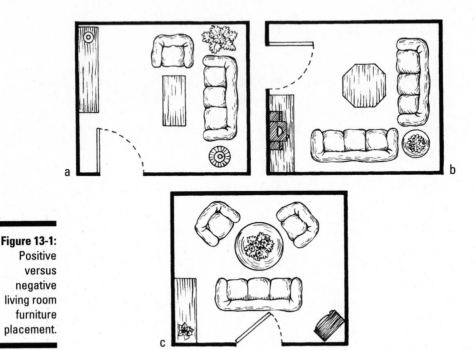

Figure 13-1:
Positive
versus
negative
living room
furniture
placement.

Guests naturally feel honored if you give them the seats farthest from the main door of the living room, but there's nothing wrong with taking this position yourself. Either way, these spots are the safest and strongest positions in the room.

Try to avoid placing a major piece of furniture with its back to the living room door (refer to Figure 13-1c). Sitting here can create a feeling of vulnerability, and the furniture can block the door.

If you can't arrange a main piece of sitting furniture to provide a view of the door, try placing a large mirror on an opposite wall. The mirror should be large enough to show the door from the sitting position. Alternatively, you can add a table with lush, green plants behind the piece of furniture to create a sense of protection.

The best living room arrangements make conversation comfortable and easy. If you need to talk across a walkway in the room, conversation is more difficult. Try to arrange your furniture so that groups of two to five (or more) people can converse in a single area. If your living room serves as a passage to other rooms, group the furniture so that coherent conversations can take place on either side of the pathway.

The Dining Room

The dining room correlates to money, career, and social life. Entertaining presents a great opportunity for you to build your network of associates and colleagues. (First you digest together, then you invest together.) The ideal Feng Shui location for the dining room is a practical one — next to the kitchen.

The larger the dining room table, the better and stronger its energy — and the more your career can grow. The best energy comes from a dining room table that's circular, square, rectangular, oval, or octagonal.

Large mirrors are very positive in the dining room because visually doubling the plates and food on the table symbolizes doubling your wealth.

If the dining room table sits beneath a beam, your career and cash flow can suffer from the extra pressure. To alleviate the problem, use the double-flute-on-beam cure: Hang two special bamboo Feng Shui flutes, one on each end of the beam. Alternatively, you can move the table out from under the beam or attach a green silk ivy vine along the bottom of the beam. (Flip to Chapter 14 for more on beams and Chapter 4 for the scoop on bamboo flutes.)

Feng Shui associates negative influences on health and money with seeing the stove while eating at the dining room table. To cure this problem, place two bamboo Feng Shui flutes over the kitchen door opening at 45-degree angles, like symbolic swords, on either side of the doorway.

Kids' Bedrooms

Children's bedrooms are important rooms in a home and need special care. In the following sections, I delve into the placement of kids' bedrooms, bed positions, bed types, colors, and other special cures.

Obtaining good room locations and curing problematic ones

Favorable locations for children's rooms include the front half of the home (especially for older children) and the Children or Family Areas of your home's Octagon (I tell you all about the Life Areas of the Feng Shui Octagon in Chapter 3). Less favorable positions are those located beyond the master bedroom or in the home's center.

If a child's bedroom and the master bedroom are equally placed in relation to the back of the home, the situation is fine, and no cure is needed. If, however, a child's room sits farther back in the home than the parents' room does, the child could tend to run the household. This problem occurs because the child (in his bedroom) has a more Commanding Position in the home than the parents do. (Head to Chapter 2 for an introduction to the Commanding Position.)

The cure for this problem is to hang a sizable mirror directly in line with and facing the child's bed and more toward the front of the home than the child's bed is. The larger the mirror, the more effective the cure. You can position the mirror within the child's room, but if this placement disturbs the child, you can place the mirror in line with the bed in a different location that's more forward in the home. As a key part of this cure, visualize the relationships in the home in harmony and appropriate balance (see Chapter 6 for insight into visualization).

If the mirror cure isn't possible, or if extra emphasis is needed, you can place a second sizable mirror in line with the master bed as long as it's farther back in the home than the bed lies.

Another potentially destabilizing factor is the child's room being larger than the master bedroom. Again, the child can exhibit out-of-control energy. One cure is to switch the two bedrooms. If you consider this option, be sure to take into account all factors regarding each of the potential bedrooms when making the decision (I cover bedroom Feng Shui in Chapter 11). If you decide not to swap rooms, you can solve the problem by using red ribbon (cut in 9-inch increments) to hang a metal wind chime just outside the child's door and a faceted crystal sphere in the center of the master bedroom ceiling.

Creating positive bed positions for children

The position of a child's bed is a big factor in determining the child's progress, maturation, and safety. Two positive choices exist for a child's bed placement: the Children Area (the center-right portion of the room) and the Commanding Position of the bedroom (I fill you in on this in Chapter 11). Placing the bed in the Children Area gives the child strength, intelligence, and energy; placing it in the Commanding Position provides general strength and stability. (Figure 13-2a shows the bed in the Children Area of the room, and 13-2b shows it in the Commanding Position for the room.)

Arrange the bed so that the head of the bed rests against a solid wall. Otherwise, insecurity and unsteadiness may mark the child's life.

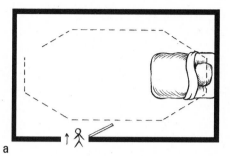
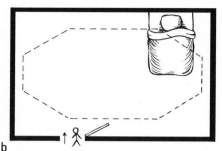

Figure 13-2: Positive bed positions for a child's room.

a   b

Note: Any of the factors that affect the master bedroom (such as a location over the garage, a slanted ceiling in the bedroom, and so on) can similarly affect a child's bedroom. Apply the cures in Chapters 11 and 14 to combat these problems.

Choosing the right bed for your child

The type of bed in which your child sleeps helps determine his or her strength and independence. Children are people too, and you can reap benefits by giving them the best possible quality of bed. In the sections that follow, I cover specific types of beds available for children and present the advantages and disadvantages of each type.

If you can't get rid of any of the negative bed types, you can apply this cure: Run a realistic-looking, green silk vine all the way around the edge of the mattress. Also, place healthy green plants in the bedroom to add living chi. The sensory input of green life energy (even if it's artificial) helps balance and harmonize your child's energy.

Discovering the ideal children's bed

The ideal bed for a child follows the same guidelines for adult beds (see Chapter 11 for these). In general, though, the frame of a child's bed should stand on four legs (meaning the bed shouldn't be a platform, mattress, or box spring resting on the floor), and it should be stable, well constructed, and solid. A headboard isn't as vital for a child's bed as it is for the master bed, but if one is present, ensure that it's both solid (not made of bars) and firmly attached to the frame (not loose or wobbly, which can symbolize a lack of support in life).

Replacing too-small or outgrown beds

Some parents keep their kids in beds they've long outgrown, creating physical discomfort and stunting their children's emotional growth, as well as their advancement in school. Make sure your child has ample room to stretch out and sleep in his bed.

Rethinking day, trundle, and temporary beds

A day, trundle, or temporary bed gives a child feelings of instability and shakiness. If you can't afford a traditional bed right now, you can help stabilize your child's energy by using the special yu cure. Prepare a yu bowl, as described in Chapter 22, and then place the bowl on the floor under the foot of the bed. Attach a red ribbon cut to a multiple of 9 inches in length to the bottom of the bed and bring the ribbon down to the floor. Make sure the ribbon is long enough so that a few inches of ribbon rest on the floor, with the yu bowl sitting on top of the end of the ribbon. Now you have a straight, vertical red ribbon running from the bed down to the floor. The top part of the ribbon is attached to the bottom of the bed (via tape or glue), and the yu bowl is on the floor resting on the bottom part of the red ribbon. Reinforce this cure for the stability and tranquility of your child by using the Three Secrets Reinforcement that I present in Chapter 6. (You can also perform this cure anytime you need help stabilizing a child's chi, even if he or she already has a good bed in a good position.)

Letting go of bunk beds

Bunk beds save space wonderfully, but they don't benefit most children. Although the negative influence is generally greater for the child on the bottom bunk, sleeping on either the top or bottom bunk can cause mental repression and personality problems in children. A regular bed is definitely preferable, although bunk beds that reside in a guestroom or that are rarely slept on are fine.

Buying a new bed is the easiest cure for this situation. An alternative solution is to hang a faceted crystal sphere directly over the heads of both children's sleeping positions. For the child who sleeps on the bottom bunk, hang the sphere down a few inches from the bottom of the top bunk. For the upper bunk, hang the sphere a few inches from the ceiling.

A client of mine expressed concern that her child was depressed, physically weak, and performing poorly in school. To her surprise, I pinpointed the problem as the bunk bed on which her child slept. Although she was initially hesitant when I prescribed the cure of getting a new bed for her son, soon after the new bed was installed, she reported that her son was remarkably happier and stronger.

Dismissing combination beds

A *combination bed* attempts to combine a desk, storage space, or a wardrobe into the bed (think of the loft beds that some college students use in dorms). This type of bed saves space, but it doesn't provide the best benefit for your child in the long run. The combined energies are quite confusing, and the bed ends up doing none of its tasks well. A regular bed is a much better choice.

Looking at colors and special cures for kids' bedrooms

Blue and green are good colors for a child's bedroom. They promote growth, improvement, and a positive attitude. White is also a good color for a child's room, especially if you add blue and green accents. For a very young child, having multiple primary colors in the room helps stimulate his brain functions and develop his sensory faculties.

To settle down an overactive or unruly child, use earth tones or accents in darker colors (such as dark green) with a white color scheme.

Following are a few suggestions for improving a child's bedroom (and life):

- **To help brighten a child's intellect:** Place a bright light in the Children Area of the room. This cure can assist a child at any time.

- **To activate a child's awareness and mental capacity:** Hang a wind chime over the head of the bed and/or in the Knowledge Area of the room.

- **To balance a child's emotions and increase his self-esteem:** Hang a faceted crystal sphere over the head of the bed.

The Bathroom

The bathroom, the home's place for cleansing and elimination, is a modern convenience that can instigate several Feng Shui problems. The bathroom can affect the family's wealth and the physical body's circulation of water. It presents two general Feng Shui issues:

- The bathroom exists for the purpose of waste removal, so it carries connotations of uncleanliness and dirt.

- More important, the bathroom features several drains, including the king of drains — the toilet.

When addressing bathrooms, the chief goal is to keep the energy that circulates in the home from draining (or flushing) away — in other words, to keep the bathroom from depleting your life force. Another objective is to prevent the chi of the bathroom (sights, odors, and so on) from circulating throughout the home.

Grandmaster Lin Yun's Feng Shui school doesn't hold that the bathroom is a bad room with no proper place in the home — nor does it call for an idyllic return to primitive outhouses. However, I do recommend minimizing the Feng Shui problems of the bathroom using the cures given in the next sections. These solutions can make your home a healthier, wealthier, and happier place to live and love (and yes, go to the bathroom).

Being aware of negative locations for the bathroom

Certain bathroom locations can create particularly negative Feng Shui results. I recommend paying particular attention to the position and layout of your bathroom if your intention is to improve any Life Areas of the Octagon associated with the locations covered in the following list:

✔ **A bathroom in the center of the home:** This rates as one of the worst bathroom locations of all. The center of the home is the single most important point in the home's interior. Having a bathroom in this spot can drain your health and, by extension, negatively affect every part of your life. If your bathroom lies in the center of your home, use the four-mirrored-walls cure that I provide in Chapter 10. I also suggest you apply the standard bathroom cures given in the following sections.

✔ **A bathroom at the front entrance or as the first room you see:** A bathroom at the main front entrance to the home can significantly drain the incoming chi from the front door, debilitating the energy of the entire home. This arrangement can create significant problems for all parts of your life. (Refer to Chapter 10 for specific bathroom location cures.)

✔ **A bathroom in the Wealth or Fame Areas of the Octagon:** Humans possess a natural preoccupation with acquiring and keeping money, making the Wealth Area (the back-left part of the home) a vital area of concern for virtually everyone. A bathroom in the Wealth Area can drain your current funds and lower your potential future wealth.

Also keep an eye on a bathroom situated in the Fame Area of the Octagon. This area is the home of fire, which may be energetically put out by the water energy of the bathroom. Use the cures in the following sections for a bathroom in the Fame Area of your home and flip to Chapter 3 for basics on the Feng Shui Octagon (also called the *Ba-Gua*) and its Life Areas.

Considering positive and negative bathroom layouts

The layout of the bathroom hinges on one main factor — whether you can see the toilet when you stand in the bathroom doorway. If the toilet is immediately visible when you open the bathroom door, as in Figure 13-3a, the effect is negative. The best location for the toilet is behind the bathroom door, as in Figure 13-3b, or behind a wall, which makes it invisible from the doorway. Cure a poorly placed toilet by hanging a faceted crystal sphere from the ceiling halfway between the bathroom door and the toilet; see Figure 13-3a for an example. (Or you can use a small screen to conceal the toilet so it's not visible from the doorway.)

Figure 13-3: Negative bathroom layout showing cure (a) and positive bathroom layout (b).

 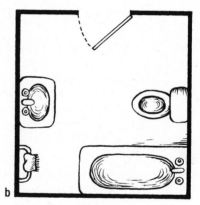

Employing basic bathroom cures

A few simple Feng Shui solutions reduce the draining effects of any bathroom. The cures I present in the following sections apply to the three danger-level bathroom locations explained in the earlier "Being aware of negative locations for the bathroom" section, but you can also apply them for good measure to any bathroom in your home.

I recommend the following policy to my clients: When in doubt about a Feng Shui situation, apply the cure. This way you'll be covered — and amazed at the positive results!

Keep the bathroom door shut

Keeping the bathroom door closed is the most basic and fundamental of all bathroom cures. It's simple, short, and to the point, yet it makes a real difference in the energy quotient of the home. If your children or hard-to-train guests constantly leave the door open, you can apply a special trick: Replace the standard hinges on the bathroom door with special spring door hinges from the hardware store. These hinges close the door even if others don't remember to.

Hang a full-length mirror on the outside of the door

Hanging a full-length mirror on the outside of the bathroom door works in conjunction with the cure in the preceding section. How so? Basically, a full-length mirror yields very good effects if you keep the bathroom door shut, but it yields almost no positive effects if you don't keep the door closed. Here's how this cure works for you:

- ✔ Energetically, it helps the chi within the home flow away from the bathroom so it doesn't drain out.
- ✔ Perceptually, the mirror makes the bathroom vanish from your attention because the view in the mirror reflects another part of the home.

Keep the toilet lid down and drains closed

The main energetic problem posed by bathrooms involves their drains; stopping or blocking them up helps avoid the loss of chi. Men, this cure asks that you develop one teensy little new habit in your daily life, and it's the same one your mother tried to teach you: Keep the toilet lid down! (You didn't know your mother was a Feng Shui master, did you?)

In addition to keeping toilet lids down, I recommend you keep a stopper in the tub and/or shower and sink drains when they aren't in use. Both of these cures help retain energy in your home and in your life.

Applying additional bathroom cures

You can apply the following suggestions à la carte for your individual bathroom (and life) situations:

- ✔ **Install small, round mirrors above the drains to provide additional lifting power.** The mirrors' lifting power counteracts the downward-pulling effect of the drains and retains vital chi in the household. Affix a 3-inch round mirror on the ceiling above each drain in the room (with the mirror side facing down) and visualize the chi being lifted up. The most important location for this mirror is above the toilet, but it can also help when you affix it above the sink and tub and/or shower drains. (I show you an example of this cure in Figure 13-4.)

✔ **Add plants for life.** Many bathrooms are somewhat grim and lifeless, but you can easily change their energy with healthy green plants. If your bathroom or green thumb doesn't support real plants, you can substitute realistic-looking artificial plants, which work just as well.

✔ **Spruce up the place.** If your bathroom feels stark and bare, warm it up with some healthy and pleasant décor. The Chinese say that a clean and beautiful bathroom helps the household stay healthy and happy (and they're right!). Feng Shui color recommendations for bathrooms are white along with brighter-colored accents. But you can also apply your own taste and enjoy the results. Add artwork, colorful candles, and/or positive scents to your bathroom and watch your health and attitudes take an upward turn.

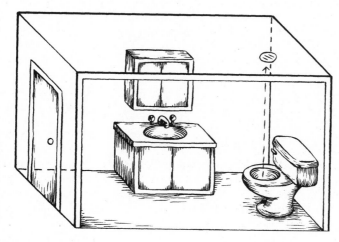

Figure 13-4:
Mirror above toilet/ drain cure.

The Garage

An attached garage is actually part of the home, even though most people don't consider it as such. Based on its condition and chi, an attached garage can affect any Life Area of the Octagon. The continuous effects of vehicles going in and out of the home (including noise, fumes, and chaotic energy) can disturb the chi of any Life Area. For example, depending on its energy condition, a garage in the Marriage Area can put a strain on your relationship with your spouse or partner. Check out the Octagon of your floor plan to determine in which Life Area your garage lies and turn to Chapter 3 for more information regarding the Feng Shui Octagon.

According to the principle that the first thing you see affects you, if you usually enter your home through the garage, the condition of the garage strongly conditions your personal energy. If you constantly view a messy, dark, and dirty garage, you can feel frustrated and cranky for no good reason. Apply old-fashioned elbow grease to the situation and spruce up the space as much as possible. The whole home — and the family living in it — will feel much better as a result.

The ideal situation is to have a detached garage, which, though more inconvenient, is better for the energy of the home in general. (Detached garages actually have a greater effect on the energy of your land.) For more on the Feng Shui of outbuildings, see Chapter 7.

The Basement

As the foundation that supports the home, the basement affects the home as a whole, including its residents — you and your loving family. This is true energetically, in terms of chi; tangibly, in terms of air flow quality; and symbolically, in that dust, dirt, and unused items "below" the main floor may represent repressed energies that you may be in denial about or would prefer not to look at.

If your basement is damp, scary, dark, or packed to the gills with stuff you haven't touched for years, why not grab a shovel, mop, broom, and dustpan and clean it up? Not only is doing so valuable for your health, especially in terms of air quality and home hygiene, but it can also resolve or clear up long-standing issues, problems, and life situations that you were unaware of or had gotten used to. Particularly good benefits come from checking the humidity level of your basement to ensure it's not a breeding ground for mold.

Basements typically feature more *yin* (dark, passive) energy than *yang* (bright, active) energy. Yin energy isn't a bad thing; in fact, life can't go on without it. However, the goal is to maintain an appropriate balance between yin and yang energy in the home. Feng Shui experts propose that this balance in home environments is struck with slightly greater active yang influences than passive yin energies. Problems occur when an environment such as a basement becomes overly yin: dark, damp, stuffy, stagnant, still, neglected, and cavelike.

You can manage to live with a basement comfortably through good Feng Shui. My goal is to help you create the best circumstances in your life, whether you're living above or below the Earth. So carefully consider the factors and cures noted in the following sections, especially if your home features an occupied basement bedroom.

Note: The following factors are reduced if your home has a *walkout basement,* a basement where you can walk straight out into the yard from the room, often through a large, sliding glass door. This type of basement is typically surrounded by the Earth on three rather than four sides. Consequently, it enjoys more natural light and fresh air (yang influences) than more traditional basements.

The more time you spend in the basement, the more influence the basement's energies have on you. But even if you seldom venture into your basement, you benefit greatly by making sure it has good, positive energy.

Improving light levels

Basements are darker than rooms on a home's upper floors because they typically have fewer, smaller, and/or higher windows accessing less natural light. Dark and dim environments are depressing and can make you more tired or even lazy.

To cure low levels of light, simply add more and brighter lights. I recommend using full-spectrum light bulbs, which imitate the Sun's light and provide added mental and physical benefits. (Flip to Chapter 15 for more information on the power of lighting.)

Optimizing air quality

Basements often have limited air access, poor circulation, and fewer negative ions in the air. This is detrimental because negative ions in an environment are critical for physical and emotional health. Healthy environments, such as unspoiled beaches, mountains, and forests, all have high-quality air that's charged with negative ions.

To cure poor air quality in a basement, keep the area clean (after all, dust and dirt affect air quality) and add as many living plants as you can. Plants thrive under natural lights — all the more reason to perform the cure I advise in the preceding section. Another option is to open basement windows frequently to freshen the air. If your windows don't already have screens, install some so you can leave the windows open without worrying about insects entering your space. You can also consider adding a high-quality air purifier.

Utility Rooms

Utility rooms include mudrooms, back or side entryways, mechanical rooms, and laundry rooms. The basic Feng Shui rule for all these rooms is the same: Keep them neat and clean.

Chapter 14

Sprucing Up the Bits and Pieces

. . . .

. . . .

*I*n this chapter, I present a veritable potpourri of cures for the individual features that make up and adorn the living spaces in many homes, including doors, windows, walls, ceilings, beams, hallways, stairways, posts, and fireplaces. All of these parts affect the energy of a home; here, I show you how to alter them to improve their energetic effects. Read on to gain the solutions.

For best results, intensely visualize your desired outcome when applying the cures. (Visualization really works! The details on it await you in Chapter 6.)

Doors and Doorways

A door's primary purpose is to admit the good things you want; secondly, it excludes bad, negative, and harmful things. A door relates to its respective home or room as the mouth does to the body, so the energy of your doors and doorways is a key contributor to the overall Feng Shui of the space.

Though the main door is the most important one (see Chapter 9 for details), all doors in a home have an effect on the home's energy — and your energy. The two essential Feng Shui aspects of doors are how the energy gets to and into the door and how it flows into and affects the room.

The energy of a space is conditioned in large part by the way it enters the space, which is primarily through a door. The energetic function of an entry is to channel energy into the space it addresses. The visible side of this function is the people who walk through the door; the invisible side is the *chi,* or life-force energy, that circulates into the space. In general, desirable energy flow characteristics in a home or room are smooth, balanced, and harmonious; undesirable energy flow characteristics include blocked, chaotic, stagnant, rushing, or piercing.

In the sections that follow, I outline common door/doorway problems and present cures for each one. You'll be pleasantly surprised how quickly they improve your situation if you're experiencing the negative effects of a misbehaving door.

Taking a look at good and bad door alignments

In Feng Shui, doorways positioned across from each other in a hallway can either agree or disagree energetically depending on how they're aligned. The following points offer a short course on door alignments and how they can affect you (see Figure 14-1):

- ✔ If the doors are the same size and completely aligned with each other (as in Figure 14-1a), they agree, which is good — no problem here.

- ✔ If the doors are completely unaligned (as in Figure 14-1b), this is also fine. Move along.

- ✔ Doors that are slightly misaligned — called *biting jaw doors* — can result in disagreements and conflicts between the occupants of the rooms (not shown in figure). Cure these doors by hanging a crystal or wind chime in the hall between the two doors.

- ✔ If the doors are obviously misaligned, cure this by mounting vertical mirrors from top to bottom at the two wall positions shown in Figure 14-1c.

- ✔ If one door is larger than another that's directly opposite it (as in Figure 14-1d), the larger door devours the smaller one. This negative situation is acute if the larger door is a bathroom and the smaller door is either a bedroom door or a kitchen door. The cure is to hang a faceted crystal sphere in the hall between the two doors.

Addressing four or more doorways in a row

As you proceed down a hallway, passing through four or more doorways can create a negative condition called a *heart-piercing arrow,* a particularly harmful form of the poison arrow problem that I describe in Chapter 7. When you have four doorways in a row, each doorway gradually compresses and focuses the chi until it functions like a shooting arrow that pierces the personal chi of the residents, potentially leading to problems along the midline of the body. If this hallway terminates at a bathroom or a bedroom, the situation becomes acute. (See Figure 14-2.)

The cure is simple: Hang two or more faceted crystal spheres between the doorways and along the pathway through the doorways.

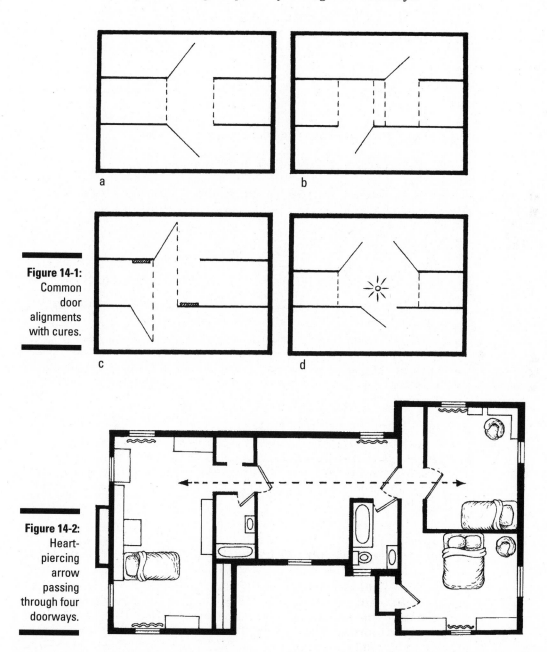

Figure 14-1: Common door alignments with cures.

a

b

c

d

Figure 14-2: Heart-piercing arrow passing through four doorways.

Curing clashing doors

When one door physically collides with another at any point of its swing, the condition is called *clashing doors*. Among other things, doors correspond to voices — specifically the voices of adult residents. Therefore, clashing doors can induce conflicts and arguments between members of the household. This principle applies to any pair of doors in the home, whether inside, outside, closet, or otherwise. For example, if the master bedroom door swings open and hits a closet door in the bedroom, the energy of these doors striking each other can create marital discord and confusion between the partners. Similar situations can ensue in any other area of the home.

Cure clashing doors by hanging a bright-red drapery tassel from each doorknob of the clashing doors on the sides where they touch. (See the later "Hallways" section for help curing multiple doorways in a small space.)

Setting stuck doors free

If doors in your home can't open easily, don't work correctly, or get stuck on the floor or the frame, the energy within them can't flow smoothly. Worse yet, if one of these problems exists at the main front door, the entire household can experience problems (see Chapter 9 for more details). If the master bedroom door sticks, your relationship may have unnecessary conflicts, and your career may become blocked or stifled. Restroom door problems can wreak havoc on your taxes and accounting, stuck dining room doors can damage your financial welfare, and jammed kitchen doors can have a negative effect on both wealth and health. The cure for stuck doors is to realign, repair, or replace the faulty door(s).

Relieving a reversed door

In Feng Shui, a door that opens near a wall, making the view of the space very small at first, is called a *reversed door*. This situation can create a negative effect on the senses upon entering the room. The cure is to change the door so it opens to the wider part of the room, allowing a more open visual perception. However, if this cure proves impractical in your situation, you can apply a mirror to the wall near the door as shown in Figure 14-3. This mirror visually opens the space, providing a feeling of freedom and flow where constriction formerly prevailed.

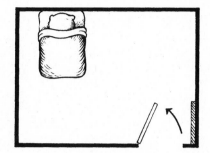

Figure 14-3:
Door open-
ing to tight
space with
mirror cure.

Treating angled doors

Whether you enter a residential space in a straight line or at an angle affects both the quality of your experiences and your overall life course, profoundly conditioning your body, mind, and spirit. A straight entry symbolizes smooth, balanced energies, whereas an angled entry implies off-balance or off-kilter effects. Feng Shui refers to angled doors with the colorful phrase "wicked doors that bring evil chi." (To see an angled door, check out Figure 14-4.)

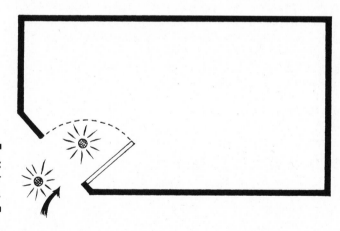

Figure 14-4:
Angled door
with cures.

Problems created by angled doors include physical maladies (spinal, bone, and joint issues), emotional distortions, accidents, and big heapin' platters o' bad luck. Consequently, curing angled doors is important. Although any angled door is unfortunate, the greatest problems result from an angled front, master bedroom, or office door. The cure? Hang two metal wind chimes or faceted crystal spheres, one outside and one inside the angled door, as in Figure 14-4.

Windows: The Eyes of Your Home

How you see out of your windows strongly influences your view of life, your energy, and your daily activities. Windows that open outward rate better in Feng Shui than those that open inward, sideways, or upward. Also, windows that open widely allow more positive energy to enter compared to those that open only slightly.

Your view out the window is a good metaphor for your relationship with the outside world. Literally, windows represent how you see your present world; symbolically, they represent how you view your future. If the view is depressing, blocked, or chaotic, this influence finds its way into your psyche. Windows are also energetically connected to the eyes; broken, stuck, or blocked windows can induce eyestrain and other vision problems. I present several specific window issues, along with cures for each one, in the following sections.

Windows that are blocked from the inside or outside

If the view from your windows is blocked, both your career and future can suffer. In addition, blocked windows can promote depression, stagnation, and frustration. For the growth of your career — and to see bright possibilities in your future — I recommend you remove obstructions that keep you from seeing the street (or any front view) from your front windows.

Note: If things outside your domain block your view, such as a nearby building, you can help your situation by hanging a faceted crystal sphere from a red string cut to a multiple of 9 inches in length in the window, slightly above eye level.

I also recommend keeping the vegetation next to your home from extending above the bottom of the windows. If bushes, trees, or other obstacles cover your windows (even partially), trim them back to allow for a clear view from the interior. If you have a large tree in front of your window, you can trim some of the branches and either hang a faceted crystal sphere in the window (inside the home) or hang a wind chime with a pleasant sound between the tree trunk and the window (outside the home).

A client once had tree branches blocking several of her front windows, prohibiting a clear view of her street and front yard. After trimming the branches to allow a much wider view, she felt more encouraged in life, moved ahead more quickly in her career, and experienced greater income.

Windows blocked from the inside of the home are just as bad as ones blocked from the outside. Want a simple cure? Move the offending bookcase, box, or other item away from the window; see the world more clearly; and enjoy a smoother career and social life.

Stuck, malfunctioning, sealed, or broken windows

Windows in the home should work smoothly and easily for maximum visibility and good eyesight. Windows that malfunction, are cracked or broken, or are painted shut can induce eye problems or issues for the children of the household. The cure is to repair the windows so that they work perfectly.

If a stuck window proves impossible to fix, you can attach a 3-inch round mirror to the windowpane, with the mirror side facing inward. This cure lets the window and home breathe, relieving energetic pressure and stuffiness. You can apply this same solution to high-rise windows that are meant to be inoperable.

Windows overwhelming doors

In Grandmaster Lin Yun's Feng Shui school, windows symbolically represent the voices of children in the home, another good reason to fix any window problems soon. An overabundance of windows can cause the parents' voices to be unheard and encourage the children to start running the household.

Determine the balance of windows to doors purely by intuition and feel, not by a mathematical ratio. (Here's my standard recommendation: If in doubt, do the cure — and see the benefits.) You can cure a plethora of windows by hanging a faceted crystal sphere in front of each one to balance their overabundant energies.

Windows that are too high, are too low, or come down too far

If a window is positioned very high in a wall and prevents you from seeing out, you can feel uneasy, controlled, or stifled, especially if the high windows are located in the bedroom. This problem isn't a major one, though, so if these types of windows don't bother you, no cure is necessary.

If, however, you feel that this situation is troublesome, hang a mural or painting that depicts an outdoor scene on the wall. Position it below a too-high window or above a window that's too low. If you're not a fan of nature art, hang a mirror in either of these positions rather than a painting (the larger the better). This is also a good cure to do if you have no or too few windows in a space.

A window that comes down too far (in other words, it has a bottom sill that's quite close to the floor) can sometimes make residents feel overexposed and vulnerable. In this case, it's okay to obstruct the lower portion of the window a little. Use potted plants to cover the window to at least knee height or higher. One client with too-low windows who always felt her neighbors were watching her performed this cure and suddenly felt comfortable and free in her neighborhood.

Skylights

According to the Feng Shui principle that says your home is energetically connected to your physical body, skylights can represent having a hole (or other possible problems) in the back of the body or the head. The most dangerous skylight is one that's added to the home while you're residing there; this event may result in unfortunate accidents involving the back or head. Although any added skylight is a possible danger, skylights added near the entrance or center of the home, in the kitchen, or in the master bedroom are especially suspect. These situations can potentially affect both financial and physical well-being.

Cutting a hole in the roof of your home (or having workmen do the cutting) without applying proper Feng Shui precautions can foreshadow future surgery or accidents and result in head-related injuries. Recommended precautions include choosing a fortunate date and time to begin the project (see Chapter 23) and performing the Rice Blessing before starting the work (see Chapter 21). You can also perform the Rice Blessing to help alleviate negative effects if you've installed a skylight in your home in the past.

You can cure a skylight by hanging a faceted crystal sphere from the center of it (see Figure 14-5). In this case, a clear suction cup is best for attaching the sphere.

Figure 14-5:
Skylight
showing a
crystal cure.

Angled Walls

According to Feng Shui principles, angled walls (which run diagonally across a floor plan) can be a negative feature in any home. Why? Because the slant results in rushing chi, which can flow too fast and throw things off balance (out of harmony) in the home. ***Remember:*** Energy circulates throughout your home all the time — whether you see and feel it or not.

Make angled walls a high priority to cure if they're located in a room or Life Area where you're currently experiencing problems. For example, if an angled wall stands in the Marriage Area of your bedroom and your relationship has been plagued by arguments since you moved into the home, consider this angled wall a prime place to cure. Of course, you can always physically move and straighten the slanted wall; however, this usually isn't a practical solution. I share two effective cure methods that are far easier to implement in the following sections.

Method 1: Stabilizing the wall's energy

A good way to handle the chi of an angled wall is to place a cure at each end of the wall (see Figure 14-6). For example, place a healthy green plant at each end of the wall to anchor the energy of the angle. Or put a lamp at one end and a plant at the other. This method effectively controls and harnesses the powerful energy of the angled wall, allowing you to make the angled wall your friend and benefactor rather than a troublemaker.

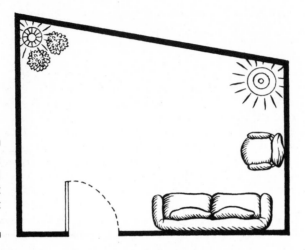

Figure 14-6:
Angled wall
with light
and plant
cures.

Method 11: Slowing down or diffusing the energy flow

A slanted wall creates an imbalance in whatever room it's in, with increased pressure and restriction toward the narrow end and expansion toward the wider end. To slow down or diffuse the flow of chi in your home, hang a wind chime or a faceted crystal sphere from the ceiling at the center of the angled wall. This cure makes the energy in your home flow more peacefully.

Another effective cure is to mirror the entire slanted wall to reflect the opposite wall, which gives the slanted wall the illusion and feeling of being square. If you use a partial mirror, make it as large as possible and position it so that it reflects the narrow side as closely as possible, especially if the angled wall is near an entry.

Ceilings

In general, the ideal ceiling is a flat one that's proportionate to the size of the room and the home — not too high, not too low. If your ceilings fit this description, you're off the hook. Multileveled, slanted, uneven, and other seemingly interesting ceilings, on the other hand, are worthy of consideration for Feng Shui cures. All of these ceilings can cause confusion, mental instability, mood swings, and differences of opinion among the home's residents, as well as blood pressure and blood sugar level problems.

A home with a one-level ceiling for the whole home (or per floor of the home) is preferred. Having one level of ceiling per room (rather than a multileveled ceiling) is also important.

During a Feng Shui consultation, I noticed that the ceilings of a client's condominium were extremely high (anywhere from 18 to 30 feet tall) for a fairly small structure; they were also multileveled. The home felt like a tower, and the ceiling over the master bed was more than 15 feet high and slanted. I wasn't surprised when the client reported that the previous occupant became imbalanced and completely wrecked the home. The multiple design factors likely conspired to create an unfortunate influence on the psyche of the resident. Using the cures given in the following sections helped the couple feel much more relaxed and mentally stable in their home.

Note: If your ceiling issues seem difficult for you to handle even with the information in the following sections, consider contacting a professional Feng Shui consultant for recommendations (head to Chapter 24 for info on selecting a consultant and the appendix for consultant sources).

Dealing with slanted ceilings over the bed

Generally, a slanted ceiling over your bed can make for an unpleasant situation. A slanted ceiling over the head of the bed presses down on the heads of the sleepers, creating mental pressure, headaches, strife, troubled sleep, and the constant desire to get up and leave the room. The cure is to hang a wind chime or faceted crystal sphere directly over the head of the bed, as shown in Figure 14-7. Alternatively, you can place plants or upward-shining lights, or you can hang two bamboo Feng Shui flutes vertically in the sword shape beneath the slanted ceiling to provide a lifting effect (see Chapter 4 for the scoop on bamboo flutes.)

Applying general ceiling cures

For a multilevel ceiling, you can install false ceilings to create the appearance of a more level and even surface. This cure is pretty pricey, though. A less expensive cure is to artistically drape fabric overhead throughout the open space to break up the lines and replace the hard angles with softer flows of energy.

For yet another ceiling fix, hang large mobiles or crystal chandeliers from the ceilings. High-quality crystal chandeliers are an especially effective solution for a multilevel ceiling.

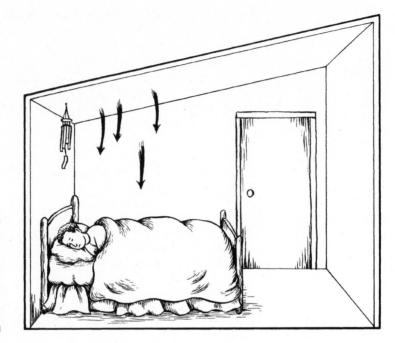

Figure 14-7:
Slanted
ceiling over
bed with
wind chime
cure.

Beams

Many times, beams act as oppressive forces that can create division, repression, and a feeling of suffocation among the occupants of a home. Any place where people enter, sit, or lie down can receive negative effects from an overhead beam (unless the beam is very high, very small, or hard to notice; in these instances, residents may receive little or no negative effects from the beam). A beam over the stove can depress your finances and physical health. Over the desk, a beam can block your career, and a beam above the dining table can hurt both your career and your social life. The worst Feng Shui beams are ones that go over the bed; they depress the marriage and the couple's health.

I provide Feng Shui cures for troublesome beams in general and above-bed beams in the following sections.

Resolving beams throughout the home

In my consulting experience, bamboo Feng Shui flutes have the greatest curing power for oppressive beams. If you don't want to hang flutes, you can hide the beams with fabric or a false ceiling. You can even paint the beams the same color as the ceiling. (If the beams' color already matches the ceiling but they still feel oppressive, hang a Feng Shui bamboo flute at both ends of the beam, as recommended in the following section.)

Curing a beam over the bed

The ideal bedroom ceiling is flat across the whole room. It's neither too high nor too low and is beam free. A beam over the bed can create unseen pressures on the bed and on you — physically, mentally, and emotionally. If you sleep with a partner, a beam above your partner can urge him or her to flee the relationship, and if the beam runs between you and your partner, it can split you apart. Additionally, beams that run across a bed can create physical problems in whatever body parts they cross. For example, a beam over the pelvis area of the sleeper can cause hip and pelvis maladies, and a beam across the stomach can create indigestion and stomach pain.

One great solution to above-bed beams is to hide the beam(s); if your ceiling is high enough, you can visually screen off the offending beam(s) with any type of false ceiling. Otherwise, the best cure for beam-over-the-bed situations is to hang two special bamboo Feng Shui flutes on the beam at 45-degree angles, placing one at each end of the beam. (Refer to Chapter 4 for visual guidance on hanging bamboo flutes.) The symbolism of the flutes provides a powerful uplifting effect and creates relief from the pressure and oppression of the beam.

If the beam over the bed runs along a peaked ceiling, the cure contains two parts:

1. **If at all possible, move the bed so it's under the highest part of the ceiling, taking into account Commanding Position principles if feasible**

   I cover the Commanding Position of the bed in Chapter 11.

2. **Hang two flutes at 45-degree angles on the wall over the bed, underneath the beam, as in Figure 14-8.**

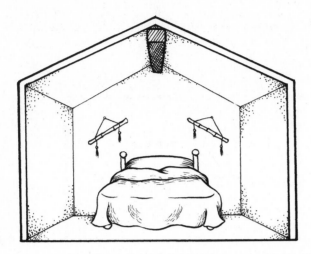

Figure 14-8:
Bed under peaked ceiling and beam with flute cure.

My client Larry, a real estate investor, was distraught when his wife decided to leave their marriage. During the session, I discovered that a beam ran the length of his bed, directly over the area where his wife slept. A few days after Larry hung a bamboo flute at each end of the beam — the recommended cure — his wife returned to the home and the relationship.

Hallways: A Home's Main Energy Arteries

Hallways are main energy arteries of the home that conduct chi, information, and people through the space. Consider these factors for a hallway: length, width, number of doors, lighting, and — most importantly — feel. The best hallways feel open and clear, with a free flow of energy. In the next sections, I detail common hallway issues and simple, yet effective, solutions. (For information on the best door alignments within a hallway, see the earlier "Doors and Doorways" section.)

Hallways with too many doors

A hallway that contains too many doors in a small space can cause fighting within the family, and you can find yourself continuously using up all the money you earn. The easiest fix is to mirror all the wall spaces in this hall (see Figure 14-9). The best option is to mirror the entire wall surface; a lesser but still helpful cure is to place sizeable rectangular or square mirrors on each wall.

Another cure is to hang one to three wind chimes or three faceted crystal spheres along the hallway to calm and modulate the flows of energy. For a grander solution, install leaded crystal light fixtures or, better yet, chandeliers (if space permits).

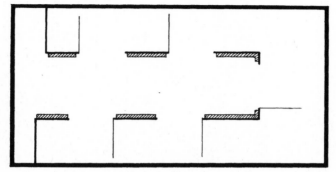

Figure 14-9: Multiple doors in hallway with mirror cures.

Long and narrow hallways

If a hallway is very long and narrow, people passing through it can experience an oppressive or tight feeling. A long, narrow hall can conduct rushing chi that moves too quickly, potentially harming the home's energy. To increase the feeling of space and freedom and add brightness, hang sizeable square or rectangular mirrors (either way, the larger the better) on one side of the hallway (both sides is even better).

A bathroom or an occupied bedroom at the very end of a long hall can bode ill for the residents — even more so if the bed or toilet is visible from the hallway. For the bedroom, moving the bed to a better site in the room may be the best option. If that's not feasible, apply the same cures as for a hallway that contains too many doors (see the preceding section) to cure the rushing energy.

Stairs

Stairways are pathways that bear chi and people. They also connect levels of a residence or structure. Depending on the construction, the energy of a stairway either feeds the floors to which it connects or prevents a free flow of energy between the floors. The following sections focus on spiral staircases and how to cure their problematic effects. (For information on outside stairs leading to the front door, see Chapter 9.)

Transforming spiral staircases

Spiral stairways create many Feng Shui problems, especially if you install them after living in the home. Their energy drills down into the ground like a bore or augur, pulling chi and fortunes downward. This downward energy spiral affects the room and the Life Area where the stairway is located.

Spiral staircases can also cause health issues. If the landing faces the front door, illness or brain disease can result. If the staircase is located in the center of the home, residents can experience heart problems.

First things first: Ensure the spiral staircase features risers (a lack of risers can lead to unforeseen accidents). Then add one or more of the following cures as you see fit:

- ✔ **Wrap an artificial vine of green ivy along the stair banister, from the bottom all the way to the top (see Figure 14-10).** The symbolic living energy of the vine stimulates growth and life and counteracts the negative effect of the stairs. This cure is the best one to perform for this situation.

- ✔ **Hang a faceted crystal sphere or wind chime at the top of the stairway.** This cure draws the energy up the stairs and reverses the downward energy spiral.

- ✔ **Place large, healthy green plants (live or artificial) in the open space below the spiral staircase.** The rising energy of the plants provides a symbolic upward antidote to the downward-spiraling energy of the stairs.

Figure 14-10:
Spiral
staircase
with green
vine cure.

When performing cures on spiral staircases, visualize your life being dramatically uplifted and improved, particularly in the Octagon Life Area where your staircase resides (see Chapter 3 for details about the Octagon).

Looking at assorted stairway problems and simple cures

The following stairway problems are easily cured; if left untouched, though, they can create unpleasant feelings and thoughts.

- **Dark, tight, or claustrophobic stairs:** These stairways are frightening, depressing, and oppressive to the residents who navigate their paths. Treat this problem by shining lots of bright and pleasing light on the stairs.

- **Rickety, unsafe stairs or a missing or broken banister:** Stairways with these features can make your life unstable and can be a literal health hazard. The cure? Fix 'em!

I present additional stairway cures in Chapter 9, including cures for stairs with missing risers, the *mandarin duck stairway* (a stairway at the front door where one stair goes up and the other goes down), stairs that lead to a blocking wall, and stairs with difficult turns. These cures apply equally to indoor and outdoor stairs.

Pillars, Columns, and Posts

Pillars, columns, and *posts* are all terms for the same physical structure; in this section, I refer to pillars, columns, and posts that are inside the home. They can block flows of chi and send negative arrows throughout the rooms they inhabit. Cure pillars or columns that stand in the center of a space by mirroring all four sides of the pillar or column. *Note:* If these structures stand near a wall, applying the cure is even more important.

Another cure is to place a potted plant, preferably one with flowers, at the base of the post. A vine from the plant should be trained to grow circularly up the post. Alternatively, you can hang four potted plants, one on each side of the post. The plants should feature irregular lengths of vines hanging down to decorate the post. (A post that stands in the corner of a rarely used room generally isn't harmful.)

Fireplaces

Fireplaces affect the household based on their location in the Life Areas of the Octagon (turn to Chapter 3 for more information about the Octagon). Fireplaces located in the Fame, Family, and Knowledge Areas are either good or neutral. On the other hand, fireplaces located in the Career, Children, Helpful People, and Health Areas are negative. The final two Life Areas, Wealth and Marriage, can be either positive or negative fireplace locations, so I recommend curing them as well.

To cure a fireplace located in any part of your home, simply place a total of nine healthy green plants (either real or realistic-looking artificial ones) around the fireplace and on the mantel, as in Figure 14-11. The green energy adds life and balance to the area. For a smaller version of this cure, place just one healthy, large plant in front of the mouth of the fireplace.

If you don't have a green thumb, you can cure your fireplace woes by hanging a large mirror over the fireplace. The mirror, which represents water, helps balance out the fire chi.

Figure 14-11:
Fireplace with nine green plant and mirror cures.

Chapter 15

Power-Boosting Your Home's Energy

From lighting up dark, dreary rooms to fixing broken items and systems, keeping your home clean and colorful can enhance its useful energies. In this chapter, I cover key tactics for perking up the energy of any home.

Lighting Up Your Life to See Positive Results

According to Feng Shui principles, adding light to a space can increase its chi and help make positive changes in your home and life. The type and quality of the lighting in your home and workplace can either improve or harm your health, moods, prosperity, and destiny. In the following sections, I go into detail about the overall quality of the light in your environment. (Turn to Chapter 4 for additional tips on applying light cures to specific parts of your home.)

A key area to infuse with good lighting is your entryway — both inside and outside your front door — because light levels in this area help set the mood for the energy of your entire home. In addition, bright light in the entryway can assist your career and fortune. Another good principle is to ensure that all key rooms of the home (the bedroom, kitchen, and dining room) contain strong, bright lights, even if you don't keep them on all the time. **Note:** You can install dimmer switches for these lights if you enjoy lower lighting levels; just make sure the lights can potentially be turned on brightly at any time.

Nurturing health and life with natural light

Grandmaster Lin Yun's Feng Shui school regards the body-mind system as the primary environment for practicing Feng Shui. What does this mean? That in Feng Shui terms, you're even more important than your home or bedroom. One good way to take advantage of this principle is to receive more light from nature. The light created by the Sun and the Moon is the best type of light for both your body and your mind; receiving sunlight and moonlight activates, energizes, and balances you.

You can enjoy natural lighting by going outside more often, like during your lunch hour or, at a minimum, during your morning and afternoon breaks. This practice is especially good for people who are inside sealed office buildings all day without access to natural light. *Note:* If you can see out a window while you work, that light helps immensely, but because of the way clear glass filters sunlight, this situation isn't as beneficial as being outside in direct sunlight.

The latest findings by light researchers indicate that the human body has a physical need to consume natural light on a regular basis. Sunrise, midday, and sunset are particularly effective, mood-enhancing times to receive the Sun's light. (Energetically, the best time is between 11 a.m. and 1 p.m. standard time.) You can benefit from the Sun's maximum energy at midday; just be cautious about getting too much direct exposure. You can also receive good-quality light by walking through woods. The filtered and dappled light that comes through the trees creates a unique calming effect.

A little-known but highly effective method for receiving light from nature is gazing at the Moon — the longer the better. Moonlight produces calming, cooling, and refreshing effects that increase feelings of hope, peace, and optimism. Seeing the Moon (preferably between 11 p.m. and 1 a.m. standard time) during any part of its cycle is helpful, but the light of a full Moon is most beneficial. In fact, the ancient energy masters prescribed the special practice of staring at the full Moon all night — a method described as powerful enough to heal 108 diseases.

Mental (or internal) uses of sunlight and moonlight offer additional benefits to the body and spirit. To discover one such use, check out the Great Sunshine Buddha Cure I present in Chapter 22.

Taking advantage of natural-light substitutes indoors

Spending too much time exposed solely to artificial light can greatly affect your energy, moods, sleep patterns, and work abilities. If your environment receives little natural light or you spend lots of time indoors, you can supplement your light diet by using full-spectrum bulbs available for both incandescent and fluorescent lamps. True full-spectrum lights aim to reproduce the beneficial light of the Sun, whereas the old-style (non-full-spectrum) fluorescent lights, for example, give off a cool, blue light and emit less light from the warmer, yellow end of the spectrum.

For a better but more expensive solution, you can install special lights that specifically provide huge amounts of healthy light. (One available brand is OttLite; search the Internet for sources.) Many people find that these lights work wonders for their depression or seasonal mood swings, a condition called *seasonal affective disorder* (SAD), during the winter months. By providing exposure to full-spectrum light — the kind Mother Nature intended — these lights help stimulate the pineal gland, suppressing melatonin, which is a sleep hormone that's overproduced by SAD sufferers.

Recognizing the importance of improving interior lighting levels

The best type of interior lighting is bright and pleasant without feeling harsh. Dimly lit rooms are fine as long as you can turn on a bright light at any time.

Check to see whether the rooms in your home are equally lit on both sides. A researcher found that people tend to feel comfortable and remain in rooms lit on both (opposite) sides, but they tend to leave quickly from rooms lit on only one side.

One key area of the home to keep well-lit is the bedroom. This room should contain at least one light that brightly lights the entire space by itself (this solution works even if you don't often use the bright light). A bedroom containing only dim light can represent a bleak future, cause you to be depressed and moody, and make it difficult for you to find a partner or enjoy a happy relationship.

Bright lighting is also essential in the kitchen. You need enough light to cook well, but bright light in the kitchen can also improve your mental health.

Adding Life with a Splash of Color

Color adds wonderful aesthetics to an area, and just about everyone loves it. In addition, the energies of specific colors create different types of effects on humans. With Feng Shui, you can use colors to change your life circumstances in specific ways.

You can choose from many color options for your Feng Shui adjustments. These color methods — all of which are covered in the following sections — include

- ✔ Choosing the best colors to adorn the individual rooms of your home
- ✔ Using colors associated with the Life Areas of the Feng Shui Octagon
- ✔ Applying any of the three special Feng Shui color systems as taught by Grandmaster Lin Yun's Feng Shui school

All three of these methods, which I delve into in the sections that follow, are quite valuable as paths for performing cures in your home and life. None of them are Feng Shui requirements as such. Rather, you can use them as and when you see fit, like when you need a boost in a corresponding part of your life.

Recognizing good colors for rooms of the home

Grandmaster Lin Yun's Feng Shui school advocates particular families of wall colors as being the most energetically sound for main rooms of the home. From painting an entire room one color to accentuating a room with several colors, applying the following color principles to the indicated rooms can enhance your health, moods, and good fortune:

- ✔ **Master bedroom:** The best colors for this room include pink, peach, blue, and green. Pink is the color of love in Feng Shui, and peach represents high attractiveness to the opposite sex.

  You can use either peach or pink to attract a mate, but if you use peach, switch to pink after the relationship solidifies to prevent a wandering eye.

- ✔ **Kitchen:** White is a good color for the kitchen because it shows off colorful food to the best advantage. Accent colors for kitchens include red and/or black.

  Lots of black — which in Chinese energy theory is the color of water — should be avoided because it can put out the vital fire energy of the stove.

✔ **Children's bedrooms:** Kids' rooms are best in green and blue; these colors help children grow and flourish. White is also favorable. Use darker colors only to settle down or calm a child.

✔ **Living room, den, and family room:** Multiple colors and shades work well in these rooms. Earth tones — especially yellow, gold, and shades of brown — are very agreeable, providing grounding and centering in these key rooms. Green and blue are also favorable, adding cheer, life, and growth.

✔ **Dining room:** Pink, green, and blue are the best colors for a dining room. These colors bring positive chi to social gatherings.

Using the colors of the Feng Shui Octagon's Life Areas

Cures using the colors of the Feng Shui Octagon's Life Areas are easy and effective to perform (see Chapter 3 for more details on the Octagon). You can use color to positively adjust the energy of any Life Area. Table 15-1 features a list of the nine Life Areas and their corresponding colors. You don't have to feature these colors in the respective Life Areas of your home to have good Feng Shui. However, if you want to perform cures for a specific part of your life, placing corresponding colors in the specific Life Areas of your home, lot, or room's Octagon is a powerful way to do so.

Table 15-1	**Colors of the Feng Shui Octagon's Life Areas**
Life Area of the Octagon	*Colors for Empowering This Life Area*
Helpful People	Gray, black, white
Career	Black, midnight blue
Knowledge	Blue, green, black
Family	Green, blue
Wealth	Purple, green, blue, red
Fame	Red
Marriage	Pink, white, red
Health	Yellow, earth tones
Children	White

Most of the Life Areas have multiple colors; for example, the Wealth Area uses purple, green, blue, and red. Be sure to visualize positive, desired life results when applying your new colors (refer to Chapter 6 for tips on visualization).

You can apply the following color cure methods as your personal needs and circumstances dictate:

> ✔ **Use the color or colors of the Life Area as the main color scheme for a room in the corresponding area of the Octagon.** For example, to improve your marriage, decorate a room in the back-right part of the home (the Marriage Area) with the color pink.

> ✔ **Place items (either large or small) featuring a color of the Life Area you're targeting in the respective Life Area location of the space.** For example, if you want to increase your wealth, you can place something purple in the Wealth Area of your home (or yard or bedroom).

Employing the three special Feng Shui color systems

This section gives you special color adjustment methods with special energetic and spiritual capabilities. The two color methods I present in the previous sections provide powerful transformation; using the color adjustment methods I present in this section is like adding jet fuel to the mix — they're that effective.

Any of the three special Feng Shui color systems can initiate powerful and dramatic life results when you use them in any part of your home. Think of them as "all-purpose magic" you can bring to bear on any situation. They're also good if you don't know of any cure to use for a situation. You can choose from the three methods to enhance your home's energy based purely on intuition.

To implement a cure using one of the special Feng Shui color systems, you can install one item (such as a painting or other work of art) that contains all the colors, use multiple items to get all the colors in the space, or paint and/ or decorate as you see fit using one of these color groups. (Keep in mind that there's no need to limit yourself to only one of these color systems. You can use one, two, or three of the systems throughout your environment if you prefer.)

> ✔ **Special Color System I:** Also known as *The Colors of the Five Elements,* this system uses all five of the Element colors together — green, red, yellow, white, and black — to powerfully invoke harmony, balance, creation, and prosperity. The colors represent each of the Five Elements (Wood, Fire, Earth, Metal, and Water, respectively). When all Five Elements are present, you can use them anywhere as an all-purpose cure (see Chapter 5 for the full scoop on the Five Elements).

✔ **Special Color System II:** This system, also referred to as *The Six True Colors,* uses the colors white, red, yellow, green, blue, and black — a unique group of colors that symbolizes healing, blessing, and luck. This combination brings extra oomph to help you in almost any situation that needs it.

✔ **Special Color System III:** Also known as *The Seven Rainbow Colors,* this system uses all the colors of the rainbow (red, orange, yellow, green, blue, indigo, and purple). Applying this rainbow of colors as a cure helps bring positive feelings, good luck, and harmony to everyone in the environment.

Keeping Things Shipshape and in Working Order

A venerable Feng Shui principle states that your home represents and is connected energetically to your physical body as well as your mind, emotions, and spirit. This connection means that many things are happening in your environment that have positive and/or negative effects on your health and well-being. In other words, the general maintenance and condition of the systems and appliances in your home can energetically affect your physical health.

Although physical ailments often stem from multiple causes and factors, many individuals find significant relief from disease and environmental sensitivity by fixing problems that relate to faulty systems in their homes. The sections that follow provide simple cures you can apply to the systems of your home to maintain a healthy flow of energy.

Maintaining your plumbing, foundation, and electrical system

All home systems relate to your own physical systems. For example, the things that circulate and move in your home have a connection to the things that flow within your body. When the flow in your home's systems is smooth and optimal, its effect on you is benign or positive; when the flow is hindered or stopped for any reason, the energetic effects on you are less than desirable. The next sections explain how to cure plumbing, foundation, and electrical system problems.

Plumbing problems

The plumbing systems of the home correspond to the circulatory and digestive systems of the physical body. Problems in these areas can result in many physical ailments, sometimes of an unusual or puzzling nature.

- ✔ **Stopped and clogged drains:** Problems with pipes and drains relate directly to the digestive and eliminative functions of the body, specifically the intestinal and excretory systems. Clogged drains symbolize a difficulty in the internal flow and issues with processing and releasing. The cure is simple: Clear the pipes! Reinforce this cure with the Three Secrets Reinforcement (see Chapter 6) and let the benefits flow.

- ✔ **Leaking pipes:** On the physical level, leaks correspond to urinary and kidney issues. In addition, water leaks in the home are immediately suspect for money problems or issues in your wealth scenario. Numerous people experience unexpected financial gains and clear up money problems by fixing their leaky faucets, problem toilets, or faulty pipes.

Leaks don't need to occur only inside the home to cause problems — leaks anywhere on the property can affect you as well. Stay aware of what's going on in your home and on the land around it.

Foundation problems

The foundation is the basis for your home's structure. Look out for problems including foundation defects and cracks, earthquake damage, excessive moisture, and water infiltration into areas such as basements. Problems in the basement can cause family and job instability and bring about unusual health problems.

To cure foundation problems, have a foundation repair expert assess your situation and quote you a cost for repairs. If the problems aren't fixable or are simply impractical for you to fix right now, I recommend that you or a Feng Shui specialist perform the Rice Blessing ceremony (see Chapter 21 for the how-to) as a way to energetically bless your home. (The Rice Blessing ceremony is also beneficial to perform after completing any home foundation repairs.)

Electrical problems

The electrical system of the home correlates to the body's nervous system. Fixing faulty wiring, lights, fuse boxes, transformers, phone lines, and computer systems is a good Feng Shui practice for restoring positive chi flow. These fixes can help eliminate physical problems (such as muscle spasms and other nervous system issues) as well as psychological and emotional difficulties (including memory loss, nervousness, and irritation).

Making sure air is flowing

The heating and air conditioning system in your home relates to your lungs and ease of breathing and blood circulation. This breathing link isn't simply a symbolic connection; proven relationships exist between dirty, debris-filled air ducts and residents who suffer from allergies, breathing difficulties, and respiratory ailments.

You can cure such problems by hiring a professional cleaning company to clear out your home's ducts at least once a year. Also, be sure to clean or change your furnace and air-conditioning filters regularly (check your owner's manuals to find out the right maintenance schedules for your appliances). Another good remedy is to use a high-quality vacuum cleaner, preferably one that uses a sealed canister system and features true high efficiency particulate air (HEPA) quality filtration.

Checking the roof for potential issues

The roof of your home relates to both the head and the back. Leaks and holes in the roof can represent problems with the head or spine and are best fixed immediately. Take care when cutting holes in the roof, though; this activity can lead to unexpected accidents or problems involving the head or brain.

If you plan to cut any hole (no matter how small) in your home's roof, you can ensure greater safety by performing the Rice Blessing (outlined in Chapter 21) the day the project begins. A stronger method is to perform this cure both at the beginning and the end of the project. In addition, I advise making the first cut in the roof between 11 a.m. and 1 p.m. while visualizing that the workers and the home's family members experience freedom from harm. (Find visualization tips in Chapter 6 and cure-timing pointers in Chapter 23.)

Fixing or replacing malfunctioning or broken elements

Malfunctioning items pose Feng Shui problems; nonworking or poorly working equipment in your environment creates the energy of decay, which energetically relates to the property. Make sure everything on the premises works correctly by removing or repairing anything that needs attention as quickly as possible.

The following list of examples gives you an idea of how items in disrepair affect you. The cure for each instance is quite clear: Fix it!

- ✔ **Burned-out light bulbs, missing bulbs, and broken fixtures reflect a dim future and indicate bad luck.** When bulbs go out, the best practice is to replace them as quickly as possible with bulbs that are at least as bright as the old ones.

- ✔ **Broken and malfunctioning clocks represent time running out on you.** Clocks that keep time poorly encourage confusion and missed appointments.

- ✔ **A broken garbage disposal indicates digestive and excretion problems.** This situation affects all members of the household.

- ✔ **Stove problems harm the pocketbook and the body.** Stove maintenance is so important that I devote an entire section to curing the stove in Chapter 12.

- ✔ **Broken bed elements are a top Feng Shui priority because the bed affects just about every part of your life.** Repairs to the bed are essential for good Feng Shui. See Chapter 11 for more information about beds.

Chapter 16

Improving Your Apartment with Feng Shui

Multiunit living has its benefits and challenges. Any of the following sound familiar?

- ✔ **The benefits:** You never have to mow the lawn or repair the roof. And if you're lucky, you have a great big pool at your disposal.

- ✔ **The challenges:** Units tend to be smaller than detached homes, neighbors are closer, and walls are thinner (as evidenced by the fact that you can hear some oaf blowing his nose or playing bongo drums on the other side of your unit). Also, units have fewer green spaces — not to mention less psychic space.

Sure, it may look like the challenges of multiunit living outweigh the benefits, but never fear — Feng Shui is here! Whether you rent or own your unit, Feng Shui can help you make the most of any multiunit living situation. The cures in this chapter are sure to smooth the snags and resolve the ruffles that come with apartment living.

Note: In this chapter, the word *apartment* also refers to condos, lofts, town homes, and other forms of multiunit living.

Addressing the Common Fate Principle

Living in the same building with other occupants — your lovely neighbors — means you may share more with them than simply a structure. According to Feng Shui teachings, sharing a common roof means sharing a common fate — a fact that's otherwise known as the *Common Fate Principle.*

If you feel that sharing a fate with your neighbors may be less than desirable (like if you don't want your health and relationships to match those of your illustrious neighbors), you can apply an effective remedy by performing one or more of the following solutions as you see fit:

- **Hang a bamboo Feng Shui flute horizontally or at a 45-degree angle over the inside of your front door.** Bamboo flutes energetically bring peace and safety — qualities that help protect you and your home. I give you the lowdown on hanging angles for bamboo flutes in Chapter 4.

- **Perform the Citrus Water Blessing inside your unit.** Also known as the Interior Chi Adjustment, this ceremony, which I show you how to do in Chapter 21, can help clear any negative energies in your space and infuse fresh, clean, and positive energy into your home. Both of these effects can serve as powerful forms of protection.

- **Perform the Rice Blessing around the exterior perimeter of your apartment building or around the perimeter of the apartment property.** This ceremony, also known as the Exterior Chi Adjustment, can help clear known and unknown issues, whether they're physical, emotional, spiritual, or financial. Chapter 21 has step-by-step instructions to help you perform this ceremony.

Examining Your Building's Structure

People often direct too much of their Feng Shui attention to the interior of their unit, but keep in mind that the structure of the building is also important in determining the overall Feng Shui situation. If you're trying to decide which multiunit residence to live in, check out what's happening in the building's exterior and its surrounding factors. (I note the surrounding factors to look for in Chapter 7.)

In the following sections, I focus on several scenarios related to your building's structure: the height of your unit within the building (in other words, how close you live to the ground), the effects of having a garage in your building, and the location of elevators and stairwells.

Living up high in the sky

Modern building methods make it possible for millions of people to live and work high above the ground in multilevel apartments and high-rise offices. From the Feng Shui point of view, living in a high unit affords at least one advantage: You typically get a commanding view of your surroundings, which helps you feel on top of the world. However, when residing in a lofty position, it's possible to start to feel too high, ungrounded, and precariously perched. Why? Because human energies are actually connected to the Earth's magnetic fields. If you're living higher than, say, the third floor, you may feel subtly wobbly and ungrounded, as well as mentally confused or uneasy. If you find yourself in this position, Feng Shui can help you make the best of it.

The Feng Shui solution is to perform grounding cures in your unit to solidify and stabilize your life. Placing sizable green plants or large, smooth stones in all four corners of the apartment or in all four corners of the bedroom (or both for extra effect) are effective cures. Another, and possibly more effective, option is to perform the cure for the garage under the master bedroom; turn to Chapter 11 for the details (although this cure is specified for the master bedroom, you can perform it in the living room or even in multiple rooms).

What else can you do? Besides moving to a lower unit, a good solution is to install plants, plants, and more plants with lots of soil in their pots for grounding. Other cure items that also contain Earth element energy are earthenware (pottery), objects of earth tone colors, and cubic shapes. *Note:* Like every cure in this book, be sure to apply the Three Secrets Reinforcement (see Chapter 6) when you do these cures for maximum effect.

Sittin' on pins: Pillars in the garage

Some apartment complexes feature a big garage that takes up the whole ground floor. This amenity is supposed to enhance security and make parking more convenient for the residents. The problem, however, comes to the residents who live on the floor directly above the garage (and to a lesser extent those on floors above that).

Sitting on top of a large, vacuous space in which vehicle movement constantly disturbs the area's chi can wreak energetic havoc in your life. In addition, the entire building may be energetically precarious because it sits on pins (support pillars in the garage) rather than a visually solid support structure. The cures for this situation are the same as the ones I present in the preceding section.

Dealing with elevators and stairwells

When you live in a multiunit building, people are often coming and going — and making plenty of noise as they take the elevator or clomp along the stairs. I once visited a friend's apartment, and people came and went 26 times from the elevator in the hall in the space of an hour. Even though you can block out the sounds and vibrations as time goes by, they still affect your energy and your results.

Generally, farther away is better when it comes to noisy elevators and stairwells. The closer your unit is to the elevator or a stairwell, the more disturbances caused by the comings and goings of others can influence your life and decisions by affecting your energy. The cure? Hang a special bamboo Feng Shui flute horizontally over the inside of your front door (see Chapter 4 for flute-hanging details).

Optimizing Your Living Space

In the next sections, I present several techniques you can use to make the most of your apartment living space, including resolving entrance issues and improving oddly shaped units.

Defusing entrance issues

The front entrance is the most important Feng Shui area in any home, and multiunit buildings can have more complicated entrance situations than other residences. For one thing, there are multiple entrances to negotiate: the main entrance to the building, the entrance to the elevator and/or stairway(s), the entrance to one or more hallways, and (finally!) the entrance to your unit. Also, one or more of these entrances may be convoluted, dark or poorly lit, narrow, or confusing, all of which can cause various Feng Shui calamities. They can even be dangerous in some cases. To reach the front door of many units, you almost need to crawl through serpentine labyrinths of passageways, halls, and turns. Your unit's entrance may be virtually nose to nose with the entrance across the hall. These conditions can cause you to experience greater energetic obstacles if you're trying to get ahead in your life, career, or relationship.

Making the most of your unit entrance isn't merely an option but a necessity. If moving or getting the landlord to perform an overall building cure isn't possible, I suggest using the kitchen sink method, which means throwing everything at the situation. As much as possible, make your entryway clear, open, and free. You can

✔ Give it nice, bright lighting.

✔ Use mirrors to open the space if needed.

✔ Install fountains to create flow.

✔ Hang chimes to encourage the flow of energy to your front door.

Choose cures from the preceding menu that fit your needs and enjoy the energetic shifts that come when your entryway cures start working.

Resolving an oddly shaped unit

Take a look at the overall shape (the outline of the floor plan) of your unit. Is the shape regular or irregular? A loose rule of thumb is that symmetrical shapes, such as squares and rectangles, are good and that irregular shapes may be positive or negative depending on the specific details. So how do you know whether an irregular shape is helpful or harmful to your energy and your life? One way is to diagnose projections and missing areas in your apartment.

✔ *Projections* (expanded or extra sections) in a particular Life Area mean positivity for the corresponding part of your life. Reinforce projections to enhance the positive results.

✔ *Missing areas* (parts of the space that are "cut out" or not present) represent deficits or problems in the Life Area in which they're located. When living in a multiunit residence, you're usually limited to applying interior Feng Shui solutions for missing areas in your unit's design because you don't have authority over the apartment building's exterior. Don't fret, though, because you have many options from which to choose; check them out in Chapter 8.

Taking on a teeny living space

Space (or lack thereof) is a common reality of apartment life. To counter the boxed-in feeling that a small living space causes, I suggest performing one or more of these cures (reinforce them all with the Three Secrets Reinforcement I present in Chapter 6):

✔ **Get rid of some of your stuff.** If it isn't absolutely necessary, toss it, sell it and use the cash for Feng Shui cures, or donate it to charity if you want to feel better about getting rid of it.

✔ **Employ large mirrors wherever possible to expand the space.** This cure creates the pleasant perception of a more expansive living space.

> ✔ **Apply faceted crystal spheres to energetically create a feeling of expansion, cheer, and lightness.** These spheres help introduce a quality of spaciousness to a room, psychically providing more "space" for the occupants. The centers of rooms are good spots for crystal cures.

Common issues in small homes are a sense of being cramped and a lack of energy flow. An elegant solution to this problem is to introduce one or more strategically placed fountains. I introduce fountains and other water cures in Chapter 4.

Making the most of multiuse rooms

Because apartments often contain fewer rooms than detached homes do, using your rooms for multiple purposes is natural. Unfortunately, this practice can lead to boundary issues within your home. One solution is to separate the spaces with curtains or large, attractive screens (a favorite strategy because they're moveable). Screens and curtains provide important visual blocks that supply needed separation.

If putting up a curtain or screen isn't possible, you can apply the faceted crystal sphere cure between areas of use to energetically divide spaces, balance your brain cells, and harmonize energy flows.

Giving yourself some breathing room

Do your paper-thin walls shiver when the fan blows or your neighbor has a house party? Does it seem like your neighbor is your roommate? Mirrors offer a multipurpose cure for closed-in unit living. Following are two ways to use the power of mirrors:

> ✔ For a particularly obnoxious or scary neighbor, mount a Ba-Gua mirror (see Chapter 7 for an illustration of one) on the adjoining wall surface, facing toward the other party (the back of the mirror should be facing you). You can cover this mirror with some artwork if you prefer. Just be sure to hang the mirror with a feeling of compassion, intending harmony for all concerned. The mirror can deflect unwanted or unfriendly energy emanating through the wall.
>
> *Note:* If you don't know which direction to point the Ba-Gua mirror, or if you want an all-purpose protection cure, you can simply put the mirror above the front door, ideally on the outside of your unit and facing out. If this is impossible, put the mirror at the top of the door on the outside or place it above the door on the inside but facing outward.

✔ If neighbors are friendly but a bit too present in your space, place large, traditional mirrors on adjoining unit walls facing into your space; this cure perceptually pushes your walls out farther, distancing the other party. Mirrors also brighten, lighten, and cheer up a space. The larger the mirror, the better. Just be sure to use high-quality mirrors that are free of any distortions.

Delving into Details That Make a Big Difference

Sometimes the littlest things make the biggest difference, which is why the sections that follow show you how to make small adjustments — such as increasing the natural chi in your environment and improving your air quality — that can really enhance the positive energy in your apartment.

Neutralizing harmful nearby influences

Taking a look at the floor plans or the actual interiors of units directly adjacent to yours is useful so you can address potentially threatening influences. Here are some situations to watch out for:

✔ **Toilets in adjacent units:** Next-door toilets situated directly back-to-back on a common wall with your bed or stove can cause problems.

✔ **Stoves in adjacent units:** A next-door stove that's directly back-to-back on a common wall with your bed or toilet is also problematic.

An effective cure for both situations is to put an inward-facing mirror on the common wall with the threatening feature. In other words, the shiny side of the mirror should be facing toward you, and the back of the mirror should be toward the toilet or stove in the neighboring unit. The bigger the mirror, the more effective the cure. If, however, hanging a large mirror is impractical or impossible, you can use a 3-inch round mirror. See Chapter 10 for further information on fixing your home's layout.

Often in multiunit living situations, you don't know exactly how things line up above you. So you may want to visit your upstairs neighbor or ask your property manager to show you the floor plan of the space above yours. One key feature to find out about in the apartment above you is the location of the toilets. The liabilities of a toilet located above your bed, dining table, or stove are similar to, but may be even worse than, those in adjacent units; flip to Chapter 10 for details and cures.

Helping out in the kitchen

Apartment kitchens present a couple major issues. First, they're small. To energetically expand an apartment kitchen, install mirrors between cabinets and counters (or on any available walls) — the more mirrors (and the bigger they are), the better.

Second, apartment kitchens that are in the front of the unit are too close in proximity to the front door — a position that may sabotage your finances and your health. (**Note:** The same problems occur if the stove sits farther back within the unit but is still directly visible from the front door.) Symbolically, the back of a space affords more protection than the front because the back is farther from the main point of entry; any threat has to go through the rest of the home to get to the back. The stove, being the main energy generator in the home, is vitally linked to both money and health, so it's best to have it located in the back half of the residence.

One of the most powerful solutions for an apartment stove placed too close to the front of the home is to virtually move the stove farther back within the home. You do this by placing a mirror in line with the stove and farther back in the home, with the stove clearly reflected in the mirror. Needless to say, the larger the mirror, the better the cure. Complete this cure by performing the Three Secrets Reinforcement (see Chapter 6).

Following are a few more remedies for a stove that's placed too far to the front in an apartment:

- ✔ Hang either a wind chime with a soothing, pleasant ring or a faceted crystal sphere halfway between the front door and the stove.
- ✔ Hang either a wind chime or a faceted crystal sphere directly over the cook's head.
- ✔ Install a screen or a beaded bamboo curtain to visually block the view.

If your kitchen is at the front of your apartment but you can't see the kitchen entrance (or front entrance, if applicable) when you're standing at the stove in a cooking position, install a mirror near the stove so you can clearly see the front door and doorway reflected in the mirror while standing in the cooking position. If the door is more or less behind you, you can situate your mirror as shown in Chapter 12. If, however, the door is at an angle to you or to your side, then a mirror located directly behind the stove is unlikely to perform the needed remedy. In this case, you may need to put the mirror to the side of the stove so you can see the door.

But what if you have multiple doorways to remedy or the proper mirror is somehow inconvenient? I have two excellent solutions to this dilemma:

- ✔ **Use a convex mirror.** The 180-degree view this type of mirror gives you allows you to see all relevant doorways.

- ✔ **Use a silver gazing ball.** This is essentially a spherical mirror; it gives you a view that's similar to what you get with a convex mirror (and sometimes even wider).

Bringing the outside in with natural chi

A key issue with many units is that they provide little or no yard or garden space. This lack of natural energy can be depressing as well as confining, so why not bring some natural energy inside to counteract this syndrome? The most direct route is to install some fountains or plants, spring for an aquarium, and toss some nice bird feeders on your deck. Before long, your cozy little unit will feel more like a nature preserve.

Another option is to install a photo-quality wall mural of powerful and awe-inspiring natural scenery. Search the Internet for the term "wall murals" for hundreds of options, many of which are in the neighborhood of $100. Thanks to the wonders of modern technology, you can enjoy Niagara Falls, the Grand Canyon, Mount Fuji, or the Serengeti in the comfort of your apartment. (As a bonus, most murals come with self-adhesive already installed, making them easy to place on your walls.)

A more upscale approach is to commission a trompe l'oeil painting that covers one or more of your walls to promote a feeling of expansion or depth rather than limitation. (*Trompe l'oeil* is the type of painting that gives the illusion of a three-dimensional scene with depth and perspective.) Stick with nature scenes for the best results.

Fixing stubborn windows

Landlords often have a funny way with windows. Some like to paint them shut; others like to nail them closed. Still others prefer prison-chic and barricade the windows with iron bars. If your windows don't open easily, or at all, needless frustration, hassle, and even claustrophobia can result.

Here's a simple solution: Open the windows! If they're broken and won't open, get the broken parts fixed. If the edgings are painted shut, you can buy a window-edging tool at your local hardware store and use it to open them. If the windows are covered with opaque material or unneeded bars, find a way (or hire someone) to remove these as well. Don't suffocate in your living space. When you cure your window problem and complete that cure with the Three Secrets Reinforcement (see Chapter 6), better energy flow will result, and you'll breathe easier. (*Note:* If you happen to live on a ground floor in a dangerous neighborhood, it may be best to keep the bars on the windows.)

Windows in a home correspond to the residents' vision, so treat window problems as a high priority and take action as soon as possible. Windows also represent the voices of children (whereas doors represent the voices of adults). A Feng Shui colleague once told me that every client she has ever consulted who had children and significant window problems also had significant issues or problems with the children. The connection with children can occur with any window issues in the home, not just those in children's bedrooms or ones located in the Children Area of the Feng Shui Octagon (I tell you all about the Octagon in Chapter 3).

Clearing the air

If you live in a high-rise with central air conditioning and heating, your windows may just be panes of glass that don't open. Whole-building air and heating means you're likely not the person in control of how often the filters and vents get cleaned out. Find out your building's maintenance schedule and try to make sure the filters get changed regularly.

A powerful cure, and one of the best investments you can make, is to generate fresh oxygen in your home by buying some plants. Not only do plants make your place look great and inviting but they also remove toxins from the air. Plants such as gerbera daisies, English ivy, peace lilies, and dracaena are known to remove harmful substances such as formaldehyde, benzene, and trichloroethylene from the air. These chemicals are used in cleaning products, paints, adhesives, and varnishes. So take a trip to your local garden center and stock up on air-cleaning plants, potting soil, and pots.

If you and plants just don't get along, then invest in the best air purifiers your budget allows. Breathing fresh air means having fresh and bright thoughts.

Chapter 17

Using Feng Shui in Your Office to Enhance Your Career

In This Chapter

▶ Relying on the Octagon and the Five Elements in the office

▶ Inspecting your office floor plan and making it work for you

▶ Assuming the Commanding Position at work

▶ Finding a good desk for a great career

*I*n addition to paying attention to your home's Feng Shui, you also need to consider the Feng Shui of your workspace. Although the Feng Shui of your home almost always affects you in a deeper, more fundamental way than the Feng Shui of your personal workspace, performing workplace Feng Shui is still a very valuable method of improving your life. The proper application of the methods in this chapter leads to an improved career, greater opportunities, and more income. Sound intriguing? Get ready to discover ways to improve your career by performing Feng Shui in your personal workspace and in your home office.

After you've applied the solutions in this chapter, if you want to take further steps in using Feng Shui to enhance your career, you may want to consult a professional Feng Shui practitioner. Turn to Chapter 24 and the appendix for help finding a consultant.

Using the Feng Shui Octagon and the Five Elements in Your Office

The Octagon and the Five Elements can help you maximize the power of your office space. Apply the simple methods in the following sections to implement these powerful systems. (Flip to Chapter 3 for basics on the Octagon and Chapter 5 for details on the Five Elements.)

The Octagon

Place the Octagon over a scale drawing of your office, room, or cubicle exactly like you would for any other room (see Figure 17-1). After you map out the Octagon, you can apply cures to any Life Area requiring help in order to meet your intentions.

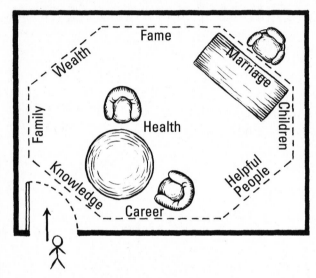

Figure 17-1:
Placing the Octagon on a scale drawing of your office.

Depending on its shape, your office may be missing one or more Life Areas; these absent Areas reflect missing energy in the corresponding part of your life. For instance, if your office is L-shaped, one or more Life Areas are missing, which can negatively influence your business life. If the Wealth Area of your office is missing (for example, if a corner is "cut out" of the room in the back-left section), you may find it harder to bring in money. After you spot a missing area, you can correct its harmful influences by performing a cure, such as hanging a faceted crystal sphere to energetically complete the area. Turn to Chapter 8 for help determining whether your office has missing areas and applying the aforementioned cure.

The meanings of the nine Life Areas of the Octagon (eight sides plus the center) at work are similar to those you use when applying the Octagon to your home. Table 17-1 lists the additional correspondences for the office.

Table 17-1	Meanings of Octagon Life Areas for the Office	
Area of Environment	**Traditional Correspondences**	**Additional Correspondences for the Office**
Front right	Helpful People, Travel	Suppliers, Customers, Co-workers
Front center	Career, Journey	Promotion, Career Growth
Front left	Knowledge, Self-Cultivation	Education, Learning, Personal Growth
Middle left	Family	Team Members
Back left	Wealth, Money	Profits, Income, Paychecks
Back center	Fame	Reputation, Recognition, Marketing, PR
Back right	Marriage	Key Partnership(s)
Middle right	Children	Employees
Center	Health	Health (of employees and of the business)

Keep these tips in mind as you plan your office cures using the Octagon:

- All Octagon meanings are symbolic rather than literal; for example, if you're a manager, your employees aren't literally children (even though sometimes they may seem that way).

- All the Life Areas of the Octagon are important. Table 17-1 simply gives you added insight into where to employ Feng Shui solutions at the office. Enhance the Life Areas that need help, but keep paying attention to all the other Areas as well.

- You can use the Life Areas in your office to perform cures for your home life, work life, or both; the choice is up to you and based purely on your intention. For example, you can perform a cure in the Marriage Area of your office to enhance your marriage (home life), your partnership at work (work life), or both. Why? Because all cures are designed to adjust the energy of you — this is the secret of Feng Shui.

The Five Elements

You can use the Five Elements anywhere you work, whether that's in an office, a cubicle, or your home. The *Five Elements* are natural phases of energy (Wood, Fire, Earth, Metal, and Water) that occur in every environment, and Feng Shui gives you the opportunity to take advantage of their powers to further your career. Each of the Elements' natural positions happens to correspond to one of the Life Areas of the Octagon, as detailed in the following sections.

Five Element cures are effective even if you don't fully understand the meaning of the Five Elements, much like how you can taste spices in your food even if you didn't see the chef put them in. Apply the cures and find out for yourself. (To discover more about the nature and uses of the Five Elements, see Chapter 5.)

Orienting the Five Elements in your office

Orienting from the main entry of your workspace, place the Five Elements on your floor plan in their natural locations on the Octagon.

- **Wood Element:** Center of the left side of the space, the same location as the Family Area

- **Fire Element:** Center of the back side of the space, the same location as the Fame Area

- **Earth Element:** Center of the space, the same location as the Health Area

- **Metal Element:** Center of the right side of the space, the same location as the Children Area

- **Water Element:** Center of the front side (the side containing the door) of the space, the same location as the Career Area

Finding cures for your career

The purpose of the information in the following sections is to show you how to use the Elements that help you the most. You don't necessarily need to employ all five of the Elements to obtain great benefits (although you certainly can); just use the ones you need.

Wood

Wood helps you reach higher, grow into new aspects of life, put down solid roots, and break through obstacles. To increase the growth, expansion, and upward movement of your career, place any of the following items in Wood's natural location:

- A lively green plant

- Any object or piece of art containing the colors green and/or blue

- A rectangular or columnar object, especially one positioned upright, such as a stereo speaker or wooden file cabinet

Fire

Fire provides you with lots of energy and movement and increases your circle of influence. It can also help you become more active, better known, and more powerful. To enhance the Fire energy of your career, place any of these objects in Fire's natural location:

✔ A candle or bright light (the brighter the better)

✔ A red object

✔ Something triangular or pyramid-shaped, with the point directed upward

Earth

Earth creates balance, peace, connection, and stability. Earth cures are good if you're experiencing changes and transitions and want to feel more solid and grounded. People and companies in rapidly moving industries can benefit by applying Earth cures. To invoke the increased presence of Earth in your environment, you can accentuate your office with one of the following:

✔ An earthen item, such as pottery, a ceramic statue, or a smooth stone

✔ Yellow or earth-colored pieces

✔ Square or cube-shaped objects

If possible, put the Earth objects or colors in the center of the space; this is the natural location of the Earth Element. Otherwise, put them as close to the center as is convenient for you.

Metal

Metal is the agent of communication, creativity, codes, and keys. It unlocks doors and conducts energies from one place to another. If you need to make better connections with people or move more quickly and fluidly, the Metal Element is your friend. You can put these cures in the natural location of Metal to enhance its power:

✔ Anything made of Metal, such as a chair, table, lamp, or art object

✔ An item or picture containing the color white

✔ An object or image with a circular, domelike, or spherical shape

If a wall in the natural location of Metal (the center of the right side of your space) is already white, this is already a positive placement. Just apply your intention and the Three Secrets Reinforcement and voilà! You have a cure.

Water

The Water Element is manifest in two types — moving and still. Moving Water brings money and people, making it a prime choice for any business. Still Water improves depth, wisdom, and clarity.

To increase either type of Water, you can

✔ Apply the colors black or midnight blue in Water's natural location.

✔ Place something in the location with an undulating or wavy shape.

Here are two great cures for improving the energy of moving Water:

- ✔ Install a fountain in the natural location of Water.
- ✔ Hang a photo or painting of a waterfall, river, or ocean.

To generate increased still Water, place an image of a large, calm lake in Water's natural location.

Working with Your Office Layout and Floor Plan

If you work in a corporation and aren't a top executive, you probably don't have much choice over where your office is located, but you can arm yourself with knowledge about the good and bad positions in your building. In the sections that follow, I show you cures that can work for almost any office or cubicle.

The positioning and quality of your office space

Generally, the farther your office is from the front door and toward the back of the building or suite your company occupies, the stronger your position is in terms of energy. First, power tends to accumulate near the rear of the building. Second, the people near the front take the brunt of the incoming traffic and noise. The energy of the space in the front influences people to serve, whereas the people near the rear of the building tend to rule. For individual offices located on floors above ground level, being located as far away from the main entry point to the floor, such as the elevator, is generally more powerful.

You can find exceptions in some offices, but over time, this rule plays out: Unless you run the company, someone else or the existing conditions dictate your workspace location. Of course, if you can choose your work location within a building, all other factors being equal, the one closest to the back is a stronger pick and can provide you with more power.

Be sure to use common sense when applying the principle of there being more power in the rear of an office building. If you can choose between two offices — one in the front of the building that's large and spacious and also has great lighting and a good position for the desk, and one in the back of the building that's cramped, dark, and depressing — the better choice is obviously the front office with the better conditions and feel.

What can you do if you want to increase the power of your office position and career but you find it impossible to switch offices? Other than finding a new company to work for (or sneaking in at night and changing the location of your office building's front door), you can perform the symbolic mirror-moving-the-desk cure. Hang the largest possible mirror (I recommend one that's at least 3 feet across) on the wall of your office that's closest to the back of the building (you can hide it behind a piece of art if you prefer). The mirror should face your desk, and your desk should be visible in the mirror (unless of course you intentionally cover the mirror). This cure works well because it doesn't diminish the power of anyone else; it simply increases your power and energy. Visualize that this solution energetically places you farther back in the building to increase your power and stability.

Private offices versus cubicles

The continuous corporate emphasis on cost-cutting and profit maximization has led to a related, yet unfortunate, drive to squeeze the maximum possible usage out of every square inch of office space — not to mention out of employees.

Corporate settings use two general seating arrangements: individual offices (one room per worker) and the more impersonal cubicle. The move to more people sharing space, whether in cubicles or not, contributes to an admirable flattening of hierarchies within corporations. However, the downside is sterility as well as a lack of privacy and personal space; you may feel like a unit in a machine rather than a person with individual needs and desires.

The following sections reveal how to use Feng Shui to improve your personal office situation, whether that's a private room or a cubicle.

Having a room of one's own

The ideal office is a room of your own with a regular shape (preferably square or rectangle), natural lighting (at least one window), a solid door you can close, and a good position for your desk. One of the great advantages of having your own office is that you can usually perform more decorative Feng Shui adjustments than if you work in a cubicle. Of course, not every company can afford, or desires, to put every employee in his or her own individual space.

Following are cures you can perform depending on how your private office deviates from the ideal Feng Shui conditions:

✔ **Irregular room shape:** Use a faceted crystal sphere, mirror, or plant to correct the space. (Refer to Chapter 8 for details on applying these shape solutions.) If your office is extremely irregular, you can have inexplicable setbacks and continuous frustrations at work. If you can't switch offices, apply the special nine-green-plants cure. Add nine healthy, new plants (not sickly, old ones) to your space all on the same day. If convenient, you can place the plants near particular irregularities in the room, such as strange angles, posts, cramped areas, and so on. Otherwise, just stick them where they fit best. Use the Three Secrets Reinforcement (see Chapter 6) and visualize your job and career going very well.

✔ **Projecting corner, post, pillar, column, soffit, or ductwork:** Many offices contain features that break up the energy flow of the room or, worse, shoot poison arrows at your sitting position at the desk (*poison arrows* are angles, edges, or points aimed at key areas; see Chapter 7). Place a sizable plant in front of the troublesome feature or hang a faceted crystal sphere between the feature and your sitting position at the desk. (Refer to the post cures I present in Chapter 14 for more information.)

✔ **Solid versus glass walls:** If your office contains one or more glass walls that make you feel even a little vulnerable, hang miniblinds to cover the glassed-in area. Blinds are effective even if you don't use them often; their presence gives you added protection. If you can't perform this solution, use red ribbon cut to a multiple of 9 inches in length to hang faceted crystal spheres from the ceiling in front of the glass wall. Use one sphere and length of ribbon for every 5 linear feet of window space.

✔ **Improper lighting:** If you suffer under fluorescent lighting, like the majority of office workers, you may be able to replace the tubes yourself with healthier full-spectrum ones (also called "grow lights") from the hardware store. If you can't replace them (either physically or because you aren't allowed to change the lighting), bring in some supplemental full-spectrum light in the form of floor or table lamps. Working solely with overhead light is uncomfortable for the eyes, and supplemental lighting is a source of relief for your eyes and mind.

Surviving and thriving in a cubicle

A cubicle is sometimes a trickier Feng Shui situation than an office room. Cubicles are unfortunate paradigms of vulnerability for the individual worker. One of the chief problems is that you don't use a real desk but instead work from a countertop, unless of course you work in one of those large, manager-type cubicles. However, just because you work in a cubicle doesn't mean you can't do plenty to improve your situation. By judiciously applying the following Feng Shui cures, you may find yourself in your own office sooner than you thought; see Figure 17-2 for cure placements.

Seeing the entrance

The first and most important priority is to make sure you can see the entrance to your cube from your desk. Try to move your sitting position first, but don't seriously cramp your work style. If you can't move, don't stress out about it. If, however, you *are* able to switch your sitting location, follow the tips in the later "Putting Yourself in the Commanding Position at Work" section.

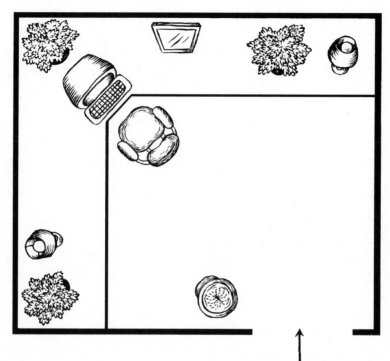

Figure 17-2:
Cubicle
with plant,
fountain,
and mirror
cures.

If you definitely can't move your sitting position, you can place an 8-x-10-inch (or larger) mirror in a picture frame or on a small stand to reflect the entrance of the cube so you can see whether anyone is approaching. Many people habitually use the reflections in their computer monitor to see who's approaching them because needing to see who's behind you is a natural human instinct. The problem is that the reflection in a monitor's screen is distorted, unclear, and unreliable. A mirror is therefore much better.

Adding living energy and water features

The second priority is to bring living, flowing energy into your workspace. These features are important ways of compensating for the small size of your space and the constant traffic flowing past your cube.

If you can bring several (three or more) healthy plants into your space, you can stimulate more active, vibrant energy. A nice fountain near the entrance of your cube can also work wonders. Not only can it stimulate more salary coming your way but it can also help uplift your mood and diffuse any negative flows of chi (human or environmental) in the vicinity of your workspace.

If space or social realities preclude having a fountain in your workspace, you can receive some of the same benefits from a photo (the larger the better) of flowing water, such as a waterfall or river.

Uplifting the overhead storage

Many cubicles provide storage space starting about 30 inches above the desk space. This setup crowds your head and symbolically makes moving up the corporate ladder more difficult. I recommend hanging faceted crystal spheres from the storage bins, one for every 3 to 4 linear feet of the length of the bins. The spheres can help uplift the oppression of the space and brighten your outlook on work and life.

Putting Yourself in the Commanding Position at Work

In the interior of the home, bed position is the single most important factor; in your office, desk position takes the honors. An auspicious desk position can mean the difference between an easy, smooth, and progressing career and one filled with hardships, setbacks, and problems.

Using Commanding Position desk principles

The best Feng Shui position for the desk fulfills the principles of the Commanding Position, which I introduce in Chapter 2. First, keep in mind that the position of the desk relative to the office door is more important than the compass direction the desk faces. Second, know that achieving the Commanding Position means that your desk position aligns with all four of the following principles at once:

- ✔ The desk is as far from the door as possible. (Such positioning gives you more control over your space as well as time to react to what comes in the door. It makes you calmer, more resourceful, and more confident at work.)
- ✔ The desk position allows you to see as much of the room as possible.
- ✔ The door of the office is clearly visible from where you sit, allowing you to see who's entering.
- ✔ The desk isn't in the direct path of the door.

Seeing the door equals success

A vital aspect of the Commanding Position principle applied at work is that you can see the door from your desk position. Seeing who or what's approaching is a fundamental element of power and success at work. If your back is to the door, you're in the symbolic victim position, which makes it easier for others to take advantage of you. If your side is to the door, the effect is the same, although somewhat less.

Note: Seeing the door from your desk means you can glance up from your work and clearly see the doorway without having to shift your position in your chair. Figures 17-3a and 17-3b are examples of powerful desk positions.

If you find it impossible to turn your desk to see the door, arrange a mirror on your desk or, even better, place a larger mirror on your wall so you can see the entry. Simple and easy, this cure is a career (and life) saver. I show you what the mirror cure looks like in Figure 17-3c.

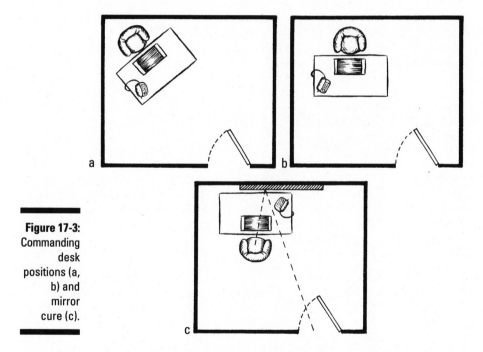

Figure 17-3: Commanding desk positions (a, b) and mirror cure (c).

Some people insist that facing the door is distracting. They don't like to be bothered by every passer-by because they want to get a lot of work done. Other people think they can find inspiration sitting with their back to the door so they face out a window with a nice view — despite the fact that a window view actually distracts from the tasks at hand. If you fall into either category, I understand your position. I really do. However, as a minimum cure, I recommend you use the mirror alternative so you can see the door whenever you want. Your control of the situation makes a real difference.

Understanding other key desk placement factors

Although the tips in the next sections don't carry the weight of the Commanding Position, they can help you gain success in the competitive world of work and career.

Stay clear of the wall

Unless you work in a very large office, you're usually better off without any furniture behind your desk chair. In addition, having at least 3 feet of space behind you while you're at your desk is good. If you hit the wall as you back your chair up, frustration and anger can result.

Avoid having a threatening window or door behind you

Sitting with your back to a solid wall is ideal in an office setting. A window creates some vulnerability but isn't a Feng Shui emergency. In fact, if the window affords good lighting, it can be helpful to your work. If, however, the window makes you feel uneasy, that's a problem; hang a faceted crystal sphere or wind chime from the ceiling, about one-third of the way down the window. If the window is quite large, you're bound to feel insecure, so use drapes or blinds to make the window look smaller.

If a door is behind you, the situation is much worse; the crystal or chime cure for the previous window problem is a minimum recommendation. In this case, the best option is to hang the cure directly over your sitting position at the desk, as shown in Figure 17-4. See whether you can move your desk to a better all-around position. In addition, hang a curtain or tapestry or place a decorative screen to hide the door. (A door that leads to the outside behind you is particularly undesirable. Unless you have a really large office, you're better off without any outside door in the room.)

Keep extremely heavy, large, or tall furniture out of your space

Furniture that dominates the space makes less room for you and your energy to flow; it can hold you down, and it can even be depressing and scary. (Ever feel like everything is falling on your head?) The cure is simple: Get rid of large bureaus or bookcases you don't often use, or trade them for more space-saving and suitable items. Use your common sense, hold on to things you do need (like filing cabinets and bookshelves), and remember that you use only 20 percent of your items 80 percent of the time.

Figure 17-4:
Door behind
desk with
wind chime
cure.

Making Sure You Have a High-Quality Desk

Second in importance to the position of the desk (see the earlier "Putting Yourself in the Commanding Position at Work" section) are the qualities and energy conditions of the desk itself. The best desk is energetically solid and complete. A flimsy, weak desk can't support your career to the greatest degree possible. I find that my clients definitely benefit from using the energetically and physically strongest desk — a choice that pays them back in many career dividends over the years. If your workspace is large enough, go for an executive desk, which typically comes in two sizes, 30-x-60 inches and 30-x-72 inches.

Trying to use any of the following desk substitutes to pursue a serious career in business can block your progress:

- A writing table or dining room table
- A dormitory or miniature desk
- A door or piece of plywood mounted on filing cabinets

Although a sturdy desk is key, using a desk that's extremely large and heavy can be impractical. Let common sense and your individual budget guide your desk selection.

Also consider the completeness of your desk. A desk protects your front, and a desk chair protects your back. Therefore, the front panel of your desk is a vital part for protection, strength, and security at work. The best front panel extends down to the floor, whereas a partial panel leaves real vulnerabilities and weaknesses in your work life (see Figure 17-5). The cure for a missing or partial front panel is to get a desk that has a full front panel.

Figure 17-5:
Full and partial front desk panels.

Of course, side panels are important too. Some desk models have only partial side panels, so buyer beware. A vulnerable desk is one that has only legs to support a flat surface — no side or front panels. With this type of desk, you can find yourself besieged from all sides and unable to gather and hold power in the corporate world.

Wondering where to put your computer on your sturdy, properly sized desk? The ideal placement for a computer monitor is on the desk in front of you, in a position that still allows you to see the door of your office. Placing the computer on a credenza behind you generally detracts from your power to the degree that you work on the computer and can't see the door of your office. If you must turn your back on the door to use your computer, you can restore good Feng Shui by placing a mirror that gives you a clear view of the door when you're facing your computer screen.

Part IV

Going to the Next Level: Using Feng Shui for Life Change

The 5th Wave   By Rich Tennant

"I'm never sure whether your mother's adjusting the Feng Shui in the house or just lost her keys again."

In this part . . .

Here, I provide you with powerful, practical assistance so you can get started right away with Feng Shui. First, I give you a simple and effective action plan that takes all the detailed information that I give earlier in the book and boils it down into practical action steps. Then I get right into specific help for three areas of life I know you want to boost: your money, your relationships, and your health. If you want things to be much better in your home, heart, and health, dive right in for some effective solutions. Next up, I reveal an incredible-yet-little-known way to apply Feng Shui with amazing results — by using its principles to select the most beneficial home the next time you move.

And that's not all. Some of the most amazing Feng Shui methods have been kept secret for centuries. My job in life is to break the rules, spill the beans, and rip off the covers so you can get a whole lot more of what's comin' to you. In this part, I share with you special blessing ceremonies that lift negativity, clear up the bad-luck soap operas playing on *Your Life* TV, and help you feel happier, footloose, and fancy-free. (These ceremonies also bless your house so things can improve gradually.)

If these benefits aren't enough, I give you another whole chapter that's crackling with higher-level cures that you can apply directly to your own energy. Sounds freaky, yet works wonderfully.

Chapter 18

Hitting the Ground Running: Your Fabulous Feng Shui Action Plan

In This Chapter

▶ Reducing Feng Shui confusion

▶ Assembling the details you need to achieve positive outcomes

▶ Focusing on the Three Life Pillars

▶ Examining the energy of your lot and home

Reading about Feng Shui is one thing; applying it effectively and strategically to your life is another. To succeed at this goal, you need an organized and knowledgeable approach to help you start performing cures and effecting real change in your life. What you need, in short, is a plan.

This chapter may well be the most important one in the whole book because it presents a clear and understandable process for applying Feng Shui knowledge to create powerful, life-changing results. Most of the solutions in this chapter are explained in more detail elsewhere in the book, which is why I refer you to relevant chapters throughout. The point of this chapter is to give you a collection of action items you can get moving on so you can start seeing positive changes in your life as soon as possible.

You can empower your life by using the simple cures I present in this book; in fact, thousands of people have used this book to create a brighter and more exciting future for themselves. Yet some difficult or uncertain situations may benefit from the assistance of a professional Feng Shui consultant who can help you pinpoint where problems lie and customize cures to remedy them. (Chapter 24 has key tips for finding the right consultant for you.)

Avoiding the Road to Confusionville

When you begin delving into Feng Shui, it's not uncommon to feel somewhat confused (or even overwhelmed). After all, a ton of Feng Shui information exists, some of it conflicting, and sorting it all out can seem a little exhausting. The following sections give you two practical, surefire ways to avoid Feng Shui confusion.

Sticking with the methods of one Feng Shui school

Applying multiple methods from different schools of Feng Shui to your life at the same time is a recipe for chaos. Although there's definitely more than one valid approach to Feng Shui, attempting to use several of them at once can set you up for failure. Think of it as trying to combine the waltz and the mambo into one dance — both styles are based in true dance principles, but the two simply don't mesh.

A smoother, more effective path is to apply the methods of only one Feng Shui school to your life at a time. In other words, choose the methods of the Feng Shui school that's the best fit for you and stick to them.

If you want to use the approach offered in this book, then you don't need to consider compass directions or your birth date when assessing your Feng Shui. These methods are valid and relevant in other Feng Shui schools, but Grandmaster Lin Yun's Feng Shui school doesn't use them. I suggest you put aside other schools and Feng Shui books, at least for now. Give your full focus to this school and give it a fair shake. (I don't claim that this is the best or the only valid method. I simply recognize that if you take a smorgasbord approach, you're likely to end up with scattershot results.)

If you've already had a Feng Shui consultation in your current home and it was effective, my recommendation is to continue working with the same consultant if you want more of the same results. If the effects weren't satisfactory, look carefully to see whether you did all that was recommended and exactly as it was prescribed. If you did, then you may want to consider a different Feng Shui consultant or method.

Performing a limited number of cures at once

You don't want to try to do every cure in this book (or in any other Feng Shui book) at one go, any more than you want to take every herbal remedy from an herbal remedy book. Doing dozens of Feng Shui cures all at once simply because they're listed in a book is neither practical nor desirable. The best approach is to do the cures you need, not all the ones you read. Turn to Feng Shui cures when you need to address a real Feng Shui problem or when you want support for a desire or need you have in a particular part of your life.

Start by performing ten or so good, strong cures aimed at a specific part of your life. Then observe that part of your life and notice what occurs. When you see results start to happen, you begin to realize just how powerful a tool Feng Shui really is — as well as the kinds of results it can accomplish. Odds are, at that point, you'll feel like picking up the pace. (See the later section "Honoring the Importance of Focus" for more information.)

Gathering the Information You Need for Success

When you have an accurate representation of both your lot and your home's floor plan on paper, you're in a much better position to assess your situation and ensure success in your Feng Shui endeavors. The sections that follow go into detail about these important documents.

Obtaining an accurate lot plan

If you own your home, you should've received a lot plan with your title papers upon closing on your home. If you don't have one, can't find your copy, or you rent rather than own, you can obtain a lot plan by visiting your local housing authority or by searching your county's online geographic information system (GIS) service. When accessing your county's (or other jurisdiction's) GIS service, if it has one, just enter the legal address or the parcel number to see information about your property, including an outline of the lot. *Note:* If you live in an apartment, the management office may be able to provide you with a plan of the entire building and/or one showing the building on the lot.

Be aware that legal lot lines are often different than fence lines or other visual markers. It's best to investigate and find out for sure before you apply a cure to your lot (like the ones in Chapters 7 and 8) that's near the lot's edges.

Acquiring an accurate floor plan of your home

When you buy a home, sometimes you receive a floor plan of the space. If you never received a floor plan, or if you're simply unable to locate your copy, you're stuck measuring the floor plan of your home. You can go the tried-and-true tape measure route, or you can obtain a laser measuring tool from a home-improvement store. Either way, when you measure, be sure to include all doors, windows, and skylights. (It also helps to draw in the placement of your furniture.)

Keep in mind that taking the extra time to draw your environment to scale helps you accurately assess your home.

After you have your measurements, you can either draw your floor plan freestyle or use one of many floor plan design software programs to create a printable floor plan. Yet another option is to head to one of several floor planning Web sites, such as floorplanner.com, that you can access for little to no cost; just type in your measurements, create a floor plan, and print out a hard copy of it.

Use the largest paper that you practically can to draw or print your floor plans. Seeing the plan in a larger format allows you to better see what you need to change.

Note: If you live in an apartment or condominium, see whether you can also obtain a plan of the entire floor (or building) where your unit resides. This way you can see where your unit sits in the overall plan.

Honoring the Importance of Focus

Before you apply Feng Shui changes, take an in-depth look at your life, decide which part of it you most want or need to change or improve by performing the life-assessment exercise in Chapter 1, and then focus on that part. Focus is a key factor when you're trying to create change. I've seen people diverted and scattered by attempting to improve too many parts of their life at once. Working on just one part of life at a time makes it easier to see when changes are truly occurring. So if you want more money *and* a new partner, for example, address these things one at a time. When you see things moving in the right direction, you can start to consider the next part of your life that you want to change. For instance, if your financial situation improves, then you can focus on finding that new partner.

Always be sure to perform the Three Secrets Reinforcement (see Chapter 6 for step-by-step guidance) as part of each cure that you do because it supplies more than half of the effectiveness of your cures.

Keeping records ensures continuity. I suggest you record all your Feng Shui activities in a Feng Shui notebook or journal. For every cure you do, note the following:

✔ What the cure was

✔ The date you performed the cure

✔ Whether you performed the Three Secrets Reinforcement (should *always* be yes)

✔ The intention for the cure

✔ Comments and status notes (for example, something you need to do to complete the cure)

I suggest you also keep note of the life changes that occur in the part of your life you want to improve. So if you're gunning for increased wealth, for example, keep note of *any* life changes (positive or negative) related to your wealth.

Addressing the Three Life Pillars

Focusing on Feng Shui's Three Life Pillars allows you to achieve a powerful return on your Feng Shui efforts. When you address the Three Life Pillars, you effectively focus your attention on one or more of three energy spots in your home:

✔ Life Pillar I: The front door of your home

✔ Life Pillar II: Your master bed

✔ Life Pillar III: Your kitchen stove

Each of these Pillars is a critical energy point in your home. If the energy is disharmonious in one or more of these parts of the home, the corresponding part(s) of your life may well be affected. I recommend starting your Feng Shui practice with the Three Life Pillars to develop a good Feng Shui foundation for your home. You can then build on this foundation and perform additional Feng Shui cures as needed.

The Three Life Pillars are by no means an entire Feng Shui system or approach. Rather, the Three Life Pillars provide a solid foundation because they're easy to grasp, relatively easy to apply, and very effective. Why are the Three Life Pillars so effective as a set? Because each Pillar simultaneously affects multiple parts of your life in very significant ways. Here's an overview of how each Pillar affects you on a daily basis:

✔ **The front door** affects income and cash flow, opportunities, health, protection and security, and your life in general. It's the single most important spot in your home and includes the entryway areas, both inner and outer.

✔ **The master bed** (including its position and construction) is your key spot for love, marriage, and partnership. It's also vital for health, career, and wealth.

✔ **The kitchen stove** is your home's energy generator. It's therefore the most important spot for wealth and is very important for health. The stove also affects marriage, career, and family relationships.

As you can see, the Three Life Pillars contain enormous power to affect key parts of your life for good or ill. The Three Life Pillars should top your list of Feng Shui factors to assess and remedy from the start. (You can profitably address the Three Life Pillars even before harnessing the Feng Shui Octagon, covered in Chapter 3, to enhance individual parts of your life.) Consider the following sections a starter list to help you get moving immediately.

The front door

Initial things to correct around the front door include the following (see Chapter 9 for more in-depth information on improving this Life Pillar):

- **Poison arrows aimed at the door:** Get rid of or block these.
- **Glass in the front door:** If security is an issue, consider replacing the door with a solid one.
- **A door that isn't working right:** Get rid of squeaks.
- **A blocked door:** Remove obstructing items or hang a wind chime if the block is a structural feature.

If you've done all the preceding tasks and desire further improvement, here are some additional things you can do:

- Place a bright light at the front door to increase positive energy in your career and in every part of your life.
- Paint the front door red (use this cure if you need power or attraction).
- Hang a wind chime outside the door for attracting good energy and for protection.

The master bed

Following are some initial things to correct around the master bed (see Chapter 11 for more in-depth information on enhancing this Life Pillar):

- **A poorly placed bed:** Make sure the bed is in the Commanding Position. If this isn't possible, be sure the bed is out of the bedroom door's path.
- **A bedroom door you can't see from the bed:** Place a mirror so you can see the door.
- **Doorways near or aligned with the bed, or large windows near the bed:** Hang a wind chime or faceted crystal sphere halfway between the door or window and the bed to handle the problem. (Note that the doorway issue excludes closet doors but includes in-suite bathroom doors.)

- ✔ **Oppressive beams over the bed:** Correct by hanging a bamboo flute on each end of the beam.

- ✔ **Poison arrows aimed at the bed:** Remove or block these.

- ✔ **Slanted ceilings:** Hang a faceted crystal sphere over the sleeper's head.

In addition to fixing the preceding items, you can create specific life improvements by hanging a wind chime or faceted crystal sphere at one or more of the following spots:

- ✔ Over the foot of the bed for career support

- ✔ Over the middle of the bed for health support

- ✔ Over the head of the bed for an overall life boost

The kitchen stove

Initial things to correct around the kitchen stove include the following (see Chapter 12 for more in-depth information on getting this Life Pillar up to snuff):

- ✔ **A stove that doesn't allow you to see the kitchen entrance(s) directly while you're cooking:** Place a mirror so you can see the door to the kitchen when you're standing at the stove. Ideally, you should place the mirror on the wall behind the stove itself, but you can also place the mirror to the side of the stove. (Note that convex mirrors are a great option here because they give you a dramatically wider view.)

- ✔ **A door that points at the cook from behind or to the side:** Hang a wind chime or faceted crystal sphere halfway between the door and the cook's position.

- ✔ **Poison arrows aimed at the stove:** Block or remove these.

- ✔ **Stove malfunctions, such as nonworking burners:** Repair any such issues.

In addition to fixing the preceding items, for additional life help you can hang a wind chime or a faceted crystal sphere over the cook's head for blessing and protection.

Analyzing the Energy of Your Lot and Home

After tackling the important internal elements of your home (see the earlier "Addressing the Three Life Pillars" section), you should turn your attention to the larger picture of your home's energy (while still remaining zeroed in on the life priority you're working to change, of course). Here's a starter list of important things to pay attention to:

- **Check the balance of the lot and topography.** Topography charts the contours (ups and downs) of a lot, and the lot shape is the legal outline of the property itself. If your lot is flat, this is likely a neutral factor. Move on to the next topic. If it isn't flat, turn to Chapter 7 for cures that can help.

- **Diagnose the lot shape for balance.** If you live in a single-family residence, the shape of your lot is important. If you live in an apartment or condominium, you can check both the lot's shape and the building's shape. If you have *missing areas* (portions seemingly "cut out" of the home or lot shape) or slanted sides, apply the cures in Chapter 8. If your lot shape is very odd or imbalanced, you can perform the Rice Blessing Ceremony I describe in Chapter 21 to compensate for this problem.

- **Analyze the shape of your home.** The shape of your home is either balanced or imbalanced. See Chapter 8 for more information about this situation and effective ways of curing it.

- **Analyze the floor plan.** Figure out where key rooms, specifically the master bedroom and kitchen, are located. Also check the center portion of the home to see whether it contains the stove, a toilet, the furnace, or the fireplace. If it does, you can find the right cure for the scenario you're facing in Chapter 10.

- **Map the environment using the Feng Shui Octagon and the Five Elements.** By applying one or both of these mapping systems to your lot plan and home floor plan, you can see where to do cures to improve key aspects of your life. See Chapter 3 for information on the Feng Shui Octagon and Chapter 5 for details on the Five Elements.

Chapter 19

Taking Care of the Big Three: Your Money, Honey, and Health

*W*herever I go in my Feng Shui travels, I always have people asking me, first and foremost, for help in these three parts of their lives:

✔ Money

✔ Relationships

✔ Health

If you've read the previous chapters in this book, you have a good theoretical and practical start to your Feng Shui knowledge. So where do you go from here? I call this the caviar chapter because it's where you discover Feng Shui techniques that support money, love, and health.

Generating Cash Flow

Have hard economic times affected you? Whether you're doing well financially or need a boost, the next sections give you some specific Feng Shui cures for increasing your wealth.

Hitting the hot spot in the bedroom

The Wealth Area of the bedroom — the room where you spend roughly a third of your life — is a very significant location for your money situation. Paying attention here can reap real dividends. An effective cure for activating the

Wealth Area of your bedroom is to hang a colorful mobile within it. Be sure to hang the mobile from a red ribbon cut to a multiple of 9 inches in length. (See Chapter 3 for details on applying the Feng Shui Octagon to your bedroom to identify the room's Wealth Area; flip to Chapter 11 for additional cures you can employ in your bedroom.) A second option is to use a faceted crystal sphere rather than a mobile.

Placing your desk in the Commanding Position

You can more easily achieve success when your desk is placed in a Commanding Position (Chapter 2 introduces this principle). Repositioning your desk properly puts you in a position of leadership and control — not least of yourself. (Ever notice that you can run faster and farther with the wind at your back than you can with the wind at your face?) Placing your desk in the Commanding Position (farthest from and facing the door) makes nature work for you rather than against you, giving you several advantages:

- ✔ Your decision making flows easier.
- ✔ You feel more relaxed, focused, and in control.
- ✔ Your confidence naturally increases.
- ✔ Your progress seems assisted as if by invisible hands.

In addition, your money-making power may increase (along with your chi) because of this auspicious — need I say lucky — shift to the Commanding Position. Not bad for a cure that requires no monetary output and only minor muscular investment. For more cures to apply to your desk, see Chapter 17.

Knowing the right things and the right people

If you want to increase your cash flow, you have to possess the right knowledge and know the right people. Fortunately for you, you can use Feng Shui to help make sure your Knowledge and Helpful People Areas are hoppin' and poppin' with great energy.

Knowledge is critical for wealth building, so continuing your wealth education is vital and a lifetime pursuit. Special bamboo Feng Shui flutes are your friends here because they represent upward growth; install one or two of these in the Knowledge Area of your home or bedroom. (For flute pointers, including hanging angles, see Chapter 4.)

Because water represents cash, put a lively fountain in your Helpful People Area (you choose which one) and visualize the right people bringing you stacks of cash.

Putting Pizazz Back into Your Partnership

Who doesn't want to add a spark to his or her love life? Feng Shui can help! The sections that follow describe some specific cures for strengthening relationships.

Positioning your bed for good fortune

Bed placement is a prime factor determining the quality of your marriage and love life. It also plays a key role in the quality of your sleep, which significantly affects your personal strength, including how strong you are throughout the day — and throughout a date.

According to the principle of the Commanding Position (see Chapter 2), the ideal position for the bed is usually as far from the bedroom door as possible. If your bedroom door is

- **In the right-front part of the room:** The best position for your bed is in the back-left corner of the room.
- **In the left-front part of the room:** The bed should be in the back-right corner.
- **In the middle-front part of the room:** You can position the bed in either corner so long as it's far away from the door.

Wherever you move your bed, place it with the head firmly against the wall and with the door in plain view. (If your bed doesn't fit into any of the previously mentioned position options, see Chapter 11 for remedies.) After your bed is in the strongest position possible, watch your romantic life gradually (or suddenly) take a turn for the better.

Planting new life

A new plant or tree means new life. To attract a new partner, or to add new life and oomph to your current relationship, try planting a healthy plant or tree in the back-right corner of your property — also known as the Marriage Area (see Chapter 3 for more about this Life Area). First, get a plant or tree that you find beautiful and energizing. Then dig, plant, water, and love. Watch as the growing energy of the plant adds growth and new energy to your relationship with that special someone.

If the plant or tree has colorful flowers, so much the better. Any color is good, but pink is especially effective. (See Chapter 4 for an introduction to other plant-related cures.)

Removing distractions from your bedroom

The watchwords for bedroom Feng Shui are simplicity, peace, and beauty. In the bedroom, an important rule of thumb is that anything not directly connected to resting and relating to your partner detracts from the relationship. If your sleep or love life needs a boost, consider removing the following from your bedroom:

- Work-related objects, such as your desk, briefcase, and work papers
- Computers (laptop or desktop)
- Phones of all kinds (if you keep these in your bedroom, you may as well sleep with an alarm under your pillow)
- Your TV and sound system (you can survive without these technological gadgets, I promise)

Bookcases and large piles of books stacked around the room are also distractions. Although the books contain many interesting ideas, few of them really involve sleeping and relationships — the intended functions of the bedroom. Removing most of the books and all the shelves from your bedroom helps reduce mental turbulence, improve sleep, and make relaxing and relating much easier. (Check out Chapter 11 for more on bedroom Feng Shui.)

Enhancing multiple Marriage Areas simultaneously

If you're looking for help reviving a flagging relationship, snagging a new love, or making a great relationship hit new heights, try putting effective cures in multiple Marriage Areas simultaneously to tip the playing field in your favor. Start by identifying at least three Marriage Areas (pick more for an even stronger overall cure) that lie within your domain. To do so, orient yourself from the front entrance to the room or property and zero in on the back-right portion of the space — that's the Marriage Area. I recommend focusing on the following three Marriage Areas at a minimum:

> ✔ Lot or property
> ✔ Home
> ✔ Master bedroom

If you crave more potency, you can toss in Marriage Areas in one or more additional rooms of the home, including the living room, dining room, kitchen, or office. For the biggest bang of all, you can include the Marriage Area of your bed (this is the top-right corner of the bed when orienting from the foot of the bed).

For each of these Marriage Areas, perform a Minor Additions cure of your choice (I cover these in Chapter 4); you can use the same cure item for each Area, or you can opt for placing a different cure item in each Marriage Area. For instance, you can place one or more birdfeeders in your property's Marriage Area, place a bright light in your home's Marriage Area, hang a crystal sphere in your bedroom's Marriage Area, and hang a large mirror in your living room's Marriage Area. The point here is that you're curing all the Marriage Areas at once for maximum effectiveness. Just remember to reinforce your cures using the Three Secrets Reinforcement (see Chapter 6 for details) and visualize your relationship flourishing and in harmony.

You can apply the same method to any other Area of the Octagon, whether it's the Fame Area, the Health Area, the Children Area, or some other Life Area of your choosing.

Maximizing Health and Vitality

In the following sections, you find out how to remove poison arrows, take advantage of your home's center to truly boost your health, optimize and protect the cook, and take care of pesky beams.

Deflecting poison arrows

Poison arrows are a real health threat, and they can occur either inside or outside the home. A *poison arrow,* as I note in Chapter 7, is a sharp angle, point, or protruding corner that's aimed at an important spot in the home, such as the front door, bed, stove, or desk. These arrowlike points may be anything from a neighbor's protruding roof ridge at the front door to sharp edges of furniture or wall corners that protrude into the room.

Following are simple, yet effective, cures for poison arrows. Be sure to visualize greater health when applying any of them (head to Chapter 6 for more information on visualization).

✔ For outside arrows, place a Ba-Gua mirror over the front door (refer to Chapter 7 for details about the benefits of Ba-Gua mirrors).

✔ For interior poison arrows, you have several options:

- Remove (or redirect the point of) the offending object.

- Cover the object with cloth, a curtain, or a silk vine.

- Hang a faceted crystal sphere in front of the point to diffuse its sharpness.

- Move the affected object out of the path of the poison arrow and into a new location.

Centering your home for healthy living

The center of the home relates to your health and is a prime place to apply Feng Shui health cures (flip to Chapter 10 for all you ever wanted to know about the home's center). Because mobiles invoke energy circulation and flow, hanging a mobile in the center of your home can be an effective health cure. Reinforce the mobile by visualizing greater health and perfect circulation in your body and your home (see Chapter 6 for details).

Saving the stove and the cook

Your kitchen stove is a primary factor in determining the health of your family. The cook's feelings while cooking affect the food you eat and in turn your body's health and energy. By extension, these feelings can affect your health, your life, and the lives of those living in your home. For this simple yet profound reason, stove position is a vital Feng Shui factor. Ideal stove placement allows you to see all entryways to the kitchen so you're not startled when cooking. This Commanding Position keeps you protected and makes you feel safe while cooking the food that nourishes you and your family. (Turn to Chapter 2 for an introduction to the Commanding Position.)

An island stove — a stove located in the center of your kitchen — is ideal because it can face the door coming into the kitchen, but these stoves are pretty rare in today's homes. More commonly a stove is found along one wall. Therefore, the more common cure for poor stove positioning (a stove against a wall) is to put a mirror behind the stove. The mirror should be at least as wide as the stove, and as tall as possible. The main purpose of installing a large mirror behind your stove is so you can see the doorway(s) into the kitchen, but this cure also symbolically doubles your stove's burners. (Those are two important effects from one cure.) Complete this cure by visualizing greater health and happiness while doing the Three Secrets Reinforcement I describe in Chapter 6.

Here's a cure that can improve the health of your family regardless of your stove position: Hang a wind chime or faceted crystal sphere from a red ribbon cut to a multiple of 9 inches in length directly over the cook's position at the stove. The positive chi and either the ringing sound of the chime or the prismatic light created by the crystal bring good energy, luck, and opportunity to the household. The flow of the kitchen's chi, particularly the chi around the cook, is harmonized by the chime or sphere, resulting in better-quality chi in the food. Both cures help harmonize and calm any chaotic chi that may be circulating in the kitchen, thereby helping to reduce kitchen accidents and mishaps (which are clear health issues, as every chef knows).

Want more information on kitchen Feng Shui? Head to Chapter 12 for the scoop.

Curing exposed beams

Exposed beams can create oppressive downward energetic flows that can induce health, psychological, and other life problems. The beams needing the most attention include beams over the bed, stove, desk, dining room table, or front door. A good way to cure such a beam is to hang two bamboo Feng Shui flutes at 45-degree angles on the offending beam, one at each end. (Turn to Chapter 14 for more on beams and Chapter 4 for more about flutes.)

Other beam cures include painting the beams to match the ceiling, hiding the beams with a false ceiling, and camouflaging the beams with decorative cloth.

Enhancing Wealth, Relationships, and Health All at Once

If you like to get the most results for your efforts, then the following sections are for you. In them I provide cures that can help you in all three of the big parts of your life — money, relationships, and health — all at once. Now that's what I call efficiency!

Evening out the shape of your lot and home

The shape of your home's lot is a prime factor determining your destiny and your luck (good or bad). An uneven lot shape means uneven opportunities — life in general is hard work, and cash is harder to come by. Look at a drawing of your lot; if your lot shape is a square or rectangle, good for you. If not, do the following (see Chapter 8 for more guidance on performing these cures):

> ✔ Correct missing areas by installing lights, planting trees, or raising flagpoles.
>
> ✔ Fix angled sides of the lot (those that look angled or appear tilted on the lot drawing) by installing lights at each end of the slant.
>
> ✔ Correct lots with more than four sides or that are otherwise oddly shaped by placing a tall green flag at each corner of the lot.

If your home's shape is missing some areas (for example, if your home is L-shaped rather than square or rectangular), pay close attention. Adding any one of the following items to energetically complete a missing area in your home creates balance and strength, making it easier to attract and retain money, partnerships, and physical health:

> ✔ A large mirror
>
> ✔ Living plants
>
> ✔ A faceted crystal sphere

Keeping your front pathway unblocked

The pathway to your front door and the space around the door primarily affect how the *chi* (energy) is — or isn't — attracted into your home. The condition and quality of the energy that circulates inside your home (and affects you directly) is determined by how much energy can come through the front door. So keeping this path clear allows more energy to enter and circulate in your home, nourishing your health, wealth, and relationships. So clear a path and allow the energy to come in. Try the following (and flip to Chapter 9 for general information on creating a welcoming entry):

> ✔ Remove items such as shoes, bikes, toys, newspapers, dead shrubs and trees, and other obstacles.
>
> ✔ Trim back living plants so the path to the door is free and open.

Perform the Three Secrets Reinforcement (see Chapter 6) and watch as more and better energy flows into your home and life.

Brightening your front entrance

A dark entrance implies a dark future, a difficult career, and difficulty attracting money (not to mention difficulty getting your key in the door). Adding light to your home's entrance is an easy and effective way to increase the vitality of your entrance so it creates positive and bright feelings. So go ahead and put bright lights — the brighter the better — near your entrance. (As an added bonus, this cure also increases the energy level of the entire home.)

Chapter 20

Looking Before You Leap: Selecting Your Next Home with Feng Shui

In This Chapter

▶ Recognizing the benefits of using Feng Shui when selecting a new (to you) home

▶ Beginning the Feng Shui home-selection process properly

▶ Analyzing predecessor energies in a home you're thinking about

▶ Considering Feng Shui principles as you focus on a home's features

. . . .

Feng Shui isn't just for improving the home you're already in. One of the best times to apply Feng Shui is actually *before* you rent or buy a home. That's right. Feng Shui is even more advantageous when you apply its principles in the selection of your next home. By using Feng Shui knowledge and principles, you can pick the best home available to you — one whose energy and structure supports and enhances, rather than undermines, your well-being. Choosing a new living space based primarily on emotion and unconscious factors (like 99 percent of folks do) rather than on energetic principles puts you at a disadvantage. What's more, you may end up with a home that — without serious energy repair — can do your life more harm than good.

Wisely selecting a home with good Feng Shui features means the home will require less remedial Feng Shui after you move in. It's best to start off from a place of strength and stability rather than a place of imbalance and weakness. Even if you're buying a fixer-upper, good Feng Shui should still be a factor in your decision. It can mean the difference between turning a good Feng Shui situation into a fabulous one and trying to turn a bad Feng Shui situation into a passable one.

In this chapter, I explain how Feng Shui can make the home-selection process a pleasant experience and start you off on the right foot by helping you set your intention and make your list of desired home traits *before* you go house hunting. I also describe how to determine whether specific home features are

Feng Shui–friendly and how to analyze the energies of the people who previously lived in a home.

The principles in this chapter also apply to the process of building a new home and to remodeling, but in-depth treatment of these topics is beyond the scope of this book. If you're planning to build a new home or remodel an existing one, I recommend you work with a professional Feng Shui consultant who has specific experience in these areas. (Turn to Chapter 24 and the appendix for help finding a consultant.)

Understanding How Feng Shui Can Help You during the Home-Selection Process

You've probably experienced the stress, confusion, and needless expense that can ensue from selecting a new home. The process of choosing a new place to live is, for most people, loaded with unconscious tendencies. It often triggers primal energies and emotions, including notions of survival, safety, and rank. For example:

✔ People tend to project their hopes, desires, and fears into the process of selecting a home. Financial concerns (debt, fears of long-term commitment, job worries, and so on), family issues (including conscious and unconscious plans to have and raise children), marital/relationship issues (commitment, future plans, doubt, and so on), career plans, and more come into play when you seek a new place to live.

✔ Leaving your current home and finding another one can stir up painful childhood memories, feelings of leaving beloved places and friends, and adjusting to new circumstances. Also, everyone has deep memories of childhood hopes, dreams, and fantasies that can be powerfully activated when deciding on a new place to live.

✔ How you think society and your peers regard you is an enormous factor in choosing where you live. Your home is a reflection of you and a tangible form of your self-image. Consciously and unconsciously, people desire a home that looks good in the eyes of others and makes them feel good about themselves. People naturally hope to avoid a home that reflects a "step down" in self-image.

✔ The home-selection process typically involves time pressure, whether self-imposed or determined externally by career, family, financial, or other pressing needs.

When you're choosing a home, any or all of the preceding concerns are operating in you at levels you may only be dimly aware of, which is part of the reason why choosing a home can induce confusion, uncertainty, and stress. The combination of these factors can leave you energetically drained and emotionally overwhelmed. In this state, you may stumble through the home-selection process, making unfortunate choices and decisions that will affect your future accordingly.

So how do you transform this mess of pressure, fear, hope, and opportunity into a conscious, creative, and joyful process that results in a practical and uplifting home that supports your daily well-being and helps you realize your life goals? Select your next home by using Feng Shui. Doing so represents upgrading your life, both consciously and energetically. By using Feng Shui, selecting your next residence becomes a catalyst for personal growth and transformation.

Here are the three foundational steps for selecting your new home with Feng Shui:

1. **Make a commitment to become more conscious of the process beforehand and as you go through it.**

2. **Have objective guidelines to keep yourself on task during the process.**

   Get as clear as you can about what you want and what you don't want in a new home. (In other words, set your intentions for your new residence; see the later "Setting your intention" section for more on this.) Resist the tendency to give in to fear or panic as you deal with the many aspects of the home-selection process.

3. **Write down your goals, create a plan, and stick to it.**

   Writing down your goals is a key part of the home-selection process. Commit to these goals by signing and dating the document.

You can (and should) use Feng Shui to find a better home

I once had a client who diligently used Feng Shui to improve both his business and professional life. His income went up dramatically, and his relationships improved. A year later, he called to ask me to consult with him on his new, larger, pricier home. I was happy to hear that his circumstances had improved, but my good cheer diminished when I surveyed his new home and realized how many Feng Shui problems it had. My client had chosen his new home without regard for Feng Shui principles based on the mistaken assumption that Feng Shui was only relevant after the purchase was complete. He now had a bigger home with *worse* Feng Shui properties than his former, more modest environment. (In Feng Shui, bigger isn't necessarily better.)

After watching several clients go through a similar process, I saw that using Feng Shui principles to find a home can dramatically affect your new life in your new home for the better. It's a look-before-you-leap type of Feng Shui principle.

Selecting your home with Feng Shui assistance adds power, clarity, and balance to the entire process. It helps you maintain the energy level you need to rise above the frustrations that are often encountered during a move and encourages you to be resourceful, happy, and engaged throughout the process.

Starting Off the Feng Shui Home-Selection Process on the Right Foot

When you're ready to choose your next home, use the information in the following sections to guide you. These sections reveal the importance of setting your intention and making a list of features you want and need in a new home.

Setting your intention

The first thing to do is identify your intention(s) for your new home. What are the general and specific life benefits and changes you hope to experience in this new residence? Here's an example: "My home is a place of peace and relaxation. My career flourishes in this location, and in return I take pride in my home, care for it, and maintain it and its surroundings to the best of my ability. I have great neighbors and many exciting opportunities. Family and friends are happy and safe here."

Now it's your turn. Take a few moments to set your intention before moving on. This step, simple as it may seem, creates a path in your search for a new home that aligns with your intentions. (Flip to Chapter 6 to see more about setting your intention.)

Making a list and checking it twice

In my consulting work, I've seen that the best way to find your ideal home is to first make a list of everything you want in your new home. Start by writing down all the qualities and elements you're looking for. Don't hold back; let your first pass be completely unfiltered. Then take a second pass to start clarifying what you really want and need in your new place.

Being clear on what you're looking for is the first step in attaining your desires. Keep clarifying what you want until your final list can fit on one sheet of paper.

The following sample criteria can help you start figuring out exactly what you're looking for in a home (feel free to customize this list, adding your own criteria as needed):

✔ Desirable neighborhoods/cities

✔ Type of surroundings (urban, suburban, countryside)

✔ Location characteristics (type of neighborhood, length of commute to work)

✔ Undesirable location characteristics (noise, weather, traffic)

✔ Type of home (single-family residence, apartment, condominium, town home)

✔ Size of home and number of rooms:

- Single story or multiple stories

- Square footage: Min_____ Max_____

- Number of bedrooms: Min_____ Max_____

- Number of bathrooms: Min_____ Max_____

- Additional rooms (den, office, playroom, and so on)

- Size of kitchen and master bedroom

- Size of other rooms (living room, den, family room, home office, and so on)

- Basement or no basement

- Size of garage

- Size of lot/yard

- Outbuildings (greenhouse, tool shed, and so on)

✔ Buying:

- Amount of down payment

- Monthly payment maximum

- Total price maximum

✔ Renting/leasing:

- Maximum monthly payment

- Minimum and maximum length of lease you're willing to sign

✔ Setting the date:

- Time frame: How long do you plan to stay in the new home?

- Urgency: By what date do you want to be in the new home? (Or by what date do you have to be in it?)

- Start date: When are you ready to start the home-selection process?

If a home you're viewing doesn't meet at least 85 percent of the criteria on your list (more is obviously better), move on to the next one unless the lack is compensated for by stunning new features your original list didn't contain. (Note that it's okay to redo your list during the home-selection process.)

Evaluating a Home's Feng Shui Features

After you confirm that a home fits your criteria list (see the preceding section), you're ready to check out specific features of the home and determine whether they agree with positive Feng Shui principles. I recommend you follow all (or at least the great majority) of these guidelines:

- **Choose a favorable terrain.** A lot that slopes down and away from the home at the rear of the property can cause financial troubles or other calamities for the home's occupants. The home's energy drains (or flows) away from this land formation, potentially draining money, health, and career success. A superior lot choice is land that lies flat behind the home; an even better lot is one where the land slopes gently upward behind the home, helping to retain chi and prosperity. (Flip to Chapter 7 for more details on optimal Feng Shui for outdoor spaces.)

- **Select a home that sits even with or above the street level.** A home located on ground that's below street level can inhibit your career, social life, income, and health. The lower the main floor of the home is in relation to street level, the more pronounced these effects will be. I recommend choosing a home that's level with the street (one that's above the street is even better). This home placement puts you in more of a Commanding Position relative to your physical surroundings and uplifts your overall destiny (see Chapter 2 for the scoop on the Commanding Position).

- **Find a street with positive energy.** The energy of society (people, money, traffic, mail, and so on) connects to your home through the energy of the street. Therefore, a strong flow of energy to the home is very positive. On the other hand, a too-busy street can have a negative effect, disturbing your home's chi and actually pulling energy away from the home. In this situation, you can lose career energy, opportunities, and money. (In this case, earplugs and a blindfold aren't a clever Feng Shui solution.) As described in Chapter 7, the ideal street allows reasonable activity and movement, feeds the driveway and property, and isn't too heavily trafficked.

Steer clear of a home facing a T-intersection or Y-intersection (they can threaten your safety), one-way streets (these often pull away your opportunities), dead ends (things in your life can come to a halt), and steeply sloping streets (these make it easy to feel off-kilter in life).

✔ **Seek out a neighborhood that's brimming with positive energy.** The flora, fauna, people, and structures around the new home should be supportive of wealth, growth, peace, and happiness. Refer to Chapter 7 for more on positive and negative neighborhood factors.

✔ **Find a balanced home and lot shape.** Regularly shaped homes and lots tend to lead to more balanced lives. Check out the shapes you're considering living in and take note of their projections and missing areas (if any) because these can mean either positive fortune or problem circumstances. (I cover projections and missing areas in Chapter 8.)

✔ **Look for a master bedroom in the Commanding Position.** Because the master bedroom is the key room in any home, its position in your new home is important. Finding a home with a master bedroom in the back of the home is preferable. A master bedroom located in the front of the home can generate chaos, disharmony, and/or a separation. (Flip to Chapter 11 for the full scoop on bedroom Feng Shui.)

Assessing the master bedroom's other Feng Shui characteristics, such as shape and especially the availability of a Commanding Position for the master bed, is also important when considering a new home. If you find your dream home but the master bedroom isn't auspiciously located or shaped, you can remedy any defects with specific Feng Shui cures found in this book. (Turn to Chapter 8 for bedroom shape cures, Chapter 10 for bedroom location solutions, and Chapter 11 for other bedroom cures.)

✔ **Select a protected kitchen.** The ideal kitchen is located in the back half of the home and is free of exterior doors. It's also not visible from the front door. (Turn to Chapter 12 for more information on kitchen Feng Shui.)

✔ **Locate a good loo.** Avoid bathrooms in the center of a home and, if possible, in the Wealth Area of the home's Feng Shui Octagon (flip to Chapter 13 for various bathroom cures and Chapter 3 for details on the Feng Shui Octagon).

✔ **Choose the most positive predecessor energy you can.** The energies of the people who lived in a home before you can have a significant effect on how your stay goes in that home. Look for the best predecessor situation possible (I help you figure out how in the next section), and use blessing ceremonies if you find that you need to repair any predecessor chi (I present blessing ceremonies in Chapter 21).

Assessing and Addressing Predecessor Energies

Predecessor energies in your living environment — the lingering energetic influences of previous occupants — vitally affect the Feng Shui of your home. These energies fall into the category of invisible factors because they aren't visible to the eye, unlike stains on the carpet. Feng Shui methods allow you to uncover these effects and either avoid or cure them as needed.

Feng Shui asserts that energetic influence is a two-way street: The energies of a home affect its occupants, and the energies of the occupants affect the home. Furthermore, occupant energies remain in a home long after the occupants leave. Such invisible energetic influences, whether positive or negative, exert a subtle influence on you as soon as you occupy a home that has had previous occupants.

Negative effects may come from predecessors who moved out of the home because of bankruptcy, divorce, illness, death, job loss, or similar negative events. (*Note:* Depending on your goals, if the previous resident moved because of divorce, illness, a lost job, bankruptcy, or a death, you may want to consider a different home!) Chronic poverty, sickness, and conflict — including physical or emotional violence or abuse — also generate negative effects. I recommend avoiding such negative predecessor energies if at all possible. However, performing blessing ceremonies can help clear these energies from a home; see Chapter 21 for details.

Most people looking to rent or buy are typically unconcerned with predecessor energies. They tend to pay attention to how the home looks but not to how it feels. The attitude is fairly nonchalant: "The home looks great, honey! So what if Charles Manson just left this morning? He cleaned the carpets and painted the walls! (Don't ask why. What a guy!) Gimme the keys!" However, Feng Shui says that paying attention to energy is vital and that the outer appearance of a home isn't always the most important factor. You benefit by taking an interest in the fortunes and life patterns of the people who are leaving a home because these energy patterns will be affecting you too if you occupy that home.

Predecessor energies deal with a wide range of factors. To keep things manageable, I present the most reliable methods to help you assess and address "new property" issues. I recommend consulting a qualified Feng Shui professional in this especially important area (see Chapter 24 and the appendix for guidance), but the tips found in the following sections will stand you in good stead.

Technically, predecessor influences go back through the residents of a home — all the way to the original occupant. These influences also include the intentions with which the home was built and the energy of the builder. (Some Feng Shui professionals even analyze the way the land was used before any homes were built in the area.) For simplicity's sake, focus on the predecessor with the greatest effect — the one who lived in the home directly before you.

Dealing a one-two punch to predecessor energies

The first step in dealing with predecessor energies involves knowing how to spot them and how to recognize good and bad energetic influences, so get busy finding out the history of the home and its previous occupants. Ask questions. If you don't know the predecessors and can't get any information about them, you need to rely on your innate Feng Shui antennae. In other words, trust your gut feelings and intuition (or as Obi-Wan Kenobi says, "Use the Force").

When you check the history of a home, also look for changes made to the original building structure, including remodeling, additions, rebuilding, demolitions, fires, and so on. If major remodeling has been done to the home, the energy of the site can remain chaotic and nonintegrated for years — or until Feng Shui comes along.

If the predecessor energies are negative and in opposition to your life goals, your best strategic option is to avoid choosing that home. However, this option isn't always practical. So if you end up occupying a home that features negative predecessor chi, I recommend you perform Feng Shui blessing ceremonies to remove or change the negative energy, thereby bringing blessings and prosperity to the site.

Performing blessing ceremonies whenever you move into a new home is a good idea, whether you're aware of negative predecessor energy or not. Flip to Chapter 21 for details on performing blessing ceremonies.

Note: Apartments frequently abound in problematic predecessor energies due to frequent tenant turnover. With many people randomly moving in and out over the years, negative influences are almost inevitable — not least from the constant disturbance of the continual moving.

Getting a handle on Initial Momentum

What I call *Initial Momentum* — the period where the ideas, thoughts, ambitions, and energy you arrived with prevail — generally lasts about two years. At the two-year point, your life results begin to adapt more fully to the Feng Shui of the home. (Keep in mind, though, that this principle is only a rough rule. As usual in Feng Shui, your mileage may vary depending on all the factors involved.)

Say, for example, that you and your spouse, happily married for four years, move into a new home that was put on the market because the couple who owned it was getting divorced. For the first couple years in this new home, your marriage is still pretty good. But in time, somewhere around the energetic turning point, the two of you may begin to argue, and one or both of you may start to entertain thoughts of a trial separation — or even divorce! I've seen this situation happen many times. And you know what? It isn't necessarily just the two of you. The problems you're experiencing may be due to the lingering separation energy of the previous couple. The energy of their arguments, pain, and divorce has seeped into the walls, carpets, and atmosphere of the home. You landed in the thick of it, and you energetically managed on your own for a couple years. But now look at the mess you're in!

Negative predecessor influences can gradually undermine the best of intentions. So why not nip them in the bud before encountering them by using some simple Feng Shui solutions? (If your relationship is already suffering, taking action late in the game is better than never acting at all.) For help sorting out the positive and negative influences, see the next section.

Reading the predecessor factors

When you're considering a new home, ask the first two questions in the sections that follow to assess whether the predecessor energies of the place are positive or negative. The third question can help you analyze the factors of the home you're currently living in.

Why did the previous occupants move out?

Determining why the home's previous occupants moved out is very important. The energy associated with moving is the final energy that the resident leaves in the home. The reason for moving is a significant dynamic that stirs up a lot of energy and emotion, and the home resonates with these influences after the family is gone. Table 20-1 shows the positive and negative reasons for moving out of a home. (**Remember:** All other Feng Shui factors being equal, avoid choosing a home with negative predecessor energies and select one with positive predecessor energies.)

Table 20-1	Negative and Positive Reasons for Moving
Positive Predecessor Reasons for Moving	*Negative Predecessor Reasons for Moving*
Growing family	Injury/death
Marriage	Divorce
Prosperity	Bankruptcy
Promotion/new job	Lost job

Positive Predecessor Reasons for Moving	Negative Predecessor Reasons for Moving
Good fortune	Lawsuit
Moved to larger home (because of improved situation)	Moved to smaller home (because of financial or other problems)

If you currently live in a home with negative predecessor factors, you can perform Feng Shui blessing ceremonies to help remove and clear these energies. (If you're living in a home where the previous resident died, you may want to skip directly to the blessing ceremonies detailed in Chapter 21.)

How did the previous occupants' lives go while living in this home?

After finding out the occupants' reason(s) for moving out, determine the general behavior and emotional patterns of the occupants while they lived in the home. Pay particular attention to Feng Shui aspects that affect these fundamental life concerns: money, marriage/relationship, and health. If possible, find out any significant incidents that happened during the occupants' stay in the residence, both positive and negative, including major accidents, sickness, bankruptcy, and death.

Of course, you can't always interview the previous occupants. Even if you can, discovering details about their past is difficult in some cases, although many people are happy to talk about why they're leaving. If you really want to find out such information, you often can. Realtors and rental agents, who often know things about their clients and neighbors, can be good sources of information. Getting even a little information is better than getting none at all. Ask point-blank, and you may find out things that deeply inform your home selection.

How has your life gone since moving in?

If you've been living in your current home for more than a few months, you're now your own predecessor. You've infused your "new" home with your basic energy patterns, and the energies of all the events, inner and outer, that you've experienced since you moved in. These energies are added as causal factors to the energies of the previous occupants and now permeate your residential environment.

If you've increased your wealth since you moved in, you're more likely to continue gaining riches because of your own residual influence. Conversely, any negative patterns you've experienced since moving in may also continue unless you do something to cure them. Life runs in trends and patterns that tend to self-perpetuate unless they're consciously and intentionally altered. (Improving your property's energy shows the real and invisible influence that Feng Shui has on people's lives.)

Banishing negative energy with a home blessing

My client Mary lived in a home for 25 years before our first Feng Shui consultation. Things went well for Mary over the first eight years in her home. Then her mother died in the home. Unaware of Feng Shui principles, Mary did nothing to clear her home of the negative energy of her mother's death, with all the trauma, confusion, and grief that brought. Without knowing it, Mary was living with a negative influence that weighed, day and night, on her health and emotions and affected the entire family. Two years later, her husband lost his high-paying job and couldn't find another one. They were unable to continue paying for their daughter's college education, so the daughter was forced to move back into the home, putting an additional financial and emotional burden on the family. A negative cycle was in full swing and continuing to gain momentum, and none of the family members knew it.

A pattern was set in motion, starting with Mary's mother's death. The energy grew increasingly negative, with each negative incident accelerating the downward spiral. Eventually, Mary's husband died, which made things very dark indeed. I learned these details as I interviewed Mary during our first Feng Shui consultation. Her situation was astounding — a clear pattern of tragedy spiraling down into calamity event by event. Every three to four years, with seeming regularity, some new trauma or life blow occurred. Mary seemed to be getting more than her share of hardships. The time had clearly come to turn things around, and Mary was ready. The Feng Shui solution was simple: the Rice Blessing (or Exterior Chi Adjustment), which I present in Chapter 21. As we performed the ceremony, the sense of energy lifting and feelings lightening in her home was palpable. The downward energy spiral ended, and a new and more positive pattern began. To this day, Mary continues to feel better and freer.

Significant negative incidents and patterns, if left uncleared, can gain cumulative and powerful momentum. Think of a snowball rolling downhill. (See the nearby "Banishing negative energy with a home blessing" sidebar for an example that was resolved with the help of Feng Shui.)

Chapter 21

Creating New Energy with Feng Shui Blessing Ceremonies

. . . .

In This Chapter

▶ Assessing invisible elements and energies

▶ Discovering the benefits of Feng Shui blessings

▶ Providing pointers for (and answers about) blessing ceremonies

▶ Applying various blessings involving rice, citrus water, and flowers

. . . .

Grandmaster Lin Yun's Feng Shui school addresses both *visible elements* (physical features and energy flows of the home and property) and *invisible elements* (energetic features such as wishes, desires, visualizations, intentions, and so on) for practicing Feng Shui. This book gives you a foundation in both visible and invisible elements and tells you how to use both of them in performing your cures and in checking out your Feng Shui situation. However, the invisible factors are the more significant of the two areas in terms of cause and effect.

Two types of invisible elements are *predecessor factors* (energies of the people who came before you; see Chapter 20 for details) and *invisible occupants* (including ghosts and spirits) that may be present on the property. (The worst part is that they don't even pay rent!) A problem in either category can generate all kinds of unwanted effects in your life. In addition, other types of invisible Feng Shui factors are at work on most properties. These factors include the intentions of current and previous owners as well as major positive and negative events that have occurred on the site.

In this chapter, you find out about *blessing ceremonies,* which are highly effective cures for addressing and improving all types of invisible energies on your property. I also present several highly effective blessing ceremonies that can counteract negative issues and enhance positive unseen energies. (*Note:* Though the ceremonies in this chapter have roots in various traditions, the specific methods are unique to Grandmaster Lin Yun's Feng Shui school.)

Dealing with Unseen Occupants in Your Home

Many people are uneasy with the idea of unseen visitors living with them in the same home. People also tend to believe (perhaps wishfully) that most homes are naturally free of invisible residents such as ghosts or spirits. Another common belief is that spirits are inherently negative and that the living residents are much better off if the invisible residents are cast out all at once. If only it were that simple!

According to Feng Shui, most residences generally have one or more spirits living in them, and this condition is perfectly natural. From a Feng Shui perspective, you don't necessarily want to have a home that's completely empty of spirits — you just don't want negative spirits, or energies, disturbing your environment. Grandmaster Lin Yun's Feng Shui school calls this type of spirit *hungry ghosts* and offers several strategies for dealing with them.

Feng Shui acknowledges two basic kinds of spirits or energetic influences: *benign* (positive spirits that promote harmony, good luck, and blessings) and *negative* (unhappy spirits that promote disharmony, bad luck, and unhappiness). The Feng Shui task at hand is to invoke positive spirits and energies and increase the benefits derived from them while giving nasty ones their walking papers. Blessing ceremonies help you do just that. Performing blessing ceremonies on a site allows you to communicate with the unseen realms through time-sharpened methods that help clear negative energies and strengthen positive ones, including your energy, your family's energy, and your home's energy.

The Advantages of Feng Shui Blessing Ceremonies

Grandmaster Lin Yun's Feng Shui school includes many powerful blessing ceremonies, also called *Major Chi Adjustments,* for changing all the *chi* (or energy) of your home, property, and life at once. Whereas regular Feng Shui cures may powerfully affect one or two parts of your experience, blessing ceremonies can simultaneously improve all parts of your life and environment.

I find blessing ceremonies to be so effective that I call them the "Big Guns" of Feng Shui. You can see the same improvements by doing one blessing ceremony on your property as you can when you perform numerous Feng Shui adjustments (proper placement, minor additions, and so on). Of course, non-ceremonial cures have their place (in fact, the best results come from using both regular cures and ceremonial methods). It's just that blessing ceremonies come in handy when the situation is urgent or when nothing else has worked.

In the following sections, I cover a number of good reasons and occasions for using Feng Shui blessing ceremonies.

Reasons for employing blessing ceremonies

Applying Feng Shui cures in as many ways as you can is bound to produce positive results. But you may find in some instances that more is necessary. Blessing ceremonies are good for the situations described in the next sections.

You should always perform blessing ceremonies with an attitude of reverence, sincerity, and compassion and with the best intentions in mind for all the people involved. When performing ceremonies (or any type of Feng Shui cure), never use negative intentions toward anyone or anything (these have an unfortunate way of backfiring). I provide instructions for setting your intention and performing the Three Secrets Reinforcement in Chapter 6.

Clearing unwanted predecessor energies

If you suspect your home and/or life are enduring the negative effects of one or more inauspicious predecessors (see Chapter 20), Feng Shui ceremonies can help alleviate your situation, often dramatically.

Relieving multiple Feng Shui problems at once

Suppose you have a handful of Feng Shui problem areas and you're able to fix some of them but not others. If you're feeling overwhelmed by your Feng Shui situation, a blessing ceremony can help move the energy throughout your space and blow a powerful breeze of change and healing through your home.

Solving a pesky Feng Shui problem

When you have a Feng Shui issue for which you either don't know the cure or can't afford to implement the optimal solution, a blessing ceremony may be just the ticket. In this case, a blessing ceremony is an effective solution that can remove some negative influences, compensate for other influences, and increase the overall positive energies of a site.

Alleviating a general feeling of negativity and depression in the home

Sometimes a home has an overall feeling of gloom and doom; other times it simply puts you down in the dumps. If the general feel of the place doesn't change to one of overall cheer, health, and uplifted energy after you perform a few Feng Shui cures, a blessing ceremony can help change the quality of the entire home's energy. It's very common to notice a freer, lighter, and happier feel immediately after properly implementing a blessing ceremony.

Setting the tone in a new residence or office

The crucial moving-in time is a prime window of opportunity for improving a site's energy. Performing a blessing ceremony to remove inauspicious energies before you move into your new residence is the best way to set in motion positive energy in your new home, office, or business location.

Good occasions for blessing ceremonies

Performing blessing ceremonies in your home or office can remove the negative energies and improve the positive energies. Some of the purposes for which you can beneficially use Feng Shui blessing ceremonies include

- ✔ Inviting blessing, prosperity, and good fortune
- ✔ Blessing a homesite upon moving in
- ✔ Clearing negative predecessor energy
- ✔ Changing your luck from bad to good
- ✔ Improving your energy after an accident or an unexpected negative event
- ✔ Removing the chi associated with sickness or death
- ✔ Releasing negative ghosts, spirits, or other unwelcome visitors

Keep in mind that performing a blessing isn't absolutely necessary for your site to have good Feng Shui. Blessings are potent tools that are very helpful in times of need, but they aren't required practices.

Frequently Asked Questions about Feng Shui Blessing Ceremonies

Got a question regarding Feng Shui blessing ceremonies? This section should solve anything that's puzzling you about this important subject.

- ✔ **Do I need to change or go against any of my religious beliefs for Feng Shui blessings to be effective?** Definitely not. These practices work for anyone and everyone, regardless of one's religion or faith (or lack thereof). Don't worry, though — no conversion is required. I recommend you incorporate your personal beliefs and practices into the ceremonies that you perform. Whether you're Christian, Hindu, Muslim, Buddhist, Jewish, atheist, or undecided, incorporate your prayers in these Feng Shui ceremonies so they feel right to you. The practices that are most meaningful to you can have the greatest effects on your body, psyche, and environment. Just keep the basic structure and steps of the ceremony intact.

✔ **Do I need to perform a ceremony exactly right for it to be effective?** If you follow the essential steps of a blessing ceremony with a positive attitude, sincerity of heart, and clear intent (the ingredients of any powerful Feng Shui cure), you can experience corresponding positive effects. Do the best you can to follow the ceremony steps closely and hold positive expectations. Attention to detail is important, but attitude and spirit are more so.

Apply the inner Feng Shui of self-control by adhering to the positive and relinquishing the negative influences within. As I tell my clients, Feng Shui is meant for stress relief, which requires stress release, not stress creation. So lighten up, have fun in the present, and look forward to the future.

✔ **Do I need special training to be able to implement these blessing ceremonies?** Yes, most definitely! What you absolutely must acquire to proceed are a human body (your own, by the way), the ability to read, and a copy of the comprehensive Feng Shui manual called *Feng Shui For Dummies,* 2nd Edition. With these three elements in place you should have no problems!

On a more serious note, blessing ceremonies are part of the advanced levels of Feng Shui practice. Any art or skill always has details and nuances that can't be picked up from a book but can only be developed through direct experience. Although the knowledge in this chapter can enable you to perform blessing ceremonies and enjoy positive, life-changing results, direct training from a qualified Feng Shui teacher brings the energy of the practices to a much stronger level. After applying the methods in this book, if you're interested in increasing your knowledge and skill in Feng Shui, you can always contact a teacher in your area to receive further training. (See the appendix for help finding a Feng Shui teacher.)

✔ **How do I know whether the ceremony worked or was effective?** As with any method, art, or skill, results vary due to innumerable factors. Sometimes you may feel or notice immediate effects after performing Feng Shui cures. Other times the results may come more gradually and improve your life over time. My advice? Just be patient and observant.

Tips for Performing Feng Shui Blessing Ceremonies

If you've never performed a blessing ceremony, your first effort can feel a bit daunting. Follow these tips to get the most out of any blessing ceremonies you perform:

✔ **Calm down.** Get into a peaceful state of mind before beginning a blessing ceremony.

✔ **Begin fully prepared.** Gather all the materials you need for the ceremony before you start.

✔ **Have the steps of the ceremony in front of you.** Open this book to the appropriate page or have the steps written out so you don't fumble and distract yourself as you perform the ceremony.

✔ **Don't rush.** Dedicate the time you need to perform the ceremony properly. Your state of mind and ability to focus on the matter at hand make a big difference in the ceremony's success.

✔ **Make sure you won't be disturbed as you perform the ceremony.** I recommend turning off your phone(s) and other electronic gadgets. Also, ask that other people don't intrude on the proceedings.

✔ **Call a trained professional if needed.** If you don't feel ready to perform a blessing or you want assistance, call a Feng Shui professional who can perform it for you. (Flip to Chapter 24 for guidance on finding a Feng Shui consultant.)

Out with the Old, In with the New: The Rice Blessing

The Chinese name for the Rice Blessing ceremony is *Yu Wei;* English speakers call it the *Exterior Blessing* or an *Exterior Chi Adjustment.* The *Rice Blessing* adjusts chi by shifting the energy to a higher level of dynamic coherence and harmony. In my consulting practice, this cure has consistently demonstrated its effectiveness and power. My clients report a host of benefits, including relief from financial and legal problems, improved family harmony, and better health. Among other things, the sections that follow reveal the realms in which the Rice Blessing can aid you, explain how it works, and walk you through performing it.

What the Rice Blessing can do for you

You perform the Rice Blessing around the perimeter of your property, and it energetically uplifts everything on the site. Applied properly, this ceremony clears and changes the energy of these three realms:

✔ **Your land:** The Rice Blessing improves the energy of all parts of your property. The energies of the ground, water, air, vegetation, wildlife, and invisible elements (think spirits) are adjusted and improved.

✔ **Your home:** The Rice Blessing energetically upgrades the main living structure and any other buildings on your property.

> ✔ **You and yours:** The Rice Blessing helps humans (and other living beings) on the property live easier, happier lives by smoothing out the energy and circumstances.

How the Rice Blessing works

Rice is a symbol of blessing. (At Western weddings, handfuls of rice are sometimes tossed on the bride and groom to wish them good luck in their new life.) In the Rice Blessing ceremony, the rice is specially prepared and empowered before being tossed around the perimeter of the property using three specific methods. The three-way tossing of the rice performs three energetic tasks that I detail in the following sections. (See Figure 21-2, later in this chapter, for a visual guide of the three tossing techniques.)

Uplifting the chi

You uplift the chi at the site by tossing the rice straight up in the air as high as possible (with your palm up) in a gesture called the *Uplifting Mudra* (a *mudra* is a spiritual or energetic gesture). This tossing method uplifts the chi and brings lightness, joy, and freedom to the site. Good things now come rushing your way!

Feeding the hungry ghosts

Hungry ghosts is a Chinese cultural term symbolizing the problems, injustices, chaos, pain, and negative emotion that may reside on a site. When you throw the rice with the *Giving Mudra,* a gesture that involves tossing the rice out from the property and horizontal to the ground with a Frisbee-like motion, the hungry ghosts can feed on the positive energy of the rice and become satisfied. Then they can feel free to leave the site or even transform into beneficial guardians of the property. The result? Cured problems and increased satisfaction for the site's residents.

Planting new seeds of growth

The *Planting Mudra,* in which you plant new seeds for growth, involves tossing handfuls of rice straight down toward the ground. It symbolically implants your wishes and intentions — along with positive, fresh energy — into the soil so that new things (the fulfillment of your needs) can spontaneously spring up and flower profusely.

Items to gather for the Rice Blessing

Before you begin the Rice Blessing, assemble and prepare the following items:

✔ **A large bowl:** A large-sized mixing bowl or salad bowl works well; I recommend buying a new one for the ceremony.

✔ **Five or more pounds of uncooked rice:** The amount of rice needed varies based on the size of the property. Anywhere from 5 to 8 pounds works for an average-sized yard; more rice is necessary for larger properties. Use regular white or brown rice, not minute or instant rice. (Sorry, Uncle Ben!)

✔ **About ¼ teaspoon of cinnabar powder:** *Cinnabar* is a Chinese medical herbal mixture with special properties. It has been ceremoniously scattered in ancient Chinese temples and imperial burial sites for thousands of years.

Keep these precautions in mind when using cinnabar:

- Remember that cinnabar is for external applications only; be sure not to ingest it in any way.

- If you have a cut or open skin on your hands, you can use latex gloves for protection.

- Don't inhale cinnabar dust or let it get in your mouth or eyes.

Most people find cinnabar difficult to obtain and should exercise care when applying it. If the idea of using cinnabar seems a bit daunting, hire a Feng Shui professional to perform the Rice Blessing in the context of a formal consultation. (See Chapter 24 and the appendix for help finding a consultant.)

✔ **A newly purchased, unopened bottle of high-proof liquor:** Specifically, you want liquor that's 100 proof (or 50 percent alcohol by content) or higher. (Note that 80-proof liquor can also be effective if that's the highest-proof liquor you can find.)

The stages of performing the Rice Blessing

The Rice Blessing is performed in two stages: First, you prepare the rice with the special methods I describe; then you take the rice outdoors to do the ceremonial tossing. After these stages, you reinforce the blessing. Follow the steps I outline in the next sections to perform the Rice Blessing.

Preparing the rice

You can prepare the rice on a kitchen counter, dining room table, or any other convenient area. Just make sure you follow these steps:

1. **Begin by holding your hands in the Heart-Calming Mudra and reciting the Heart-Calming Mantra nine times.**

   In the Heart-Calming Mudra, your left hand is on top of your right hand; the palms are up, and the thumbs are touching. The Heart-Calming Mantra goes like this: Gate gate, para gate, para sum gate, bodhi swaha (pronounced *gah*-tay *gah*-tay, *pair*-uh *gah*-tay, *pair*-uh *sum gah*-tay, *bo*-dee *swa*-ha).

   A mantra or prayer from your own religion (or even a personal prayer) works as well; the point is to use a mantra or prayer that has spiritual significance to you. Whatever you use, be sure to repeat it nine times.

   A mantra is different from a mudra. A *mantra* is a word or phrase with spiritual significance and energy, whereas a *mudra* is a hand gesture that invokes a spiritual state in the person holding the position. Turn to Chapter 6 for more information regarding these two powerful energetic elements.

2. **Fill a large bowl with rice until it's three-quarters full.**

3. **Add ¼ teaspoon cinnabar powder to the rice.**

   The cinnabar empowers the mixture to remove negative forces and spirits from the property; it also adds powerful positive energies and auspicious blessings.

4. **Add nine measures of liquor to the cinnabar and rice.**

   You can measure nine capfuls or just pour nine splashes of liquor into the bowl — the nine measures don't need to be equal. The liquor helps energetically strengthen the rice-and-cinnabar mixture.

5. **Mix the rice, cinnabar, and liquor together using the middle finger of your left hand if you're a woman or the middle finger of your right hand if you're a man while reciting the Six True Words (or another mantra) 108 times.**

   Figure 21-1 illustrates this step from the perspective of a man. As you're reciting the Six True Words, which I reveal in Chapter 6, visualize the deity of your choice entering the rice in spirit and infusing it with the power to bless and cleanse your property.

   As an optional aid to counting, you can use a *mala* (an Indian rosary) or any other rosary containing 108 beads. Count one bead for each repetition of the mantra and stop when you get to the end of the rosary.

Figure 21-1:
Rice
Blessing
ingredients
and mixing
procedure.

Tossing the rice

Follow these steps for the stage of tossing the rice:

1. **Take your bowl of rice and go to the property's Mouth of Chi.**

   The *Mouth of Chi* is the property's entrance — typically where the driveway meets the street (see Chapter 9 for the full scoop on the Mouth of Chi). If your home doesn't have a driveway, go to where the front walkway meets the public sidewalk or street (or the main front entry to the property).

2. **At the Mouth of Chi, vigorously toss three handfuls of rice straight up and as high as possible into the air, using the Uplifting Mudra, as shown in Figure 21-2, and reciting the Six True Words with each toss.**

   I explain the Uplifting Mudra in the earlier "Uplifting the chi" section. As you perform this step, visualize the energy of your site — and your life — being raised, empowered, and uplifted.

3. **Toss three handfuls of rice outward, parallel to the ground and aiming toward the exterior of the lot, using the Giving Mudra (see Figure 21-2) and reciting the Six True Words with each toss.**

   Refer to the earlier "Feeding the hungry ghosts" section for information about the Giving Mudra. While enacting this step, visualize your problems disappearing and all negativity leaving the site.

4. **Toss three handfuls of rice straight down to the ground, using the Planting Mudra, as shown in Figure 21-2, and reciting the Six True Words with each toss.**

   I describe the Planting Mudra in the earlier "Planting new seeds of growth" section. Be sure to visualize the positive things you desire in life springing up all around you and growing strongly, starting now, with each throw.

5. **Proceed around the perimeter of the property in a clockwise or counterclockwise fashion, according to your choice.**

   Figure 21-3 illustrates one of the possible ways in which you can proceed. Wherever you intuitively feel that you should, stop and toss the rice as directed in Steps 3 and 4.

   For best results, each time you toss the rice, recite the mantra and visualize according to the tossing method that you're performing, as described in Steps 3 and 4. Outward tosses disperse and remove problems and negativity, and downward tosses plant new energies for growth.

6. **Complete the circuit, and when you return to the entrance, finish the tossing stage by throwing three final handfuls of rice toward the sky.**

Figure 21-2:
Rice
Blessing
tossing
methods.

Figure 21-3:
Rice
Blessing
path around
perimeter of
property.

Reinforcing the blessing

The Rice Blessing isn't complete until you reinforce it with the Three Secrets Reinforcement (see Chapter 6). Flick nine times outward with your middle and ring fingers. Repeat your mantra or prayer of choice nine times while visualizing that your ceremony was effective and seeing your desires coming true quickly and easily.

Frequently asked questions about the Rice Blessing

Check out the following frequently asked questions and their explanations to clear up any lingering uncertainties you may have regarding the Rice Blessing:

- ✔ **What should I do with the rice that's scattered on the ground, and how long should I leave it there?** The best course of action is to leave the rice on the ground alone as long as possible because the rice is a blessing for the property. Ideally, the rice should remain outside for at least 24 hours.

- ✔ **I live in an apartment building and can't perform this ceremony around my building unit. How can I bless my apartment?** You can perform the Rice Blessing around the apartment building's exterior or, if desired, around the whole city block. You can also perform a variation of the ceremony by tossing the rice around the interior perimeter of the apartment. In this variation, I recommend leaving the rice on the floor for a minimum of 24 hours before vacuuming it up. If you can't apply any of these options, you can perform the Citrus Water Blessing on the interior of your home; see the later related section for details.

✔ **What if pets or birds eat the rice?** I've never seen or heard of any animals being harmed by this ceremony, so this situation doesn't seem to be a problem. (If animals do eat the rice, perhaps they can get the blessing!) The idea that birds explode when they eat rice is an urban legend. Problems for wildlife occur only when you use cooked rice, which isn't appropriate for the Rice Blessing anyway. However, if you're truly worried, you can use grains such as millet, wheat, or barley for this blessing rather than rice.

✔ **What if I have extra rice left over?** You can ceremonially throw a few final large handfuls using the upward-tossing motion until you use up the rice.

✔ **What should I do with the bowl after the cure?** First, you should wash the bowl and your hands thoroughly because you never want to ingest cinnabar. After the bowl is clean, make sure you never use it for kitchen or eating purposes.

Results from the Rice Blessing

Immediately after performing the Rice Blessing, the home and property typically feel lighter, freer, and more cheerful, and the lighting in the home appears brighter. (In fact, some people mention that after the Rice Blessing, their home almost looks like it glows.) Over the longer term, my clients report that they experience freedom from problems and blocks, their interpersonal relationships and health improve, and life just feels better. Increased flow of funds may also follow.

The Citrus Water Blessing

The *Citrus Water Blessing,* a type of Interior Chi Adjustment, uses the freshening power of citrus, specifically its fragrance, and water, along with mantras and visualizations, to change and refresh the energies of a building. You perform this blessing on the interior of your home in order to energetically cleanse and bless the building and its inhabitants, bless the building upon moving in, or ensure an auspicious grand opening for a new business. This blessing removes a multitude of negative influences and helps correct and compensate for known and unknown Feng Shui problems. The Citrus Water Blessing also helps create new beginnings and fresh starts in life even in the most unfortunate circumstances. The sections that follow clue you in to how the Citrus Water Blessing gets the job done, what you need to perform it, and how to do it.

How the Citrus Water Blessing works

Whereas the Rice Blessing (which I cover earlier in this chapter) acts on both the ground and the building, the Citrus Water Blessing works specifically on the building itself. Accordingly, it has great power to promote and enhance freedom and good fortune.

Items to gather for the Citrus Water Blessing

Gather the following items in advance of performing the Citrus Water Blessing:

- ✔ **Nine oranges:** For a large home, you can use 18 or 27 oranges.
- ✔ **A large bowl:** Any large mixing or salad bowl works well.

Performing the Citrus Water Blessing

To perform the Citrus Water Blessing, you must first prepare the orange peels and large bowl of water. Then you do the active phase of the cure throughout the building's interior. Finally, you perform the Three Secrets Reinforcement to reinforce and further strengthen the blessing.

Here's how to prepare the oranges and water:

1. **Recite the Heart-Calming Mantra (or your own mantra of choice) nine times while holding your hands in the Heart-Calming Mudra.**

   I explain how to perform the Heart-Calming Mudra and pronounce the Heart-Calming Mantra in the earlier "Preparing the rice" section.

2. **Fill a large bowl three-fourths full with water.**

3. **Cut 9 round pieces of peel from the skin of each orange for a total of 81 round pieces of orange peel.**

4. **Tear all the round pieces into much smaller pieces of peel and place them into the water.**

   The fruit pulp isn't used in the ceremony, so you can dispose of it any way you want (that includes eating it).

Sprinkle the citrus water in this manner:

1. **Take the bowl containing the water and orange peels to the front door on the inside of the building.**

2. **Holding the bowl of water in one hand, dip the fingertips of your other hand into the water and, with the Expelling Mudra, sprinkle the water around the entryway inside the building (as in Figure 21-4) while reciting the Six True Words (or your own mantra).**

   In the *Expelling Mudra,* you hold your index and pinky fingers out and flick your middle and ring fingers out from your palm. To discover what the Six True Words are, see Chapter 6.

   As you perform this step, make sure you're visualizing and feeling all the bad luck and negative chi being removed. Also, see and feel new blessings and positive energy being infused into your environment. Envision your goals and desires coming true quickly and easily.

3. **Proceed through the entire building, dipping your fingertips into the water and sprinkling it throughout the building as you go, all the while continuing to recite the Six True Words.**

   Visualize that all the negative energy is being removed.

   The visualization is the most important part of the Citrus Water Blessing. The stronger your mental imagery, detailed imagining, and/or feeling of future results, the better your cure will perform.

4. **Sprinkle the water everywhere, moving through the building clockwise or counterclockwise as your intuition guides you.**

   Sprinkle water on all the floors and in all the rooms (including the basement and garage if they're attached to the home). Also sprinkle water on the walls, floors, furniture, ceilings, objects, and so on. As an extra step, you can even sprinkle the water in closets, cupboards, storage spaces, and the area underneath the beds.

5. **Return to the front door.**

   Don't attempt to use all the water. You can simply toss any leftover water outside and dispose of the peels.

To complete the Citrus Water Blessing ceremony, perform the Three Secrets Reinforcement, visualizing and feeling that the blessing is completely successful and seeing your intentions coming to life. (I describe how to perform the Three Secrets Reinforcement in Chapter 6.)

Figure 21-4:
Sprinkling
method for
Citrus Water
Blessing.

The Fresh Flowers Home Blessing

The *Fresh Flowers Home Blessing* (also known as the *Fresh Flowers Fragrance Cure*) is a very effective remedy that uses the power of fragrance to adjust the chi of a home's interior. This blessing ceremony involves putting successive sets of fresh flowers in a central location to bless and positively adjust your home's chi.

To perform this blessing, put flowers in water and place them in a visible, central spot in the home. Fresh-cut, newly purchased flowers are best, but flowers picked from your garden can also work. After three days, change the flowers. After another three days, replace the flowers again with fresh new ones. You've now placed three sets of flowers consecutively for three days each. (*Note:* If the flowers begin to wilt before their three-day period is up, go ahead and replace them.) Perform the Three Secrets Reinforcement (see Chapter 6) each time you put new flowers in place and visualize the fresh new results you desire in your life.

Make sure the flowers have sufficient water to help keep them from drooping. The final set of flowers can stay in place after the nine-day period is complete, but you should remove them from the home as soon as they lose their freshness.

Chapter 22

Unleashing the Genie: Personal Feng Shui Empowerment

In This Chapter

▶ Using secret wealth and protection methods

▶ Stabilizing your life, boosting your energy, and strengthening your marriage

▶ Performing a physical energy practice

▶ Improving your health with meditation

*T*his chapter reveals secret methods you can use to adjust your personal *chi* (your energy or life force). Although the best results can come from applying both personal and environmental Feng Shui cures, these methods work whether or not you perform any Feng Shui cures in your home. They use special, unusual, and transcendental ways of changing and improving personal energy. They employ elements from multiple cultural and folklore traditions and carry Indian, Tibetan, Chinese, and Western influences. The eclectic nature of these cures adds to their potency and makes them priceless cultural treasures. But that's not even the best part — these methods are inexpensive in addition to being highly valuable and effective.

The secret cures I present in this chapter retain their potency better if you don't reveal their procedural details or the fact that you're performing them. Such secret cures strongly emphasize visualization and intention as catalysts for their unusual levels of effectiveness. *Visualization* involves using your mind's eye to see what you want before it happens; *intention* refers to the clarity and strength of your desire for the cure (in other words, knowing what you want and intending strongly for it to happen). See Chapter 6 for more details on visualization and intention.

The secret cures in this chapter aren't meant to replace the Feng Shui cures your home may need to improve the corresponding parts of your life. They're part of inner Feng Shui — internal energy practices you can use to directly adjust and enhance your chi and change your life path in particular areas of need.

Putting Bad Luck to Bed

In the following sections, I present two special Feng Shui cures for the bed (which is an all-important Feng Shui location): the Red Cloth Protection Cure for vitality and stability and the Red Feet on Bed Cure for wealth and protection.

Giving yourself a boost: The Red Cloth Protection Cure

The *Red Cloth Protection Cure* can enhance your life in a number of ways and can be used in relation to almost any intention or desire. The beneficial effects of this cure include

✔ Improving your health and vitality

✔ Revitalizing or injecting passion into a marriage or relationship

✔ Boosting your spirits and energy

✔ Recovering from an unusual illness

✔ Gaining wealth, prosperity, and protection

To use the Red Cloth Protection Cure, first decide what you want to improve. Then perform the cure with this intention by getting a red piece of cloth as large as your bed and place the cloth between the mattress and box spring. Reinforce the cure with the Three Secrets Reinforcement (see Chapter 6) and visualize your results while performing it.

I recommend using a bright red sheet for this cure; this shade is more effective than off-shades of red (such as maroon). I also encourage you to purchase a new red flat bedsheet because one whole piece of cloth is stronger than two pieces sewn together.

Note: Parents can perform the Red Cloth Protection Cure for a child using the child's bed. When performing the Three Secrets Reinforcement during the cure, be sure to visualize the needed results for the child.

Doing fancy footwork: The Red Feet on Bed Cure

The *Red Feet on Bed Cure* is applied to the four feet (or bedposts) that hold up the bed. This cure helps strengthen one's ability to obtain money and provides strong protection for the occupants of the bed and the household.

For this cure, you need

> ✔ **Four 9-inch square pieces of new and unused red cloth:** Bright red is the only recommended shade of red.
>
> ✔ **Four old-style Chinese coins:** These coins are round with a square hole in the center; they usually measure about 1 inch in diameter. You can find a source for them in the appendix.
>
> ✔ **Four pieces of bright red ribbon:** Cut the ribbons to a multiple of 9 inches in length (typically 18 or 27 inches).

To perform the Red Feet on Bed Cure, follow this simple procedure:

1. **Set a red cloth square next to one of the bedposts.**

2. **Place a Chinese coin in the center of the red cloth**

3. **Lift up the bedpost and then slide the cloth underneath it so the coin lies directly beneath the post.**

4. **Set the bedpost down so it rests on top of the coin.**

5. **Bring the red cloth up, wrap it around the post, and tie it securely with one of the red ribbons.**

   The bedpost will look like it has a little red bootie on it.

6. **Perform the same procedure for the other three bedposts.**

7. **Reinforce this cure with the Three Secrets Reinforcement.**

   The most important thing here is to see and feel yourself becoming wealthy and very protected. (I explain how to perform the Three Secrets Reinforcement in Chapter 6.)

Getting Personal with Feng Shui

The next sections get you familiar with special personal cures, which include the Yu Bowl Cure to build strength in various parts of your life, the Orange Peel Bath Cure to restore your personal energy, and the Marriage Cure to encourage a long and happy marriage or relationship.

Building strength and stability with a yu bowl

The *Yu Bowl Cure* involves preparing a special bowl called a *yu*. A yu bowl has a shallow base, a wide body, and a shallow mouth (refer to Chapter 4 to see a drawing of one and flip to the appendix for a source for finding one). The body of the bowl, which is wider than the mouth, symbolizes accumulated or stored energy.

Before using the yu bowl as a cure, first put nine smooth round or small stones inside the bowl. Fill the bowl three-quarters full with water and add in a fresh, green, leafy twig. Take the bowl outside and expose it to the sky for a few moments. Next, place the bowl under your bed or on your nightstand and perform the Three Secrets Reinforcement (see Chapter 6). Repeat this process for an additional eight consecutive mornings for a total of nine consecutive mornings; keep the same stones, but change the water and the twig each time. After performing this cure for nine days, return the stones to the earth. Now the bowl is ready for use in special cures that can strengthen and stabilize your life, relationships, and career.

To add strength to your life and positive weight to your endeavors, leave the empty yu bowl on your nightstand or under the bed indefinitely. If you want to empower your career, set the bowl on your desk. Be sure to treat the bowl as a sacred object and reinforce either cure using the Three Secrets Reinforcement while visualizing your desired goals being accomplished quickly. (To stabilize a child, perform the variation of this cure I give you in Chapter 13.)

Refreshing personal chi with the Orange Peel Bath Cure

The *Orange Peel Bath Cure* is a highly effective way to restore personal energy, shed bad luck, protect yourself against spiritual or emotional attack, and recover from strange or difficult illnesses. It's a simple personal chi adjustment cure that offers profound energetic help in times of real need and calls upon the revivifying energetic properties of the orange. How so? This cure uses the mystical powers of fragrance to effect profound change. (Citrus is renowned for its power to freshen and purify, and it can powerfully assist human chi.)

To perform the Orange Peel Bath Cure, follow these three easy steps:

1. **Tear the peels of nine oranges into small pieces and put them into bath water.**

2. **Take a bath with the orange peels in the water.**

3. **After your bath, perform the Three Secrets Reinforcement and visualize yourself healthy, fresh, and free from harm, disease, and ill will.**

   I tell you all about the Three Secrets Reinforcement in Chapter 6.

Promoting a long and happy marriage with the Marriage Cure

With so many marriages ending in divorce and with many relationships never even reaching the marriage zone, many people have clearly mastered the art of short, intense relationships. But maybe you're ready to try something new and different — for instance, a long and happy marriage. If you're someone who desires a long, fulfilling marriage or relationship, the *Marriage Cure* may be the one for you. This cure isn't designed to get you a new partner, but it can promote relationship longevity and happiness with your current partner. It's very potent when performed properly and with great intention.

Here's what you need to perform the Marriage Cure:

- ✔ **One photo of you and one of your partner:** The photos should be approximately the same size, and each picture should show only one person (see Figure 22-1a).

- ✔ **A really long red string or ribbon, all in one piece (not tied together):** To determine the length of ribbon needed, multiply the width of the pictures by 100. For example, if the photos are 3 inches across, the string needs to be at least 300 inches long.

- ✔ **A brand-new red envelope:** Make sure your envelope is big enough for your photos to fit inside. Most stationery stores offer red envelopes in various sizes; any type is fine as long it seals and is large enough to hold your photos.

Follow these steps to a long and happy marriage:

1. **Place the photos so they're facing each other.**

2. **Write your full name and the word "matrimony" on the back side of your partner's photo, and on the back side of your photo, write the word "matrimony" and your partner's full name.**

3. **Under the light of the (ideally full) moon, bind the photos together (face-to-face) by wrapping a red-colored string around them 99 times, as in Figure 22-1b.**

4. **Visualize that you and your beloved are perfect mates, destined for each other and brought together from many miles apart.**

5. **Place the string-wrapped photos in a red envelope (as shown in Figure 22-1c).**

6. **Put the envelope beneath your pillow (see Figure 22-1d) and sleep with the envelope in this spot for nine consecutive nights.**

7. **On the tenth day, take the red envelope to a place with moving water and throw the envelope into the water (see Figure 22-1e).**

   A river or ocean works well for carrying the envelope away; a barely moving brook or stream may not have a strong enough current for a good cure. If you go to the ocean, make sure you throw the envelope into it when the tide is going out.

   If you can't get to a body of flowing water, you can bury the photos in your backyard instead — the Marriage Area is a good spot — and, at the same time, plant a new, healthy tree on top of the envelope. The Marriage Area of the yard is the back-right portion of the lot (see Chapter 3 for more details on this Life Area of the Feng Shui Octagon).

8. **Visualize that your marriage or relationship is made in heaven and will last forever.**

9. **Reinforce the cure with the Three Secrets Reinforcement presented in Chapter 6.**

If you perform this cure, your relationship can move to a new depth of love and commitment that may surprise and delight you and your partner.

Figure 22-1:
Marriage
Cure steps.

Letting the Sun Shine In

The *Great Sunshine Buddha Cure* is a physical energy practice that helps your body circulate its energy in a more healthy and vibrant manner. It purifies, clarifies, and strengthens your energy system and promotes physical and mental health. This cure is easy, requires no training, produces tangible results — and it feels great! You can perform the Great Sunshine Buddha Cure as many times per day as you want.

The Great Sunshine Buddha Cure has three parts (which are shown in order from left to right in Figure 22-2). In Grandmaster Lin Yun's Feng Shui school, visualization is the most important part of Feng Shui. If visualization isn't easy for you, you can internally feel, hear, or sense the corresponding sensations according to the following instructions.

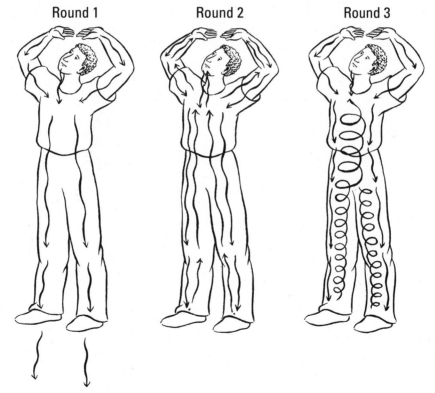

Round 1 Round 2 Round 3

Figure 22-2:
Great
Sunshine
Buddha
Cure.

Performing the three-part cure one time through is one repetition of the Great Sunshine Buddha Cure. After you complete one (or more) repetitions of the exercise, perform the Three Secrets Reinforcement (see Chapter 6) while visualizing yourself feeling healthy, refreshed, clear, and revitalized.

Great Sunshine Buddha: Round 1

Follow these steps for Round 1 of the Great Sunshine Buddha Cure:

1. **Stand with your feet shoulder width apart and your hands at your sides.**

2. **Visualize a bright, shining Sun 2 to 3 feet above your head and directly in front of you.**

3. **Raise your arms above your head and slightly in front of you with the palms facing the Sun and visualize that the sunlight contains positive, spiritual, and healing energy within it.**

   For extra power, visualize a spiritual figure in the Sun that's shining his or her light toward you along with the Sun's rays.

4. **Inhale, visualizing the healing golden light and warmth from the Sun pouring into your body through the centers of your palms and the point between your eyebrows as you draw in air.**

   See the healing golden sunlight flooding and filling your body. See the light fill you and also feel it energetically.

5. **When your body is full of light, start to exhale, visualizing all the golden light going straight down through your feet and into the ground.**

6. **Return your hands to your sides.**

Great Sunshine Buddha: Round 2

Follow these steps to perform Round 2 of the Great Sunshine Buddha Cure:

1. **Raise your hands over your head with your palms toward the Sun.**

2. **Inhale energy from the Sun into your body through three points —
both palms and the mid-eyebrow point.**

   Visualize and feel the warm sunlight flooding into your body, filling you to the bottom of your feet.

3. **When the light reaches the bottoms of your feet, immediately exhale while seeing and feeling the light quickly bounce back up through your body, out through the three bodily points, and into the Sun.**

4. **Return your hands to your sides.**

Great Sunshine Buddha: Round 3

Follow these steps to perform Round 3 of the Great Sunshine Buddha Cure, completing the cure:

1. **Raise your hands over your head, palms toward the Sun.**

2. **Inhale energy from the Sun into your body through the three points — both palms and the mid-eyebrow point.**

   Visualize the warm sunlight flooding into your body, filling you from the top down to your feet.

3. **When the sunlight has filled your body, start to exhale and visualize that the light is beginning to swirl in a spiral manner up through your body.**

   As the light swirls upward, it collects these negative energies:

   • Sickness and harmful chi

   • Negative emotions and thoughts

   • Bad luck and negative energy or negative potential of any kind

4. **Continue to exhale and visualize the light exiting the three bodily points and returning to the Sun.**

   When the light hits the Sun, the negative energy is instantly, completely, and permanently burned up.

5. **Return your hands to your sides.**

If you want to meditate, now (after performing the Great Sunshine Buddha Cure) is a good time to do so.

Feeling Clean, Clear, and Refreshed with Meditations

Two special meditation methods — Supreme Yoga Stage 1 and the Five Elements, Five Colors Meditation — can help improve your health and physical energy circulation. These two meditations are nonsectarian; anyone of any belief system or religion can use them.

> ✔ **Supreme Yoga Stage 1** positively adjusts your energy by increasing intelligence and stability.
>
> ✔ **The Five Elements, Five Colors Meditation** helps heal the organs by restoring them to proper functioning and returns the body to health.

Supreme Yoga Stage 1

Supreme Yoga is one of the highest forms of meditation in Grandmaster Lin Yun's Feng Shui school. Nine stages of Supreme Yoga exist, each of which cultivates different aspects of the body and psyche. The method I outline in the following sections is the first stage of the set.

Understanding the benefits of Supreme Yoga Stage 1

Supreme Yoga Stage 1 is good for healing insomnia and clearing neuroses. It improves the health and cultivates one's spiritual development and psychic abilities. It can restore energy when you're tired and can also help you recover from so-called incurable diseases. Potent and highly effective, this method operates purely on the inner level (it entails no environmental adjustment) and fine-tunes the most important Feng Shui environment of all — your energy and body-mind system.

Performing the meditation

The steps of Supreme Yoga Stage 1 are as follows:

1. **Sit, stand, or lie down in the position that's most comfortable for you with your hands in the Heart-Calming Mudra.**

   Turn to Chapter 6 for information on the Heart-Calming Mudra.

2. **Repeat the Heart-Calming Mantra or your mantra of choice nine times.**

   The Heart-Calming Mantra is as follows: Gate para gate para sum gate bodhi swaha. (Flip to Chapter 6 for a pronunciation guide.)

3. **Imagine everything around you becoming very still and quiet.**

4. **From a far distance, hear the sound "Hum" gradually approach you, getting louder and louder as it grows near (see Figure 22-3a).**

5. **Hear and feel the sound enter your body at the point between your eyebrows and see the sound become a small white ball of light.**

6. **See the white ball drop down inside your body to a point that's four finger widths below your navel, in the center of your body.**

   In Chinese medicine, this point is called the *dan tien*, or energy field.

7. **Visualize and feel the small white ball at the dan tien making nine small, horizontal circles in a clockwise direction.**

8. **Visualize the white ball dropping to the bottom of your torso and then moving up the front of your body, over your crown, down your back, and to the bottom of your torso again.**

    Visualize the white ball traveling around your body in this manner two more times for a total of three circulations (see Figure 22-3b).

9. **Visualize the white ball returning to the dan tien.**

10. **See and feel the white ball becoming very hot and bright like the Sun, radiating heat and light.**

11. **See the white ball circulating all throughout the interior of your body, still radiating heat and light (see Figure 22-3c).**

    The white ball can circulate rapidly or slowly, and it can move in a random or precise manner. Just make sure that as the ball circulates, you're visualizing its movement, heat, and light opening up your body's circulation on all of these levels:

    - **Physical circulation:** The flow of blood and lymph, nervous activity, air, water, digestion, and chi throughout the body is enhanced. Your body is energized, clarified, and healed.

    - **Mental and emotional circulation:** Old and stagnant emotions such as fear, anger, and hatred are cleared; mental stagnation, including rigid ideas, ignorance, and confusion, is replaced with clarity, wisdom, and free-flowing awareness.

    - **Energy circulation:** Your body's energy is free-flowing and circulating well throughout your system. Energetic blocks are dissolved, and your energy is smooth, balanced, and powerful.

    If any parts of your body need extra healing, visualize the small white ball circulating in these parts a little longer.

12. **Allow the small white ball to return to its position at the dan tien when you feel the circulation is complete.**

13. **Complete the meditation by holding your hands in the Heart-Calming Mudra and reciting the Six True Words, or another mantra of your choice, nine times.**

    The Six True Words are as follows: Om Ma Ni Pad Me Hum.

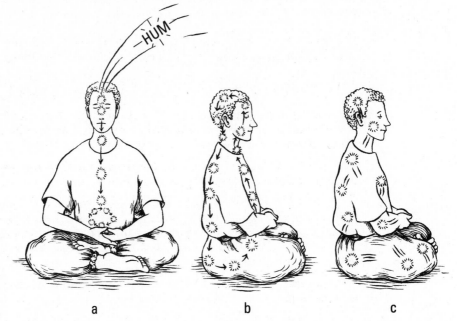

Figure 22-3:
Supreme
Yoga
Stage 1.

a   b   c

The Five Elements, Five Colors Meditation

The Five Elements, Five Colors Meditation applies the power of the Five Elements (see Chapter 5) and their corresponding colors to five internal organs of the body. Chinese medicine believes that these five organs are the most important ones in the human body. Each organ correlates to a particular energy of the Five Elements.

✔ The lungs relate to Metal.

✔ The kidneys relate to Water.

✔ The liver relates to Wood.

✔ The heart relates to Fire.

✔ The spleen relates to Earth.

When all Five Elements are balanced and functioning normally in your body, your life achieves profound balance and harmony. This harmony greatly enhances and energizes your being on the physical, emotional, mental, and spiritual levels. In other words, the Five Elements, Five Colors Meditation brings you profound benefits on every level of your being.

To carry out the Five Element, Five Colors Meditation, perform the following internal steps:

1. **Hold your hands in the Heart-Calming Mudra and chant the Heart-Calming Mantra, or other mantra of your choice, nine times.**

   See the earlier "Performing the mediation" section for the Heart-Calming Mantra and turn to Chapter 6 for a visual of the Heart-Calming Mudra.

2. **Visualize that everything around you is in deep silence and you're one with all of nature; imagine that everything has dissolved into a complete void.**

3. **Visualize every part of your skeleton from your skull downward turning into red-hot molten iron.**

   Inch by inch, heat is moving downward from your skull to your jaw, neck, spine and ribs, pelvis, thighbones, calf bones, arms, fingers, and finally to your toes. All the bones of your body are turning steadily into molten iron — hot, strong, and red, like steel in a smelting furnace. Your skeleton is intensely radiating heat and light.

4. **Envision, through the molten heat of your skeleton, that the following is occurring:**

   - All negative causes and effects that have accumulated from your previous, current, and next lifetime are cleansed and purified.

   - Negative energies stored in your body-mind system through wrong actions of body, speech, emotion, and thought are also being cleansed away.

   - All negative chi, bad luck, and illness of body are being removed and burned away.

5. **Imagine a pink lotus flower with eight petals arising from the bottoms of your feet.**

   The lotus flower begins to wrap its petals around your red-hot skeleton, moving up from your feet to your legs, pelvis, chest, back, arms, and so on.

6. **Visualize that all of your vital organs (lungs, heart, stomach, liver, and so on) are emerging as 100 percent newborn pink lotus flesh and that you're being reborn from this new pink lotus material.**

   Composed entirely of pink lotus flesh, your body is completely new and pure.

7. **Envision a smaller pink lotus with eight petals blossoming in your heart.**

On the blossom appears either a small Buddha or the deity of your own religion. See the image of the deity growing gradually and filling your body completely until you and the deity are one. You now have the deity's same image, color, and shape. You're one with the deity, and the deity is one with you. Your head possesses the deity's perfect wisdom, your heart its great compassion, and your body its infinite power.

8. **Starting with your lungs, visualize the color of each key organ gradually changing according to the Creative Cycle of the Five Elements.**

   I describe this cycle in the sections that follow.

Lungs: Natural color white (Metal)

See your lungs as white. Now, visualize your lungs changing color from white to black (Water) to green (Wood) to red (Fire) to yellow (Earth) and back to white (Metal) again.

Visualize that all lung disorders are gone, both lungs are emitting light and radiating heat, and you're breathing normally.

Kidney: Natural color black (Water)

See your kidneys as black. Now, visualize your kidneys changing color from black to green (Wood) to red (Fire) to yellow (Earth) to white (Metal) and back to black (Water) again.

Visualize that any kidney disorders are gone and your kidneys are emitting light, radiating heat, and functioning normally.

Liver: Natural color green (Wood)

See your liver as green. Now, visualize your liver changing color from green to red (Fire) to yellow (Earth) to white (Metal) to black (Water) and back to green (Wood) again.

Purifying three lifetimes

Buddhist practitioners of inner Feng Shui believe that negative causes and effects have accumulated through multiple lifetimes. However, you don't have to believe in past lives to receive tremendous "this lifetime" benefits when performing the Five Elements, Five Colors Meditation.

Just visualize that all of your negativity from the past, present, and future portions of this life are being cleansed away while all of your positive energy is being greatly enhanced. This concept is called *three-lifetime purification*.

Visualize that any liver disorders are gone and your liver is emitting light, radiating heat, and functioning normally.

Heart: Natural color red (Fire)

See your heart as red. Now, visualize your heart changing color from red (Fire) to yellow (Earth) to white (Metal) to black (Water) to green (Wood) and back to red (Fire) again.

Visualize that any heart disorders are gone and your heart looks like a sun, emitting light, radiating heat, and functioning normally and strongly.

Spleen: Natural color yellow (Earth)

See your spleen as yellow. Now, visualize your spleen changing color from yellow (Earth) to white (Metal) to black (Water) to green (Wood) to red (Fire) and back to yellow (Earth) again.

Visualize that any spleen disorders are gone and your spleen looks like a sun, emitting light, radiating heat, and functioning normally.

The entire body

Visualize that your entire body is now filled with the light of the deity in your heart. All of your internal organs are metabolizing healthily and are radiating spiritual light toward the following:

- **Millions of deities (or any entities of your own religion) throughout the universe:** Their spiritual light radiates back toward you.

- **The six realms where sentient beings exist:** In Buddhism, these realms are named as follows:

    - The heavenly realm

    - The jealous gods realm

    - The human realm

    - The animal realm

    - The hungry ghost realm

    - The hell realm

  If your religion differs, you can broadcast the light to the realms that fit with the cosmology of your religion (such as heaven, hell, earth, or other variations). Visualize that all the beings in these realms go from suffering to happiness and from happiness to ultimate peace. Now their spiritual light radiates back to you.

> ✔ **Your spiritual teacher or leader, if you have one, or a spiritual mentor or friend:** His or her spiritual light radiates back to you.
>
> ✔ **Your family, friends, and relatives from afar:** Bless them. Their spiritual light radiates back to you.
>
> ✔ **Your home and office:** Eliminated of evil spirits, bad luck, illness chi, and negative chi, your home and office are cleansed and purified, radiating positive luck. Your light returns to you.

Now make a wish for whatever you want. As you visualize your wish coming true, with your hands in the Heart-Calming Mudra, recite the Six True Words (Om Ma Ni Pad Me Hum) or a personal prayer or mantra nine times.

When you finish this meditation, your circulation is enhanced, your organs function more smoothly, and your energy is positively adjusted. Your internal energies are balanced and harmonized, creating a centered body, mind, and feelings. You feel calm and peaceful — probably like you're ready to do some more Feng Shui cures!

Part V
The Part of Tens

The 5th Wave   By Rich Tennant

"What do you mean you don't think the Feng Shui is right?"

In this part . . .

If you hate wasting time and you're ready to happily waltz into better times, this part is for you. Here, you find tens and tens of Feng Shui methods to end the madness and mend the sadness. With ten essential pointers to ensure your Feng Shui packs a punch; ten guidelines on how to pick a qualified Feng Shui consultant; ten special tips for selling your home using Feng Shui; and ten unique art pieces created by Feng Shui Grandmaster Lin Yun Rinpoche, this part helps bliss your life, bless your loft, and blow away your loss. All in all, this part is a treasure-trove tried-and-true, a bounty basket through and through.

Chapter 23

Ten Principles for Success with Your Feng Shui

In This Chapter

▶ Listening to your intuition and surroundings

▶ Following and improving on your Feng Shui instincts

▶ Seeking help with cures and using special timing to enhance them

*F*eng Shui isn't a one-trick pony — some gimmick you use once or twice and then put away in the closet with your ab machine. Instead, Feng Shui is a multifaceted tool that enables you to see beneath the surface of your environment, understand how your environment affects you, and rearrange your life on a whole new level. Beginning Feng Shui is like embarking on a journey — it leads you to new discoveries, knowledge, and more of what you really want and need in life.

Every journey in life needs guideposts. Let the following ten guiding principles help you refine your new skills so that your Feng Shui can take you all the way to the winner's circle.

Just like everything else in life, you get out of Feng Shui what you put into it, so use the best materials you can find and afford for your cures. Consider your Feng Shui remedies an investment in your future.

Note: If options exist, choose the strongest cure you can for the situation at hand. In many cases, I've sprinkled tips throughout this book to indicate which cure is the most potent. In cases where I haven't noted the most potent cure, stretch a little and use your intuition to select the best one. Why settle for a partial solution? By applying your full commitment to each cure, your results will be profound and highly gratifying.

Retain Your Energy

Feng Shui recommends that you keep the specific details and purposes of your cures to yourself. Keeping the particulars of your cures private is a way of containing their energy. (Loose lips don't just sink ships — they also leak energy.) You can safely discuss the subject of Feng Shui and let others know that you use it, but telling people outside of your household the fine points and purposes of your cures unnecessarily leaks energy from your life.

Pay Attention to Life's Feedback

Life itself is the ultimate, unerring feedback mechanism for the Feng Shui process. The events of your life are inseparable from and interactive with your environment. Take notice of your life events and actions after you perform cures and look out for signs of the changes you seek. If you're not seeing the desired results, or if the effects aren't coming fast enough for you, you may need to perform additional cures in the corresponding parts of your life.

Follow Your Intuition and Act with Urgency

Allow your *intuition* — your inner knowing — to guide you when deciding which cures to perform, as well as when, where, and how to apply them. (If you don't believe in intuition, by all means, use the Force.) After all, you're the one living in your home, and your feelings are connected to its energy. The key is to pay attention to your feelings and act on them.

I recommend that you perform your cures within three days of receiving them from your consultant or recognizing the need for them on your own. In any case, the sooner you can perform your cures, the better. The three-day period is a special opportunity window that significantly increases the effectiveness of cures. A Feng Shui problem area is like a wound to your environment's energy, and this condition directly affects you whether you realize it or not. The longer you wait, the more damage the situation does.

For example, if you cut your finger with a rusty knife, would you think, "Hmm . . . I really ought to wash and bandage this cut, but a football game is on TV right now, and tonight is the dinner party at the Wilsons' house, and I'm kind of busy at the office this week. Maybe I'll do it next Saturday." I doubt it. Well, the same idea applies when dealing with Feng Shui wounds. (Feng Shui solutions are called *cures,* hint hint.) So don't procrastinate — fix the problem as soon as you discover that something is broken. (If you can't complete a cure within the three-day period, at least get it started within this time frame.)

Fine-Tune Your Feng Shui

Use the feedback that life gives you to help you reach your goals. What happens in your life after you apply a cure tells you how to fine-tune your Feng Shui. If, for example, you perform a wealth cure and your funds increase just one-third of the amount you desire, be encouraged — this result is progress! Plus, you've discovered the art of using cures to create new wealth. Maybe you're not Warren Buffett yet, but if you keep practicing, you'll increase your profits as your skill improves.

Keep on Keeping On

Continue performing cures, cures, and more cures! Feng Shui is a continuous process, not a one-way trip to your destination. The need for Feng Shui arises every time you need a boost, buy new furniture, or simply notice the need for change in any part of your life. The more cures you perform, the more the energy of your home aligns with your needs and supports your goals. You gain skills by continuing to do cures over time.

A positive frame of mind works wonders both in life and in Feng Shui, so expect results before they appear and then celebrate them when they come. As you continue to make positive changes (and your Feng Shui eyes sharpen), you may notice new parts of your home that pop out at you because they need balancing. Go after 'em with a vengeance!

If you feel stuck or unclear about a Feng Shui issue, you can seek spiritual guidance from whatever spiritual source you feel connected to — your heart, God, Jesus, Mary, Buddha, Allah, the Tao, Scooby-Doo, even Obi-Wan Kenobi (alright, just kidding on the last two). Ask for help in selecting and performing the right cures. Visualize that this source is coming to your aid and guiding your actions and thoughts. You may be surprised at what you receive, and the resulting cures can produce wonderful benefits.

Work on the Mundane as Well

This principle is more or less a common-sense disclaimer: Put diligent attention and effort into fulfilling the mundane requirements of your life as well as into your Feng Shui practice. If you desire wealth, diligently study and practice the principles and techniques of creating wealth. Feng Shui isn't a substitute for gainful employment; it can't magically fill your bank account while you drink beer and watch soap operas in your perfectly Feng Shui-ed home. Feng Shui enhances your life's work in progress and creates a supportive environment in which you can further your dreams. So perform cures in your home and do your work in the world. The combination of intelligent effort, dedication to self-improvement, and powerful Feng Shui cures is the best recipe for your success.

Continue to Increase Your Knowledge

If you practice Feng Shui attentively, your ability to notice Feng Shui trouble spots and adjust them to your advantage continuously increases. Eventually, you become like the captain of a well-organized, smoothly operating, and aesthetically pleasing ship. And this ship is your living and working environment — your life as a whole.

Attending classes on Feng Shui and reading additional books can help you keep progressing in the world of auspicious placement.

Keep the Faith

Keep an open mind regarding your Feng Shui efforts. There's no such thing as a cure that doesn't work. What matters is that you do enough and you do it in the right direction. (***Remember:*** For every action, there's an equal and opposite reaction.) Some people perform cures and feel disheartened when they don't see immediate results, but then they experience powerful, desired life shifts weeks or months later. Predicting the precise results from any specific cure is impossible. However, God is in the details of the cure, and details are what Feng Shui is all about. So continue to perform cures with sincerity and great intention, and use the Three Secrets Reinforcement (see Chapter 6). Then you can patiently and confidently expect the well-deserved results to appear in time.

Enlarge the Team

If you need help performing a Feng Shui cure, enlist your spouse, partner, or other members of your household. Numbers mean *synergy* (a combined force), so the more positive intentions involved in your cures, the more the Feng Shui problem can be transformed.

If a Feng Shui situation seems out of your league or you simply want to advance to the next level with professional help, seek assistance from a qualified Feng Shui practitioner in your area. (Flip to Chapter 24 and the appendix for help finding a local Feng Shui consultant.)

Employ Special Timing for Stronger Cures

Feng Shui teaches that special timing can make your cures stronger. Two special time periods each day provide windows of opportunity: 11 a.m. to 1 p.m. and 11 p.m. to 1 a.m. (standard time). These periods — when day becomes night and night turns into day — add significance to any solution you perform, giving extra momentum to a Feng Shui cure.

Good dates to perform cures include the day of the new moon or full moon, your birthday, New Year's Day, Chinese New Year's Day (which differs every year, so check an almanac or the Internet for the exact date), or any other day that holds special significance for you. (You can also consult the Chinese almanac or another book of auspicious dates for help selecting dates and times to perform your cures.) Performing cures on special dates and times is especially helpful for enhancing the effects of the special cures, such as blessing ceremonies and personal cures, given in Chapters 21 and 22.

If the special dates and times aren't convenient for you, perform your cures whenever you can. It's always better to move ahead now and see progress than to wait for a special date or time to come around.

Chapter 24

Ten Tips for Finding the Right Consultant and Sticking with the Plan

Doing Feng Shui on your own is great — in fact, it's the focus of this book — but sometimes having a trained set of eyes to analyze your situation can make all the difference. The right professional can help you move in leaps and bounds beyond your solo capacity. Think about it this way: No matter how good you get at cleaning your own carpets with that supermarket rental carpet machine, you'll never achieve the results a professional can guarantee. The same principle applies to Feng Shui.

Here are just a few reasons why a professional consultant can help you get better results:

✔ Professionals have more information, knowledge, expertise, and experience than you do and you probably ever will, no matter how many books you read.

✔ By definition, you can't see your own "blind spots." In other words, it's impossible for you to objectively see and evaluate your own situation. Only a professional outsider can do this.

✔ A good professional challenges you and helps you reach your goals in ways you can't on your own. This is the reason why top professional athletes always have coaches. If they do, why shouldn't you?

✔ A pro can get you out of a rut and back on track toward your full potential if you're stuck and don't know what to do to get moving.

Guarantee the best results for yourself by taking two vital actions: Hire a qualified consultant and do your cures — you know, the ones your consultant provides. The ten pointers in this chapter help set you on the right path. Be sure to also check out (and use!) the great tips for Feng Shui success that I share in Chapter 23.

Gauge Your Commitment Level

Before starting the process of working with a professional consultant, stop for a minute and assess just how committed you are to the process. Your results will be less than stellar if you're ambivalent about committing to Feng Shui or unclear about your goals. (If you need help setting Feng Shui–related goals, turn to Chapter 1.)

Feng Shui isn't interior design, something designed to "make you feel better," psychotherapy, or a quick-and-easy life fix. In the right hands, Feng Shui is a potent tool for stimulating growth and changing your life. To get these changes, you must be willing to surrender your resistance and confusion. You must also be willing to "get your hands dirty" creating changes, no matter how hard or easy that may be. You may have to face the things you've been avoiding, perhaps for a long time, and change them. It isn't always easy or convenient, but it is worth it.

Set a Working Budget

Knowing upfront how much you're able to spend on Feng Shui cures for your home makes the process more straightforward. Decide with your spouse or partner (if you're living together) what an appropriate budget is for you in order to create substantial and powerful life changes.

Nail Down Your Intentions

Get clear on your intentions before you start looking for a Feng Shui consultant. Ask yourself this question: What do I truly want to get out of Feng Shui?

Focus on the parts of your life that you most want to change. You benefit when you limit your attention in one consultation to a single part of your life (two at the most). Focusing all your energy for change on just one or two parts of your life (such as money and/or health) helps you more in the long run by creating clearer focus and better results. *Note:* The parts of your life that you decide to change don't have to match the Life Areas of the Octagon exactly (see Chapter 3 for a description of each Life Area); just ask for what you want.

Some clients mistakenly think they'll get more for their time and money if they ask their consultant to help them resolve numerous life issues in one consultation. For instance, I once had a client request I help him in 17 different parts of his life in one consultation — a true recipe for frustration (both mine and his). This tactic is both unrealistic and unproductive. Avoid this pitfall by applying the necessary focus. You'll see more tangible results and experience dramatically less confusion if you do. After you've improved your money situation, for instance, you can switch your focus to family, health, or whatever you'd like to improve in the next consultation.

If you're just starting out in Feng Shui, remember that a big part of the game is simply achieving your first tangible results. After that, the floodgates can open. The best way to proceed is to meet with your spouse or significant other (wine, candles, and Barry White tunes in tow) a couple days before your consultation begins. Talk about your life and the part that feels like it needs the most changing right now. Then write it down. At the consultation, tell your consultant what your intention is for change. (If your consultant doesn't ask you for your goals or intentions, find a new consultant.)

Find a Real (Professional) Consultant

The best consultant is a trained professional who has a successful track record making his or her living as a Feng Shui consultant. Getting together with a friend (or a part-timer) who has read some Feng Shui books and trying to figure things out together can be tempting, but this approach has inherent limitations. Also, beginner's luck doesn't necessarily apply when it comes to Feng Shui. Think about it: Would you go to a dentist who makes his or her primary living as a delivery driver?

Consulting in Feng Shui involves much more than knowing some Feng Shui information. First and foremost, it involves proper training from qualified masters and teachers; development of technical Feng Shui skills; intuitive gifts for observation, judgment, and counseling; and the ability to match solutions to situations and guide people through the Feng Shui process. Turn to the appendix for a source of qualified consultants.

Discover What's Involved in a Consultation

You need to find out what's included in a consultation before you hire a consultant. This way you know whether what's offered meets your needs. When first contacting a consultant, be sure to ask the following questions:

✔ Is your consultant ready, willing, and able to help you achieve your life goals by using Feng Shui? (Ask specifically about your needs to determine this. See the earlier "Nail Down Your Intentions" section for more information about outlining your needs.)

✔ What services are involved in the consultation?

✔ How many home/office visits will your consultant provide you?

Make Sure the Vibe Is Right

Ultimately, knowing whether the consultant you're considering is the right one for you comes down to a gut decision. After gathering information and talking to the consultant, always trust your intuition to guide you to the right decision.

Get Specific Action Items

A consultation should always involve you receiving clear advice for specific and practical changes you can make to your home that should result in positive life changes. Vague generalizations or confusing instructions are a red flag.

If your consultant gives you a cure you can't do, check with the consultant during the consultation to see what can be done. If the consultant gives you a cure you *can* do but don't *want* to do, ask more questions and get more clarity. Sometimes the changes you resist turn out to be the most effective, beneficial cures you do. (See the next section for more about the importance of performing every cure your consultant gives you.)

Make sure you take clear, accurate notes on the cures your consultant recommends. It helps if both you and your spouse or partner (if you're living together) take notes during the session. (Don't just rely on an audio recording of the consultation; written notes are always best.) Check your cure list with the consultant before he or she leaves to ensure that everybody's on the same page.

Just Do It — All of It!

After you have a consultant you trust, the next part is simple: Follow his or her instructions. One of the most important factors in reaping the benefits of good Feng Shui consultation is to do all the cures you receive.

Picking and choosing from the list of cures and then performing only the ones you feel like doing or the ones you think will work is a recipe for failure. Would you do that with post-op instructions from a brain surgeon? I don't think so! If you trust the consultant, then also trust his or her recommendations. You haven't given the process a fair shot unless you perform all the recommended cures. Missing one cure could mean the difference between minor, less satisfying results and enormous, life-changing ones. Give the program a chance before you change the recipe.

Track Your Cures and Keep Your Eyes Peeled: Change Is A-Comin'

Keeping track of your cures is critical for success. I have all my clients track their cures (and the results they experience) with a cure-tracking sheet, and we go over it together regularly. Tracking your cures helps you in these important ways:

- It helps you not lose track of valuable cures your consultant gave you — something that can easily happen if you don't have a comprehensive, organized way to track the whole process.

- It assists you in completing the cures. Remember, no cures — no results!

- It helps you stay honest. You may find it easy to think, "Man, I've done so much Feng Shui. Where the heck are my results?" But when you check your cure-tracking sheet, you may find that you've actually done just three or four cures and merely thought about all the others you were supposed to complete. It happens more often than you may think. (This is the "hope, pray, and dream rather than work" version of Feng Shui — definitely not recommended.)

- It assists you in doing them more quickly. Because you're organized, you get more done faster and easier. So what are you waiting for?

- It helps you track your results and aids your consultant in helping you get results.

Your cure-tracking sheet should feature the following information for each cure:

- The exact cure as your consultant gave it to you

- The date you received the cure

- Your intention for the cure (health, wealth, and so on)

- The current status of the cure (still pending, in progress, or complete)

- Your comments (for instance, notes on what needs to happen next for the cure, remaining tasks to complete the cure, or questions to ask the consultant about the cure)

Document Your Life Changes

Carefully document what's happening in your life after you do your cures. If you're looking for changes in money, for example, record *anything* that has changed in your life regarding money. And know that many times the changes come in different ways than you expect. (Kind of like life, right?)

Also, remember that you're not in charge of the way change happens. I once had a client who asked for help in the wealth department. A few weeks after the consultation, she called to say that nothing had changed. Upon further discussion, it turned out that she'd actually received some additional hours at her job, an unexpected tax refund, and a surprise check from her insurance company for an old claim. So why was she saying she hadn't seen any results in the money part of her life? Because she hadn't gotten a raise at work — the specific way she desired to get increased money. Because she was fixated on new money coming solely from a raise, receiving cash from three additional sources equaled "the Feng Shui hasn't worked" in her mind. Don't fall into this beginner trap. Embrace all the positive changes that come your way, keeping your mind open about how your results can happen.

Chapter 25

Ten Tips for Selling a Home with the Help of Feng Shui

*F*or many people, selling a home seems like a stress-fest; it falls somewhere between living with your in-laws and going on a blind date that turns out to be your ex. Feng Shui can not only lessen the pain of the home-selling process but also help preserve your precious sanity.

Selling a home first requires getting qualified buyers to view and show interest in your home. The Feng Shui cures in this chapter activate energy to attract the right people to buy your home. Some of these cures address the entrance, where people first view the home. After all, first impressions matter. (Chapter 9 delves into the importance of entryways.)

After you find a buyer and are preparing to leave the property, it's time to address your powerful energetic attachment to your home with the guidance I provide in this chapter. This step is helpful even if you consciously want to move. One way to face this psychological obstacle is to dispose of the mountains of unused belongings tucked in your closets and garage. Such accumulated baggage can be emotional and physical dead weight that anchors you in your current residence. Consider it dangerous contraband confiscated by customs before you move into your new home.

For additional help with the topics in this chapter, check out these other great *For Dummies* titles (both published by Wiley): *Home Staging For Dummies,* by Christine Rae and Jan Saunders Maresh, and *House Selling For Dummies,* 3rd Edition, by Eric Tyson and Ray Brown.

Note: More factors than I can cover in this short chapter need to be considered when selecting a home. I recommend contacting a Feng Shui professional for assistance when choosing your next residence to ensure you choose wisely with the help of Feng Shui methods. See Chapter 20 for in-depth information on choosing a home, and flip to Chapter 24 for details on finding and working with a Feng Shui consultant.

First Things First: Taking Care of Business

When selling a home, the following three factors, placed in order of importance, are more significant than any Feng Shui cures you can apply:

✔ Setting the right (read: realistic) price

✔ Employing the right real estate agent

✔ Having and following the right marketing plan

Although price is the most important of the three, neglecting any of these factors makes selling your home a very difficult job. Feng Shui cures can't induce buyers to act against their own best interests. Here's what I mean: If the price for your home is set unrealistically high, Feng Shui cures, even effective ones, can't magically make your home sell. So take care of these basics first and then add the powerful cures I provide in the rest of this chapter to gain the best of both worlds.

Activating Your Helpful People and Money Energies

The Helpful People Area of the home is extremely important at sale time (see Chapter 3 for details on how to locate the Helpful People Area in your home). Selling a home requires many helpful people, including real estate agents, bankers, brokers, family members, escrow agents, and, of course, your buyer. So the best cures for this Area are ones that create activity and flowing energy. You can install a wind chime, mobile, or fountain in the Helpful People Area of your home and/or lot and see tangible benefits. The energy of these cures helps create flow, which helps draw the first key ingredient of home sales your way — a qualified buyer. Visualize your home selling rapidly when you install the aforementioned cures, and be sure to use the Three Secrets Reinforcement I describe in Chapter 6 to fully activate the cure.

The other important ingredient in the sale of a home is money. Thus, the Wealth Area is also a prime area for home-sale cures. A chime, a faceted crystal sphere, or a fountain in this Area can effectively attract money. (Turn to Chapter 3 for more details about the Wealth Area.)

Applying cures in the Helpful People and Wealth Areas of your home can also help you find a good real estate agent and gather the necessary funds when you're buying a new home.

Enter Buyer, Stage Right

Two moments can make all the difference in selling your home:

- ✔ When potential buyers see the exterior and curb appeal of your home for the first time
- ✔ When potential buyers open your home's front door and first see the interior

You have to make sure both of these moments have maximum "wow" power. Stage, polish, and enhance your home to the best extent possible.

When you get ready to sell your home, make a point to attend at least five real estate open houses in your area. Carefully note what the owners did that made you want to buy the home, what they could've improved on, and what things made the house unattractive to you. Then go home and improve the way your house is presented even more, fixing any problems you find.

If you've done everything you can and your home still isn't selling, consider employing a professional home stager — preferably one with Feng Shui knowledge.

Sending Out Your Message with Sound

An effective Feng Shui house-selling cure is to activate your entrance with sound energy. Sound — especially clear, bell-like tones — promotes the energy of awakening, alerting, calling forth, and sending out messages. When you put your home up for sale, hang a beautiful-sounding wind chime near your front door. The melodious sound of chimes not only awakens and draws chi to your entrance but also energetically attracts people to your front door. It greets the visitors and makes them feel welcome.

When hanging your chime, visualize the house selling rapidly and easily —
and for the right price. (Flip to Chapter 4 for more information on sound cures
and Chapter 6 for tips on visualization.)

Enhancing the Visibility of Your Entrance

If your entrance isn't visible from the street, you may have a natural block to
selling your house. For a good cure, install bright lights to illuminate the front
area. You can also install lights along the pathway up to the front door. If the
main entrance to your home is dark or shadowed or set into the front of the
house (a funnel-like entrance), mount a bright light just outside the door to
light the front entrance. Adding light to the front of your house energetically
"activates" the entrance — the most important part of the house.

If energy is lively at the entrance, buyers are much more likely to view and
purchase the home.

Removing Obstacles from Your Entryway

If the main entryway (or *Mouth of Chi*) is blocked, possible buyers tend to
stay away. Talking with your mouth full is an apt metaphor here. If your trees
or shrubs block the entrance, I recommend trimming them back so the chi
can flow freely toward the front door. When the chi can flow freely toward
the entrance, buyers are much freer to visit the home, greatly increasing your
chances of making a sale.

Letting the Good Times Flow with Fountains

Fountains can not only help bring you more income but also bring you new
contacts and help you increase your opportunities. All three benefits of these
virtuous devices are invaluable when you're selling a home, so fountain away!
In other words, place one or more fountains in key locations to stimulate
buyers coming with fountains of cash. Use as many fountains as you need to
make things happen.

Places to use fountains profitably include

- Just outside your front door
- Just inside the front door

> ✔ In the Helpful People and Wealth Areas of the home and/or for your property (as I explain in the earlier section "Activating Your Helpful People and Money Energies").

Reinforce each of your fountain cures by visualizing your house selling quickly and for the right price. (Flip to Chapter 4 for more information on using fountains as Feng Shui cures.)

Cleaning Like Your Sale Depends on It — 'Cause It Does

Cleaning is number one when it comes to selling. After all, one of the biggest turnoffs is seeing and then thinking about moving into someone else's dirt. The solution: Clean, clean, clean! In fact, clean even more than you normally do, putting extra emphasis on the kitchen and bathrooms.

Having another set of eyes never hurts, so ask your real estate agent to check how well you've done. It also doesn't hurt to perform the Citrus Water Blessing, which freshens the energy of your home (I describe this cure in Chapter 21).

Start Moving Now

In the outer realm, selling a house is based on the price and the market, but in the inner realm, it depends largely on the seller's personal energy and willingness to move. Many sellers consciously think they want to leave, but they energetically hold onto their homes because of fear, resistance to change, and emotional attachment. To keep this mind-set from holding you back as you try to sell your home, get some energy moving as soon as possible.

The more dead weight you toss off your property and out of your life, the more energy you free up to move yourself out. So detach from all the material things you don't need and free yourself of stuff you won't be taking with you when you move. Have a garage or yard sale, donate goods to a local charity or halfway house, give things to friends and neighbors, or simply throw unwanted belongings in the back of a truck and take them to the dump. The sooner you clean out your home, the sooner you'll find yourself emotionally — and energetically — ready to move into a new home.

If you rent a storage space, don't forget to evaluate the personal value of the stuff you keep in there and get rid of what's no longer important or wanted. Every object you let go of decreases your energetic attachment to your home.

A final way to get a good start on moving is boxing up in advance the things that you're planning to move to your new home. The more ready you are to move, the easier (and more urgent) selling your current home and finding a new residence becomes.

A Little Birdie Told Me: The Birdseed Cure

If you're not drawing a sufficient number of prospective buyers to see your home, you can employ a special ceremonial solution — sprinkling birdseed. This little-known method helps you attract new opportunities (buyers and real estate agents) and send out positive messages ("Honey, we sold the house!"). It may be just what the doctor ordered for your home-selling needs.

Birds have been used for centuries to send messages (think of homing pigeons and falcons), and they're regarded as potent symbols of life change. The *Birdseed Cure* uses this concept in a mystical manner to powerfully change your circumstances.

To perform the Birdseed Cure, you first need to buy a large bag of birdseed. Then, right after waking in the morning, scatter handfuls of birdseed all the way from the street in front of your home right up to your front door. As you sprinkle, walk the normal path that you take to get to the door, visualizing the right opportunities and messages coming to you. Continue doing this every day — without missing any days — until you've done it for 9 or 27 days consecutively. Reinforce this cure with the Three Secrets Reinforcement (see Chapter 6) and visualize your home selling quickly and for the right price.

If you live in an apartment or other domicile where you can't sprinkle birdseed up to your front door, a good substitute for the Birdseed Cure is the Fresh Flowers Home Blessing, which I describe in Chapter 21.

Chapter 26

Ten Unique Calligraphies to Bless Your Life

In This Chapter

▶ Discovering the significance of the calligraphies

▶ Using the calligraphies to enhance your life

*T*his chapter contains a special bonus: ten special works of art created for you by Grandmaster Lin Yun, master of Feng Shui and traditional Chinese calligraphy. Chinese culture reveres calligraphy and painting as the only two true art forms, and highly skilled masters of the brush are few and far between.

Each of the ten calligraphies in this chapter contains a special meaning and energy. Grandmaster Lin Yun infused this art with his unique chi; simply viewing each calligraphy can help adjust your energy and energize your environment. You can enjoy them as works of art, or you can apply them as cures in key rooms of your home or in specific Life Areas of the Feng Shui Octagon (see Chapter 3 for details on the Octagon).

To apply a calligraphy as a cure, photocopy it or cut it out and hang it on a wall, with or without a frame. I recommend you apply the "Auspicious as You Wish" calligraphy to any area where you have a specific wish or desire that you want to come true.

Each calligraphy is followed by the English translation of the Chinese characters. (The translations are provided by Crystal Chu.) Traditionally, Chinese calligraphy includes the place and/or date where the art was composed. In the following pages, this information comes after each calligraphy translation.

Buddha

May the observer [of this calligraphy] be blessed with a smooth life.
May the chanter be blessed with peace.
May the receiver be blessed with prosperity.
May the keeper be blessed with longevity.

Composed by Grandmaster Lin Yun while chanting infinite numbers of mantras at the study of disciple Crystal Chu.

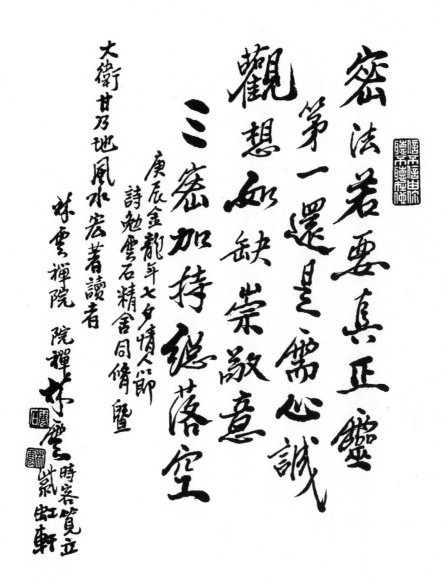

Secret Cures Poem

If you want your secret cures to be really effective,
First you have to have a faithful heart;
If your visualizations lack respect and sincerity,
Even with the Three Secrets Reinforcement, you will still come up empty.

*Written by Grandmaster Lin Yun on the Seventh Day of the Seventh Lunar Month,
also known as Chinese Valentine's Day, to encourage all disciples of Grandmaster
Lin Yun, as well as the readers of David Kennedy's book on Feng Shui.*

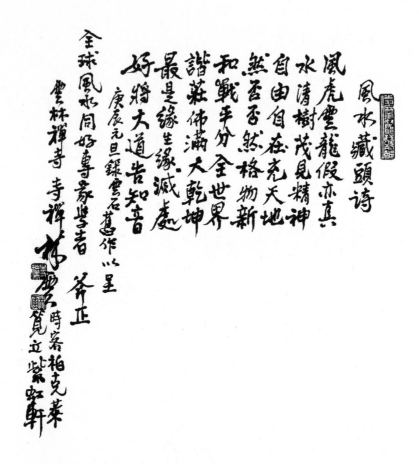

Hidden Title Poem on Feng Shui

Tigers appear in wind, and dragons emerge from clouds,
These images seem real yet untrue.
Water is clear and trees are lush,
From these we sense vital energy.
Freedom and ease fill the heaven and earth
Whether this is true or not,
We will get new knowledge after we've analyzed it.
Peace and warfare are spread equally throughout the world;
Humor and seriousness also fill the entire universe.
The ultimate is when karma begins and karma ceases
So it's best to share this teaching with those of common interest.

Grandmaster Lin Yun composed this poetry while visiting the study of disciple Crystal Chu. Written on New Year's Day, 2000, from a previous poetic composition. This poem is presented to all the Feng Shui founders, experts, and scholars in the world.

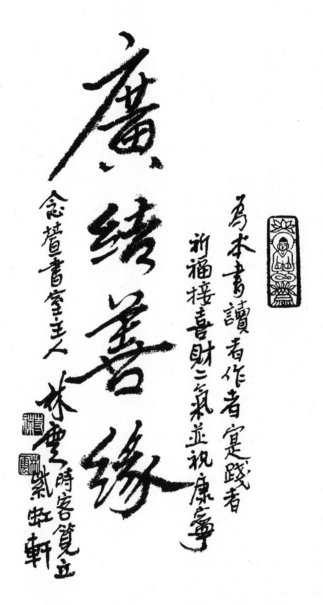

Good Karma Should Be Widely Connected

To bestow blessings upon the reader, author, and user of this book. May they receive prosperity, lucky chi, wealth chi, good health, and peace.

This calligraphy was composed by Grandmaster Lin Yun while visiting the study of disciple Crystal Chu.

One Shall Receive Great Benefits from Opening This Book

To bestow blessings upon the readers of David Kennedy's Feng Shui book.

This calligraphy was composed by Grandmaster Lin Yun while chanting mantras on New Year's Day at the study of disciple Crystal Chu.

Auspicious as You Wish

To bestow blessings upon David Kennedy's Feng Shui book. May its author, readers, publisher, and their family members all receive prosperity, wealth, wisdom, and safety.

Composed by Lin Shi while chanting infinite numbers of mantras at the study of disciple Crystal Chu. (Lin Shi is the other given name of Grandmaster Lin Yun.)

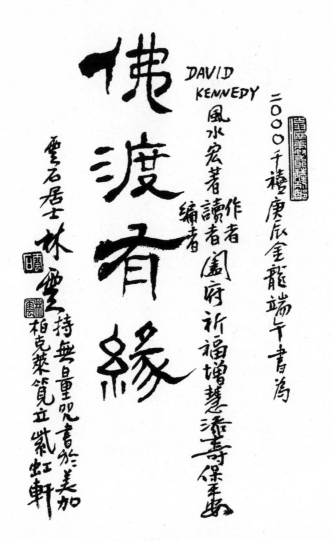

The Buddha Liberates Those with Good Karma from All Suffering

Written in the Millennium Year of the Golden Dragon for David Kennedy's Feng Shui book.

May its author, readers, publisher, and their family members all receive wisdom, longevity, and safety.

Composed by Grandmaster Lin Yun while chanting infinite numbers of mantras at the study of disciple Crystal Chu.

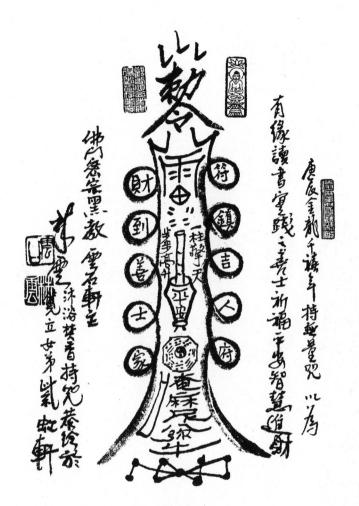

Taoist Talisman for Wealth and Safety

Taoist Talisman [showing the following blessings]: "Highest Supreme Order," "Five Thunder Protectors," "Bamboo Flute in Vase" to bring safety, while catapulting and elevating your success and well-being, "Eight Trigrams," "Six Syllable Mantra: Om Ma Ni Pad Me Hum," and "Tracing of the Nine Star Path."

This Talisman will bring safety to the residence of the blessed one. Wealth will arrive to the residence of those who do good deeds.

Respectfully composed by Grandmaster Lin Yun at the study of disciple Crystal Chu. Written in the Millennium Year of the Golden Dragon while chanting infinite numbers of mantras to bestow blessings upon readers and users with good karma. May they receive prosperity, safety, wisdom, and wealth.

Treasure Box

To bestow the acquisition of wealth upon the author, readers, and publisher of David Kennedy's Feng Shui book.

Regarding Wealth

Don't assume that seeking wealth is the same as being greedy.
Money just may bring relief
In hard times when you're needy.
Yet if it is acquired and used
Without a proper method,
It'll be easier to capsize a boat
Than to carry it afloat.

Composed by Grandmaster Lin Yun while chanting infinite numbers of mantras at the study of disciple Crystal Chu.

The Tao Reaches Heaven and Earth

For the readers and author of this book, as well as spiritual cultivators.
May their whole families be blessed with prosperity, auspiciousness, and
wisdom.

*Composed by Grandmaster Lin Yun while chanting mantras at the study of dis-
ciple Crystal Chu on New Year's Day, Millennium Year 2000.*

Appendix

Feng Shui Resources

・・

*T*he following sources offer Feng Shui products, training, and further information.

Yun Lin Temple Feng Shui Objects

Many authentic Feng Shui objects are available through the Yun Lin Temple, most of them exclusively designed or chosen based on Grandmaster Lin Yun's Feng Shui school. Following the principle of Minor Additions, Grandmaster Lin Yun's Feng Shui school uses special objects for Feng Shui cures. These items include special bamboo Feng Shui flutes, Ba-Gua mirrors, Buddha statues, wind chimes, Chinese coins, firecrackers, yu bowls, faceted crystal spheres, and crystal bracelets and necklaces. All Feng Shui objects have been blessed at the Yun Lin Temple to enhance their effectiveness. To order these Feng Shui objects or for more information, contact:

Yun Lin Temple
Phone 510-841-2347
Fax 510-548-2621
E-mail info@yunlintemple.org

David Daniel Kennedy

There's a better life out there waiting for you, and David Daniel Kennedy can help you attain it through Feng Shui. Whether you've successfully applied Feng Shui on your own or you don't know where to begin, David Kennedy can help you tap into the full potential of the power of Feng Shui in order to

- ✔ Create increasing wealth and abundance
- ✔ Revitalize your relationship and create new harmony in your home
- ✔ Improve your health and vitality
- ✔ Jump-start your career and attract new opportunities

Join the thousands of people who have improved their lives, their homes, and their businesses with the help of David Kennedy, who offers Feng Shui classes, home and business consultations, and practitioner trainings nationwide. Visit his Web site for Feng Shui information, manuals, classes, and schedules. To inquire about taking classes, finding cure items, or locating a teacher or consultant in your area, contact:

David Daniel Kennedy
1563 Solano Ave., Suite 127
Berkeley, CA 94707
Phone 888-470-2727 (toll-free)
E-mail info@daviddanielkennedy.com
Web site www.daviddanielkennedy.com
Facebook www.facebook.com/daviddanielkennedy
Twitter @ddkfengshui

Index

• *Q* •

Apple & Macs

iPad For Dummies
978-0-470-58027-1

iPhone For Dummies,
4th Edition
978-0-470-87870-5

MacBook For Dummies, 3rd
Edition
978-0-470-76918-8

Mac OS X Snow Leopard For
Dummies
978-0-470-43543-4

Business

Bookkeeping For Dummies
978-0-7645-9848-7

Job Interviews
For Dummies,
3rd Edition
978-0-470-17748-8

Resumes For Dummies,
5th Edition
978-0-470-08037-5

Starting an
Online Business
For Dummies,
6th Edition
978-0-470-60210-2

Stock Investing
For Dummies,
3rd Edition
978-0-470-40114-9

Successful
Time Management
For Dummies
978-0-470-29034-7

Computer Hardware

BlackBerry
For Dummies,
4th Edition
978-0-470-60700-8

Computers For Seniors
For Dummies,
2nd Edition
978-0-470-53483-0

PCs For Dummies,
Windows
7 Edition
978-0-470-46542-4

Laptops For Dummies,
4th Edition
978-0-470-57829-2

Cooking & Entertaining

Cooking Basics
For Dummies,
3rd Edition
978-0-7645-7206-7

Wine For Dummies,
4th Edition
978-0-470-04579-4

Diet & Nutrition

Dieting For Dummies,
2nd Edition
978-0-7645-4149-0

Nutrition For Dummies,
4th Edition
978-0-471-79868-2

Weight Training
For Dummies,
3rd Edition
978-0-471-76845-6

Digital Photography

Digital SLR Cameras &
Photography For Dummies,
3rd Edition
978-0-470-46606-3

Photoshop Elements 8
For Dummies
978-0-470-52967-6

Gardening

Gardening Basics
For Dummies
978-0-470-03749-2

Organic Gardening
For Dummies,
2nd Edition
978-0-470-43067-5

Green/Sustainable

Raising Chickens
For Dummies
978-0-470-46544-8

Green Cleaning
For Dummies
978-0-470-39106-8

Health

Diabetes For Dummies,
3rd Edition
978-0-470-27086-8

Food Allergies
For Dummies
978-0-470-09584-3

Living Gluten-Free
For Dummies,
2nd Edition
978-0-470-58589-4

Hobbies/General

Chess For Dummies,
2nd Edition
978-0-7645-8404-6

Drawing
Cartoons & Comics
For Dummies
978-0-470-42683-8

Knitting For Dummies,
2nd Edition
978-0-470-28747-7

Organizing
For Dummies
978-0-7645-5300-4

Su Doku For Dummies
978-0-470-01892-7

Home Improvement

Home Maintenance
For Dummies,
2nd Edition
978-0-470-43063-7

Home Theater
For Dummies,
3rd Edition
978-0-470-41189-6

Living the
Country Lifestyle
All-in-One
For Dummies
978-0-470-43061-3

Solar Power Your Home
For Dummies,
2nd Edition
978-0-470-59678-4

Internet

Blogging For Dummies,
3rd Edition
978-0-470-61996-4

eBay For Dummies,
6th Edition
978-0-470-49741-8

Facebook For Dummies,
3rd Edition
978-0-470-87804-0

Web Marketing
For Dummies,
2nd Edition
978-0-470-37181-7

WordPress
For Dummies,
3rd Edition
978-0-470-59274-8

Language & Foreign Language

French For Dummies
978-0-7645-5193-2

Italian Phrases
For Dummies
978-0-7645-7203-6

Spanish For Dummies,
2nd Edition
978-0-470-87855-2

Spanish
For Dummies,
Audio Set
978-0-470-09585-0

Math & Science

Algebra I
For Dummies,
2nd Edition
978-0-470-55964-2

Biology For Dummies,
2nd Edition
978-0-470-59875-7

Calculus For Dummies
978-0-7645-2498-1

Chemistry For Dummies
978-0-7645-5430-8

Microsoft Office

Excel 2010 For Dummies
978-0-470-48953-6

Office 2010 All-in-One
For Dummies
978-0-470-49748-7

Office 2010 For Dummies,
Book + DVD Bundle
978-0-470-62698-6

Word 2010 For Dummies
978-0-470-48772-3

Music

Guitar For Dummies,
2nd Edition
978-0-7645-9904-0

iPod & iTunes For
Dummies, 8th Edition
978-0-470-87871-2

Piano Exercises
For Dummies
978-0-470-38765-8

Parenting & Education

Parenting For Dummies,
2nd Edition
978-0-7645-5418-6

Type 1 Diabetes
For Dummies
978-0-470-17811-9

Pets

Cats For Dummies,
2nd Edition
978-0-7645-5275-5

Dog Training For Dummies,
3rd Edition
978-0-470-60029-0

Puppies For Dummies,
2nd Edition
978-0-470-03717-1

Religion & Inspiration

The Bible For Dummies
978-0-7645-5296-0

Catholicism For Dummies
978-0-7645-5391-2

Women in the Bible
For Dummies
978-0-7645-8475-6

Self-Help & Relationship

Anger Management
For Dummies
978-0-470-03715-7

Overcoming Anxiety
For Dummies,
2nd Edition
978-0-470-57441-6

Sports

Baseball
For Dummies,
3rd Edition
978-0-7645-7537-2

Basketball
For Dummies,
2nd Edition
978-0-7645-5248-9

Golf For Dummies,
3rd Edition
978-0-471-76871-5

Web Development

Web Design
All-in-One
For Dummies
978-0-470-41796-6

Web Sites
Do-It-Yourself
For Dummies,
2nd Edition
978-0-470-56520-9

Windows 7

Windows 7
For Dummies
978-0-470-49743-2

Windows 7
For Dummies,
Book + DVD Bundle
978-0-470-52398-8

Windows 7 All-in-One
For Dummies
978-0-470-48763-1

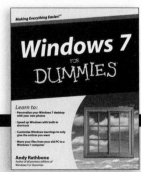